The Broken Ladder

Despite becoming a global economic force, why does India win so few Olympic medals and have so many people living in poverty? Why have opportunities not become available more broadly? How can growing individuals assist with the task of building a growing economy?

Krishna presents a refreshingly unusual perspective of emergent realities, drawing on the stories of everyday lives, of people like you and me and those less privileged. Through decades-long investigations, living in villages and slum communities, the author presents eye-opening details of missed opportunities and immense untapped talent that can be harnessed, with tremendous consequences for equity and growth.

Offering possible solutions for inequality and those in need, *The Broken Ladder* is a comprehensive and fascinating account of development strategies in a fast-growing, yet largely agrarian, developing economy.

Anirudh Krishna's research investigates how poor communities and individuals in developing countries cope with the structural and personal constraints that result in poverty and powerlessness. He has written five other books and more than sixty journal articles. Awards include an honorary doctorate from Uppsala University in 2011. Before returning to academia, Krishna worked for fourteen years with the Indian Administrative Service, managing diverse rural and urban development initiatives on behalf of the government. He has consulted with the World Bank, the United Nations, national governments, and a variety of development support organizations.

The Broken Ladder

The Paradox and Potential of India's One-Billion

Anirudh Krishna
Duke University

CAMBRIDGE
UNIVERSITY PRESS

University Printing House, Cambridge CB2 8BS, United Kingdom

One Liberty Plaza, 20th Floor, New York, NY 10006, USA

477 Williamstown Road, Port Melbourne, VIC 3207, Australia

314-321, 3rd Floor, Plot 3, Splendor Forum, Jasola District Centre, New Delhi - 110025, India

79 Anson Road, #06-04/06, Singapore 079906

Cambridge University Press is part of the University of Cambridge.

It furthers the University's mission by disseminating knowledge in the pursuit of education, learning and research at the highest international levels of excellence.

www.cambridge.org
Information on this title: www.cambridge.org/9781108402507

DOI: 10.1017/9781108235457

© Anirudh Krishna 2017

First published 2017
First paperback edition 2020

A catalogue record for this publication is available from the British Library

ISBN 978-1-108-41592-7 Hardback
ISBN 978-1-108-40250-7 Paperback

Additional resources for this publication at www.cambridge.org/delange

Cambridge University Press has no responsibility for the persistence or accuracy of URLs for external or third-party internet websites referred to in this publication, and does not guarantee that any content on such websites is, or will remain, accurate or appropriate.

CONTENTS

List of Figures   *page* vi
Acknowledgments   vii

1   The Dollar Economy and the Rupee Economy   1

2   Beyond-5-km Villages: Where the Lights Aren't Shining Brightly   27

3   Up and Down in the City   51

4   Preventing Future Poverty   74

5   A Deep Pool of Talent   98

6   Attitudes, Experiences, and Information   128

7   Democracy at the Doorstep   150

8   Looking Ahead: Growing the Economy – and Developing Individuals   178

Notes   194
Bibliography   248
Index   298

FIGURES

1.1   How wealthy or poor are the people of different countries?   *page* 14

2.1   Household possessions decrease with smaller towns and more distant villages   32

5.1   India is consistently underrepresented among Olympic medalists   105

5.2   India performs poorly on per capita patent applications   106

7.1   The Tiered State   155

ACKNOWLEDGMENTS

I owe debts of gratitude to the many people from beyond-5-km villages and city slums who agreed to talk to me and the research teams, especially to those, like Chintalamma, Chandru, Jaitram, Keshu, and Vasundhara, whom I have pestered on multiple occasions. I am thankful to each member of the research teams, with many of whom, including Sanwarmal and Mansoor, I am in correspondence.

To the government officials who spoke to me – including Deepak and Avinash and Dinesh and Amarjit and Amarjeet and Nair and Mitra and GVK and Shobhan – I owe debts of gratitude. To Rajan, for being unswerving; Pradeep Deb, for our arguments about bureaucratic authority; Arijit, for the overview; Anil, for specific advice; KP, for his all-too-rare old-world values. To the many patwaris, gram sevaks, constables, agricultural supervisors, and other street-level bureaucrats who spoke to me in confidence.

To Sunisha Ahuja, Anurag Behar, Hardy Dewan, Sharad and Kirti Iyengar, Rajiv Khandelwal, Mrinalini Kher, Pramod Kulkarni, Ramesh Ramanathan, Pankaj Shah, and many other NGO leaders who readily gave of their knowledge and their experiences. To everyone in my village – especially Laloo and Arjun and Hira. In the city nearby – to Mishraji and Mahesh and Porwal and Seema.

At Duke University, I owe thanks to lots of people, starting with Bob Conrad, who challenged me to think harder about the role of globalization; Gary Gereffi, for directing me to new learning about regional competencies and global value chains; Herbert Kitschelt, for guidance about citizen-provider relations; Phil Cook, for explaining winner-take-all; Sunny Ladd, for helping me sort through education; Pablo Beramendi for discussions about the state and decentralization; Manoj Mohanan, for insights about health care at the grassroots; Erik Wibbels, for slum-and-satellites and other conversations; and Alma Blount and David Guy, for writing consultations. To a large number of students who helped with this work, and whose inputs have made a critical difference, including Adam Hosmer-Henner, Vijay Brihmadesam, Kaijie Chen, Madhav Dutt, Chad Hazlett, Gautam Joseph, Aditya Joshi, Grady Lenkin, Sharique Mashhadi, Sarah Nolan, and Emily Rains.

I owe a special debt of gratitude to Angela Zoss, Data and Visualization Services, Duke University Libraries, for helping convert complex numbers into comprehensible visualizations.

To my academic colleagues who helped hone these arguments (but share no responsibility for the blemishes that remain). Thanks are due especially to Adam Auerbach, Mehtabul Azam, Poulomi Chakrabarty, Pradeep Chhibber, Vegard Iversen, Niraja Jayal, Surinder Jodhka, Devesh Kapur, Mukul Kesavan, Atul Kohli, Shobhit Mahajan, Phil Oldenberg, David Rueda, Mark Schneider, Kunal Sen, M. S. Sriram, and Tariq Thachil.

To Virpal Singh and Devendra Bajpai for help with analyzing nationally and regionally representative data. To Varun Aggarwal and Swapnil Agarwal for sharing my belief in social mobility. To Subroto Bagchi, for constructive criticism and encouragement. To Anurag Sharan, who quarreled with everything I said. To the anonymous referees, who provided a wealth of useful criticism.

To the grant-making agencies and other organizations that helped make different parts of the research possible, including Bass Connections at Duke University, the Ford Foundation, the International Growth Center, the Centre for the Study of Law and Governance and the Institute of Advanced Study at Jawaharlal Nehru University, Jana Urban Foundation, Disha, Sarathi, and Seva Mandir.

To my editors, Meru Gokhale and Anushree Kaushal at Penguin Random House India and Robert Dreesen at Cambridge University Press for their faith, encouragement, and recommendations.

To Chutki and Jag and Arvind and Sonia and Aditi and Abhay for making me think harder. To Vidya, most of all, who never fails to tell me when it's time to stop working and start living. I dedicate this volume to the memories of three mentors: Milton J. Esman, who showed me how to think critically about development assistance; Mitha Lal Mehta, who made the link between ideas and implementation; and Ram Narain Meena, who taught me to look at different perspectives.

1 THE DOLLAR ECONOMY AND THE RUPEE ECONOMY

Keshu believes that he took the right decisions, but things did not work out as he had hoped. He was determined to remain in school even as his companions dropped out. Nearly all children started primary school in his village, but by middle school, a four-kilometer walk, most had stopped going to school. In high school, ten kilometers further, Keshu was the only student from his village. He worked hard, and he earned good grades. Through his years of studying, Keshu's parents lightened his household chores, and they cut back on household expenses. Buoyed by the faith that going to school would lead to a better life, they invested in Keshu's education.

In 2006, he passed the senior secondary examination, becoming the first high school graduate from his village. The moment of reckoning had come, and it turned out to be a time of disappointment. He looked high and low for more than a year, but Keshu was not offered any worthwhile employment. Studying further was beyond the family's means. He had to get a job and start making a living.

He wakes up early and walks for an hour to get to a seasonally dry riverbed, where he digs for sand that is used for construction. It's the type of low-paid work that many men from his village have taken up, including several with only a year or two of education. It is dispiriting that he does the same work as they, despite staying in school for much longer. But Keshu's experience is hardly unique. Many others who persevered with education have failed to gain the advantages they had expected.

As illiteracy vanishes and a different generation takes over, the problems of India's development are changing. Change has been rapid in the vast countryside, deeply affecting the residents of India's half-million villages. Up to forty years ago, hardly any schools existed in rural areas. Public schools in considerable numbers began to be erected a few decades after national independence. The insertion by the state of schools in their midst was accompanied by a vast change in the mindsets of people in villages. Widely shared norms began to emerge: all children must get an education, and everyone should give their support to this widely respected initiative.[1] Over the years, the situation has arisen that once basic survival needs are met, rural families spend their very next bits of money on children's education.[2] Large gains in education have been achieved because of this combination of state provisioning and public motivation: very few village grandmothers or grandfathers have any formal education, but more than 90 percent of the new generation have at least a few years of school education. Still, very few complete high school, and only a tiny proportion go to college. And those who do graduate from high schools and colleges are rarely able to gain a substantial advantage. It has increased their efficacy as democrats and as citizens, and it has helped elevate their social status – both of which are considerable achievements; however, the newfound faith in education has, more often than not, failed to produce the anticipated and hoped-for gains in earnings. Men with high school diplomas and college degrees work as delivery boys, making no more than uneducated lorry loaders.

India's rapid economic growth has in many ways helped improve the lives of its poorer people, but in other respects, the effects of growth have been deficient. Keshu's family has a cell phone now. Until quite recently, there were none in their village. Children no longer have to walk to high school: there is a paved road now, and there are public buses. Some families in his village own motorcycles and televisions. In other respects, however, things are no different than they were earlier. Keshu's father works as a *mazdoor* (a day laborer) in the nearby city, doing the same work for as long as Keshu remembers. They have lived in the same home since Keshu was born. Education did not help him advance. No other avenues to a better life are visible.

There is no lack of effort on their part. Everyone in the family works hard: they have to; there is no other option. A sister takes care of the cattle and goats, going far into the forest for fodder and firewood. Another sister labors on public projects and people's farms. An older brother goes out to Mumbai each year to work for a few months as a construction laborer. Because their income is below the official poverty line, the family has a BPL (below poverty line) card, which qualifies them to get subsidized food rations. Some years ago, a government agency gave them free packets of seeds and fertilizer. Another government program gave them a brood of chickens.

Despite these efforts and the outside assistance they have received, the family makes a bare existence. What their farm produces, even in good monsoon years, is not enough for the table. Misfortunes occur with frightening regularity. Two years ago, a cow that she was milking slipped and fell against Keshu's mother, breaking her hip and left leg. Treatment was expensive. They sold her silver anklets to pay for her care, and they contracted debts, but her leg and her hip healed poorly, and she cannot walk two steps without falling. A few months after this incident, on his way back from Mumbai, Keshu's migrant-worker brother was robbed of the money he had saved and was bringing back to the village.

The prospect of moving down in life seems more plausible than that of moving up. It is a meager and a precarious existence. Any sudden shock can pitch them into poverty that endures. The risk of shocks is ever-present.

Instead of helping make their lives easier and less uncertain, public officials often end up making things more risky. Many families in Keshu's village planted a second crop during the winter season, drawing water from wells with the help of electricity. One day, a new procedure was announced for registering one's electricity connection with the authorities. Under the new dispensation, Keshu's family was required to submit a fresh application and obtain a new connection. Two years later, they were still waiting for their application to be approved by the concerned officials. Meanwhile, electricity supply to their well was cut off, and the winter crop remained unirrigated. A bolder neighbor, seeing his crops withering, set up an illegal connection. Arrested by the police, he has since been embroiled in a potentially ruinous legal action.

What went wrong? Why have growth and education not delivered higher returns for people like Keshu? What can be done to make things better in the future for these and other people who have been poorly served by the gravy train of globalization?

Alternative Views

A range of answers to these questions has been offered by scholars of different persuasions. They have disagreed about the most important causes and effects. Commonly, however, a bird's-eye view was taken. Scholars considered the questions of development with the perspective of an entire nation.

Two bird's-eye views dominated a debate that was waged in the opening years of the new millennium. One view held that India's democracy provided the basis for more effectively improving the lots of poorer people. By making representations, mounting protests, amassing public pressure, and mediating with public officials, civil society organizations would help direct policy makers' attentions toward the concerns of the less well-off. Such as a view was presented, for instance, by Jean Drèze and Amartya Sen, who concluded a magisterial examination asserting that "the democratic politics of India do offer opportunities for the most deprived Indians 'to reflect on their own strength,' and to demand that the critically important inequalities that ruin the lives of so many people in the country be rapidly remedied."[3] Democracy would help cure the problems of poverty. Democracy, growing stronger, would enable poorer people to climb higher.

A contrary view was presented by the other side in the debate. Faster national economic growth – by creating employment, raising tax revenues, and closing the gaps in infrastructure requirements – would help everyone advance, providing better opportunities to richer and poorer individuals. Promoting national economic growth represented the surer path to individual successes. The ills of poverty would be healed by faster growth.[4]

Both views in the debate have pointed to actions that are urgently required. Promoting rapid economic growth is necessary, and strengthening democracy is essential, for improving the collective well-being of a nation.

However, growth and democracy are wide-ranging and far-away notions that exist at some remove from the everyday lives of ordinary people. Neither democracy nor growth reaches out automatically with beneficial effects for all people. Only those who are able to make the connections are able to gain the protections of democracy and to benefit from growth in the nation. For many others, the ladders leading up to the benefits of democracy and growth are broken.

Democracy in India is not yet a fully-built institution. Elections are regularly held and fairly conducted, and poorer Indians vote in large numbers, but in the years between elections, poorer individuals have little access to decision makers and few opportunities to influence public decisions. With notable exceptions, civil society actions by poorer people are far from common.[5] Things are improving, but we are not at the point where a poor Scheduled Caste woman can walk into a rural police station and expect to have her rights enforced as a routine matter of public justice. Making and strengthening the links that connect a citizen to her democratic remedies is a task that still needs to be completed.

Similarly, there is no guarantee that economic growth in a country will help resolve its poorer people's problems. There are many problems that growth can more assuredly resolve – raising the country's international profile, helping enlarge the numbers of airlines and airports, financing better roads and school buildings, etc. But growth does not suffice to improve an individual's situation – unless there is a tight connection between an individual's capacity and her prospects for moving upward. Where many individuals, like Keshu, work well below their potential, these prospects are dimmed. The rate of growth is lower in such situations, and progress in poverty reduction is slower and more tenuous.

Once again, it is a matter of making better connections. People climb out of poverty individually – they are not "lifted out" by other people. How can better ladders be constructed that help hardworking people across the board climb as high as they are individually able?

Over the longer term, economies continue on a growth path when yesterday's job seekers become tomorrow's job creators. How to bring the largest number of individual efforts to bear more productively on the project of building national economic growth is the critical question before a nation.

A View from Below

To complement what the bird's-eye views have shown, I have adopted a worm's-eye perspective. I look at diverse situations of development from the vantage points of different individuals.

Some of the characters in this book are drawn from a village in central India, nearly every resident of which is technically poor.

They live rich and complex lives. There's happiness and joy; poverty is only one dimension of a person's existence.[6] But apart from the two schoolteachers who live in this village and teach in its primary school, nearly everyone else has a hand-to-mouth existence.

I made a home in this village more than 10 years ago, and I have lived there for several weeks each year. I decided to buy property in this village after conducting years of field research in the extended area. A friend mentioned that a piece of land was up for sale, and impelled by a romantic urge, I took up the opportunity, becoming an instant curiosity in the village. Some villagers thought I was setting up a nongovernmental organization (NGO); others speculated that I would build a resort hotel. I could do little to dispute these fanciful notions. I carried on with my research activities in the wider area, while living in my new home in the village. A handful of fellow villagers became my friends in the first few years. Since then I've struck up friendships with many more residents. I have not tried to "uplift" these people in any manner. I do not run development projects in this village, and I do not undertake any formal research. It's hard to conduct formal interviews with people who are one's friends, and it's hard to become friends with someone you've had to grill for information.

I've learned a great deal, however, by walking around and talking to people. That's the bulk of what I do when I am in the village. In the process, the villagers' suspicions have abated. My neighbors ask how long my *chhutti* (vacation) will last on each occasion. We talk about each other's children. My closest friends in the village include my immediate neighbors, the two schoolteachers and their families, and some who are among the poorest in the village. Dignity, good humor, and a sharp wit, I have found, have little association with poverty or with riches. I have made friends, in particular, with a group of young people. There are walks around the village that take you through breathtaking scenery, and some young people have volunteered to serve as my guides and walking companions. In the process of speaking with them and with their siblings and parents, I have learned much that would otherwise have escaped my attention.

The learning I acquired from this close-up view in one Indian village was supplemented by the field studies that I conducted over 20 years in diverse parts of rural and urban India. Looking within remote rural villages and urban slums, I learned of many things that I hadn't known existed.

In one multistate research project, I compared across a group of sixty-six villages to see how each village had performed in six different kinds of development programs. These programs were different in many respects – they related to different sectors (health, education, employment generation, etc.); some were implemented by government agencies and others by NGOs; some were purely grant-funded while others required a local contribution. For each program, I assessed a village's performance in relation to a few important criteria – yield per acre in the pasturage project, percentage survival in the tree plantation program, the share of the eligible student population who completed the education program, etc.

It turned out, however, that no matter which measure I employed and which development program I considered, one type of villages consistently had high performance scores while another type consistently showed poor performance. The first type of villages, the high-performing ones, were not located in a cluster, nor were they different from those of the second type in terms of village population or other factors, including religious and caste compositions, levels of poverty, market access, or extent of commercialization. Literacy levels mattered a little for distinguishing between high-performing and low-performing villages. What mattered most, however, was whether villages acted collectively for mutual benefits – some villages did while others didn't. Across a wide range of tasks, people in the first type of villages knew how to cooperate for shared gains, and they mounted effective collective actions. People in other villages did not have the same capacity. Performance suffered in the second type of villages, despite the planners' best intentions.[7]

This finding turned upside down much of my earlier thinking about development practice. It is not simply the nature of the policy or program that matters for development performance. There is a definable quality that some villages have, which other villages don't, that is critically important. Otherwise, why would performance levels spill over across widely varied program types with different modes of implementation?

The realization that local-level differences matter in an important way led me, for the first time, to see the merit in a worm's-eye perspective. My respect for the worm's-eye view has subsequently grown, for it has allowed me to see other facets of development more clearly.

In another research project, I investigated households' poverty dynamics – their movements out of poverty (or into poverty) over a period. In twelve villages in Rajasthan, where I looked initially, I found that some households in each village had moved out of poverty during the preceding twenty years, but simultaneously, other households had fallen deeply into poverty. Poverty was created at the same time it was reduced. Every village had experienced the same two-faced dynamic. Curious to examine the nature of this dynamic, I expanded this inquiry into three other states of India, examining a large group of diverse villages and urban areas. Later still, I looked at these trends in different parts of Kenya, Uganda, Peru, and Bangladesh and in one region of the United States of America. I found that it was the same story everywhere: Of two close neighbors, one overcame poverty, and the other became impoverished. Within every one of more than 400 rural villages and urban neighborhoods where I looked, some people had escaped poverty while others had fallen into persistent poverty.

You need a microscope to see these things, though. A "macroscope" does not spot individuals' different realities.

A third research project reaffirmed my faith in the worm's-eye perspective. This project is concerned with social mobility: What are the chances that a talented and hardworking child born to poverty will reach a high position? How many such children have actually succeeded? What can we learn from their journeys that can be of benefit to other children in similar starting positions?

I met many inspiring individuals during this inquiry, and it jarred me to learn of the struggles they've had and the obstacles they've encountered. Many talented and hardworking individuals fall along the wayside, because they lack the necessary guidance and support. The ladder leading upward is broken in many places. Very few are able to climb high starting from a low position.

Through these and other research projects, undertaken with the generous support of grant-making agencies, colleagues, friends, and research assistants, I was able to collect original interview data for more than 40,000 individuals. This book builds on these and other bodies of information.

In addition to collecting original data, I analyzed a variety of nationally representative data that helped cross-check my smaller-scale findings. I learned a great deal from reading other scholars' studies; from the published reports of journalists, government departments, and international organizations; and from discussions with NGO leaders and government officials.

Gaining access to public officials was easier in my case because I had worked for fourteen years as a public official. I was recruited to the Indian Administrative Service (IAS) in 1982, after graduate work at the Delhi School of Economics and Harvard University. I developed and implemented a number of development programs during my period of employment with the government, and I learned a great deal about designing and implementing development programs and about the tasks of governance. But after a sojourn in academics – first as a Hubert Humphrey Fellow, and then, a PhD student at Cornell University – I changed career tracks and returned to a teaching and research position. I have kept up with many former colleagues who serve in different tiers of public administration. These conversations have sharpened my insights about the workings of "the system." I am not blinded, however, and neither are my former colleagues, to the poor quality of governance that the average Indian routinely experiences.

Examining the questions of development with a worm's-eye view in the context of India has significance as well for other countries. People in other countries, especially those with large agrarian populations until recently denied schools and hospitals and all-weather roads, are facing very similar situations. A tiny part of the population in these countries has the preparation that is required for becoming globally competitive. This small part is catapulted into the international economy. The rest, a larger number, who lack resources and preparation, fall far behind. Many, who work with crude technologies, eke out a bare existence. But it is not only in poorer and largely agrarian nations, such as India or Kenya or Guatemala, where global economic integration has been accompanied by growing polarization. Among richer countries, too, the promise of free trade has been marred by increasing joblessness and employment insecurity. India's experience in dealing with the emergent trends is, therefore, worth following closely. How can India better improve the prospects for people like Keshu while simultaneously growing its globally influential economy?

Layered Development: The Dollar Economy and the Rupee Economy

A nearly closed economy until the early 1990s, India was cut off from many imports and from most global trends and fashions – a deliberate choice of policies made by its leaders to support their strategy of state-led industrial development, launched soon after the country achieved national independence. Fifteen years into the implementation of this development strategy, by the mid-1960s, a vast industrial estate had come into being, the likes of which had not been seen before in India, or indeed, in many other developing countries. State-of-the-art steel and chemical plants, dams by the dozen, heavy industries and armament factories, and other wonders of modern technology dotted the country-side, the majority owned and managed by the Indian state, and the rest strictly regulated.

By the 1970s, however, the wheels began to come off this experiment with state-led economic development. The red tape of state-led growth in time became infested with worms. Cronyism and corruption became endemic. The economy drifted along, narrowly avoiding shipwreck, until, by the mid-1980s, the leaks had become too many. Following the dual crises of the early 1990s – ballooning government deficits and a balance-of-payments crunch – the Indian economy began to sink rapidly. India asked for and received a bailout from the International Monetary Fund (IMF), and with it came structural adjustments. Policy changes commenced in the 1980s to liberalize the economy, freeing it by degrees of state control, were quickly ratcheted up. These policy changes, welcomed by many in India and resisted or condemned by relatively few, had the effect of opening up the Indian economy.[8]

Life after globalization has become better in many ways. Economic growth rates have remained high in all but a few years. The stock market has soared, attracting international investors. India's space operations have become the envy of other countries. There are numerous Mercedes, Maseratis, and McLarens on the streets of New Delhi and Bengaluru. The number of dollar billionaires has soared. Indian companies have become the new multinationals.[9]

Still, very few Indians have the kinds of assets and conveniences that are commonly associated with the middle class in Western countries. Less than 3 percent of Indian households have computers at home with internet connections; less than 4 percent of families own cars; less than 4 percent have credit cards; less than 2 percent travel abroad in any year; and less than 2 percent are invested in financial markets.[10] Every percentage point of the Indian population translates to more than 10 million people, so the absolute numbers are breathtaking. In terms of proportions, however, no more than one in every 20 Indian households has the markers of international middle-class status.

Differently placed individuals have received varying rewards, for globalized growth does not reward everyone equally. It is especially good for individuals who own globally scarce resources or who have a specialized educational qualification. Where before they could sell their resources and skills mostly or only within their home country, they can now transact freely across the globe. The market for their knowledge and their products has grown, greatly boosting the incomes of such individuals.

A pattern of layered achievements has come into existence. Some in India have become part of an international or *dollar economy*, sharing lifestyles and Facebook links with peers in the Western world. These are not, of course, the only kinds of people who live in India. Others who neither have a specialized education nor own a globally scarce resource are in the *rupee economy*, the less affluent part of the country.

It is difficult to precisely delineate the boundary between them, but the distinction between the rupee and dollar economies is substantial. There are individuals whose pay packets are dollar-comparable, and there are stores and restaurants in India that charge dollar-equivalent prices, where a cup of coffee costs what it does in the West, about $5, or approximately 350 rupees. But there are also other stores and eateries, in side streets and back alleys, where people of the rupee economy can buy their cups of coffee or tea for as little as 20 rupees.

A rough idea of the relative proportion of people in the rupee and the dollar economies can be gained by looking at the spread of incomes in the country. In 2012, 13 percent of all Indians had monthly per-capita incomes below 500 rupees; another 22 percent earned between 500 and 1,000 rupees; and a further 30 percent had incomes between 1,000 and 2,000 rupees, making for 65 percent in all who lived below the threshold of two thousand rupees monthly or a little over sixty rupees daily. It's hard, with that kind of income, to buy a dollar-economy coffee and almost impossible to stay in a dollar-economy hotel.

A sliver of the population had monthly per-capita incomes of more than 10,000 rupees. These are the dollar-economy people – who make up no more than 3 percent of the country's population.[11]

The economic importance of these dollar-economy people grew rapidly in the years after globalization. The incomes of the top 5 percent increased twice as fast as those of the bottom 5 percent.[12] The richest 1 percent, who owned 30 percent of the country's private wealth in 2000, increased their share to 50 percent by 2014.[13]

Opportunities have improved vastly in the years after global-ized growth, most visibly and rapidly for people with large amounts of investible capital and others who have a specialized education. For others, the increase in earnings has been relatively small. Software engi-neers, for example, quadrupled their average take-home pay in the 1990s. Doctors and lawyers and other professionals also began mak-ing more money. For people at the lower end of the education scale, however, the gain in average earnings was a pittance.[14]

Globalized growth has little use for people whose educational qualifications are below a certain threshold. The threshold level of edu-cation required for making real gains has been rising higher in richer and in poorer countries. The so-called college premium has grown. In today's job market, even an undergraduate education, except from a handful of prestigious universities, is not enough for making a decent living.

Unfortunately, few Indians have a college education. The pro-portion is growing, but is still quite small. Among rural adults aged 25–34 years, only 4.4 percent had college degrees in 2008.[15] Hurting from the costs and not seeing the benefit clearly, large numbers of young people drop out before completing high school. They gravitate toward the informal sector, where the wages are low and the job is uncertain.

Few people in India have a regular or formal job, one that comes with social security benefits and legal protections. More than 90 per-cent of all working individuals are employed in informal positions. The informal sector is where child laborers are found, minimum wage laws go unimplemented, and health and safety precautions are rare. All but a few construction workers, coolies, rickshaw pullers, lorry loaders, seam-stresses, and domestic help go into constituting the informal (or what in India is also called the unorganized) sector. Some small shopkeepers and businesspeople are also included within it, but day laborers, the *maz-doors*, constitute the largest chunk of the informal sector. Such people – like Keshu, his brother, and his father – have no assurance that the job they have today will still be theirs tomorrow. On some days, they are able to find paid work; on other days, they come home empty-handed.[16]

Day-to-day struggles to make ends meet crowd out the scope for future planning. For poverty is not only about low average earnings;

it is as much, and arguably more, about suffering a downfall and the nagging uncertainties of daily living. You're never sure if there will be money to keep the wolf from the door. That's still a lurking fear for millions in India.

Policy Stretch

Undertaking the twin tasks of building the economy and ridding the country of desolation is not going to be easy or straightforward. There is no known road map that India can simply adapt from other countries.

These tasks are made more difficult by the wide array of human needs and social circumstances that policy makers confront in India. In the first of his three books set in this country, Nobel laureate V. S. Naipaul used the metaphor of an onion to describe Indian society, with its layer upon layer of caste differences and economic distinctions. People in diverse layers have vastly different lifestyles, and they rely on different technologies. The technologies and instruments that you used 30 years earlier are still in use, although far from you and in a lower layer of society.[17]

The layering of Indian society has become more complex in the period after globalization, presenting another challenge for development policy. The best in India compete head-to-head with the best in the world – software developers, chess players, graphic designers, Bollywood producers, and recording artists, to name but a few. In other respects, India continues to have among the lowest positions internationally. The worst schools in India are among the worst in the world, declining from year to year in terms of quality. Maternal and infant mortality rates are high in India, and undernutrition is widespread. There are outbreaks of plague and *kala azar* (black fever), medieval diseases that most of the world has long forgotten.[18]

India has a long list of impressive achievements. But the chronicle of its non-achievement is also lengthy.

As a result, the country represents a paradox, juxtaposing, on the one hand, an impressive growth record and some of the hottest investment opportunities, and on the other hand, the largest number of poor and undernourished people of any country. Visually, it is a land of contrasts – "nowhere is inequality more in your face than in India"[19] – beggars beside glass-walled office towers; hovels huddled below

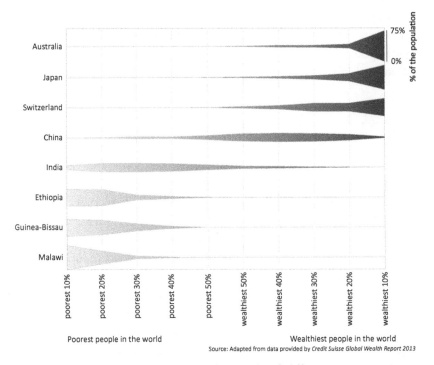

Figure 1.1 How wealthy or poor are the people of different countries? *Source:* Adapted from data provided by *Credit Suisse Global Wealth Report 2013*.

elevated highways; animal-drawn carts neck-to-neck with late-model luxury cars; modern airports and roadside mechanics.

Figure 1.1 depicts this paradox in a graph. The horizontal axis is divided into successive 10-percent segments of world wealth distribution. The poorest people on the planet are on the left of this graph (and the wealthiest are on the right). Different countries are depicted on the vertical axis. Each country's wealth distribution is shown in the form of a streamgraph, a band of different widths from left to right. Its width at any particular point depicts the share of the country's population that belongs to the corresponding 10-percent segment of the world wealth distribution. If a large share of a country's population belongs to the world's wealthiest 10 percent (as in Australia), its streamgraph is widest on the right-hand side. Conversely, if the largest share of a country's population is of the world's poorest 10 percent (as in Malawi), its streamgraph has a broad part on the left side.[20]

In Australia and Japan, almost the entire population falls within the top 50 percent of world wealth distribution, with more than half of these countries' populations belonging to the wealthiest 10 percent. There are many globally rich people in these countries, but virtually no globally poor ones. Conversely, nearly 40 percent of the population of Ethiopia and 60 percent of the population of Malawi belong to the world's poorest 10 percent. The entire population of these countries is contained within the world's bottom 50 percent.

So much is not surprising. Some countries are rich and their people are rich, while other countries and their people are poor.

It is difficult, however, to uniquely classify a country that has a streamgraph like India's. A significant share of India's population is contained within the top, the bottom, and every other 10-percent segment of the world's wealth distribution. Few other countries have the same spread between space-age rich and stone-age poor people.[21]

Inequalities of wealth are also large in China, but while China's rich compare with the rich in India, China's poorest citizens are better off than their counterparts in India.[22] China's poorer people receive better-quality education and health care, and they have a greater chance of upward mobility. But in India, for many people like Keshu, the ladders leading upward are broken.[23]

What does the future hold? Will India end up looking like Japan or like Switzerland at some point in the future? That's the rising-tide hope. But it's not going to be fulfilled, unless the forces that have propelled a small group into the global elite are directed with equal vigor toward the remaining population.

What needs to be done in order to make India a better place is, however, a complex and multi-stranded question. The coexistence of dollar-rich and rupee-poor people, with their different ambitions and disparate needs, places an enormous burden on the state, which needs to tackle rich-country problems while at the same time dealing with the kinds of problems that rich countries overcame a century earlier. Pit latrines, country roads, and two-room schoolhouses must be built at the same time as maglev railroads and state-of-the-art airports. National leaders are well aware of this need, simultaneously to speak to the widest range of policy concerns. Consider, for instance, the manifesto of the Bharatiya Janata Party (BJP), which won the national election of 2014. It promised to "build world-class centers of excellence of scientific research in the fields of nanotechnology, material sciences, thorium technology, and brain research," while at the same time pledging to "create an open-defecation free India" and to provide safe drinking water for all – a strange mix of promises that spans the known public policy spectrum.[24] The manifesto of the Congress Party, in power at that time, presented a similarly wide range of pledges and targets.[25]

Such a stretch of policy needs – responding simultaneously to stone-age and space-age needs – has not been mounted in the past by any rich country. India will have to hew a new development path, taking on at the same time what had been thought to be sequential stages of development.

Other developing countries are facing similar situations, and they will also need to forge newer strategies of national development.[26] The decisions that India takes in this regard will, therefore, have broader consequences.

The Argument in Brief

The argument that I will develop in the rest of the book is built around a few key aspects:

- Globalized growth in a largely agrarian society
- The broken ladder
- Pervasive vulnerability
- Divisive attitudes in an information-poor society
- The tiered state and its deficits

To begin at the beginning, it needs be understood that what is often spoken of as "India" in the business news is only a tiny part of this country. Two thirds of India's population lives in its rural areas, a total of more than 800 million people, but the situations of individuals in this part of the country are rarely mentioned in news bulletins. The rupee economy is dominant in rural India, and there are few signs of dollar-economy progress.

The average villager's income is far below that of a big-city resident. Their lifestyles are different. Less than 1 percent of rural families had computers at home in 2011, compared to more than 10 percent of urban families. Other markers of progress – cars, credit cards, air travel – are also disproportionately associated with people in cities.

Differences between cities and villages predate this era of globalization, but these preexisting disparities have grown larger in the past few decades. Across large parts of the world, "global integration has created a new strategic role for major cities," with the biggest cities becoming "highly concentrated command points" in the organization of the globalized economy. "These changes in the functioning of cities have had a massive impact."[27] Smaller towns and rural areas have fallen far behind the biggest cities. "Proximity in geographic, cultural, and institutional terms allows special access, special relationships, better information, powerful incentives, and other advantages in productivity," considerable advantages that "are difficult to tap from a distance."[28]

Villages in India located closer to towns have benefited from the country's economic achievements. In remoter villages, however, the benefits of growth are smaller and harder to detect.

Close to 60 percent of India's villages are located more than 5 kilometers from the nearest town or city. These people's conditions have not improved much in the years after globalization. Measured on some parameters, their conditions have deteriorated. Today, the average Indian farm family operates less than 1 hectare of land – a pocket-sized farm, unable, even in good years, to produce enough for the family's requirements (see Chapter 2).

Because of the resulting economic compulsions, millions of people have moved from rural to urban areas. It is estimated that anywhere between 80 and 150 million people are on the move each year. Most of them are unable to set down roots in the city. More than 90 percent return to their villages after working in the city, some for a few days, others for a few months, and relatively few for the whole year.[29] Only a tiny fraction, no more than 3 to 5 million people annually, are able to move permanently from villages into cities.

As a result of this peculiar kind of rural-urban migration, very different from the kinds that were experienced earlier in Western countries, the rural share of the Indian population has not declined rapidly. From nearly 70 percent in 2001, the rural share of India's population fell to a little over 67 percent in 2011. In earlier decades, too, the rate of changeover was on the order of 2 to 3 percent.[30] Even as it was falling in proportional terms, India's rural population grew in size – from 743 million in 2001 to 833 million in 2011, larger than the combined populations of the United States, Russia, Mexico, and Brazil.

For a long time to come, India's rural areas will be populated by tens of millions of people. This large part of the country's population has been poorly served by its government. Compared to urban areas, public investments in rural areas have languished.

This relative neglect was sometimes justified by the faith that the rural would soon be transformed into the urban. The faith was belied in one part by the large number of people who continued to stay on in rural areas, and in another part, by the experiences of people who had moved in the past to cities. A small minority of such internal migrants, better educated and in a higher social layer of the social onion, has made significant advances, but a large majority did not achieve significant lifestyle improvements. The number of people living in slums has burgeoned. Many have lived in slums for generations. Sons follow fathers and uncles into low-paid informal positions; there are few signs of upward mobility (see Chapter 3).

Two sets of factors – those operating on the supply side and those on the preparation side – are responsible for why better outcomes were not obtained by the majority. Supply-side factors help explain why, despite fast macroeconomic growth, relatively few good jobs were created. More than 90 percent of all new jobs are of an informal kind – uncertain, low-paid, and with little prospect of career advancement. These supply-side weaknesses have been compounded by parallel weaknesses on the side of preparation. Few people coming into cities have had the kinds of qualifications that are required for getting a good position. The consequences have been deleterious for an equal-opportunity society. Things are not what they used to be at the time of assembly-line manufacturing. In today's world, you need at least a high school, if not a college, education. Lacking this kind of preparation, the majority who have come into cities have gravitated, by and large, into insecure and poorly paid positions. They cope without advancing.

Realizing more fully the potential of urbanization will, as paradoxical as it might seem, require making prior investments in India's villages. Improving their standards of preparation is necessary before encouraging people to move from rural areas to cities. When they are better prepared, more people coming into cities will live in homes and apartments, and fewer will live on sidewalks and in shanties.

Investing in villages should be a national priority. That's an important part of what it will take to equip the nation for globalization.

Equally important is the need to stabilize people's lives by diminishing the risk of falling into poverty. Official statistics tend to depict a rosy picture of fast-declining poverty, suggesting a situation in which people are only moving up and out of poverty. But India has one of the highest rates of poverty creation internationally. Between 3 and 5 percent of the country's population falls into poverty each year, adding to the large number of people already in poverty. Any sudden shock, any large disruption of money flows, can serve to pitch people into poverty. Vulnerability to shocks is pervasive. Many who moved out of poverty continue to feel its gravitational attraction.

The Indian government has mounted a series of programs intended to assist people in poverty. The most important programs are implemented nationwide, benefiting tens of millions of people whose lives would otherwise have been harder. The programs of the government have grown in size, dwarfing the expenditures made by NGOs and foreign aid agencies. The sophistication and coverage of these programs has steadily increased, and stricter measures have been introduced to stem corruption.

Despite their greater coverage and more sophisticated designs, the contribution these programs make to long-term poverty reduction is uncertain. First, the programs of the government do hardly anything to prevent people's descent into poverty. There is no preventive policy. Second, the assistance they receive makes it easier for these families to cope from day to day, but without overcoming the factors that keep people in poverty. Subsidized food rations help poor families survive. Cash wages from the rural employment guarantee program – up to 100 days of minimum wages for rural families wishing to do manual labor – also add to the household budget. But rarely is this money enough to constitute an investible surplus. Hardly anyone who labors at a government worksite has a son or a daughter in college (see Chapter 4)

Assistance to poor people must be continued – it helps keep the wolf from the doors of millions of families – but other efforts must also be mounted. High vulnerability at one end – the risk of falling into poverty – combines with low upward mobility at the other end to keep millions of families trapped in the zone of poverty.

Only too rarely are poorer people's children, no matter how talented or hardworking, able to do much better than Keshu. Many climb up, only to come crashing down. Very few are able to achieve escape velocity.

There's a low chance that a child born to poorer parents in India will become a high-paid official or upwardly mobile business executive.

The award-winning feature film *Slumdog Millionaire* is a pleasant fiction; uplifting because of its sharp contrast with the lived reality.

The ladder leading upward is broken in many places. Human talent is the greatest productive resource that a country possesses. India, more than other countries, has been wasteful of its vast reservoir of human potential. Whether seen by way of Olympics medals won, patents claimed, new businesses registered, or academic papers published, India's performance in relation to its human resource is poor compared to other countries (see Chapter 5).

The failure to provide a high-quality education to the majority is an important part of the reason why relatively few individuals have been able to make significant achievements. But lack of good-quality education isn't the only obstacle that kids from poorer neighborhoods routinely experience. Other obstacles have equally pernicious effects, especially the absence of clearly signposted career pathways and the lack of better role models. Information about the better careers is hard to come by; there are no superior role models in neighborhoods where no one has risen to high position.

The lack of information places an additional burden on people who already suffer from multiple burdens. An information-poor society restricts people's life chances. Information, like education and health, needs to be made available as a public service.

Changing attitudes and beliefs is another rarely acknowledged, but equally important, task. Working on these "soft" factors is as important as fixing the hardware of development. Attitudes, values, and beliefs are responsible for constraining many individuals' life chances. "The attitudes of those who make, implement, and influence policy [uphold]...a division of labor between people who work with their minds and rule and people who work with their hands and are ruled," validating the practices of hiring poor children as employees. "Even those who profess to be secular and reject the caste system are imbued with values of status that are deeply embedded."[31] Scheduled Castes and Scheduled Tribes have been restricted on account of the beliefs and values held by others in society.[32] "City-dwellers are mostly ashamed of rural India . . . seen as inescapably backward."[33] These and other beliefs and values hold back many individuals' development. But attitude and values are rarely brought within program designs and plan documents.

The important role that these elements play in people's lives was revealed to me in an incident that occurred some years ago in a village of Andhra Pradesh. I was in Nalgonda district along with members of a research team that I had recruited and trained for studying household poverty. The research team had started its work, and a community meeting had commenced with a brisk give-and-take, yielding important information about how different households had moved out of (or fallen into) poverty. Not wanting to disrupt the flow of the discussion – I speak virtually no Telugu – I took off for a walk and was admiring the ancient temple architecture.

Hearing a shout, I turned around. He was 14 years old at the time, and his right leg was crippled by childhood polio.

"*Telugu raadu*," I apologized.

"But I speak English!" Chandru declared. I learned that he studied in the 9th Standard and liked being in school.

"Which subject do you like the most?" I inquired.

"Mathematics," he said, and I felt glad. Like a nerd sometimes does upon meeting another, I wrote three math questions and handed them over. My questions did not in the least faze Chandru. He rapidly wrote out the answers. My next three questions were harder, and the three that followed were harder still, but each time Chandru took only a moment to respond, and each time he responded correctly.

Then, with a mischievous grin, he swiveled the notebook around, grabbed the pen, and wrote out three questions that I was to answer.

The boldness of this act caught me by surprise, but that was not as bad as the embarrassment which followed. I answered the first two questions that Chandru had posed, but I found myself struggling with the third question.

Luckily for me, Chandru's father came upon us at this time, and I had an opportunity to redirect the conversation. The father spoke not a word of English. The son stepped in to translate for us. We started speaking about the crops and the weather, but as soon as I politely could I posed the question:

"What do you wish for your son to become?"

"He reads every mathematics book that he can find," the father told me, "and he wants to become an engineer. But no one in this village can help him. No one from around here has ever become an engineer."

"Besides," he added after pausing for a while, "it could be very expensive. My daughters were married just a few years ago. And we don't have the money for a college education."

Surely, I felt, if lack of money was the impediment, then it should be easy to find a way out of the situation. With the help of some people I knew in the state administration, I came to learn of a fully funded government fellowship that was available. Persisting, I procured the prescribed application forms, and I learned about the application deadline and the selection procedures. In a detailed letter that I mailed out the next day, I sent Chandru this set of materials.

Three months later, I had another chance to go to this village. Chandru's father was unmoved by the possibility of a free college education. The mere thought that his son would become an engineer seemed like an impossible expedition.

"It is not for the likes of us," he maintained. "No one from around here has ever become an engineer. No one from here can *be* an engineer."

It was his last sentence that goaded me to undertake my first systematic study of social mobility. In a block of ten villages, all within a 10-kilometer radius of Chandru's village, the study team and I went in to inquire about the highest positions that had been achieved by residents (or former residents) in the preceding ten-year period. Our survey revealed that not one person in any of these villages had become an engineer, or for that matter, a doctor, lawyer, professor, architect, sports star, airline pilot, or news anchor. The highest position that anyone had achieved was that of village schoolteacher. That's also the position to which most young people aspired; hardly anyone expressed a desire to become an engineer or a graphic designer, positions that seemed impossibly out of reach to the majority.

Beliefs and attitudes give shape to future hopes and goals, and what was a distinct likelihood becomes a distant possibility. Aspirations are lowered in contexts where achievements have been low in the past – and the cycle gets repeated across generations (see Chapter 6).

Looking for Solutions

Fixing this situation isn't going to be easy. There are multiple tasks that need to be undertaken. Increasing preparedness, reducing vulnerability, making information more easily and reliably available, helping develop superior role models, re-forming attitudes – each of these development tasks is necessary, and each needs to be undertaken with a long-term horizon.

It's not simply a matter of allocating more money. You can't re-form attitudes, for instance, merely by forming a ministry and allocating a budget. Neither is it a matter simply of turning over development programming to the private sector. (It would be naive to think that while doing what the government does, the private sector wouldn't, over the longer term, become just like the government.) The search for such snap-of-the-finger solutions, the stuff of drawing-room conversations, is a chimerical one. There are no magical solutions.

Holding the idea of development practice as a search for cure-all solutions is not very productive. The problems of development aren't ever "solved." That's because the process of identifying problems and fashioning solutions is a continuous one; the situation is fluid and keeps evolving. Each solution gives rise to new problems, which must be resolved, giving rise to other problems and opportunities.

Take, for instance, the case of school education. At first, the problem was that there were no school buildings and no teachers in remote rural areas. Solving these problems by building schools and sending teachers to far-flung villages led to other problems – of low-quality education and low-performing schoolteachers. Solving these newer problems, perhaps by giving teachers more autonomy or by instituting more local control, might lead to consequent problems of local capture, which would, in turn, have to be tackled using newer measures.

The ever-changing scenarios, and the appearance of new downstream threats, are essential parts of the development experience. Problems mutate rather than being resolved. The process of problem solving needs to be more robust than any particular solution that it proposes. It's the process that needs to be developed first.

Capacities for iterative problem solving needs to be strengthened at different levels. Of special importance is the need to nurture problem-solving capacities at the grassroots level. More often than not, when people meet with the government, the contact is made with lower-level service providers, such as nurses, schoolteachers, and revenue officials. A large share of the problems can, and should, be resolved at these points, without having to be pushed up to a higher level.

Making these encounters at the ground level more productive for citizens requires accepting that there's a different way of administering the tasks of development. Centralized solutions pushed from the top down, which may be all right for currency control, national defense, and foreign relations, are not as useful, or as necessary, for other important tasks of development. Objectives such as improving school quality, reducing morbidity, and reducing people's carbon footprints require more than just a government department with a big budget. To achieve these ends, behaviors and attitudes need to change, assisted by processes that invoke ownership and spark creativity.

School quality will not improve, for instance, merely because another law is passed or another departmental instruction is issued. It will improve when teachers love their jobs more and when parents are more involved in setting directions. The process of re-forming the state so it can work in this fashion, empowering the grassroots and bringing decision-making closer to ordinary people, is going to be a long haul, but there isn't any easier alternative (see Chapter 7).

Hurrying slowly is the better way to move forward: acting with urgency (hurrying) while also taking the time (slowly) to be deliberate, thoughtful, and reflective.[34] The hubris of trying to solve complicated problems with the stroke of a pen, and the impatience inherent in these efforts, will have to give way before a better method.

Getting the processes right and engendering local innovation is more important than chasing after the mirage of the best solution for an entire nation, particularly one as large and as diverse as India. Flip the usual order and begin by looking at the grassroots.

There isn't need for a single national solution to all problems. Diverse solutions can be found, all effective and reliable, and each better suited to a different context. In some places, the problem of missing information may be addressed, for instance, by instituting more effective citizen-provider communications; in another place, by a stricter regimen of professional training and motivational aids; and in yet another place, through a creative combination of teacher-led and internet-based learning tools.

It doesn't matter that the solutions are different. What matters is that each of them works, that each is grounded in a local context, and that each is the handiwork of people invested in longer-term outcomes. Program and process designs are better determined through such processes of bottom-up innovation. There's a reason why NGOs thrive, despite being dwarfed by the government's programs.

The best NGOs have taken the lead in developing innovations on the ground. The number of innovators has been growing in India, and new actors have emerged, including within the private sector. Even more NGOs and corporate social responsibility (CSR) operations – but not only they, government dispensaries and school districts, too – should be motivated to become innovators. At the same time, the means must institutionalized that pick up on the best innovations and take them to the next higher level.

A national system of social innovation needs to be established, a chain that links organically from the grassroots to the apex level (see Chapter 8). Process innovations at each level should be systematically tracked, and their lessons publicly discussed and disseminated.

For guiding these efforts, ambitious but realistic goals need to be set and clearly stated. It can't be another hazy vision or another overblown promise. I propose three goals for this purpose:

(1) *A minimum threshold:* No citizen of India should live in conditions that do not come up to a minimally acceptable standard. She must have enough to feed her family a nutritious diet, a firm roof over her head, clothes she's not ashamed to wear in public, and affordable and useful education and health care.

(2) *Equality of opportunity:* She must be able to rise to the level of her capabilities, not being denied a chance merely because she is poor or rural or from a particular caste or ethnic group. There have to be more effective ways of connecting talent with opportunity.

(3) *Democracy at the doorstep:* No matter where she lives, in a big town or in a remote rural area, a citizen must have low-cost venues where she can express her discontent, be listened to patiently, and be able to obtain redress with assurance. The protections, opportunities, and benefits of democracy must be easily accessible to all.

The Wider Significance

India, which ongoing trends are cleaving into a nation of *mazdoors* abutted by a small enclave of globally competitive executives and technicians, is faced with a situation that many other developing countries are also facing. Inequality-increasing trends have gained force in this era of globalization. Technological advances, spread by global value chains, are reducing the demand for less-skilled workers and raising the demand for others who are more qualified. These effects, felt in terms of relative income gains, are being experienced in richer and in poorer countries.[35] "Across the world, the high end of the wage distribution is falling in line with that of countries where economic elites are the best compensated."[36] But at the lower end, in urban slums and beyond-5-km villages, the improvement of lifestyles is much slower, and the low end in developing countries is much lower than the low end in richer countries.

Elites in developing countries, acquiring lifestyles and world-views similar to elites in other countries, can have more in common with faraway Facebook friends than with their fellow citizens. Elites can begin to see how their futures might be more closely linked with a larger global project and less closely linked with the rupee economy of their own country. With their concerns dominating policy making, the less-well-off majority could be been rendered "invisible...their needs un-politicized, not an important part of the national blueprint."[37]

There are signs that such a trend may be emerging. People with less than cutting-edge skills, who have experienced an erosion in earnings, are becoming disaffected. Such people view trade pacts, international treaties, and other tools of globalization as working to the advantage of the 1-percent while imperiling others' situations. Disaffected by the shifting economic sands, groups in the UK voted to leave the European Union, and a sizeable population in the US came out in support of Donald Trump, led astray by sirens of nativism. In country after country, groups protesting growing globalization are becoming a new voice to which national leaders are forced to listen.

Developing countries, particularly faster-growing ones, are experiencing some of the same polarizing tendencies. The inequality increases accompanying globalization are the new normal, and countries will have to adjust to their consequences. Rising inequality has costs that keep accumulating. Widening differences in lifestyles and perspectives deprive societies of the elements that make for social cohesion.[38] The fabric of a nation, even one as diverse as India, with a background of opulent maharajahs and famine-starved peasants, will not be able to withstand the pressure-cooker world of stark and growing differences. Unless developing countries are able to move a larger proportion of their people into the right-hand side of the streamgraph (Figure 1.1), inequality will reach alarming proportions, with politics riven by newer and more violent divisions. What India does in this regard will have lessons that other countries will find instructive.

2 BEYOND-5-KM VILLAGES: WHERE THE LIGHTS AREN'T SHINING BRIGHTLY

An important source of the difference that persists between India and the advanced economies of the West is that a greater share of the Indian population lives in rural areas. The hinterland is sometimes seen as a drag on India's progress, preventing the achievement of faster modernization. But this view takes no account of the country's history of public service disparities. If one examines the situation from the ground up, taking a worm's-eye view, one arrives at a different understanding.

India's rural areas are huge and diverse. Not everyone in rural areas lives off agriculture, and the share of agriculture in rural incomes has diminished. But agriculture still remains the mainstay of the rural economy, and how much land a person owns is the measure of his status in rural society. Farmers in some parts of India have become rich from growing high-value export crops, such as cut flowers and other exotics. But the majority of Indian farmers have much simpler lifestyles. To get rich through farming, you need to own a sizeable area of farm land, at least 10 hectares (22.5 acres) according to government experts, but only 1 percent of all farm families, regarded as "large farmers" in the government's classification, have landholdings of this size. Another 4 percent, classified as medium farmers, own between 4 and 10 hectares, and they are able, for the most part, to make a decent living. All other farm families, the vast majority, are in trouble. More than 75 percent have marginal landholdings of less than 1 hectare. The same experts calculated that a minimum of 2 hectares of farm land is required just to feed a family of five, let alone providing its other necessities.[1]

For most people in rural areas, it's a struggle to survive. There are few traces of India's dollar economy in the interior.

Moreover, there has been a progressive deterioration in the conditions of the farm family that has gone largely unnoticed. From more than 3 hectares in 1947, the average size of the family plot fell to 1.1 hectares in 2003. Since then, it has fallen further. The share of marginal and uneconomic landholdings has doubled from what it was 50 years earlier.[2]

Population growth has a lot to do with this trend, as does the practice of intergenerational subdivision. But both of these factors have been known for a long time, so why has so little been done by way of rectification?

The state in India has done little to ease these transitions, and coping with this slow but relentless transition in the absence of effective supports has transformed the ways of life in rural India. Unlike the industrial revolutions of the West, which converted farm laborers into factory workers, the transformation in India is of a different nature: the grandsons of peasant farmers have become *mazdoors* in the millions. More than half of all rural residents work as irregular unskilled labor. Millions of circular migrants spend part of each year in their village (where the land is and where the family lives) and another part in a city (where there's demand for manual labor). Families are torn apart because of economic necessity. Children who grow up in these circumstances face a bleak future. If one is a circular migrant, there's little prospect of achieving a stable existence or steady income.

More effective solutions have to be found to the rural questions: How will its rural parts fit within the India of the future? What needs to be done in order to make things more promising for rural people?

Two candidate solutions can be ruled out at the start. First, you can't just ignore rural areas, thinking that sooner or later they are bound to become merged within India's rapidly growing urban agglomerations. The numbers and projections that show a rapid dwindling of the rural population just don't hold up on closer investigation. For a long time to come, hundreds of millions of Indians will live in rural areas. This large share of the country's population cannot simply be asked to wait for a dim and distant future.

The second proposal, which can also be ruled out, is to keep giving larger and larger cash doles to people in rural areas. Giving someone handouts is not half as good as raising their capacities for self-improvement. It does not lead to a life of dignity, nor are hand-outs what people necessarily desire. I have yet to meet a woman who prefers a bag of free grain to improved education for her children. Poor people, wherever I have met them, have expressed the same kind of sentiment that I heard from a woman in a Gujarat village: "We don't want free things. We need more resources and better opportunities for our children."[3] Giving handouts is not an abiding solution. In some situations it may provide the only feasible solution, but only as a temporary resort, to be used until something better, with more enduring effects, can be made available. Besides, the game is principally about growing the national pool of talent.

Investing in its rural people is critical for the future of India, essential for elevating the country's long-term growth potential. Directing growth-oriented policies almost exclusively toward city-based enterprises – while feeding rural areas on a diet of make-work antipoverty programs – is hardly best suited to a longer-term strategy of building a knowledge economy with a wide base of talent.

Two Families: The Children of Hiralal and Dhansukh

Neither rural nor urban is a precise term, nor are these terms neatly separable. There are big differences between cities (Mumbai is a city, and so is Cherrapunjee). Villages, too, are hardly homogeneous. We will look at these differences and at how they have grown, but before that, let's look at how rural and urban have come into being – the result, in large part, of millions of individual decisions.

The story of two branches of a family will help illustrate this proposition. One branch lives in the village where I made a home. The other branch lives 500 km away, in a big city.

These families trace their origins to the brothers Dhansukh and Hiralal, who were born two years apart in my village. Their people have "forever" lived in this village, meaning that for as far back as anyone can remember they've been around, like most other families of this village and many other villages.[4]

When he was only a lad – he believes he was not quite 18 years of age (it must have been around 1950) – the younger brother, Hiralal, went along with a family friend to a large city. This friend, who was much older, had been working for many years in a textile factory. Using the connections that he had developed, he helped Hiralal gain an entry-level position in the same factory. It was backbreaking work and it paid poorly, but Hiralal had a job – he was making money.

For many years, he remained in the same low-paid position. He shared a small room with five other millworkers, moving every few months because no landlord would let them stay longer. But this was a time when labor-intensive manufacturing and assembly-line production were on the rise, leading to demands for both skilled and unskilled labor.

One day, assisted by a stroke of luck and steered by some helpful contacts that he had cultivated, Hiralal was taken on the permanent rolls of the company. In the years to come, his wages doubled, but even more transformative was the change in his worldview and self-image. He had entered a different world, one where people are treated like people should be and cannot be fired without reason and notice. It was at that point that he began to feel anchored in, and welcomed by, the big city.

He moved his wife and children, who had until then been living in the village, into a small two-bedroom apartment in the city. His older son, Shantilal, after finishing high school, went to work for the same cotton mill as his father. He started out as an assistant to one of the accountants, and he rose to become chief accounts clerk. Not much is spoken about the younger son, Dheeru, but from the little I heard I could make out that he wasn't interested in studies, fell into bad company, and did not finish school. They started him out in an entry-level position, the same as his father, but Dheeru couldn't handle the drudgery. He ran away, never to return to his family.

The older son, Shantilal, the studious and hardworking one, on being raised to accounts clerk, got married and set up a family of his own. He sent his children to the best private schools, even though he could ill afford these expenses. His son, Arjun, upon acquiring a bachelor's degree in commerce, was hired by a firm of accountants. His daughter, Madhu, took a nursing degree, and she works for one of the best general hospitals in this city. Both have become part of India's dollar economy – formal-sector jobs, health care coverage, cars and computers – among the top 2 or 3 percent in the country, with lifestyles similar to the middle class in Western countries.

What became of the other branch of this family, the ones who stayed behind in the village? Hiralal moved to the city, recall, but his brother, Dhansukh, kept living in the village.

When their father died, the 8 acres of land that he had owned were divided equally between the two brothers.[5] Hiralal, who was by then well settled in his urban job, sold his half-share and returned to the city.

The older brother, Dhansukh, remained in the village, farming the half-share, 4 acres, that he had inherited. He and his wife had four children. Their two daughters got married and moved away, each to her husband's ancestral village. Dhansukh's sons, Rupa and Kantilal, kept living with their parents. Each son farmed the pieces of land that he would eventually inherit. Half of 4 acres made for 2 acres each, a pittance. A generation later, things have become worse. Rupa has two sons, Jaitram and Gopal, and they have to make do with 1 acre each. The land is no longer enough for making a living.

Their father's and grandfather's way of life is no longer viable for Dhansukh's grandsons, Jaitram and Gopal. Merely in order to survive, they need to develop additional streams of income. This makes for difficult circumstances, because the skills they have learned from their parents and neighbors – useful farming techniques, rearing animals – are of little use for bridging the gap between need and income.

There are new skills to be learned, but there are few people around who can teach these skills to young village people. So how do people in villages cope with the emergent situation?

Let's look at what the brothers, Jaitram and Gopal, are doing. Jaitram left school in 2005 after completing the 8th standard. He took up work as a general-purpose assistant on a commercial truck – washing and cleaning; changing tires; loading and unloading the cargo; fetching and carrying for the driver. He learned how to drive, and over the next ten years, he rose to become the truck driver. His brother, Gopal, who is younger by two years, also left school after finishing the 8th standard. He earns a living as a *mazdoor* in the construction industry, putting himself out to hire by the day at designated street corners, ubiquitous in every city, and known as labor *chowks* or *nakas*.[6]

It is a harsh life they lead. Jaitram and Gopal, in the rupee economy, have lifestyles that are far removed from those of their dollar-economy city cousins. Branches of the same family tree, they grow further apart in the social forest.

Indian society is a vast collection of such split-apart family trees. A hundred years ago, very few people lived in cities. Today, nearly one third of all Indians live in urban areas. One part of this increase occurred

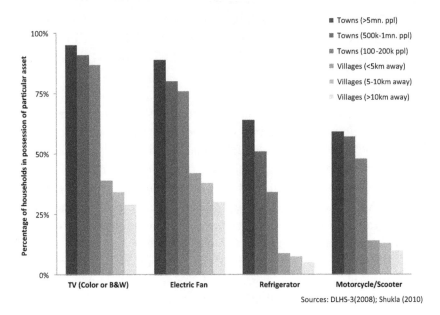

Sources: DLHS-3(2008); Shukla (2010)

Figure 2.1 Household possessions decrease with smaller towns and more distant villages. *Sources: DLHS-3 (2008); Shukla (2010)*

because of natural growth (with births exceeding deaths within cities); another part arose on account of the reclassification of bigger villages as towns; but a large part of the increase came about on account of rural-to-urban migration. City people tend to have a migrant figure in their family histories.

It is not just the branches of this particular family tree, however, that have grown far apart. There is, in general, a large separation between the lifestyles of people in towns and villages.

Beyond-5-km Villages

Compared to those who live in villages, people who live in towns own more assets and make more money. They are also better provided with infrastructure and public amenities. The deeper you venture into the countryside, the greater is the contrast in lifestyles and opportunities.

Figure 2.1 provides one illustration of the differences in quality of life between towns and villages. It shows the possession rates by households in 2008 of 4 different consumer durables: TVs, electric fans, refrigerators, and motorcycles/scooters.[7] Three types of cities are considered in this graph, ranging from the largest (with more than 5 million people) to the smallest (100,000–200,000 inhabitants). Villages, too, have been separated into three broad types based upon their distance in kilometers to the nearest urban center (town or city).[8] The first type (or "distance-band") of villages consists of those that are located within 5 kilometers of the nearest urban center (<5 km). In 2008, 31 percent of the rural population lived in such villages. The second distance-band lies between 5 and 10 km from the nearest urban center. It accounts for 27 percent of rural households. The largest share of rural households, 41 percent, lives, however, in the third and furthest distance-band, inhabiting villages that are more than 10 km from the nearest urban center (>10 km).

Classifying cities and villages in this manner helps uncover important inequalities. For each type of consumer durable, the highest ownership rates are found in the biggest cities. These rates decrease consistently as town size falls – and they fall off a cliff upon reaching rural India. For example, nearly 95 percent of residents in the largest cities owned television sets, but no more than 30 percent of residents in any type of village. Within rural India, possession rates for each type of consumer durable are highest in villages closest to towns and lowest in the furthest distance-band of villages.

Like the heights of buildings, tallest in the largest cities and shortest in the furthest village, there is a regularly declining level of asset possession. Households in the largest cities are three to six times better endowed with consumer assets compared to households in the furthest distance-band of villages. Financial assets, like stocks and bonds, are similarly distributed. Average incomes are also largest in the biggest cities and smallest in the last distance-band of villages. No matter what one's level of education, earnings are higher if one lives within a large town compared to a small town – and in a small town compared to a remote village.[9]

One category of habitations has the highest score in each case (metro cities), while another category of habitations is consistently lowest. This always-low category, which I have come to regard as "beyond-5-km villages," combines the two further distance bands (excluding only within-5-km villages). It's a sizeable group. Nearly 70 percent of all rural people – i.e., nearly *half the population of India* – live in beyond-5-km villages.

People in beyond-5-km villages not only have fewer assets and lower incomes compared to those who live in villages nearer cities; the means that enable people to earn higher incomes are also more developed in closer-by villages. All sorts of aids to business and enterprise – electricity supply, canal irrigation, paved roads, and bank branches – are more assuredly available in cities and in villages closer to cities. More than 20 percent of villages within 5 km of towns have bank branches, for instance, but less than 12 percent of beyond-5-km villages.

The distance measure helps capture the simultaneous effects of multiple encumbrances.[10] In order to get to schools, colleges, dispensaries, hospitals, police stations, and government offices, people of beyond-5-km villages have to travel greater distances, incurring greater costs in terms of time and money. Young people who live within 2 km of a town have to travel 3.3 km, on average, to attend secondary school, but those of villages situated more than 10 km from towns have to travel 13.4 km – not an inconsiderable distance, especially where roads are bad and buses are infrequent. Partly as a result, the percentage of individuals with a middle-school or higher education is 13 percent lower in beyond-5-km villages compared to the rest of the country. The gender gap in education is greatest in more remote villages: parents fear for the safety of daughters who travel great distances.[11] Surveys that I conducted showed that, compared to other locations, the quality of learning is also poorer in beyond-5-km villages.[12]

The situation with respect to health care is no different. The more rustic one's existence – the further one lives from towns – the greater are the odds of disease, malnourishment, and morbidity.[13] Villages located closer to towns are three times as likely, compared with beyond-5-km villages, to have a hospital (government or a private), and more than twice as likely to have a basic care facility, such as a primary health center or government dispensary.[14]

You don't need to know these facts in advance: when you go into villages and talk to people, it's easy to make out the difference. People in beyond-5-km villages are more likely to be poor, to work as migrant laborers with divided families, to be less well informed about various matters, and to have less confidence in their economic futures.

Accumulated advantages help the young people who live inside or near India's cities prepare in better ways for their future careers. Young people growing up in beyond-5-km villages have a different experience during their formative years. Their struggles to achieve a better life are handicapped by lower and less effective state provisioning. Extending its embrace to this large part of the national talent pool is important for the country's future development.

The state has rarely been visible in remote rural India, however – neither before national independence, nor in later years. Constructed from the top down, the state was left incomplete; a considerable gap remains between ordinary villagers and the lowest-level government office. The supply of government functions and functionaries is lower and more erratic in more distant villages. The intensity of demand for better governance is also lower: people in more remote locations are less confident that their voices will influence government decisions, and they make contact less often with public officials.

Using the measures developed for this purpose by the World Bank, I tested the relationship between quality of governance and distance to nearest town in a group of villages. The World Bank examines different dimensions of the quality of governance – including voice and accountability; political stability and absence of violence; government effectiveness in service delivery; and control of corruption.[15]

On every one of these dimensions, governance scores tend to be higher in villages located closest to cities and lower in beyond-5-km villages. In fact, there is a consistently inverse relationship between distance-to-town and governance outcomes, a regularly declining gradient of governance.[16]

Nationally representative studies uphold the same conclusions. The results of one such survey show that more than 10 percent of city residents had regular contact with different types of government officials, but the corresponding proportion in beyond-5-km villages was less than 4 percent. These are disappointing percentages overall, showing relatively little contact between service providers and ordinary citizens. Even these small percentages are smaller still in beyond-5-km villages.[17]

Two of four positions in my village school, 22 km from the nearest town, remained unfilled for more than four years; few government teachers are willing to come to this remote location. The remaining two teachers often turn up late and are frequently absent. When asked, they claim to have been held up elsewhere on account of "other official duties" (such as elections or censuses). But schoolchildren and their parents rarely ask. They could do little about it even if they knew why a teacher had gone missing, for who has the patience and the money to go 22 km to file a complaint, all the while knowing that the likelihood of getting things fixed is pretty dismal?

It is with this kind of situation that our farmers of the third generation, the trucker, Jaitram, and his brother, Gopal, the part-time construction laborer, have to cope on an ongoing basis. With their land-holdings diminished and productivity increases not keeping pace, they have had to seek supplementary earnings away from their village. But for making such external earnings they are ill prepared. The public schools and clinics that serve them are far away and of poor quality. Teachers and nurses are frequently missing. They have little confidence in their ability to hold these public officials to account: everything seems distant, costly, and shrouded in mystery. It is these realities – and not lack of hard work or absence of good sense – that account for the vast differences that have arisen between people in rural areas and those in big cities.

I cannot see how their situations will improve of their own accord or how these problems will go away as a result of urbanization. More than 800 million currently live in rural areas (of whom more than 550 million live in beyond-5-km villages). Moving such a large number off the land is not a task than can be accomplished in only a few decades. An extreme remedy, deliberately depopulating villages, has never been part of any reasonable person's toolkit for making India more urban. Building hundreds of brand-new cities almost overnight to house many millions and relocating masses of villagers, by force if necessary – a strategy given serious consideration by the technocrats of the Chinese Communist Party[18] – is an unimaginably difficult enterprise for India.

However, even as uprooting villagers and transporting them en masse to cities is not a viable option, its alternative – how to develop villages *in situ* – has not been given serious policy consideration. As a result, villagers in India live in a sort of in-between policy space: they've always had lower levels of public infrastructure and experienced a poorer quality of governance. Broken roads, decrepit school buildings, erratic electric supply, disease, and malnutrition – all these are more prevalent farther from towns and far from national highways.

Devoting resources to big cities, which are India's engines of growth and its gateways to globalization, is a matter of high priority. But it shouldn't get in the way of giving a fair deal to other citizens.

Besides, it's not a zero-sum game: the amounts do matter, but *how* the money is spent matters in addition. The government is aware that it is not performing effectively. Its schools and its hospitals are being steadily deserted – but it is not doing much to fix things at the operational levels.[19] There are severe problems, both of resource allocation and of governance, which have to be overcome using creative methods. We will return to consider these issues, but let's first look at how people in villages have been coping individually.

Far from the State's Gaze

In 2011, 69 percent of India lived in villages; only 5 percentage points less than 20 years earlier. But over the same 20-year period, the share of agriculture in the national economy fell from 31 percent to 14 percent. The spectacular rise of the services sector, including information technology, accounts in large part for this relative decline in agriculture.

However, agriculture has declined not just in relative but also in absolute terms. When one takes a de-massed view and examines trends at the individual level, the extent of the absolute decline becomes visible.

Let's return to the half-finished story of Jaitram and Gopal, our third-generation farmers, grandsons of the brother, Dhansukh, who chose to stay behind in the village. What are the different ways in which people in such situations can improve their economic conditions? I put this question to a group of people in my village. They suggested the following alternatives:

(1) By acquiring more land
(2) Through an increase in productivity (growing more tomatoes on the same piece of land)
(3) By developing a new earning source, such as an additional job, which brings in a supplementary income

Conversely, they said, an individual's situation worsens if one or more of these conditions moves in the opposite direction – less land; few productivity gains; and lack of alternative income sources.

For the average rural family dependent on agriculture, the converse is exactly what has happened. The size of the average landholding has decreased. Productivity increases have been too small to compensate for this reduction. Alternative earning opportunities of the better sort have been out of reach. Few rural individuals have the preparation required to make high and reliable earnings in this era of globalization.

Government grants, which could have helped cover some part of the deficit, are small, and in any case, they do not constitute a sustainable solution.

Let's start with agricultural land. We saw how after each generation the landholding gets partitioned. Jaitram and Gopal's great-grandfather farmed 8 acres of land – small in size, but enough for making a living. Their grandfather had half as much land, 4 acres. Jaitram and Gopal have 1 acre each. Across rural India, such extreme fragmentation has been experienced.[20]

One possible way out – expanding land under the plow – is not a promising solution. There's no cultivable land where there aren't already people.[21]

What about the second way that my village group suggested: increasing productivity, i.e., growing more wheat or tomatoes on the same piece of land? There seems to be some promise in this option. Per-hectare productivity figures for India are on the low side. India produced 1,938 kg of rice per hectare (averaged over the three-year period 1998–2000) while China produced more than 6,000 kg per hectare. Cotton yields are 640 kg/hectare on average in India and 3,130 kg/hectare in China. Sorghum yields are 801 kg/hectare in India and 1,624 kg/hectare in Thailand.[22] There's scope, this evidence suggests, for future increases. If yields can be tripled even as land sizes are halved, the ongoing decline in small farmers' situations can be reversed.

Serious efforts to raise agricultural productivity were made earlier, especially from the second half of the 1960s into the 1970s, but these efforts have decreased in intensity in recent years. During the earlier period of state-led development, between 1951 and 1991, even as the main thrust of economic development was in heavy industry, agriculture was supported by the state through a variety of measures:

- by expanding the network of irrigation canals, with coverage doubling from 8.3 million hectares in 1951 to nearly 17 million hectares in 1991;
- through investments in research and development, backed by extension services that took the latest technical advice from lab to land;
- by opening bank offices in rural areas, the number of rural bank branches increasing from 14,000 in 1980 to 35,000 in 1991; and
- by providing inputs such as seeds, fertilizer, and pesticides through a network of state-backed cooperatives.[23]

Rural leaders of the time regarded these provisions as inadequate, claiming that agriculture was being shortchanged.[24] They did not realize that worse was to follow.

Nearly all of the means adopted to support agriculture have been cut back in the period after globalization. The network of government canals has not been extended. For more than 20 years after 1991, its coverage remained static at 17 million hectares. The research and extension services of the government have become weaker and less effective, with the network of agricultural universities being "starved of funds," according to the report of a government commission, which also notes how "government agencies ... have come to play a negligible role in disseminating information on agricultural technology. By 2005, extension agencies were a source of information for only 5 percent of all farmers, a situation that is very different in China," a country that continues to maintain a robust extension agency connecting lab findings and land operations.[25]

Instead of helping people in villages overcome a difficult transition, the Indian government in the post-globalization period has turned its gaze away from rural areas. An expert group commissioned by the Indian government found evidence of a widespread "decline in public agricultural support systems."[26] Other authoritative examinations have concluded similarly, including a World Bank team, which found that public investments in agriculture have "fallen by more than half" in the period after economic liberalization.[27]

The state has, by and large, retreated from agriculture, being replaced by a different kind of political economy arrangement. Subsidies that disproportionately benefit medium and large farmers (together constituting less than 5 percent of farmers) have increased, at the expense of broader-based public investments. Supermarket chains and seed companies are the new sources of incentives and innovation. Following the money, as for-profit enterprises should and must, they disproportionately serve larger farms and better-off regions. Inequalities have been increasing in rural areas.[28]

Simultaneously, agriculture has become a riskier business. Journalist Siddhartha Deb has a harrowing tale from the southern state of Andhra Pradesh, where he met with representatives of a large group of farmers who "had chosen to grow a crop called red sorghum. They had contracted their produce to the biggest of the local seed dealers ... who had offered them an exceptionally high price for red sorghum. When the farmers finished harvesting, [the dealer] refused to take delivery of the red sorghum or to pay them."[29] World market prices had fallen sharply in the period between sowing and harvesting, and because there are no realistic mechanisms to enforce such contracts, the dealer could renege without fearing consequences. The farmers faced ruin.

Small and marginal farmers, the vast majority, neither well organized nor well represented, have little bargaining power, and they are the ones who are most acutely affected.[30] The marginalization of farm size takes away from their ability to save and invest. When public investments in agriculture were also cut back, there remained little scope for future productivity increases.

Different Ways of Coping

The share of agriculture in the average rural household's income consequently fell from 60 percent in the early 1990s to less than 30 percent by 2011, and farm families' efforts were redirected toward other sources of income. The share in rural household income of four other income sources has increased – agricultural labor, nonagricultural labor, nonfarm self-employment (setting up a trade or business), and salaried and professional positions. These sources differ widely in terms of average pay,[31] terms of employment, and conditions of entry. Not every source of alternative employment is equally available to everybody.

Two kinds of casual labor, agricultural and nonagricultural, have made up for the bulk of the decline in the share of agriculture in rural households' incomes – particularly among poorer households and particularly in beyond-5-km villages. Given a choice, few would select to work as agricultural laborers: it is the lowest-paid occupation, irregular and seasonal, with hard and often hazardous working conditions.[32] But there is freedom of entry, and so it attracts poorer and less-educated individuals. For the poorer half of families in beyond-5-km villages, the largest share of household income, more than 40 percent, is now derived from agricultural labor. Another big part of their income, more than 20 percent, comes from nonagricultural labor. Three kinds of nonagricultural labor opportunities have expanded fast: construction, transportation, and trading.[33] Informal employment is dominant within each of these sectors; most people find employment on a day-to-day basis.

Since neither agricultural nor nonagricultural labor is constant or well paying, poorer rural families diversify, taking up multiple occupations. Some combine cultivation with agricultural labor nearer home; others migrate seasonally to towns in search of work as *mazdoors*. Because men are more likely to be involved in these migration streams, a widespread "feminization" of small-holder agriculture has been reported.[34]

These are the kinds of career options that are practically available to most young village people. Gopal – the grandson of our farmer in the village – became a construction laborer not because that was what he wanted and worked toward, but because there was no better option. He, his wife, and their two children live on the 1-acre farm they possess. Gopal leaves every morning to seek work as a *mazdoor*. He earns 200 rupees on the days he finds work, spending 20 rupees each way on transportation. His wife, Koonthi, looks after their 20 goats and 4 cows, assisted by their 11-year-old daughter, who is enrolled at school but rarely attends, because herding and other household chores take priority.[35] At the time of the monsoon rain, Gopal plows their field and sows seeds of sorghum and maize, paying for tractor hours or hiring in a pair of oxen. Koonthi takes care of the weeding, sorting, fertilizing, watering, and other needs of the crop for the next few months. For a few weeks each year, when there is no standing crop, she goes to work on government work sites. She also works for payment on other people's fields. Their 9-year-old son goes to school more regularly than his older sister. When he turns 14, though, he will also be sent to work for a wage; that is the need and the custom.

Better opportunities do exist, but they are out of reach of the majority of village residents. Salaried and professional incomes, the most desirable and highest-paying alternative to agriculture, have also increased their share in rural households' incomes, but this earning source has been availed, in the main, by the sons and daughters of the richest 5 percent of rural households (large and medium farmers and business people).[36] The efforts of richer farmers to provide for a good education for their children "acquired a new sense of urgency in the mid-1990s. They sought a greater range of educational opportunities, started to give their children extra-school tutorials, and used schools outside the immediate vicinity . . . sending their children to private, usually English-medium schools" located in cities.[37]

Benefiting from the better education they have been able to receive, children of the richest farmers have prospered. The share contributed by salaried and professional jobs to the richest rural households' incomes has steadily expanded. People from this narrow social stratum have captured high-level positions in different walks of life.[38] Some among them have set up large business enterprises, becoming India's new capitalists.[39]

But simultaneously, the poorer one is and the more rural one's location – the further one lives from towns – the more difficult it has become merely to make a decent living. It is in beyond-5-km villages, far from the planners' line of sight, where a great deal of the pain of development is being experienced. People in beyond-5-km villages have been able to derive the fewest benefits from growth in this era of globalization. During some periods they have suffered real income losses, even as the national economy was growing.[40] Even for those, like Gopal, who have attended schools, making 5,000 rupees a month is a struggle.[41]

Growth, globalization, education – and as we will see, urbanization and technology – have not bestowed the anticipated large rewards on a large variety of people. Some gains were made in the agricultural economy in the seven years following 2005, and some evidence points to a narrowing of the rural-urban difference during this period, but overall the earlier pattern has continued. Instead of being directed to the areas with the greatest needs, the growth of infrastructure in rural areas has been by way of urban sprawl, with additional ribbon growth on account of highway building.[42] It seems unlikely, therefore, that the forces holding back beyond-5-km villages have been significantly weakened.

On the contrary, there is evidence of falling consumption expenditures among marginal farmers and agricultural laborers and of increases in the numbers of the undernourished. Many, including Gopal's family, are having to work much harder simply to make ends meet, a coping strategy characterized as "self-exploitation – in the form of long working hours together with low pay, and maximum participation of household members in the labor process."[43] There are reports of suicides by desperate farmers.[44]

Rural discontent, rising to the level of militancy in some regions, often spoken of as India's Naxalite or Maoist movement, is better viewed against the backdrop of these developments. Disrupting state sovereignty and the rule of law, this corridor of unrest has at times spread across vast parts of the country.[45] India's former Prime Minister Manmohan Singh, who saw Naxalite activities as India's gravest internal security challenge, considered it a result largely of failed development efforts and poor governance.[46] A report of the Indian Home Ministry was equally candid, acknowledging that "Naxalites operate in the vacuum created by functional inadequacies of field-level governance structures, espouse local demands, and take advantage of prevalent disaffection ... among the underprivileged and *remote* segments of the population."[47] The government is right to recognize that distance and discontent are related: the states where Naxalite activities were most widespread are also the ones in which a great share of the population lives in beyond-5-km villages.[48]

There's an element of truth in the charges that have been leveled of failed development efforts and poor governance in beyond-5-km villages, home to nearly half the country's population. That's hardly the best way to achieve the objective of broad-based development in a largely agrarian economy undergoing globalization.

The Policy Need

Waiting for urbanization to solve rural problems is both a dewy-eyed and an impractical expectation. Three generations ago, when Hiralal moved to the city, migration from villages was still just a trickle, assembly-line jobs were plenty, labor unions were strong, and formal-sector employment was growing.

The situation in cities has changed a great deal in the period after globalization. Formal sector jobs have grown in considerable numbers only for the most highly educated. A high school diploma, and more often a college degree, is required to achieve any considerable advancement. But few urban Indians and fewer village residents have any such qualifications. Only 15 percent of rural individuals in the age group 18–24 years were attending higher education institutions in 2008, with this proportion being much lower among poorer households and lower still among the residents of beyond-5-km villages.[49] Those without a higher education – the greatest number – vie for low-paid informal sector positions. As ever more rural people are thrown on the city economy, the supply of lower-paid workers has increased dramatically. In these circumstances, moving to a city has not helped achieve considerable improvements in living standards for the majority.[50]

The rural question has to be resolved *in situ*. The country cannot sustainably grow or equitably develop until this question is more effectively settled.

Several elements of a likely solution need to be openly debated, starting with the matter of resource allocation. One view, expressed first by Mahatma Gandhi, and repeatedly reaffirmed, including by Abdul Kalam, India's president between 2002 and 2007, demands equal priority in resource allocation between cities and villages and equal standards of infrastructure provision.[51] A succession of governments has paid lip service to this idea, but resource allocation and policy attention have continued to be biased toward urban areas, becoming worse in the post-globalization period. A report by the International Food Policy Research Institute, an institution for research and policy advice responsible to the United Nations, notes, for instance, how the Indian government's policies are "heavily oriented toward urban areas, and new public investments have privileged mostly urban areas as well as more prosperous regions . . . A similar disparity exists between urban and rural areas in terms of public investments in literacy and education."[52] Why such a strategy has been adopted is hard to justify on grounds either of democracy or of growth promotion.

The gains to be had by implementing a strategy of more equal resource allocation are considerable. Imagine, for instance, what might be achieved if the same kinds of well-resourced educational facilities that are used by the top 5 percent were to be made available to poorer kids in remote rural areas. Imagine, too, that these kids were to get decent health care and all-weather roads. It's a fair bet that there would be many more rural entrepreneurs and capitalists, creators of jobs and developers of innovations.

The rural cousins Jaitram and Gopal, the truck driver and *mazdoor*, are neither less smart nor less motivated than their cousins in the big city, but being unaware of better opportunities and lacking guidance, resources, and preparation, they have been left behind by growth, becoming part of a large underutilized portion of the national pool of talent. Ironic as it may seem in a country of a billion-plus people, shortages of qualified manpower are being acutely experienced.[53] The paradox is that simultaneously, people who are capable and desirous of gaining qualifications and obtaining employment are finding these opportunities virtually impossible to access.

Making India stronger in the future requires attending more urgently and effectively to the problems faced by this half of the population. They need more support – better and more accessible education and health care, banks and communication facilities within easy reach, more authority over their public officials, better career options, and superior role models.

A failure to provide opportunities equitably and to recognize and reward talent more widely – the broken ladder – has hurt India's performance in diverse arenas. Countries that have performed better than India have consistently brought diverse opportunities within easy reach of their populations, rural and urban.

Be it the Olympic Games, or the number of international patents received, or articles published in top academic journals, South Korea, with only 50 million people, consistently ranks ahead of India. That's because almost every Korean knows what the Olympic Games are and has a chance to attend a high school with functioning laboratories. The story is very different in India: if you are poor or if you grow up in a beyond-5-km village, it's highly unlikely that you know how to make serious bid for a place in the Olympics or have your creativity sparked by studying the sciences in a thoughtful and practical manner. In South Korea the entire talent pool, or a very large part of it, has access to diverse opportunities. Much of India's talent pool remains latent because the better opportunities are hidden and distant. That's not merely because South Korea is richer than India. Until the 1960s, the two countries had the same income level. South Korea grew prosperous by productively harnessing the creative energies of the bulk of its population; its institutions continue to connect talent with opportunity.[54]

Something similar can and should be done in India. There are admirable examples, still few in number, that demonstrate how rural Indians and those in city slums can be better engaged in diverse national efforts. We will meet some of these people, as well as noteworthy organizations that are assisting with the task of finding and developing talents. It's through means such as these – and not by way of increased handouts – that people in beyond-5-km villages can be suitably empowered.

The national dialog has to concern itself with providing more resources for developing physical and social infrastructures in rural India.[55] Equally, the dialog has to focus on the mechanisms of spending this money – who is authorized to spend it; when and for what purposes; and with whose consent and participation. Questions of institutional design and governance arrangements need to be taken up with renewed seriousness.

Resolving governance problems requires fixing institutions at the grassroots and vesting more authority in field-level officials and more discretion in village residents. The way things work presently, village residents, particularly poorer ones, including many Scheduled Castes and Scheduled Tribes, have very little say in how their day-to-day public affairs are conducted. It's a major feat, and a rare one, to have a nonperforming teacher replaced in one's village's primary school, or to get an irrigation engineer to send water down the pipeline when one's standing crop has started to wither.

When "reforms" are discussed in India, it is economic policy reforms – such as reduced taxes and tariffs and fewer inspections of factories – that people usually consider. However, there is also another class of reforms, consisting of improvements at multiple levels in the chain of governance, that require policy attention and systematic experimentation. The chain of governance begins at the grassroots levels and links upward through blocks and districts to the level of state government and ultimately to the national level. Its weakest links currently are at the grassroots level and at levels just above – but those are the very levels about which there is the least talk of reform and innovation.

A view seems to prevail that having created *panchayats*, enough has been accomplished already. *Gram panchayats*, or elected village councils, have been established across rural India, but only in a handful of states do such bodies have significant authority over local-level government functionaries.[56] Additionally, *panchayats* do not independently raise the bulk of their revenues. They are funded almost entirely by grants that flow in from higher-level links in the chain of governance.[57] Ministries of the central and state governments, who give out this money, decide in advance how it will be expended.

Apart from being short on discretionary authority and resources, *panchayats* are also unwieldy institutions. They loosely oversee a wide array of activities – including education, health care, environmental management, agriculture development, public works, conflict resolution, and local policing – that stretch the capacities of the available staff, pulling them in different directions. Moreover, the diverse functions are variously of concern to different village residents. Those who do not have children at school, for instance, tend to be less interested in and less well informed about teaching quality, and those who do not rear animals are, by and large, less aware of the quality of veterinary services. Each of these groups is a natural constituency with a related set of demands; all together, they can be a rabble pulling in different directions.

It is important for a number of reasons to strengthen *panchayats* and to enhance their functional independence. But *panchayats* in their current form are not all that is necessary for achieving effective local-level governance.

Multiple local organizations answering to different natural constituencies – parents of schoolchildren, animal breeders, seed purchasers and sellers to supermarket chains, farmers of particular watersheds, nursing and expectant mothers, and so on – are required, each empowered to take decisions and to effectively supervise personnel, and each linked up to higher-level organizations in the chain of institutions. Research in multiple countries has shown consistently how networks of grassroots organizations have accompanied exemplary rural development.[58]

Practically viable and empirically tested processes must be developed that can help keep program and institutional designs relevant and current. In the end, it is institutions and processes that matter more than one-time solutions. Attitudes need to change in tandem. Decentering state provisioning and de-massing development will require respecting villagers and trusting them with the authority to make decisions.

All of this is within reach. But it requires that age-old ways of thinking about poverty and economic development be replaced by a different vision.

Progress will not take the same path in India as it did in the West, with the peopling of industrial manufacturing accompanying the de-peopling of agriculture. Already a critical stage has been missed: employment in organized services has grown faster than employment in organized industry, which has remained almost static, eliciting charges of jobless development.[59]

The different transition that India is undergoing is converting the grandsons of peasant farmers into an army of itinerant *mazdoors* and their granddaughters into part-time marginal farmers. Ensuring more stability to their livelihoods and fixing the broken ladders they confront has to become an essential part of the national strategy. Else, we might see life becoming more difficult at the margins, with people and natural resources more ruthlessly exploited and increasingly desperate individuals adopting scorched-earth tactics.

In Other Countries

Other countries have dealt more evenhandedly with cities and villages, presenting a different legacy of economic development. Governments in East Asia, in the 1960s and 70s, energetically built high-quality infrastructures in rural areas, both to develop rural talent and draw it into workplaces in cities and to increase the competitive advantage of rural locations. The rural share of the population in these countries used to be similarly large. In 1950, for instance, 78 percent of South Korea and 65 percent of Japan was rural. The investments made by these governments in rural areas – in roads and canals, schools and colleges of good quality, hospitals and dispensaries, electricity supply, career centers, and communications – helped villagers in these countries participate more effectively in building globally competitive economies. It is notable that these investments did not have to wait on these countries' spurts of economic growth: investments in rural infrastructure were large even before their golden periods of economic development.[60]

The Indian state has not been as nurturing in its response. Except for helping build a small number of isolated islands,[61] viable solutions of the kinds that help rural individuals compete on a level playing field have not been implemented. On the contrary, and quite surprisingly – for it may have been no one's intent – public investment has been cut back, making the situation worse, particularly in beyond-5-km villages.

India is hardly the only country, however, where the gulf is fast widening between remote villages and larger cities, creating a dollar economy and rupee economy (or local equivalents) that operate in parallel. Similar situations are being experienced across a swath of countries that have large rural populations. More than 80 percent of people in Ethiopia, Kenya, Malawi, Niger, and Sri Lanka live in rural areas, for instance, and more than 60 percent in Bangladesh, India, Madagascar, Pakistan, Uzbekistan, and Vietnam. In other developing countries, too, the share of the rural population is substantial – more than 40 percent in China, Georgia, Ghana, Guatemala, Indonesia, and Nicaragua.

Studies conducted in many of these countries have found evidence of growing spatial inequalities, a widening rift between cities and villages. A disproportionately large share of the gains from globalized growth have accrued to the already better-off urban residents.[62] There is a glittering part of globalization: glass-walled skyscrapers in big cities. And then there are the duller bits in remote rural areas. "China's remarkable economic growth is a result of only a handful of urban centers such as Shanghai, Shenzhen, and Beijing... each of which is a world apart from its vast impoverished rural areas... India's growing economic spikes – city regions such as Bangalore, Hyderabad, Mumbai, and parts of New Delhi – are rapidly pulling away from the rest of this country."[63]

Why is increasing spatial inequality of this kind such a large part of the current experience of globalization? One part of the explanation has to do with what economists refer to as "agglomeration effects." Another part has to do with attitudinal shifts and policy reinforcement. Market-driven agglomeration effects help explain why financiers, suppliers of intermediate goods and maintenance services, and a mass of workers with diverse skills are commonly attracted to locations with superior infrastructural facilities and growing economic opportunities – namely, big cities. As purchasing power increases in big cities, it gives rise to specialized educational opportunities and helps nurture a range of sports and cultural activities. Specialized colleges, libraries and bookshops, theater and music, and shopping malls crop up in the small group of big cities that are inhabited by highly skilled technologists and managers and their families. As this dynamic gathers pace, the separation widens. Places that start behind fall further behind. Because they live in such conditions, people of remote villages are, implicitly or explicitly, considered less worthy by many big-city people. Increasingly, the rural is seen as part of a country's past, to be pushed aside in the rush toward Westernization.

All of this is making the world a very difficult place for hundreds of millions of rural people who do not enjoy the advantage of a level playing field, who have been told to wait patiently for generations.[64]

But murmurs of discontent, rising to crescendos of rural protest – in Thailand, for instance – show that the deepening rifts in lifestyles and prospects will not for long be meekly tolerated.[65]

The politics of growing inequality led by rising rural-urban differences have implications that will test democracies. These problems are not simply going to disappear, a side effect of economic growth, technological advancement, and globalization. Developing countries with large agrarian populations will have to be proactive in dealing with the emergent situation. If it takes the right steps, India can show the way for other countries.

3 UP AND DOWN IN THE CITY

Globalization has enhanced the economic role of bigger cities. Not only in India, but also in other developing countries, public as well as private investments have flowed into larger cities, leaving behind smaller towns and rural locations.[1] Some observers reckon that these trends – of concentrating investments, opportunities, and people in the largest cities – are necessary and beneficial, an inevitable accompaniment of economic growth and modernization.[2] A large-scale transfer of population from farms to cities occurred in countries that industrialized earlier, including England, France, Germany, and the United States. More recently, in Japan and South Korea, too, large numbers of people moved off lower-productivity farm jobs, entering into higher-productivity city-based occupations.

A similar transition has been advocated for India by some who see big cities as the economic powerhouses of the future. For promoting three national objectives, at least – establishing India's place on the world's commercial and economic map, accelerating economic growth, and removing destitution and reducing poverty – the argument is made that it is essential to make big investments in India's cities.[3]

This sense of inevitability in a vibrant urban future for India needs to be reviewed, for much of it seems to be illusory. I have no quibble with the argument that cities can be the source of great economic dynamism, and that making cities work better is necessary for a country to derive larger benefits in a world increasingly patterned by globalization. That much is well established. What is not so well founded, in my opinion, is the belief that urbanization will have the same transformative consequences for individuals. To what extent will cities in India perform the same kinds of transmission-belt roles as they did in the West, taking in a stream of farm hands and churning out an upwardly mobile urban middle class? On that question, there's much less certainty. To a limited extent and in a previous period, the Indian city did play such a role. Of late, however, its ability to play this role has been greatly diminished, on account of a series of factors needing careful consideration.

Urban History Will Not Be Repeated

Five aspects are especially noteworthy in the difference between the history of urbanization in the West and the contemporary situation in developing countries. First, and most obviously, the numbers involved in the rural-urban transition in the West were different by an order of magnitude from those involved in present-day China and India. A different demographic sequencing was followed in the West, where death rates declined with the advance of medical science, and birth rates fell shortly thereafter. The population explosion – which occurs when death rates fall sharply but birth rates linger at preindustrial levels – was of a shorter duration in these countries (and, providing further relief, a considerable part of the "surplus" population was shipped off to overseas locations in the New World). In India, however, as in many other developing countries, the duration of the population overhang has continued for much longer, with birth rates exceeding death rates without letting off for several generations. In the 50 years after national independence, India's population *tripled* from 350 million to more than 1 billion, far outstripping population growth in richer countries.[4]

The pressure of an increased population has diminished rural landholdings, and few nonagricultural employment opportunities were created in most rural areas. For generations, rural people have been coming into cities in search of better opportunities.[5]

Of late, this movement of people from villages to cities has greatly accelerated. A very large share of rural households, between 40 and 70 percent in different parts of the country, have one or more members who live and work in a city.[6] That's tens of millions of people. But here's the rub: the share of the urban population recorded by the Indian government (just over 30 percent in 2011) is tiny compared to the urban share of the population in other late-developing countries, including Malaysia (71 percent), South Korea (60 percent), and China (49 percent).[7]

How does one reconcile seemingly contradictory facts – first, that the officially recorded urban population share is relatively small, and second, that a large proportion of rural households have members who live and work in the cities of India? The simple explanation is that the official data are mistaken. At any given time, there are many more people living in India's cities than the numbers recorded in the national census.

This is a particular characteristic of an Indian city, the second factor that distinguishes it from New York, London, Seoul, and Tokyo: India's cities have very large floating populations, as do those in some other developing countries. More than 40 percent of the labor force in India's cities is constituted by a floating population, with more than 100 million coming in annually as itinerant immigrants. One sees them everywhere – construction laborers, street vendors, nannies, delivery men, waiters, parking lot attendants, and so on. Because of definitional quirks and other methodological weaknesses, however, this large and mostly poor segment of the city population has been severely under-counted in official circles, leading analysts who rely on official data to present a skewed image of the urban reality and to project an overly rosy future.[8]

Why so much rootlessness is associated with India's urban-ization story is explained by the third aspect of difference between India and the West, which has to do with the nature of the eco-nomic growth process. Unlike countries of the West, which decades ago focused on labor-absorbing manufacturing, constructing vast assembly lines to commence their modernization process (a process that China has followed more recently), India's recent economic growth has relied on high-end services of a specialized and capital-intensive nature. This strategy has added a great deal to the country's GDP, but it has resulted in creating relatively few good jobs. Of every ten new jobs created since the early 1990s, nine and sometimes all ten jobs have involved informal working arrangements – no written contract, no security of tenure, no health-care support, no old-age benefits.[9] Getting one of these jobs does not constitute an assured path to the good life. The pay is low and one's position is not secure. It seems wiser to leave the family behind in the security of the village home rather than bringing it face-to-face with a precarious urban existence. That's not how an upwardly mobile urban middle class comes into existence.

Compounding these supply-side factors, related to the small supply of good jobs, there are parallel weaknesses on the side of preparation. The fourth aspect of difference between India and countries in North America, Western Europe, and East Asia concerns the nature and quantum of investments that were made in preparing the working-age population. Compared to other countries, including Japan and South Korea (and more recently, Malaysia and China), India's investments in education and skills development have been small and of poor quality, leaving the bulk of its population ill prepared for employment in modern enterprises.

This combination of supply-side and preparation-side factors has resulted in creating a situation in which very few good jobs have been created, and simultaneously, very few people have been made capable of staking a credible claim to the better jobs – far less, of becoming job creators. These factors help understand the different experience of urbanization in India.

A fifth aspect of difference is also important: Cities in India have very little control over their own governance and development. A tiered and fragmented state machinery inherited from colonial times has been largely carried over into the contemporary period. Diverse agencies that report to different levels of government, state and federal, have authority over separate parts of city administration. The effects are seen in the form of turf wars, evasion of responsibility, and duplication of effort. Ad hoc solutions are pursued with momentary vigor, but little attention is given to the bigger picture.[10]

Because of these five aspects of difference, an individual's move from a village to a city in India has been a less rewarding and more risk-filled experience. Instead of being absorbed within high-productivity, higher-paying jobs, as in Western Europe, North America, and East Asia, workers coming to cities from rural areas in India are much more likely to become *mazdoors* (laborers) and other types of low-paid workers. They are more likely to live in slums of various kinds than in planned neighborhoods with municipal services. Many remain rootless their entire working lives, part of the large and growing floating population, characterized as "nowhere people."[11]

The economic and demographic transitions of today's richer countries took place in very different global and technological contexts.

Their history serves as a poor guide for predicting the urban futures of India and other largely agrarian developing countries. To act upon the belief that the same kinds of transformations will occur in these countries is to embark upon a quixotic mission. That's not to say that there isn't much to be gained by investing in cities. Rather, the argument I will make is that in order to realize the undeniable potential of cities, some prior steps are essential.

Paradoxical as it may seem, realizing the potential of urbanization will require making investments in rural India. Of course, there's more that is necessary, but that's an important part of what needs to be undertaken.

Diverse Arrivals: The Blue-Polygon People

Various types of internal migrants have been coming into India's cities, with short-term visitors of different kinds outnumbering the permanent relocators.[12] Neither entirely rural nor fully urban, this large portion of the Indian population has a mixed or cosmopolitan character, an extended umbilical cord that keeps alive the organic links between villages and cities.[13]

Individuals from villages located a short bus ride away come into the city as day migrants. They arrive in towns each morning and return to their village homes in the evening.

People from beyond-5-km villages cannot come and go so easily, and living in the city can be expensive, so they look for and create cheaper lodging alternatives. Several short-term single migrants get together to rent a small accommodation, sleeping ten to a room, often in shifts – or they live rough on railway platforms and city pavements. Their lives are harsh, uncertain, and risk-filled; the journeys they make are full of menace. Studies show how these types of migrants have been coping without accumulating: barely able to make ends meet, their lives have remained precarious; hardly any among them has been able to climb into a higher layer of the social onion.[14]

A third type of internal migrant, somewhat more rooted but still split to a considerable extent between a city and a village, lives within a particular type of slum settlement. These are the "blue polygon" people, so termed because clusters of their homes – four poles surmounted by a blue plastic sheet – appear as blue rectangles in satellite images, which you can see for yourself by looking at publicly available Google Earth images.[15]

Over the 16-year period 2000–2015, blue-polygon slums registered the largest increase among different types of slums in Bengaluru. In other cities, too, blue-polygon slums have proliferated.[16] Near the airport in Mumbai, close to where the airplanes come in to land, there is a vast sea of such settlements. Covered by blue tarps, these crude settlements, representing the lowest type of urban slum, are quickly becoming widely prevalent.

Blue-polygon residents are the archetypical first-generation migrants, impelled to come from villages to cities for economic reasons. "We have come here only in order to repay our debts back in the village," is a refrain I heard from many blue-polygon residents, who remit, on average, more than one-quarter of their meager earnings to the native village. But apart from aiding them in making this small amount of earning, living in the city has not placed these residents on the pathway to an ever-higher standard of living. Most blue-polygon men and women (and many older children, too) work on construction sites as irregular, daily-waged *mazdoors* earning a pittance.[17] A large majority belong to Scheduled Castes, Scheduled Tribes, and minority religions, a pattern that other slum studies have also uncovered.[18]

A typical blue-polygon abode is a 7′ × 7′ tent erected on land rented from a private owner and shared by families of between three and five individuals. Few possessions were evident within the blue-polygon dwellings that I visited in Bengaluru, Mumbai, and Patna: wooden planks balanced atop two stacks of bricks, covered with piles of shabby clothing; a couple of battered aluminum cooking vessels; a cheap mobile phone to stay connected with relatives in the village; a wood-burning *chulha* (fireplace); one or two plastic containers for storing drinking water; thumb-tacked pictures of gods and goddesses.[19]

This segment of city society, not emblematic of a shining urban future, has grown rapidly, but the official record contains hardly anything about its existence. No blue-polygon settlement features on the official list of slums in any city that I studied.

Partly as a result, blue-polygon residents have received barely any public assistance. None among the eighteen blue-polygon settlements of Bengaluru that I studied intensively was connected to the electricity network. There was a hand pump in one of these neighborhoods and a bore well in another, but residents of the remaining sixteen neighborhoods filled up at distant public water points, or they purchased drinking water at great expense from privately operated tankers. Only a tiny percentage of residents felt that they would be able to get support in times of need from employers, community leaders, government officials, political parties, NGOs, or any of the other organized agencies that other city residents can count on with more assurance.[20]

Compared to other city children, those in blue polygons have many fewer years of school education.[21] Eligibility for school enrollment, along with other social services and benefits, is virtually impossible to obtain when one's existence remains unrecognized and unregistered. Only 9 percent of residents in the blue-polygon slums of Bengaluru had Voter ID cards, 6 percent had ration cards, and only 1 percent had a Bengaluru-based Unique ID (*Aadhar*) card.[22]

Intergenerational occupational improvements are virtually nonexistent among this group of city residents. The principal occupations of current male heads of households are much the same as those of their fathers and grandfathers, the vast majority of whom also hired themselves out as casual labor. The small savings that these families are able to put aside are too often wiped out by adverse events. Illnesses, deaths and marriages, climate-change-induced droughts and rainfall failures – events occurring with great frequency – keep them trapped within a cycle of poverty. Exposed to risk in two places at once – in their city tents and in their native villages – the lives of blue-polygon slum residents are doubly precarious.[23] Driven by diminished rural livelihoods to make the trek to the city, many are unable to gain a secure foothold even after living in the city for generations.[24]

A Hierarchy of Slums with Little Upward Mobility

Other poorer city residents, including those of other and better types of slums, have also not experienced significant intergenerational improvements. These facts have also been hidden from public view, because the official databases are, once again, skimpy and selective. Slums of various kinds have been proliferating for decades, but government agencies have only recently started counting the people who live within different kinds of slum settlements.

The methodologies adopted by different official agencies are at odds with one another, but they have all underestimated the slum population. Adopting one definition of slums, the National Sample Survey Organization counted 44 million slum dwellers in 2008, but adopting another definition, the Census of India counted 65 million slum dwellers just three years later. Separately, UN-HABITAT, the international authority on low-income settlements, claimed that India had as many as 104 million slum dwellers in 2014, a number that is closer to estimates derived by grassroots investigations.[25]

Not only is the true number of people in slums not clearly known in official circles, little information is available in relation to other key questions: How many slums exist within the limits of different cities? Where are the boundaries of each particular settlement? How have individual slums changed over time? Where have conditions improved, where have they deteriorated – and for what reasons? The official record has large gaps in relation to these questions, resulting in scant official knowledge about the conditions of urban poverty.[26]

Smaller-scale examinations by independent scholars and authors have helped sketch a clearer picture.[27] A number of facts have come to light, including that slums do not constitute a homogeneous category of living arrangements.

Different types of slums have come into existence, constituting separate layers of urban existence. In examinations conducted in Bengaluru and later in Patna and Jaipur, colleagues and I were able to distinguish distinct types along a continuum of slum categories.[28]

Residents of the highest category, with the best living standards – the notified slums – have succeeded in surmounting numerous bureaucratic obstacles, over the years gaining official recognition and the considerable benefits that accrue with this status. They are better off than other slum residents. The majority in notified slums, more than 85 percent, own TV sets, steel *almirahs*, pressure cookers, and gas stoves (mobile phones have become common even among poorer people). A few families own scooters and motorcycles, but very few have washing machines or refrigerators, and almost no family has a car of its own.

Only a minority of slum settlements have been able to gain notified status.[29] Without official recognition, a slum remains an unmarked and unnamed place on the official map. Individual property titles cannot be acquired. Municipal services, such as piped water and sanitation, are provided with regularity only after a slum has been notified officially. But when notification occurs, which isn't often, it takes place at the end of a very long process.[30]

Over the longer term, there has been some improvement, though not a great deal, in the physical conditions of most slum settlements. Comparing satellite images over the 16-year period 2000–2015, a group with whom I worked found that very few among the lower or intermediate types of slums had progressed toward a higher type of slum existence. In twenty-four slums out of the random sample of forty slums that we examined, there was no change in essential physical characteristics (including building height, roofing materials, external roads, width of inner lanes, etc.). Ten slums experienced small positive changes: in some of these slums, paved road replaced unpaved ones; in others, roofs changed from a brown color (signifying cheaper construction) to a gray or white color (showing better roofing material). These changes aren't emblematic of large improvements in lifestyles, and even these small changes have occurred gradually. In only three of the forty cases we examined was there evidence of any substantial improvement. These three settlements moved up the slum typology, becoming a better type of habitation. Simultaneously, some other slums, which had existed 15 years earlier, ceased appearing in recent satellite photos – and in three settlements there were signs of deterioration.[31] In other cities, too, relatively little has changed for the majority of slum settlements, which have remained mostly as they were, experiencing few notable or sustained physical improvements.[32]

This impression of collective stasis, of entire slums stuck in place, does not change when we consider the experiences of individual slum residents. Upward mobility, virtually nonexistent in blue polygons, is only a little greater in other and higher types of slum settlements. Some individuals who live in slums have experienced positive changes, but not of the kinds that transform a person's conditions of existence. In Bengaluru's notified slums, we found that women had experienced some progress across generations. The daughters of maids, gaining an education, had become shop assistants, secretaries, and data entry operators. Among men, too, some newer occupations had arisen. Younger men are more likely to work as mobile phone repairmen and security guards than were their parents, who worked more often as peddlers and laborers. The gain in social status has been of a larger order, however, than the accompanying gain in income. (Shop assistants and security guards make about the same amount as maids or *mazdoors*, around 8,000 rupees monthly.) That has been the limit of intergenerational improvement.

People who have grown up in slums have only too rarely become higher-paid professionals. Families have continued living in slums, particularly the long-standing ones, over multiple generations. Someone achieving a higher status should have moved to a swankier address, but such instances are rare. Our surveys showed that even in the best type of Bengaluru or Jaipur slum only a minuscule number of young people were studying to be doctors, engineers, business managers, journalists, or professors. Most young men have followed their fathers and uncles into low-paying informal sector positions; very few even conceive of higher-paying careers.[33]

Studies undertaken by other scholars in other cities have depicted similar situations. Social mobility is very limited among slum residents.[34] "Children tended to ply, by and large, the same trades and occupations as their parents."[35]

Not everyone in a slum is a hardworking saint, to be sure, but neither is everyone a shirker or a hustler. Why such young people have been unable to achieve the higher rewards of city life, despite living in a city for multiple generations, cannot be put down to character flaws. The reasons for low achievement lie elsewhere. Why greater prosperity has not been more widely experienced is explained in one part by supply-side and preparation-side factors and in another part by unhelpful normative structures and inadequate public institutions.

Supply-Side and Preparation-Side Factors

Supply-side factors, recall, are related to the nature of jobs that have been created and the associated conditions of employment. Preparation-side factors help explain why individuals come into the job market with highly unequal levels of education and skills development.

A number of supply-side factors, gaining force in the era of globalized growth, have made things difficult for people with little education and low incomes. The kinds of gains that rural migrants with low educational levels could expect to make earlier are no longer possible.

There is a growing inequality of opportunity between the small number of people who have advanced degrees and the large number who don't. Measures of the "skills premium" – the difference in expected earnings between college graduates and others – have registered an increase worldwide. The situation in India is no different.

"Wages have increased significantly only after, at least, the secondary level of education."[36] A large and widening skills premium has created a separation between a small minority of highly educated individuals and the large majority of less-educated and less-skilled workers. People with a college education have gained the most, attaining more than 15 times the gains that were achieved by people with only a primary education.[37]

The gap in earnings has been widened by the adoption of the high-end services sector as the country's growth fulcrum. The share of the services sector in national income increased rapidly during the period of globalized growth. From 29 percent in 1951, the share in GDP of the services sector grew slowly over the next 30 years to reach 38 percent by 1981, but over the next three decades, the high period of globalization, this share grew much faster, reaching 59 percent by 2011.[38] Because it tends to employ a relatively small number of people, however, the services sector's share in the country's labor force remained below 30 percent, or just about half its share in national income.

Relatively few people were absorbed within the higher-productivity services sector. Many more had to make do with lower-productivity employment in other sectors.

Within services, the GDP shares of particular subsectors, including information technology, biotech, and financial services, have grown rapidly. And the employment imbalance was also larger. The numbers of highly paid positions increased, but their representation in the workforce was still tiny. Between 1993 and 2005, for instance, the number of system analysts and programmers increased by a phenomenal 572 percent – but only from 28,000 positions in the earlier year to 160,000 positions in the later year, a drop in the ocean of 1.3 billion people.

At the other end of the economic spectrum, low-wage informal sector employment grew fast, involving a much larger number of actors. The employment share of the informal sector grew from about 80 percent in the 1990s to more than 90 percent in the new millennium, both because informal-sector enterprises have grown and because formal enterprises, including many in the public sector, have been hiring larger numbers of informal workers, especially at the low end of the pay scale.[39]

Most young people in India work as *mazdoors* (laborers) and *kareegars* (small craftspeople) – and not as call center operators or software engineers. The majority who live and work in India's cities are low-paid, informal-sector workers. Demands for the services of domestic servants, drivers, and security guards have grown, and slums have grown in parallel, with some suggesting that these developments are interrelated.[40]

Different categories of employment, each with more than one million workers, which registered the largest increases over the period between 1993 and 2005, included

- bricklayers and other construction workers, whose numbers more than doubled (from 5.4 million in 1993 to 13.3 million in 2005);
- "transport equipment operators," i.e., drivers (5 million to more than 10 million);
- salesmen, shop assistants, and related workers (4.5 million to 10 million);
- maids and related housekeeping workers (1.5 million to 3.1 million);
- cooks, waiters, bartenders, and related workers (1.1 million to 2.1 million);
- hairdressers, barbers, beauticians, and related workers (1.1 million to 1.9 million);
- building caretakers, sweepers, cleaners, and related workers (1.2 million to 1.8 million); and
- launderers, dry cleaners, and pressers (from 1.4 million to 1.7 million).[41]

The structure of employment in India has come to be characterized, thus, by two opposite poles, high-end services and low-end menial positions – the *dollar economy* and the *rupee economy* – a dualistic structure, with a huge gap in the middle.[42] India has world-class engineers but not-so-great mechanics, electricians, and plumbers.

Its manufacturing sector is also dualistic with a large missing middle. At the one end, there are a large number of "own-account enterprises," tiny manufacturing units, in which production is done, quite often inside the home, by the owner-operator assisted by family labor. Such units, many of which are located within slums of different kinds, employ more than 50 percent of all manufacturing workers, but they contribute only 10 percent of the valued added by the manufacturing sector. At the other end of the spectrum, a small number of large and technically sophisticated players contribute more than 80 percent of the value added but engage less than 20 percent of all manufacturing workers. Per-worker productivity is more than 20 times lower in the tiny own-account enterprises. Despite this disadvantage, such enterprises not only have survived, but have multiplied – and for a reason: incorporated within global or domestic value chains at the lowest level, they can be cut loose at any time, taking on a greater share of the risks of manufacturing, because they lack the support of formal contractual mechanisms.[43]

In order to deal more effectively with dualism and labor insecurity and with the related slow growth of good-quality employment, a proposal was put forth in 2014 that sought to encourage the growth of advanced manufacturing within India. Over the three previous decades, the share of India's manufacturing sector in the country's GNP had remained almost static. China's growth, on the other hand, was powered by its manufacturing sector, resulting in a faster increase in higher-quality employment. Borrowing a page from the Chinese playbook, India's government launched a "Make in India" initiative, which aimed to motivate global investors to move their manufacturing operations to India.

In theory this is an excellent proposal, but in practice it constitutes an incomplete solution. Given the right incentives, global manufacturing operations will come to India, and Indian entrepreneurs will also set up high-tech manufacturing operations. Production and manufacturing productivity will increase in consequence.

For supply-side and preparation-side reasons, however, these investments are unlikely to make a significant dent in the problem of generating large numbers of good jobs. Manufacturing today involves a much greater use of sophisticated capital equipment, and it has little use anymore for people with low levels of education. Recent technological developments "have augmented the contributions made by more abstract and data-driven reasoning, and in turn have increased the value of people with the right engineering, creative or design skills. The net effect has been to decrease demand for less skilled labor while increasing the demand for highly skilled labor."[44]

The technology of manufacturing has changed radically since the time of Henry Ford. Fewer people, albeit with higher levels of education (high school, if not college), are required per unit of production.

In India, however, few city residents and even fewer village residents have been educated to these levels. Only 8 percent of rural individuals aged 15 years or more, and only 27 percent of urban individuals of the same age group, had obtained a high school diploma or college degree by 2010, many of an exceedingly poor quality, making them virtually unemployable.[45] While some among these individuals may be able to make it, the rest, a vast majority, have no real chance of entering advanced manufacturing operations.

Why the bulk of India's workforce is so poorly prepared can be attributed in some part to its legacy of skewed educational investments. Colleges and universities, including many prestigious ones, have existed in India's cities for many generations, and they have been comparatively well-resourced. But primary schools in rural areas, particularly in beyond-5-km villages, were established only some decades after national independence, and even today, India's public schools tend to be poorly resourced, low-quality operations.[46]

The Indian government continues to spend almost ten times as much per student at the college level compared to what it spends on primary school students. Education at the college level is more expensive, requiring specialized and costly infrastructure and equipment, and other countries, too, spend more at the college level. But the extent of this imbalance is much greater in India: countries whose educational systems are held up as examples to others spend only twice as much on college students as they do on primary school students. By focusing initially on delivering a high-quality school education, these countries have brought a larger and more diverse part of their population into the economic mainstream. India's skewed educational investments have hindered the preparation of the vast majority of its citizens.[47] For instance, the greater investment by China in the lower layers of its education pyramid, and the more equal stress it has placed on primary, secondary and college education, helps explain why this country has been able to vastly grow its modern manufacturing sector, creating a larger number of good jobs for its less well-off citizens – and increasing the numbers of potential job creators. Japan and South Korea, too, invested widely in developing the capacities of their people, even as they were building manufacturing plants and installing machinery.[48]

Because of its smaller and more unbalanced educational investments, fewer people in India have been able to acquire the preparation required for higher-paying jobs, either in high-end services or in advanced manufacturing. Bringing more people into India's cities will not have the same consequence, thus, as bringing more people into Japanese, Chinese, or South Korean cities.

Lower and Higher Beings

The trends just examined provide some clues as to why the urban transition in India is of a different nature from what today's rich countries experienced earlier. But why did such trends emerge in India, and not in other fast-growing developing countries – for instance, in Singapore, Malaysia, or South Korea, countries that, through the 1950s and 1960s, were at fairly similar levels of economic development compared to India?

Why do so many citizens of India – but not of these countries – work under ill-paid and insecure conditions? Why is there a growing tide of blue-polygon people and day laborers?

Part of the answer has to do, of course, with the conditions of supply and demand for labor. The earnings of laborers are driven down in situations where the jobs are few and the people are many.

But unlike the prices, say, of soap or iron ore, the price of human labor is not so much a result purely of market determination. The wage level also reflects a society's valuation of the legitimate needs of its less fortunate members. Societal values – shared conceptions of what it takes to maintain a family at some minimally acceptable standard of living – are deeply implicated in wage determination. Else, wages may be driven down to zero in periods of deep recession. The same conditions of demand and supply can lead to different labor market outcomes, depending on the prevailing normative standard.[49]

Attitudes and beliefs, as much as supply-side and preparation-side factors, are involved in producing the observed inequalities and dualism.[50] In India, the prolonged existence of a large informal sector and the broad acceptance, both legally and normatively, of the associated employment practices have made it possible for employers to make inexpensive use of the more abundant kinds of labor. "Employers use many ploys to make labor insecure. Payments are withheld ... debts are manipulated."[51] Such practices, honed over time, are widely condoned; they have come to be seen as normal and appropriate, helping create a permanently insecure segment of the working population.[52]

Objective conditions of demand and supply are not all that help explain these outcomes, for it is not only India where employers have looked for greater flexibility in hiring and firing workers. There has been a worldwide trend toward greater flexibility in the employment agreement. When workers and supplier firms can be shed or hired at will, companies can react more quickly and cost-effectively to fluctuations in market conditions. Such flexible work arrangements have helped companies deal with the fiercer competition they've had to face in this era of globalization.[53]

Countries have dealt very differently, however, with the same market forces and the same pressures for quick adjustment. European workers are also hired on short-term and flexible arrangements, but unlike their counterparts in India, they are protected by health-care benefits and old-age security; they can fall back on state unemployment benefits, including retraining and reskilling; their children attend day-care centers and public schools of a quality acceptable to the professional middle classes (whose children also attend, by and large, the same kinds of public schools and crèches).[54]

Hardly any such provisions apply to India's informal workers. The laws governing the conditions of informal employment are rarely enforced; and in the name of reforms, even these weak laws have been further weakened. What will become of these workers when they grow old, fall ill, or become disabled seems to be a matter of little concern to employers and officials.[55]

Why does a progressive formalization of informal work arrangements not figure more prominently on the policy agenda? In part, arguably, it's because of the attitudes and values that prevail, which justify giving less regard to a lower category of people, a "labor class," thought to have a lower level of human existence.

Beliefs associated in part with India's caste system help uphold ideas of higher-level and lower-level individuals and legitimize their unequal treatment.[56] Attitudes, beliefs, values, lifestyles, and employment practices reinforce each other, resulting in a hardening of discrimination and of its legitimizing influence. "The urban poor are often seen [by elites] as a distinct social segment, sharing undesirable traits and posing a threat to moral and social order ... The casual and impermanent nature of the jobs available to the poor in towns and the consequent 'floating' nature of their work enhance this image of instability, volatility and rootlessness."[57]

Effecting changes in values and beliefs is necessary. Such "soft factors" form an important part of the explanation for why the ladder leading upward is broken.

The Tiered State and Ineffective Institutions

Another part of the explanation is provided by India's tiered state structure and *its* differential treatment of individuals. Diverse social layers in India's divided cities are served in different ways by government officials.

Like the manifestations of Hindu gods, the state assumes different forms – some nurturing and benign, some capricious and neglectful, some menacing and malignant. Which among these different forms you get to meet depends on the particular layer of society that you represent. If you come before the state as a global investor, you meet with a suave official in an executive office; the conversation, its tone, and its setting will not be very different from what you'd expect to encounter in a Western capital. If you are a slum resident, however, you are confronted with a different vision of the state apparatus. This is the medieval face of the state, complete with truncheons and torture chambers, where blue-polygon youths can be beaten senseless on mere suspicion.[58]

Those who see one face of the state do not see its other faces, not at close quarters. Its least benign face has been turned toward poorer people.

The public institutions that help make the city a source of security, predictability, and economic dynamism for people in the higher layers are rarely accessible to individuals in lower layers of the social onion. While living in the city, slum residents are not *of* the city: they have little access to the better opportunities.

The story of Pachamma and her daughter Leela illustrates how people in slums live beneath a low glass ceiling. It's not usually because these people aren't bright or hardworking. More often, it's because of disconnects with institutional supports and information sources.

"When her father died at the age of forty-two," Pachamma told me, referring to her late husband, "there was none but myself to take care of Leela, who at that time was a little child of three years." Stooped from a life of hard work, with a head of white hair which she ties in a rough bun, Pachamma is a woman of about sixty years. I sat at the entrance to her two-room house; she sat facing me, on a mat on the floor. She spoke softly, almost deferentially, but there was no hesitation in her expression.

"I had no education to speak of and no other skills. There was not much that I could have done for making a living. At that time, some women of our neighborhood used to go and work in rich people's homes, cleaning their houses, cooking, doing their laundry. I started going out with these women. I have worked as a maid for 25 years."

Despite the small amount that she made, Pachamma sent her daughter to the best school in the neighborhood. "I wanted Leela to become a doctor. If there had been a doctor in the family, we would have saved my husband."

Leela did well by herself, not disappointing her mother. She studied hard. She earned good grades.

But after completing high school, Leela was faced with a difficult situation. Admission to medical college was highly competitive. Most candidates took coaching classes in order to prepare for the entrance exam, but these coaching classes were expensive, and Leela felt that she could not ask her mother for more money. She sat the entrance exam nonetheless, but she did not rank high enough to win a place in any government-run medical college. These places are highly sought after, not only because government colleges are ranked higher than private ones, but also because the cost of education is highly subsidized by the government. But what Leela was offered – a place in a low-ranked private college – entailed a high admission fee, putting it out of the reach of this family.

No one had told Leela that an NGO in her city gave free coaching classes to low-income candidates, especially women. No one had told her that bank loans were available, which she could use to pay for the expenses of a private medical education. No one had told her about dentistry or physiotherapy as other desirable and lower-cost career options. No one told her that with her high grades in the sciences she could easily have got into a course of study leading to a job in biotechnology – a field that was fast expanding. No one had told her that there were many other career possibilities – and not just the traditional doctor, lawyer, engineer, and so on. The people in her social circle knew little about other and better possibilities, however, and Leela had no other means for obtaining broader information. She was working, when I met her, as an assistant at a private pathology laboratory, a low-paid and informal job, earning 8,000 rupees monthly.

For other slum residents, too, the prospects for economic advancement have been dimmed on account of multiple and mutually reinforcing gaps in institutional provision. Even when they have title deeds to their homes, for instance, slum dwellers are rarely able to access institutional sources of finance for homebuilding or business development.[59] Hardly any of the slum residents whom colleagues and I interviewed in three cities (Bengaluru, Jaipur, and Patna) have received support from any public or private institution for acquiring job-related skills or for making connections with potential employers. A large-scale survey carried out in multiple cities similarly found that less than 5 percent of slum dwellers had availed themselves of institutional sources of home financing, compared to 20 percent of non-slum households. This survey also found that, compared to slum households, almost three times as many non-slum households had availed themselves of health insurance programs; and that households outside slums were much better connected with public officials, including school teachers, nurses, municipal councilors, and members of state legislative assemblies.[60]

Institutional disconnectedness is a fact of life for slum dwellers, who are generally unable to make the connection with multiple public institutions, except by resorting to informal leaders and patron-client networks.[61] "Their encounters with bureaucrats almost always lead either to trouble or official inaction. Their experience with the courts is virtually non-existent. The city's poorest residents have next to no contact with the press … The government provides almost nothing by way of medical facilities."[62] A number of factors, including discriminating attitudes and beliefs, help explain why poorer city residents so often confront situations of disconnectedness and lack of access.

The structure of the state, laid down in colonial and precolonial times, forms an important part of the explanation. Stratified and segmented institutional enclaves were set up in the colonial era: one set of spaces and rules for the rulers, and other sets, respectively, for richer and poorer natives.[63] Many among these tiered arrangements have outlived the dismantling of colonialism, supporting the continuation of a state that has different faces. The practices of everyday governance developed under colonial rule continue to inflect officials' behaviors. Particularly in the lower tiers of the state hierarchy, little attention has been paid to reform and modernization.

The architecture of the state set down under colonial legacy was not only tiered; it was also fragmented, another aspect that continues to hamper urban governance. City governments were designed to be weak, with little or no original authority over important matters of municipal administration. Authority for the development and regulation of land, for instance, was retained by the provincial governor, and it passed over after independence to specialized urban development agencies (such as the DDA in Delhi and the BDA in Bengaluru). Critical functions, including the police, water supply, and electricity provision, are most often not within the purview of a city government but vest, rather, with the state government. The arteries of a city – its roads and bridges and flyovers – are the responsibility of multiple agencies, loosely coordinated, that report to different departments of the central and state government.[64]

No single body has the mandate, the authority, the resources, or the professional competence required to plan effectively for a city's future.

Achieving a Better Balance

Wrapping up for now this discussion about the role of cities, let's return to the three national objectives that were outlined at the start of this chapter. In which among these objectives – entrenching India's place as a major global player, building economic growth, and removing destitution and reducing poverty – can we reasonably expect India's biggest cities to play a leading role in the near future? And for which other objectives do we need to be looking at a different balance of emphasis between villages, smaller towns, and bigger cities?

In terms of the first objective, there's no gainsaying that cities will continue to play a primary role in the future. A country's biggest cities serve as its principal gateways to global flows of goods, services, investments, and ideas.[65] Enhancing India's clout as a global economic actor requires investing in making its bigger cities work better. Infrastructures of different kinds – roads, highways, bridges, water supply and electricity; high-speed mass transportation; sports and cultural facilities – need to be built for making India's cities more globally competitive.

In terms of the second and third objectives, concerned with sustained growth and poverty reduction, it's more of an open question.

Across a large group of developing countries, the hope that the rural and agricultural sectors would grow to keep pace with city-led growth has been belied. The promise of steady progress by internal migrants and people in slums has not been fulfilled. The biggest cities have become the sites of the greatest inequality.[66]

Coming into a city does not equate any more to stepping onto a transmission belt that leads inexorably to a better future. You can join a city's multilayered society at various points; where you end up depends critically on where you had entered initially.[67] The hope that over time the lower social layers would experience progress and upward mobility has been widely let down. In other largely agrarian developing countries, too, the broken ladder is a feature of cities as much as rural areas.[68]

It is not clear, thus, how the people of India and other largely agrarian countries will unequivocally benefit from emulating the development paths of Western countries. Circumstances have changed, and as a result, it helps to take account of new challenges and new opportunities.

It's an image born of an earlier age, in which wealth was produced when large groups of workers congregated in one place to work with great masses of machinery. That's no longer the only or even the most productive kind of modern workplace. Decentralized networks of production and innovation, organized around groups of specialized smaller-scale enterprises, have sprung up to lead the way in different world regions. New technologies and new methods of industrial organization have made alternative modes of production feasible and competitive; nimbler and more innovative than the old industrial behemoths in making productive connections with global value chains and domestic manufacturers.[69] These are the kinds of options that India and other countries in similar situations should be exploring more aggressively. Investing in physical infrastructure – more roads, bridges, electricity, water supply and drainage lines, housing stock, broadband links, mass transportation, and the like – while scattering these investments across hubs, large and small, will be important for exploiting the country's untapped potential for sustained economic development. A government initiative, recently introduced at the time of writing, which sought to develop "Smart Cities," looked promising in this context.[70]

Most of all, it will be essential to invest in India's people and to greatly raise the level of their preparation. Globalization is a wager on the strong and the well trained; it has little use for people with low education levels.

Developing people in villages is an essential prerequisite for obtaining the promised benefits of investing in cities. People coming from villages to cities must be equipped with better education that can help them make more productive contributions, entering the city in a higher social layer. This is a crucially important future task, which can greatly enhance people's positive experiences of urbanization. Some noteworthy NGOs have made it their mission to make the journey from rural to urban less risk-filled and more productive.[71] These efforts need to be deepened and extended.

To conclude this chapter, let me highlight three policy recommendations that concern me, respectively, as a researcher, a former policy official, and a concerned individual. As a researcher, I am upset by the deficiencies that continue to mar the official urban databases. There are large gaps in information that have the effect of misrepresenting reality by systematically underreporting the poorest in cities. In order for there to be better urban planning, information about people in cities need to be substantially updated. Newer technologies, including satellite-image interpretation, can help considerably with the required effort.

Separately, as a former policy official, I am concerned about the organizational mess that is characteristic of municipal administration. Cities will become smarter not just by installing more computers, but by rationalizing and streamlining public administration, and making its different parts more closely integrated.[72] The failures of coordination and planning are abundantly evident: the gap between the need for and the availability of infrastructure of different kinds is large, and the backlog has grown larger. Roads and sidewalks are overcrowded; electricity and drinking water are severely rationed. Even at some minimally acceptable standard of provision, it will be decades before India is able to build the infrastructure, the housing, and especially, the institutions required by large-scale urbanization.[73]

Finally, as a concerned individual I am persuaded that while investing in its gateways to global opportunities, India must simultaneously build a decentralized system of production hubs, spread out and linked together by superior infrastructure. In parallel, and most importantly, India has to work harder at developing its people. The objective of creating more jobs needs to be supplemented with that of creating more job creators. Because of its stinting and poorly directed investments in human development, there has been little trickling down of the benefits of growth – and even less trickling up of human talent. Too many in India continue living in difficult circumstances, in rural areas and as well in big cities.

4 PREVENTING FUTURE POVERTY

I first met Chintalamma in 2005 in her village in Khammam district of Andhra Pradesh. She lived in a crude hut at the edge of a plowed field, but the clothes she wore spoke of a different existence. Her hands were rough and callused like those of a laborer, but her hair wasn't stringy and sun-bleached, unlike that of other poor women in the village. There was a faded grandeur about her. She wore a gentle expression.

She lived with her younger daughter, who was about 20 years old, and they worked from morning to night, barely making a living. We sat on a string cot under a mango tree. Chintalamma told me her story.

Ten years earlier, they'd had a comfortable life. Her husband, Rajulu, owned 10 acres of farm land. He had bought a tractor with the help of a bank loan, which he used on his farm and rented out to other farmers. He had a share in a commercial truck, which brought in another stream of income. They lived in a pleasant three-bedroom home. Their daughters attended a private school in a nearby city.

Things were going well with this family until 1998, when Rajulu took to bed with a serious illness. They consulted a number of city doctors and local healers, and they spent a great deal of money. But in 2001, three years after he had taken to bed, Rajulu died, leaving behind a financially ruined family. The tractor was sold to pay for his medical expenses, followed by his share in the commercial truck, and some of the agricultural land. After his death, the rest of the farm was taken over by Rajulu's brothers. The widow was left with the house in which she lived, their cows, some jewelry, and a little money. Soon, the cash was gone, and the cows and jewelry had been sold to pay for their living expenses. There was no money coming in, whereas their expenses continued unabated.

Her older daughter's marriage had been arranged before Rajulu died, and it was formalized a couple of years later. Chintalamma organized the wedding ceremony in a style that her late husband would have approved, undertaking all the ceremonies and the gift-giving that are expected of a high-status family.

By then, however, she had little money of her own, and she had to incur debts to pay for these expenses. By 2004, she had accumulated debts of nearly 190,000 rupees, equivalent to almost three years' wages. She tried to repay this amount by going out to work – on government work sites and in other people's homes – a state of affairs previously unimaginable for a woman of her caste rank and family background. What Chintalamma earned, usually less than the official minimum wage, was hardly enough to keep her household together. Seeing how she was struggling financially, the moneylender kept pushing up the rate of interest. A point came when she felt compelled to sell her home just to rid herself of the debt burden.

I visited Chintalamma again in 2011. She had begun to receive a monthly cash stipend of 400 rupees, given to widows by a government program, but that wasn't enough even for a week's subsistence.

She lived in a shack by the side of a field owned by one of her husband's brothers. Her younger daughter had been pulled out of school and put to work. They needed her wages for keeping things together.

In the six years between these visits to their home, I conducted extensive inquiries in different parts of India. Working together with teams of local investigators, young men and women, I studied how different households have fared over longer periods.

We met thousands of people who, like Chintalamma, weren't born poor, but who have *become* poor for reasons that could have been averted or mitigated. Poverty, I found, not only fails to be reduced; it grows. Contrary to the popular narrative, poverty is incessantly created. Millions of people are poor; millions more join their ranks regularly. In addition to the low prospect of upward mobility experienced by the poorer majority, there is also, in India, a very high risk of downward mobility. Because of the combination of these elements, a large part of the country's population is in poverty. More than one third of the world's poorest people live in India, compared to its share of less than one sixth of the world's population. In per-capita terms, India is twice as poor as the average country.

Widespread poverty in a country that is a fast-rising economic power is in large part a result of misconceptions and unhelpful attitudes and not so much a consequence of resource shortages or lack of good intentions. Poverty is not more speedily reduced because of the ways in which it is visualized and addressed by the policy makers – a product of five half-truths that have dominated the discussion:

> Half-truth 1: Economic growth is what it takes to reduce poverty, and there has been a great deal of progress in poverty reduction
>
> Half-truth 2: Income or expenditure assessed at a point of time serves as a reliable measure of an individual's situation
>
> Half-truth 3: The task of poverty reduction is to move people out of poverty
>
> Half-truth 4: An individual's rise above the poverty line represents success in poverty reduction
>
> Half-truth 5: National poverty-assistance programs are helping many people overcome poverty

Each of these assertions contains an element of truth, but each is only partly supported by the evidence. There's another side of reality, which remains hidden from sight when poverty is viewed from the top down and considered in the aggregate. That's typically what policy makers do: they try to reduce the total number of poor people in the country, ignoring the many differences that exist between these individuals. Looking at the mass of poverty and how it changes from year to year helps ascertain some important facts, but it obscures many others. The situation of people like Chintalamma, who have become poor, gets lumped together with the situations of others who have been persistently poor. How to render these different individuals assistance that is effective cannot be distinguished on the basis of aggregate analyses. Policy becomes a blunt weapon on account of gaps in poverty knowledge.

Getting beneath the surface of poverty analysis is necessary for delineating useful avenues of action. The top-down view needs to be augmented with worm's-eye view investigations.

The Half-False Nature of Half-Truth 1: Persistent Poverty in a Growing Economy

The official story is that poverty in India has steadily fallen, a consequence of economic growth in the 1990s and later. Government statistics show that the share of the population below the national poverty line fell from 45 percent in 1993 to 37 percent in 2004 and further to 22 percent by 2011. Because the country's economy was growing fast during this period, it seemed easy to connect the two things and claim that it was national economic growth that had caused the observed rapid reduction in poverty.[1] To some extent, there is truth in this claim; a growing economy creates more opportunities. Still, in two respects, the claim is only half-true. It depends, first, on how poverty is defined and measured. With some measures and according to some definitions the claim rings true, but using other measures and other definitions it doesn't. Second, there is the unresolved question of causality: How exactly has aggregate growth (at the level of the nation) flowed down through successively lower levels before reaching down to an individual and removing her poverty? What are the mechanisms by which the aggregate result was apportioned into benefits for people in poverty? Were these mechanisms sufficient to overcome the gravitational pull of poverty?

Let's take these points in order, first considering the practice of measuring poverty. It's not rocket science, but neither is it straightforward: there's plenty of room for cherry picking and arbitrariness while measuring poverty.[2]

Following a method pioneered in India in the late 1960s, poverty in developing countries is usually measured on the basis of surveys administered to a random sample of households. These households are spread across different states and districts. Trained investigators go into each of these households. They stay for a few hours, and they inquire about how much the household has spent on purchasing each of a long list of consumption items over the preceding month or fortnight. A standardized list of consumption items is used for this purpose.[3] The household's total consumption expenditure over the month, or on an average day, can be calculated by aggregating these separate items. If this amount is below fall below a specified threshold – the poverty line – this household, and all its residents, will be labeled poor. Adding up the number of poor people in the sample provides a good estimate of the percentage of poor people in the country.[4]

Although it is good for the purpose, this measure of poverty is hardly perfect, neither reliable nor suited for many purposes. A number of judgment calls have to be made, which render the measurement of poverty imprecise and problematic. Which particular consumption items should be included in the survey of households – and which items can be excluded? Should what each individual purchases directly for herself be included, or – because they clearly affect the quality of life – should public goods, such as higher-quality education, better-maintained public gardens, cleaner air, and fairer governance, also be considered? A different measure of poverty results when one answers this question one way or the other.[5]

There are also many other questions: Should households' expenditures on health care be included, or should these expenses be left out, being seen as indicators of pathology rather than of well-being? What period of recall is optimal for these surveys: a week, a month, or a year? How should differences in cost of living across different locations be harmonized to make these numbers comparable within (and across) countries?[6]

Theory does not provide a clear answer to any of these questions. Instead, thumb rules are employed; a series of judgments are made in practice. Measures of poverty "unavoidably retain an element of arbitrariness and inevitably embody some implicit or explicit normative judgements."[7]

The particular thumb rules that are employed resulting in changing the poverty estimate.[8] Applying different rules of thumb, analysts have come up with very different poverty percentages for India, ranging from a low rate of 26 percent of the population in urban areas, to 36 percent nationwide, to a high rate of 65 percent in urban (and 87 percent in rural) areas.[9]

Any assessment of how effective growth has been for reducing poverty depends, obviously, on which of these numbers one uses. In some scenarios, using numbers derived using particular thumb rules, economic growth has a robust correlation with poverty reduction, but using other thumb rules, also plausible ones, the relationship between growth and poverty reduction is much weaker.

One part of the definition of poverty that critically affects the strength of the observed relationship has to do with the selection of a poverty line that is appropriate for the circumstances of a particular country. No universal line can be specified that is good for all times and all places. Poverty is defined as "the state of one who lacks a *usual* or *socially acceptable* amount of money or material possessions,"[10] implying that as societies grow richer, and the average condition improves, the notion of the socially acceptable minimum also changes. The richest countries, consequently, have adopted a poverty line that is close to $25 per person daily; some countries work with poverty lines between $11 and $14/day; the median poverty line for developing countries used to be $2/day (and is $3.10/day since 2015). For the world's poorest countries, the World Bank has assigned a poverty line of $1.90/day (which corresponds to its earlier dollar-a-day limit). These lines are used for making comparisons across countries, after adjusting for differences in costs of living. Dollars aren't converted into rupees at the prevailing exchange rate; purchasing power parity (PPP) corrections are used for this purpose.[11]

Though it has been adjusted a few times recently, India's poverty line at the time of writing was still among some of the lowest in the world, set at a level lower even than the one applied by some of the world's least-developed countries.[12] The claim, however, about rapid poverty reduction has been advanced on the basis of this penurious definition. If one were to work, instead, with the median developing country poverty line of $3.10/day – a more appropriate standard, given India's present circumstances – the extent of poverty reduction was decidedly smaller. Between 1993 and 2009, a period of rapid national growth, the share of the population below the $3.10 poverty line fell by less than half as much as the share below the low national poverty level. The total number of $3.10-poor people *increased* over the same period.

Among all countries, India has the largest number of $3.10-poor people. Nearly 60 percent of the country's population, and more than 70 percent of rural India, were poor by this definition in 2015.

Hundreds of millions continue living in a zone of poverty (above the national poverty line but below the $3.10 level), vulnerable to falling below the lower poverty line at any instant. Investigations undertaken separately by a government-appointed commission and private investigators found that more than 75 percent of the population is poor, near-poor, or extremely vulnerable to falling into poverty.[13]

Certainly, poverty has been reduced, as claimed by successive governments, but the majority still live within the zone of poverty. Reducing poverty further and faster in the future will require better understanding the reasons that keep people in poverty and others which make them poorer.

Growth will have a positive effect, but it cannot be reliably predicted how far and how fast future growth will reduce poverty. The problem lies with a concern mentioned before: the lack of knowledge about the channels through which the effects of growth are passed down to affect an individual's situation.

The positive influence of growth must pass through a series of intermediate levels – states, regions, districts, communities, and households – before reaching the individual, but the influence gets dissipated at each intermediate level. States of India with faster growth rates have not achieved better results by way of poverty reduction.[14] Further below, at the level of communities and households, the connection between national growth and individual poverty becomes virtually nonexistent. In some neighborhoods and villages, poverty was reduced during periods of national economic growth, but in other, often neighboring villages, poverty *increased* during the same period.

The reasons behind such local-level differences are very important to uncover. Forces operating at the intermediate and the local levels matter alongside national and international factors. There are multiple points at which poverty can be attacked, and thus manifold avenues for reducing poverty in the future. The potentials of intermediate and local levels have remained hidden because of the planner's fixation with the aggregate level.[15]

Exposing Half-Truth 2: It's Not about Average Incomes

In circumstances where a great share of the population lives in the zone of poverty, the prospect of becoming poor in the future is pervasive. Whether someone is above the poverty line (however defined) at any particular moment certainly matters, but what matters as much, and arguably more, is whether tomorrow and the day after she will still be able to feed her family and educate her children.

Most poor people do not have a steady job or a regular income. Working as farm laborers or *mazdoors* or small tradespeople, their earnings not only are small; they fluctuate widely. Multiple household members work in order to make a living, many taking up more than one job, because no one occupation is dependable. A Tagalog saying from the Philippines, *isang kahig, isang tuka* (one scratch here, one peck there), illustrates the circumstances of their daily existence.[16]

For many who depend on agriculture, the vicissitudes of the seasons add another source of risk and fluctuation. No particular month's income (or expenditure) provides an accurate reflection of such a family's usual circumstances. If calculations of monthly expenditures are made right after the harvest, then one gets one set of poverty numbers, but if these calculations are made, instead, in the months of the monsoon, the hardest time of the year, when money and food supplies are both running low and there are many diseases, then a much larger number of households will be found in poverty.[17]

India, together with other developing countries, has a large number of people who experience wide fluctuations in their economic circumstances. Many among them cycle in and out of poverty, never quite escaping its clutches.[18] The numbers of these people are not separately counted by official agencies, and because their existence is not recognized, no particular assistance has been given.[19]

Smaller-scale studies have helped cover this important gap in poverty knowledge. Undertaken in different parts of India, these studies show that between 55 and 88 percent of all households had experienced poverty for the entire year or for shorter periods. These numbers are much larger than the official poverty estimate, but in many ways they more accurately reflect the everyday lives of poorer people.[20]

Take the case of Chunnilal, a resident of my village. When I first met him, more than 10 years ago, he wasn't rich in terms recognizable to city dwellers, but he wasn't poor, either. He owned four acres of land. He also owned six cows, two buffaloes, a pair of oxen, and a small herd of goats. He was saving up to buy a water pump and to deepen the well that watered his land. However, things turned out to be different. First, his father became seriously ill, requiring intestinal surgery, which cost the family close to Rs. 70,000, more than their entire savings. Another illness in the family, coming immediately after, required spending another Rs. 60,000. The herd of animals was sold, and loans were taken from friends and relatives.

For many years, Chunnilal's family teetered in and out of poverty. Getting some assistance during this period would have been very helpful. More affordable medical care would have been very welcome. Cheap loans from banks or microfinance institutions would have helped. But lacking this assistance, Chunnilal had to borrow from a moneylender, pledging the land he owned as collateral.

Seeking to repay the money he owed, Chunnilal began to work long hours at a nearby stone quarry. But a third adverse event occurring in quick succession proved to be the last straw on the camel's back. A large rock fell on him one afternoon while he was working at the quarry, breaking his leg in two places. No medical attention, or even any first aid, was available on site. After several hours of lying in agony, he was taken to the district hospital. The treatment he received was expensive but ineffective. A month later, his leg was amputated. His expenses and his debt had increased many times, even as his ability to earn an income was severely reduced. Today, this family is among the poorest in the village. Their agricultural land is in the moneylender's possession. They have no money to repay their debts. Chunnilal receives a disability grant from the government. A sum of 500 rupees is deposited every month in his bank amount. It helps, but it's a very small amount of money, equal to what he made earlier from two days' work. Survival itself has become a worry. In a final irony, his older son was pulled out of school and put to work in the same stone quarry. No better prospects were in sight.

Chunnilal, like Chintalamma, is hardly alone in undergoing a reversal of fortune. The fear of the wolf appearing at one's doorstep is not merely an unpleasant fiction. For too many in India, it's a constant dread, a threat that deters longer-term planning.

The Other Half of Half-Truth 3: Falling into Poverty

In the aggregate view of poverty that dominates the policy discussion, the notion of poverty reduction has been equated with the task of moving people out of poverty. The parallel question is rarely posed: How do people come to be poor in the first place? Was everyone who is poor today born into poverty?

Undoubtedly, one part of poverty is transmitted intergenerationally. Children of poorer parents are more likely than others to remain in poverty. Stigma and exclusion directed toward Scheduled Castes and Scheduled Tribes diminish their prospects of rising out of poverty. Compared to other households, female-headed ones are also more likely to be poor.[21] Given the right conditions, however, some among these population groups have escaped poverty, and a few have become prosperous.[22]

Contrarily, many other households, who were not poor earlier, have fallen into chronic poverty. Recent evidence, collected by disaggregated studies, shows that falling into poverty is widespread in India and in many other countries. Impossible to pick up in an aggregative view, which looks only at the stock of poverty, this phenomenon of poverty creation – of people falling into poverty – has been brought to light by a growing body of grassroots inquiries. Employing diverse methodologies, these studies have investigated the two separate flows that constantly reconstitute the stock of poverty.[23]

Between one third and one half of all poor people were *not* born to poverty, the results show; these people have become poor within their lifetimes. Poverty has an essentially dynamic and two-faced nature: many people fall into poverty, becoming the future poor, even as others, formerly poor, move out of poverty.

In more than 150 villages that I studied in four states of India, and in 70 city slums that colleagues and I investigated separately, there was not one location in which people only moved out of (or into) poverty. Everywhere, poverty creation and poverty reduction occurred in parallel: one household escaped poverty; another household, just across the road, fell into poverty. Scholars who have undertaken grassroots studies elsewhere have similarly observed the two-faced nature of poverty. They have helped uncover an essential fact that planners have long ignored: the stock of poverty is regularly reconfigured by parallel flows into and out of poverty. Table 4.1 presents results from a sample of studies undertaken in different parts of the country.

One among these studies, which considered the 13-year period 1970–82, looked at a representative sample of more than 3,000 rural Indian households. It found that 23 percent of these households escaped poverty, but another 13 percent fell into poverty. Another study adopted a similar methodology and looked at a subsequent period, 1981–99. Alarmingly, it found that the relative strength of the two poverty flows had been reversed: more people (20 percent) fell into poverty than rose out of poverty (18 percent). The same worrying conclusion – that the rate of falling into poverty has accelerated – was reinforced by a third and later study. Examining a more recent period (1993 to 2005) and a larger sample of households, more than 13,000, this study found that 22 percent of households had fallen into poverty while only 18 percent

Table 4.1. *Poverty Flows: Escape and Descent*[24] *(percent of all households)*

Region	Escaped Poverty (A)	Became Poor (B)	Net Change (A minus B)
Rajasthan	11%	8%	3%
(6,376 households, 1975–2002)			
Gujarat	9%	6%	3%
(5,817 households, 1976–2003)			
Andhra Pradesh	14%	12%	2%
(5,536 households, 1976–2003)			
Orissa	11%	12%	−1%
(800 households)			
All-India	23%	13%	10%
(3,139 households, 1970–82)			
All-India	18%	20%	−2%
(3,239 households, 1981–99)			
All-India	18%	22%	−4%
(13,593 households, 1993–2005)			

had escaped poverty. The stock of poverty increased by 4 percent, even as many households escaped poverty.[25]

Falling into poverty is not merely a temporary inconvenience: most of those who fell into it have persisted in poverty. It's not just the near poor who have fallen into poverty; many formerly well-to-do families have become acutely poor.[26]

The repeated observation of pervasive poverty creation suggests that something is deeply wrong with a policy that has a lot to say about raising people above the poverty line but contains nothing at all about preventing future poverty. The ignorance of poverty flows that has led to this unfortunate result is implicated in the continuation of large-scale poverty.

Consider what might have happened if an effective preventive policy had been in place, if almost no one had been let fall into poverty. Escapes from poverty occurring at the rate found by these studies, between 15 and 20 percent every decade, would long ago have made poverty history. Instead, the progress made by households moving out of poverty has been compromised by the unremitting flow of other households into poverty.

Poverty will not be removed until there is a more effective preventive policy. The telescope that planners have used to look at poverty from above needs to be put aside in favor of a microscopic view of the reasons that make people poor.

Micro-level studies of poverty flows have found that two separate sets of reasons are involved: one set of reasons is associated with the flow into poverty, while a different set of reasons is associated with the opposite flow, out of poverty.

That's why we need two separate poverty policies: a preventive policy, restricting the flow into, and a promotional policy, increasing the flow out of, the pool of poverty. Countries that have the lowest poverty rates have consistently adopted both types of poverty policies in parallel.[27]

No single event or household characteristic is usually responsible for pitching people into poverty. More usually, chains of adverse events are involved, like the sequence that drove Chintalamma or Chunnilal into poverty. The particular events that are most closely associated with falling into poverty vary from one region to another. In some regions, irrigation system failures were found to have made a big impact; in other regions, expensive funeral feasts have ruined families. Decentralized investigations of poverty flows will help map these vectors.

One type of adverse event is ubiquitous, however: The leading culprit everywhere is ill health accompanied by the ruinously high costs of medical treatment. More than 85 percent of households who fell into poverty in villages studied in Gujarat – and as many as 75 percent in Andhra Pradesh and 60 percent in Rajasthan – cited one or more health episodes as an important part of the event histories they recounted. Other types of adverse events – including high-interest debts; expensive wedding ceremonies and funeral feasts; recurrent droughts; and irrigation failures – were also cited as part of people's experience of falling into poverty. But these types of events are more region-specific. Health care is commonly the biggest part of falling into poverty.[28]

In comparison, far fewer people became poor on account of indolence or bad habits. Idleness, alcoholism, and drug addiction are not to be condoned, but contrary to the myth such reasons are not disproportionately part of the experience of being poor or falling into poverty. No more than 6 percent of households in Andhra Pradesh, 5 percent in Gujarat, and 7 percent in Rajasthan fell into poverty on account of any of these reasons. Other micro-level studies that have probed these reasons carefully have similarly found that personal failings aren't a big part of the reasons for becoming, or remaining, poor.[29]

Family size, too, is not uniquely associated with moving out of or falling into poverty. In the aggregate, of course, having a larger population diminishes each individual's share in GNP and so is to be avoided. But at the household level the relationship between income and numbers is more ambiguous and bidirectional. Small family size was an important factor in the experiences of 11 percent of households who escaped poverty in rural Rajasthan (they had fewer mouths to feed). Conversely, large family size was associated with 8 percent of escaping households (they had more hands to work). In other regions, too, family size had an unclear relationship with household poverty.[30]

These studies show how people do not become poor or remain poor for reasons of their own making. More often, it's because of factors beyond their individual control, which arise from their larger policy and cultural environments.

The persistently poor, too, have not remained poor for lack of trying. Despite their best efforts, one step forward was followed by two steps backward. They experienced the same kinds of adverse events far more often than others who were able to escape poverty. A loved one's illness, the death of a spouse, a workplace injury – the occurrence of adverse events such as these have combined to keep people like Chunnilal trapped in poverty.

Improving people's access to reliable and affordable health care is essential for combating the growth of poverty. Millions of families in India are one illness away from poverty. Between 3.5 percent and 6.6 percent of households in rural areas, according to various calculations, and between 2.5 percent and 5 percent of urban households, averaging to 5 percent of the entire population, fall below the poverty line each year on account of poor health and unaffordably high medical expenses.[31]

Growth in India has not made things better in this respect. For the majority in India, health care continues to be unreliable, expensive, and of poor quality.[32] An unregulated commercialization of medicine that has occurred together with globalized growth has plunged millions into a poverty trap. Thousands of people lose their shirts every day merely in order to pay for a loved one's medical treatment. Surveys by public health specialists have found that "rises in out-of-pocket costs for public and private health care services are driving many families into poverty and increasing the poverty of those who are already poor."[33] The availability of more sophisticated medical interventions is not an unmixed blessing. An elderly farmer in my village observed philosophically: "In the old days, the aged people would get sick and they would die. Their survivors would grieve and be unhappy, but after some time they would pick up their lives and carry on. Now, when old people fall sick, their children run up huge debts. Now when old people die, they leave behind financially ruined families."

Fixing health care – making it more effective and accessible but less of a gamble with bankruptcy at stake – is the critically important preventive policy. Diverse actors, medical professionals most importantly, but also other individuals, NGOs, foundations, and various government departments, can make important contributions.

Health care is very important, but it's by no means the only reason for people's descents into poverty. Other reasons for descent will also have to be tackled.

Different chains of events are variously associated with poverty descents in separate parts of the country. There is a need, therefore, for bottom-up examinations of poverty dynamics and for decentralized program designs and implementation. These are important aspects to which I will return. Let us first examine two other components of what is missing from India's agenda for poverty reduction.

Half-Truth 4: Narrow Escapes

Does it matter if some individual rising above the $1.90 poverty line achieves a new income level of $2.15 or $5.50? It does, of course, but not in official circles, where each type of ascent is counts equally in the tally of progress.

A singular focus on the aggregate number, on quantity rather than quality, has led to two kinds of tunnel vision among planners of antipoverty measures. Officials assess poverty in terms of the percentage share of the poor population. But they pay no heed to how many people actually escaped poverty (and how many fell into poverty). Nor are they usually concerned with how high above the poverty line different individuals have ascended. Consider the following example. When the national poverty rate fell from 37 percent in 2004 to 22 percent it 2011, it was implicitly assumed that 15 percent of the population had risen out of poverty (and not a single person had become poor). But the underlying facts could have been very different. It could have been, for instance, that a much higher number, 25 percent, actually rose out of poverty, but simultaneously 10 percent fell into poverty – leading to the same net change of 15 percent. But the underlying flows weren't measured, so officials were not able to tell the difference. In addition, the official statistics do not help distinguish between the number of poverty escapes that were of a marginal kind (a rise from $1.90 to $2.15) and how many others moved far beyond the zone of poverty (say, to the $5.50 level). In the official count, every escape from poverty is totted up as a success, even those that are marginal and temporary.

To get a better accounting of the nature and quality of poverty escapes, one must turn, once again, to smaller-scale grassroots examinations. These studies show that poverty escapes of the marginal kind were more numerous than those of a qualitatively better nature. Most people who escaped poverty moved only a bit above the poverty line. Very few moved higher and became prosperous. More than 80 percent of all households escaping poverty in the four states and two cities that I studied have remained stuck within the zone of poverty. Many are precariously placed and vulnerable to falling back into poverty.

The available pathways out of poverty are narrow, and they come to an end abruptly. Mainly two kinds of pathways out of poverty have been available in the regions I studied. Around 25 percent of households who escaped poverty in rural areas did so by diversifying within agriculture – investing in irrigation equipment, trying out different agronomic techniques, experimenting with new and higher-value crops, and so on. The second route out of poverty, taken by close to 75 percent of those who escaped poverty, has involved finding some kind of employment in cities. Rural people have traveled to big cities, such as Mumbai, New Delhi, Chennai, Bengaluru and Pune, several hundred kilometers from their villages, and there they work as ice cream vendors, laborers, masons, maids, sign painters, tea stall assistants, truck drivers, and waiters.

Neither pathway out of poverty has been especially enriching. That's why so few have achieved higher levels of success, and many who escaped poverty remain vulnerable to its clutches.

The extent to which a household can get ahead with the help of agriculture is limited by the amount of land that a poorer household typically possesses. In the mid-2000s, when I conducted these investigations, I found that the average landholding of a poor household was 1.1 acres in Vadodara district of Gujarat; in Nalgonda district of Andhra Pradesh it was 0.72 acre; and in East Godavari district of the same Indian state, poor households held, on average, 0.48 acre. That's not enough land even for producing the food the household needs, far less for raising it to a higher income level. Consequently, escapes from poverty using the agricultural route have mostly been of a marginal nature.

The second and more often followed pathway – which involves migrating to a city in search of employment – also has inbuilt limitations. Secure and formal jobs have been available in only a small number of cases. Even in cities and regions that experienced rapid economic growth, low-paying and precarious informal sector positions have been the most numerous.[34] One doesn't make much working as a security guard or day laborer. People who have taken informal-sector routes out of poverty have mostly joined the swelling ranks of the urban near-poor.

What is one to make of these achievements? Is there reason to celebrate, or is there cause to be despondent? Seen in one way, to the extent they have resulted in somewhat better lifestyles, these movements out of poverty should be felicitated. But seen in another way, they are indicative of a lost potential.

Imagine that someone like Einstein had been born in a poor household. Would it have been enough to raise him to become an ice-cream vendor or a day laborer?

It's not merely a rhetorical question. Among the poor, there are bright and not-so-bright individuals, and hardworking as well as lazy ones, just as there are among people who are not poor. One result of India's one-size-fits-all poverty policies is that many smart individuals work in positions that are well below their personal potentials.

No matter how capable and diligent they might be, people raised in circumstances of poverty hardly ever achieve high positions. There's need for a more encompassing poverty policy that not only works with a base poverty line that the masses must cross over, but also provides for social mobility commensurate with an individual's talent and dedication. In the next chapter, I expand on this proposition.

Probing Half-Truth 5: How Effective Are the Existing National Programs?

What the Indian government has been doing for reducing poverty is impressive in its scale of operation. A series of national programs have provided poorer people with subsidies, wage employment, and small cash transfers.

Two problems limit the impact, however, of this approach to poverty reduction. The first problem arises from an assumption inherent to the top-down and aggregative view, namely that poverty across the land will respond similarly to the same intervention – what works in Assam will also work in Tamil Nadu; within large states, some the size of France or England, the same policies and programs can be followed; that settlements across the land are essentially homogeneous: beyond-5-km villages need the same supports as those located closer to cities.

In fact, vast differences in the rates of escape and descent as well as in the underlying reasons have the effect of rendering any uniform national policy irrelevant. Many factors that matter for escape (or descent) in one Indian state matter little or not at all in other states and regions. Experiences of poverty in villages of the same state and district can be of a widely varying nature.[35]

Diverse programs and policies are required in different locations, the only exception being better health care, which is commonly required; but even here, the diseases and their causes can vary. Programs with national scope need to be supplemented with state, sub-regional, and local programs. Some impressive state-level plans have been developed,[36] but there's been notably little by way of sub-state and local innovations in the government sector.

A second problem with the national programs that have been implemented has to do with the theory underlying this approach to poverty reduction. These are excellent initiatives in many respects, and some, particularly the National Rural Employment Guarantee Program (MNREGA), add a strong element of local demand and incorporate impressive safeguards against corruption. An essential concern has been neglected, however. These programs do not address the reasons underlying poverty flows: they are not aimed at preventing or slowing down the flow into poverty, and they do little to improve the extent, far less raise the quality, of escapes from poverty.

This inattention has been costly in terms of longer-term impacts of national programs. While they help make the conditions of poverty easier to deal with, they do not nurture people's capacities to move out, and stay out, of poverty on a permanent basis.

Let me expand on this contention. Standardized program designs are implemented nationally, and the way they work is as follows. First, BPL (below-poverty-line) households are identified as those who qualify by virtue of having a plurality of characteristics – such as crude or no homes, few assets, physical handicaps, or no earning members. Households that feature on the BPL list are eligible to receive benefits from a larger number of antipoverty programs. The two largest national programs, with the biggest share of public resources, are the Targeted Public Distribution System (TPDS, which provides subsidized rations to BPL households) and MNREGA (which assures a fixed number of days of minimum-wage employment to all who show up). Other significant national schemes include the Mid-day Meal program (school feeding for grades 1–8), the *Indira Awaas Yojana* (subsidies to BPL households for constructing or adding to a dwelling), and monthly pension schemes for the elderly, the disabled, and widows.[37]

Investigations have found loopholes in the identification strategy, which enable locally powerful people to effect manipulations in BPL lists, leaving out the names of some poor people while including others who are not poor. Careful assessments show that these errors can be large, producing considerable defalcation.[38]

There is also a more fundamental problem. Even if these programs were to work in the manner intended, they would not help people overcome poverty on an assured basis. Take TPDS, for instance, the benefits of which are available to BPL households. Let's say that this assistance is successful in terms of its aims: the availability of more food at a subsidized price helps raise the benefited household above the poverty threshold. What then? Since the household is no longer poor, these benefits should cease, bringing to an end the very thing that raised the household out of poverty. Thus, even when, especially when, the exercise achieves its stated objectives, it creates dependency instead of self-reliance.

Free or subsidized things can be recommended in two circumstances – first, as an essential support for groups of people, including the elderly and infirm, who are simply unable to help themselves; and second, as an interim measure for other people. Permanently maintained subsidies cannot be supported in lieu of other programs that build capacity, helping poorer people enhance their earning capacity.[39]

Because they do little to enhance people's capacities, the existing national programs make little long-term impression on poverty. Take MNREGA, a program of mammoth financial size, lauded worldwide for its reach and ambition. When these payouts are disaggregated and seen in microcosm, they are skimpy. The government's data show that the program has been providing only a small cash supplement, amounting, on average, to no more than 3 rupees (or 5 US cents) per day per person. These small amounts do have value for poorer households, but are unlikely to produce life-changing consequences.[40]

Further, the existing programs of assistance rarely sponsor new organizational initiatives of the sort that can help poorer people assert their rights, express their demands, and otherwise fend for themselves more effectively, building useful linkages with diverse government departments and market operations. Institution building at the grassroots level has been among the weakest aspects of these programs, and neither have other individual or collective capacities been built that can help people lift themselves up on a permanent basis.[41]

Grassroots studies of poverty flows show that programmatic assistance have rarely formed a significant part of the experiences of households who escaped poverty. The vast majority escaped poverty on the strengths of their own efforts.[42]

Which is not to state that programs of support are not helpful or necessary. On the contrary, the requirement for public assistance is urgent and widespread. MNREGA and other programs need to be pursued with vigor; they need to be bolstered and revised in ways that can more fundamentally and sustainably improve people's life chances.

Two basic questions need to be asked while designing programs of assistance: What kinds of adverse reasons, whether of national or local scope, will they help combat effectively? Alternatively, what kinds of pathways out of poverty will be widened and made easier to access?

Preventing Future Poverty

Policymakers in India have vested their hopes in the idea that economic growth will eventually eradicate poverty, and until then, palliatives such as subsidized food or make-work programs will be sufficient. These formulations have not been efficacious. A large share of India's population – more than half by any reasonable measure – continues to live in the shadow of poverty, and many more remain vulnerable to becoming poor in the future.

The lower one sets the poverty line, the greater is India's success in poverty reduction. Its low official poverty line overplays the extent of progress. If the country's poverty line was to be set at a higher level, for instance, if a $4 level were to be selected, which may seem very high but which, adjusted for purchasing power parity, corresponds to only about 12,000 rupees a month for a family of five (an amount that an executive in New Delhi or Mumbai would pay for employing a driver), then more than 90 percent of all people in India would be counted as poor.[43] Despite rapid growth, the percentage below this poverty line has barely budged in 20 years.

Economic growth can be a potent measure of poverty reduction, or it can make hardly any impression. The relationship between growth and poverty reduction is probabilistic and contingent. What happens in any particular case depends not only on how these calculations are made; more fundamentally, it depends on how growth was achieved in practice. Growth in post-globalization India has been driven by the high-end services sector, staffed by highly trained specialists and other upper-layer people. Employment of the formal kind has not increased in the middle and lower layers. Insecurity and vulnerability have become more widespread. For these and related reasons, growth is not a ready antidote to the problems of vulnerability and the broken ladder.[44]

To be sure, it is not my point that the objective of faster economic growth is not worth pursuing – far from it. A faster rate of growth helps with a variety of public purposes, and faster growth should be pursued with the greatest vigor.

But growth and poverty reduction *cannot* be bundled together and regarded as a single objective. Separate policies are required for achieving more effective poverty reduction.

Let's aim to halve the percentage in $3.10-poverty over the next 10 years. It's a modest but an achievable objective. Specific policies are required for this purpose. No uniform social policy will effectively assist all poor people.

Three types of poverty assistance are required in parallel:

- *Protection and prevention* (against falling into poverty);
- *Promotion and support* (helping advance people's prospects); and
- *Survival benefits* (which help people cope with poverty on a day-to-day basis).

The first and second types of policies are more important for the longer term. Once these types of assistance are in place, the rationale for the third type becomes less compelling. Justifiable as an essential support for the disabled or weak – and an interim measure, at best, for other poor people, whose longer-term well-being is better supported by other measures – handouts should have a diminishing significance in the future.

It's important to give first priority to a more effective preventive policy. Before people can plan seriously for moving higher in life, they need to feel more secure and less vulnerable. The apparition of the wolf at their door has to fade from people's imaginations.

Among interventions to prevent the growth of future poverty, improving health care is primary. A caring health policy has been part of the arsenal employed by every country where single-digit poverty ratios have been achieved or can be foreseen in the near future. Countries such as the United States that are rich on average but which do not provide everyone with affordable access to high-quality health care have a higher poverty rate (14 percent) compared with others, such as Denmark or Japan, whose per-capita GNP is not as high, but where more generous health care is available.

Countries with much lower levels of per-capita GNP have also effectively reduced poverty by investing in health care, including many that have largely agrarian populations. In Bangladesh, Vietnam, and Thailand, countries whose recent growth record is no better than India's, people spend less, incurring fewer debts, for obtaining medical treatment.[45] Compared to people in India, the people of these countries are much better protected against the downward pull of poverty.

Public expenditure on health care remains very low in India, equivalent to just over 1 percent of GNP (compared, for instance, with 3 percent in Thailand). Even of this 1 percent, the Indian government spends a large share on its own employees, and not on the general public.[46]

Public health care expenditure needs to increase. But effecting a realistic remedy is not merely a matter of spending more money. There's also an associated question of raising effectiveness and cost-efficiency by improving the quality of governance in health care facilities. A vast and expanding network of public clinics and hospitals has been established, but the government is often unable to motivate or effectively control the health care providers who are paid with the taxpayers' money. As a result of lackluster and sometimes callous and corrupt behaviors on the parts of government medical staff, many people, including poorer ones, have moved over to private providers.[47] In the absence of effective regulations, however, the for-profit health care sector has developed its own pathologies, including over-prescription, overcharging, and unnecessary procedures. Quacks and make-believe doctors abound, particularly in beyond-5-km villages and other places with larger numbers of poorer people. The poorer one is and the less well-informed and well connected, the greater are the chances that one will be forced into an unnecessary surgical procedure, overcharged, and overmedicated, and that a stay in a hospital will end up becoming a one-way ticket to destitution.[48]

A policy to improve health care needs to have at least three components: insurance, provision, and regulation. Extending the coverage of medical insurance will achieve little in areas where there are no hospitals and no doctors. And having doctors and hospitals will not solve the problem if they charge more than ordinary people can reasonably afford to spend and treat people badly. Improving governance in the public system and strengthening regulation in the private system is a critical, and so far mostly missing, part of solving India's health care problems. Enforcing accountability from above and from below is equally necessary. Clients need to have better and more readily enforceable rights vis-à-vis their health care providers.

These elements of reforming health care can be outlined, but as yet full-blown solutions are not on the horizon. Pioneering initiatives taken up by some NGOs and a few state governments give reason for hope that broader reforms can be initiated. We will look at some among these initiatives while considering other recommendations.

It needs to be remembered, though, that although improving health care is a critical part, it is not all of poverty prevention. Many of the reasons for falling into poverty vary locally, so it is important to have a decentralized response to poverty.

Identifying and responding to contextually relevant threats and opportunities will require local initiatives. It cannot be effectively undertaken from a remote central location. Empowering local bodies will be essential for this purpose. Mounting a more effective set of poverty policies will require investing in local institutional development. Simply enacting laws or promulgating rights will not be enough. In order to become real and practical, laws and rights have to be accompanied by viable forums for deliberation and accessible avenues of action.[49] Flattening the hierarchy of government organizations, empowering local bodies with authority and resources, and extending the scope for citizens to engage with officials in an informed and egalitarian manner – these and related reforms are necessary. Simultaneously, different ways of measuring and tracking poverty are required. Methods that focus on poverty flows, not measuring stocks alone, are necessary for getting to the roots of how poverty grows and the reasons for that growth at local and higher levels.[50]

Many of these objectives, particularly involving poorer people in decision making, will be hard to achieve unless another element – divisive attitudes – is addressed in parallel. Many who make or influence poverty policy are far removed from the everyday realities of poor people. Some among them get their ideas about poverty solely from official statistics; others from the interactions that they have with domestic servants (even though rich people's maids and drivers aren't technically poor and may, in fact, count among the top 10 percent of India's people). The lack of personal familiarity among opinion makers with actual situations of poverty gives rise to misplaced ideas – and worse, to demeaning beliefs and biased values. Growing up in a middle-class family in New Delhi, I was told, for instance, that people are poor because of their own faults and character defects: they are not willing to work hard; they lie and steal; the men drink away the money earned by the women; and so on. Only much later, after I had met and spoken with hundreds of poor people, was I able to fathom that the beliefs that had been fed to me as facts were nothing more than a grandmother's stories. My cousins and aunts and uncles haven't had the same experiences, however, and they continue to believe the worst about the characters and motivations of poorer people.

Reforming beliefs and attitudes by facilitating interactions among people of different social layers will diminish the appeal of blame-the-victim ideologies and help mobilize public opinion. Relying on the official numbers alone, or on the verdicts of domestic servants, will not present a true picture of what being poor in India truly means. "No one knows more about how to survive poverty than the poor themselves,"[51] whose fortunes can evaporate quickly and for whom the threat of falling deeper into poverty is very real.

Initiatives are required concurrently on multiple fronts and by a variety of actors – including businesses, universities, foundations,

NGOs, government agencies, and richer and poorer citizens. Combating poverty has multiple avenues, and thus there are many reasons to feel optimistic. But business as usual will not do the trick. Policies that help stem the flow into poverty, making people's lives less volatile and less vulnerable to downturns, are necessary for reducing future poverty, spurring greater efforts on the parts of poorer individuals. Simultaneously, raising these individuals' legitimate aspirations together with their prospects for upward mobility will help achieve larger gains, not only in terms of social justice, but also by way of future economic development. Growth will follow when many individuals start achieving more and are less helpless against adverse events.

5 A DEEP POOL OF TALENT

Raju, my 9-year-old neighbor, knocked on the window of my bedroom. It was 6:30 in the morning. I was in my village home, brewing a pot of tea and cranking up my computer. Bhura Ram had come along with Raju. Fourteen years of age, he's another one of my walking companions. We had arranged to go for a walk that Saturday morning, but I had forgotten. I rushed through my remaining tasks, which involved sending off a couple of urgent messages, but the connection was slow, and it was a while before we could get started.

We had walked briskly for about half an hour, and we had reached the edge of a scrub forest, when Raju stopped and pointed to a low stony ridge. "That's where I saw a panther," he said. "It came down that slope, before turning around those *saalar* trees, and making its way down to the river." Running dry at that time, the river was only a hundred yards away, a few seconds for a charging panther.

"Were you afraid?" I asked Raju.

"No." He shook his head from side to side. "I was with my Papa."

We walked on, and for another kilometer we followed the curving riverbed, skirting scattered pools of water. Flame-of-the-forest trees, nondescript for the rest of the year, were ablaze with red and orange flowers.

Bhura Ram told me of the useful products that could be harvested from the trees in the area. Not to be left behind, Raju named the animals and birds that we were seeing, describing the habits of every species. They must have identified at least 15 different tree types and

25 species of birds and animals. I tried hard to absorb everything they were telling me; it was an impressive display of knowledge.

"Pheasant eggs are good to eat," Bhura Ram suggested, "but not those of a particular type of pheasant." He dove under a bush to plunder a nest, coming up with a handful of small-sized eggs that had a bluish pattern.

I was reminded of stories I had read when I was a boy, in which British schoolchildren romped around villages, riding bicycles, swimming in ponds, and raiding birds' nests, while solving complicated mysteries. I doubted that Raju or Bhura Ram would write the Indian equivalents.

What they know is remarkable; any Boy Scout would be proud. Each of them can do a dozen things that I have no hope of performing. Nine-year-old Raju can snare a hare, shin up a palm tree to get the fruit, milk a cow, cook a perfect *chapatti*, take 50 goats into the forest and bring them back at the end of the day without losing any, figure out which wells to drink from and which ones to avoid, and kill a snake with one strike of his *laatthi*. Fourteen-year-old Bhura can do all that and more: he can manage a team of oxen and plow a series of straight furrows; determine when a field needs to be watered and how much water it needs; repair the diesel pump when it's broken; build a dry stone wall; retile a roof; and mix the animal feed according to the needs of the seasons.

Quick learners with agile minds, Raju and Bhura Ram have absorbed what their parents and others in the village have taught them. But that knowledge will not take them far in today's world. Things have changed a great deal since their grandparents' time, and snaring pheasants and telling apart trees, laudable skills in their own ways, are no longer materially important. In order to get ahead, you need to acquire higher education and have other credentials. Otherwise, you become one of the many *mazdoors* who catch the first bus into town and hang about at well-known street crossings.

Unfortunately, too many growing up in situations of poverty are becoming *mazdoors*, no matter how agile their minds or how energetic their bodies. Hardly any are becoming doctors or sports stars or financial analysts. Until a few years ago, Keshu was the only person from my village to have completed high school. Since then a few others have earned high school diplomas. None among them has acquired a dependable or higher-paying job. They work as truck loaders or cleaners, shop assistants, security guards, and messenger boys in offices.

It's not just from my village that educated young people have had to satisfy themselves with such low-paying and insecure occupations. More widely, there is a pattern of low achievements among individuals from less well-off neighborhoods and poorer households.

I came to this realization after studying patterns of career achievements across a wide range of villages and poorer urban neighborhoods, a research project that was sparked off by my encounter in a village of Andhra Pradesh with Chandru, a young man we met before, who was then studying in the ninth standard. I discovered that he had a flair for mathematics. Despite being aware of this talent, Chandru's father couldn't imagine how his son might go to college and become an engineer. Instead, he felt sure that his son would not be able to go beyond some low-level local position.

Chilled by this ingrained sense of a hopeless situation, I began to ask about career achievements in a group of nearby villages. Later I expanded this search to include a wider group of villages and cities in different states of India. Table 5.1 presents the results of the initial investigations, undertaken between 2005 and 2007 in a diverse group of 105 villages, 35 each in Karnataka, Rajasthan, and Andhra Pradesh. In each village, I asked about the highest positions in any walk of life that residents or former residents had attained over the preceding ten-year period. More than 1,500 young people in these villages had graduated from high school during these ten years, and some among them had also gone to college. Yet, among those who got regular jobs (and the vast majority did not), the highest positions were usually those of village schoolteacher, army *jawaan*, or police constable. A couple of doctors and engineers show what might have been possible for other young people. But on the whole, it was a narrow range of career achievements.

Chandru's father had read the situation correctly: with a rare few exceptions, people growing up in villages, especially remoter ones, have not made it big in terms of professional achievements. They have become constables but not police superintendents; electricity linemen, but not civil engineers; foot soldiers, but not colonels.

Studies undertaken in other parts of urban and rural India have uncovered similar patterns of low achievements. Young people growing

Table 5.1 *Highest positions achieved over 10 years in 105 villages of three states (1995–2005)*

Position	Number
Accountant	3
Advocate	5
Computer operator	7
Constable	**26**
Clerk typist	12
Civil engineer	2
Doctor	2
Driver	8
Lineman (electricity)	8
Messenger (peon)	9
Panchayat secretary	6
Records keeper (*patwari*)	11
Sub-inspector (police)	6
Schoolteacher	**67**
Soldier (*jawaan*)	**41**
Software Engineer	2

Source: original survey data, 2005–7

up in city slums have performed somewhat better than people in remote villages, but they, too, have mostly ended up in low-paid, dead-end positions.[1]

Broader examinations show that social mobility – the chance that an individual from a poorer household will rise to occupy a position of relative prosperity – is low in India compared to other countries. A study by the World Bank of intergenerational income correlation (which measures the extent to which parents' incomes are reflected in the incomes earned by their children) shows that this measure is higher in India than in most other countries – higher than the US and UK, where concerns about the privileges of the 1 percent have become widespread, and nearly as high as Brazil, one of the most unequal countries.[2] Another study, which looked at the occupations of successive fathers and sons, found a very high rate of occupational persistence, signifying a low rate of social mobility in India compared to other countries.[3] The same conclusion is reported by other studies that compared the occupations of fathers and sons in India, finding that the apple does not fall far from the tree: there is substantial intergenerational continuity in occupation type and income category.[4]

Not everyone can climb to the same height. But equal talents ought to be given an equal shot at fame and fortune. Unfortunately, in India, the height to which one rises depends crucially on one's starting position. Children of poorer parents, no matter how talented and hardworking, rarely achieve positions commensurate with higher capabilities.

Aspirations are similarly limited. In two states, Rajasthan and Karnataka, I followed up my earlier inquiries by asking a subset of younger villagers – those aged between 14 and 22 years and attending a school or a college – about the career paths they wished to pursue after completing their studies. Not one among more than 1,000 young individuals whom I interviewed mentioned airline pilot or chartered accountant (or master chef or TV news anchor). Only a couple of individuals aspired to become doctors or engineers. The vast majority could think of nothing other than schoolteacher or *jawaan* or police constable, a narrow range of choices that reflected the career achievements of a previous generation. Schoolteachers and *jawaans* and police constables perform valuable and essential tasks; they are well paid compared to the majority who work in the informal sector.[5] To aspire to these positions is thus no bad thing. Still, I felt a sense of disquiet. Why do young people who grow up in these contexts not look to a wider range of career choices? In villages of Karnataka located close to Bengaluru, the hub of India's globally renowned software industry, why do young people so rarely think of becoming software professionals? What limits their lines of sight and dims their horizon? I have not had an opportunity to ask the same questions as systematically of students in elite city schools, but I can well imagine how these answers would be different.[6]

More than forty years ago, much before India's spurt of economic high achievement, when I was attending one such high school in New Delhi, a far greater percentage of my graduating class went on to become doctors, engineers, MBAs, professors, senior military and civil officials, and other types of highly paid professionals. All of us planned for such better careers.

The people with whom I studied at school were not always more hardworking or more intelligent than Bhura Ram or Raju. That's not a good explanation for the observed differences. Studies have regularly found that "IQ cannot explain why children from less-privileged social strata systematically perform more poorly than others or why children from privileged families systematically perform better."[7]

Careful investigations show that poorer people with less exposure to higher education, even those who live in remote jungles relatively untouched by modern civilization, have a capacity for analysis and a knack for processing complex information that rival those of university students.[8] I discovered this for myself when I carried games and puzzles – construction sets, Rubik cubes, jigsaw puzzles, and so on – to my village, and the children who live there, including Raju and his cousin Harsh, who was in grade 6, took them apart and reassembled them with great facility. So what explains their narrow range of aspirations and generally low career achievements? Why does India's segmented society produce a segregated set of career opportunities?

The answers are complex, weaving in a number of threads, but two sets of factors are primary. Factors on the supply side and factors on the preparation side have played important parts in creating this situation. The first set of factors is related to India's sectoral pattern of economic growth. Its high-end services sector has grown the fastest, resulting in a relatively small supply of assured and better-paying positions. That helps explain why few people have gotten higher-paying jobs, but it doesn't explain why people from poorer backgrounds have almost never attained these positions. For this part of the explanation, one has to take account of multiple weaknesses on the preparation side, including poor-quality education. Although it is of fundamental importance, education is not the only significant gap in preparation. Multiple weaknesses – including lack of information about the full range of career options, non-availability of guidance about how to get ready for the competition, and absence of better role models – combine to present almost insurmountable obstacles for millions of talented and hardworking individuals in disadvantaged situations.

In many ways, these weaknesses on the preparation side come prior to supply-side weaknesses in the explanation for low achievements. Few good jobs are created in large part because few people have the preparation they need to rise high and become job creators.

India's first Prime Minister, Jawaharlal Nehru, writing in 1961, stated: "I have no doubt that there is a vast reservoir of talent in this country. If only we can give it opportunity!"[9]

More than five decades later, opportunity is still not widely dispersed or easily available. The ladders that leads talented people upward are broken in many places. These breakages are detrimental not just for the affected individuals; they limit the achievements of an entire society.

Low Glass Ceilings for Individuals Lead to Low-Level National Performance

Multitudes of below-potential individual achievements combine to produce low levels of national performance. The size of the national pie is smaller than it needs to be. In multiple arenas, India performs well below its vast potential. A few examples will help illustrate this proposition. Figure 5.1 shows the number of Olympic medals per million of population that were won by a selection of countries. In proportion to population size, India gets the smallest number of Olympic medals – consistently placing at the bottom of world rankings. Not just South Korea, a country that is now (but wasn't always) richer than India; even Cuba, Ethiopia, Kazakhstan, and Uzbekistan regularly win many more medals than India, despite having much smaller populations. India has not budged from its bottom position in the world table, even after becoming richer. In 2012 and 2016, India won less than one-tenth as many medals per capita as China or Iran, and less than one-hundredth as many as Malaysia, Moldova or Azerbaijan.

Why does India fare so poorly? Trying to explain these results on the basis of race or genetic characteristics is facile, simply because of India's immense human diversity. The problem isn't one of relative poverty either. Other countries with low per-capita incomes have fared better. Consider Jamaica, Kenya, and Ethiopia.

It's not only at the Olympics that India fares poorly. In other fields, too, India's performance is comparable to that of a smaller and poorer country. Whether seen by way of the number of international patents filed (Figure 5.2), or articles in top-ranked academic journals, or new businesses registered, three quite different measures, India's performance in relation to its human potential consistently places it in the bottom third of world rankings, among countries such as Congo, Swaziland, and Haiti.[10]

Why is the average Chinese citizen 4 times more likely to publish a research paper than is the average Indian, and 50 times more likely

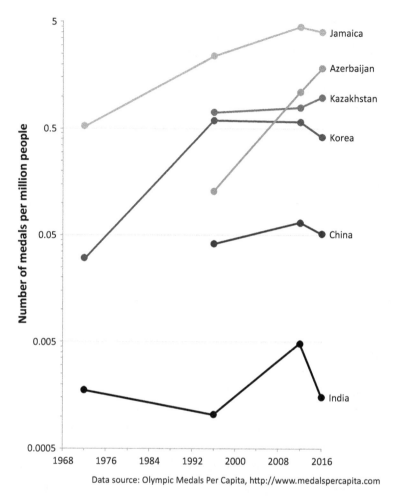

Figure 5.1 India is consistently underrepresented among Olympic medalists.

to register a patent? Why is the average South Korean 30 times more likely to establish a new business than is the average Indian, and 100 times more likely to win an Olympic medal?

Poor performance in any one of these domains could be attributed to a domain-specific cause.[11] Poor performance across diverse domains indicates that something else is afoot, something that commonly influences the country's prospects in multiple fields of achievement.

The root problem, as I see it, is one of limited and ineffective participation. Arising from the difficulties in gaining access that are

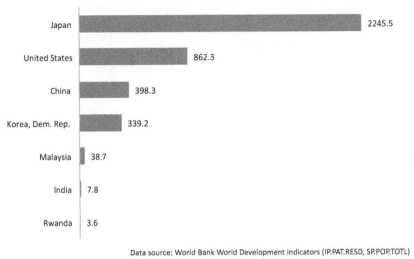

Number of patent applications per million people (2011)

Japan	2245.5
United States	862.3
China	398.3
Korea, Dem. Rep.	339.2
Malaysia	38.7
India	7.8
Rwanda	3.6

Data source: World Bank World Development Indicators (IP.PAT.RESD, SP.POP.TOTL)

Figure 5.2 India performs poorly on per capita patent applications.

faced by the vast majority of the country's population, lack of participation cripples the country's performance in multiple international competitions. The talents of Raju and Bhura Ram and millions of others are not being effectively harnessed and connected to opportunity – not in the country's leading economic sectors, not in its Olympics teams, and certainly not in its research labs and universities.

A tiny proportion of individuals is able to make it big. The rest are held back because of multiple inadequacies on the side of preparation. In diverse walks of life, only a few individuals, favored by birth or circumstance, are able to prepare effectively and compete seriously, one explanation for why the 1,200 million in India win fewer Olympic medals than the 11 million in Cuba or the 7 million in Serbia.

Building national capacities on the backs of only a small fraction of its population will not lead India steadily forward to a higher global position. Growth in the current era is not so much about factories and machines as it is about innovators and entrepreneurs. Business leaders recognize the essential reality that grooming individual talents "is at the heart of the success of free markets . . . When more people get a shot at better jobs . . . the chance of innovation and productivity leaps for the economy only increases."[12]

On grounds of equity and social justice, as much as for accelerating economic growth and promoting other national achievements, the country has to invest in developing broader pathways to greater opportunity. There are glimmers of hope, small improvements that have occurred, which are suggestive of a great potential waiting to be unleashed with the help of suitable interventions. Educational achievements have risen across the board, including among Scheduled Castes and, to a lesser extent, among Scheduled Tribes, and incomes have increased in small but significant measure in these and other disadvantaged groups of the country's population.[13] A handful of exceptional individuals – the outliers (to use a term made popular by the social commentator Malcolm Gladwell[14]) – have bucked the trend and climbed high from low starting positions. Learning from these experiences helps identify the most important obstacles and to understand how they have been overcome in practice.

Who Makes It Big in India?

I was able to identify some exemplary outliers when I worked with colleagues to survey the entering cohort of students in a selection of business schools and engineering colleges. Both types of institutions serve as gateways to highly desired career destinations, and the numbers of both types have rapidly expanded.[15] I also looked at the area of government service, which has traditionally been, and remains today, a desirable destination for young people in India.[16]

These examinations helped in identifying the kinds of people who are making it to the more desirable destinations – and conversely, the kinds who are underrepresented. They also helped in discerning the characteristics and experiences that are usually associated with successful entry. Although most new entrants share these characteristics, there are a small number of notable exceptions. Detailed follow-up interviews with these outliers helped delineate the pathways they have taken.

We examined the types of individuals who have gained admission to each of five engineering colleges, eight business schools, and three different classes of government service. Between 2009 and 2012, we surveyed more than 2,000 high-achieving individuals.[17] For reasons of confidentiality, I cannot name these business schools or engineering colleges, or use the proper names of the individuals we interviewed. One among the eight business schools we studied is consistently ranked among the top ten in India, and another two are ranked among the top fifty. Similarly, one among the engineering colleges we studied is ranked in the top ten; another two colleges belong to the second quality tier, ranking within the top fifty; and the two remaining colleges form part of a third quality tier, less desirable than the others and less competitive.[18] Within the civil services, similarly, we looked at the Indian Administrative Service (IAS), an elite cadre, and two relatively junior cadres of government officials.

What is common among the individuals who made it to these destinations? And what is different among entrants to institutions of higher and lower quality tiers?

No matter which among these career streams one looks at, one conclusion is obvious and startling. People who were brought up and educated in rural areas are at a severe disadvantage.

How to categorize a given individual as rural or urban is not straightforward. We employed alternative definitions for this analysis, starting by considering as rural someone who ever attended a rural school, even if only for one year. The proportion of rural entrants, so defined, ranges from a low of 6 percent of all new entrants in the highest-tier business school to 24 percent in engineering colleges of the third quality tier. Both figures are much lower than the proportion of rural residents of India (which was 69 percent in 2011).

When one considers a tighter and more realistic definition of rural – as someone who attended rural schools for all 12 years and whose parents live in rural areas and work in agriculture – the representation of rural students is dramatically lower. In top-tier business schools, there isn't one rural individual of this kind. In other business schools and in engineering colleges, such individuals constitute a tiny proportion (nowhere more than 3 percent of the intake). Even in the top two tiers of government service, less than 10 percent of all new entrants are rural individuals.

The obstacles associated with a rural education do not arise only on account of the quality of education. Even when they had the same marks as students from city schools in the tenth-standard board examination, rural students were less likely to gain admission to higher-tier educational institutions.[19] There is a problem of access that people from rural India face, which is experienced both at the time of gaining admission to better colleges and again at the time of securing employment. Studies that have looked directly at new hires in higher-paying positions – instead of looking indirectly, via gateway institutions – have also found very little rural representation.[20]

It is not only in higher education or good jobs that rural individuals are underrepresented. The problem of access has wider repercussions. There are very few rural people among noted entrepreneurs.[21]

Why a rural upbringing presents high obstacles in diverse fields of endeavor is worth examining closely. Before looking at outlier interviews and other pieces of evidence that help explain the rural obstacle, let's look at some other characteristics that are associated with entry into these gateway institutions.

In general, the individuals who have gained entry tend to come from better-off households. There are, encouragingly, a handful of exceptions. A small number of relatively poor individuals have also gained entry, whose families owned only one bicycle or television set (but no other asset from among the list of sixteen about which we inquired). That, however, is the limit of representation. Hardly any among the new entrants grew up in a city slum. Not one came from a family that lived below the official poverty level. If one makes the reasonable assumption that talent is randomly distributed at birth, it follows that that a significant share of India's talent pool has been excluded.

Reflecting a similar reality, the data show that relatively few individuals from Scheduled Castes and Scheduled Tribes have been able to gain entry. Their share in the civil services and in government-run institutions is broadly in line with the population share of these groups, a result of affirmative action policies, which in India are called "reservations." But in the privately owned engineering colleges and business schools, even lower-tier ones, the share of Scheduled Tribes, is as low as 1 percent (compared to their 8 percent share in the country's population). Similarly, the share of Muslims is less than half their population proportion, underscoring the conclusions of a government committee, which found that the disparity in graduation rates between Muslims and others, already large, had further widened after 1970.[22]

Multiple disadvantages combine to greatly diminish individuals' chances of entry. The share of individuals who are poor *and* rural, or rural and Scheduled Caste, or Scheduled Tribe and a woman, suffering two disadvantages simultaneously, is close to zero, even within the lowest-tier educational institutions. But such joint limitations are common in practice – more than 75 percent of Scheduled Castes, and more than 90 percent of Scheduled Tribes, are rural according to any definition.

The most heartening part of this story relates to the strides that have been made by women. The share of women entrants in each of these institution types is substantially larger than what it used to be a generation earlier. At the time of our surveys, 17 percent of the recent intake into the top-tier business school, 37 percent in the top-tier engineering college, and 21 percent of recent recruits into the IAS consisted of women – not yet 50 percent, but evidence of a rising trend, a continuing improvement.[23]

The downside of this otherwise positive trend is that the women who have gained entry are mostly of urban origin. A large majority belong to wealthier households: their fathers are well paid professionals, and many of the mothers are also highly educated and employed in high-paying positions. Other studies that have observed the greater participation of women have also remarked on this element of elitism.[24]

In general, among both men and women, the parents of new entrants tend to be highly educated individuals employed in well-paid professional positions. Hardly any of these fathers or mothers have professions of the types that individuals in slums tend to have; a tiny number have informal-sector occupations. On the other hand, as many as 94 percent of all fathers of Tier 1 business school and engineering college students had regular employment in the government or the private sector, or they owned and managed businesses, enjoying high and steady incomes.

More than 90 percent of new entrants had fathers with college degrees *and* mothers with at least a high school education. These proportions are far higher than those prevailing in the general population. In 2005, when these students were at school, the proportion of households in which *both* the mother and the father had least a high school diploma was very small – in rural areas no more than 7 percent, and in urban areas no more than 15 percent.[25] That's a stunning degree of exclusion, because if having two parents who are educated to these levels constitutes some kind of condition of entry, then no more than 7 percent of all rural Indians and no more than 15 percent of urban Indians would fulfill this condition. The rest, more than 90 percent, will get left behind, not because of any lack of effort on their own part, but simply because their parents are less educated.

Why should the parents' education level matter so much, when it is the child who is being educated? That's something that we need to look at closely. It's not obvious why a rural upbringing and the parents' background should make for such a large distinction.

One other fact that came up in this analysis also belies any simple explanation. As many as 88 percent of Tier 1 business school students studied in schools where the medium of instruction was English. In engineering colleges, too, these percentages are very high, as also among the newly recruited IAS officials. But in India as a whole, at the time these students were in school, only 13 percent of high schools had English as the medium of instruction.[26] Studies show that studying in an English-medium private school does not lead to better test scores, nor are English-medium schools of better quality compared to schools that teach in Indian languages.[27] So why should going to an English-medium school make such a big difference?

Overall, this examination of desirable destinations corroborates what we had seen from the source side earlier (while examining career achievements within poorer communities). A small proportion of Indians is in competition for the better-paying opportunities; a very large part of the overall talent is left to wither on the vine, which bodes poorly for overall national performance.

Examining the backgrounds of India's teams for recent Olympic Games produced a similar analysis. A large number of India's ace athletes have parents who are also eminent sports personalities and thus more able to show the ropes to their children.[28] Other top athletes come from affluent families and were encouraged and supported financially by their parents.[29] Another large number were able to train for the competition by virtue of having jobs in the military and public-sector undertakings.[30] There are, of course, a handful of athletes, including the boxer Mary Kom, the wrestler Amit Kumar, the archer Deepika Kumari, and the sprinter Dutee Chand, who did not have these starting advantages and were still able to make it to the highest levels of competition. But these are the outliers, the exceptions to common practice.[31]

Overcoming Obstacles

What should be done so talent can more broadly connect with opportunity? Theories about social mobility are still in an early stage, and they serve as a poor guide to action.[32] Learning from the outliers' experiences is thus very important. The nature of the obstacles that deter others can be identified, and how to surmount these obstacles is highlighted.

Among the 2,000 or so individuals who made up the entering cohort of the various gateway institutions that my colleagues and I examined, we were able to identify only a few dozen outliers. These are the individuals who – despite getting all their education in rural schools, despite having less educated and often illiterate parents, despite being from disadvantaged groups, and so on – nevertheless made it onto fast-track career pathways. We interviewed nearly all of these outliers at length, and we uncovered several commonalities in their experiences. I will cite extracts from only four among these outlier interviews. Very similar points are emphasized in the other interview transcripts.

Let me begin with an extract from the interview with Shivana Prasad, who gained admission to a second-tier engineering college. Here's what she told me:

> Just being highly intelligent doesn't suffice. One's mind has to be trained and one's skills have to be sharpened to get admission in a good place.
>
> Poor schooling is a major constraint. I did not have good schooling in my village.
>
> But once a person has been well educated, he might still not find a good college, because good opportunities to excel aren't made available to him. The contacts and connections that the student's parents and relatives have are also limited. Lack of inspiration and absence of good role models is related. Students may feel that the aim is unclear and unachievable.
>
> In my case, my cousin, who had studied in nearby city, guided me. He had done a course in polytechnic. He helped me with my school work and gave me books to read. He guided me about engineering colleges.

Varun Sheshank, another individual educated throughout in rural schools and belonging to a Scheduled Caste family, whose parents are poorly educated, narrated the following story, which has similarities to Shivana's story:

> There is practically no teaching taking place in villages. Even where it is taking place it is insufficient for a village boy or girl to compete with urban area students.

The parents basically are from rural background. There is no input and guidance about career from them.

If a student from a rural community wants to get into premium engineering colleges like IIT and NIT then he will need proper coaching as entrance exams today have become very competitive and without coaching one finds it hard to get into such institutions.

In rural communities there is poor infrastructure. There is no knowledge. Students of urban area know more about jobs and about coaching classes.

In my case I was helped by a rich relative who paid for my one year in a coaching institute, and he also gave me regular guidance.

A third outlier, Venkata, a young man from a poorer household in a beyond-5-km village, narrated the following account of his journey:

The experience of the teachers themselves ... they are so bound by what they know. They were not very well trained, these teachers.

They used to [impose] a lot of things on us ... only what they know; not allowing us to experiment, asking us 'With these studies, what job you will get? Why don't you go back and do some small work at home?'

The challenging thing I faced right from primary school, then high school, everywhere teachers used to say, 'Why don't you do a small diploma course and join some small mechanic?' Then I said 'No, let me try to do something more.' Then I went for 10+2. After that the teachers said, 'You have completed, now why don't you do teacher training? You can become a teacher.' That's all they knew; they are not exposed to what is available outside ... nothing about business, what happens in international affairs, nothing about internet. There were no such facilities in my village also.

My uncle, who manages a clothes store in the city, gave me financial support and motivation. He kept on saying 'Study hard and you will make it.' He found out about college admissions. He talked to his friends and gave me advice. He helped me to meet people who are doing different jobs.

These and many other outlier interviews revealed that there is nothing intrinsic to being rural that acts as a handicap to higher achievement. Rather, there is a certain set of factors that goes together with living and studying in a rural area – and it is these factors, more than rural-ness itself, that raise the obstacles to higher achievement.

A content analysis of multiple outlier interviews helped identify the major handicaps that were commonly experienced. The majority of interviewees cited more than one among the following list of factors:

- Poor-quality school education
- Lack of information about better career pathways
- Absence of role models
- Lack of enabling facilities, such as libraries, career counseling, and coaching centers
- Financial hardship
- Attitudes – diffidence on one's own part and condescension on the part of outsiders

The last factor, which was highlighted in Venkata's account, is related to attitudes – in this case, those exhibited by his teachers. Despite seeing how talented and how determined he was, they kept pushing him toward one or another low-paid career alternative. Perhaps they did not know about other and better career alternatives; that is what Venkata surmised. Or perhaps they knew but could not imagine how someone like Venkata might fit into the pathways that, in their minds, were associated with children from better-off households.

There's also a larger problem of attitudes and expectations. Layer jumping is very uncommon, almost startling, in the segmented society. When a *mazdoor's* child makes it into some gateway institution, it's an occasion that makes for newspaper headlines.[33] And when, despite encountering dismissive attitudes and obstacles, they are able to make it into higher education institutions, Scheduled Castes and Scheduled Tribes, non-English speakers, as well as people with deep rural backgrounds face discrimination at the time of job recruitment.

Just as disabling is their information-poor environment. Children who grow up in poorer neighborhoods, whose parents are not well educated, suffer from an acute lack of knowledge about the range of career pathways. The fourth and last outlier interview that I will cite, an account provided by Suraj Kumar, a young man who grew up in a city slum, elucidates this point about the poverty of information.

> Families where the parents are less educated lack the environment necessary to prepare for competitive exams. Such a family may

not have enough faith that so many years of additional education would result in some additional benefit.

Such students also suffer lack of preexisting network of friends or relatives and lack of proper information regarding the methods and means of becoming successful. For many years I did not know what to do in the future.

No one in my circle dreamed big. I also faced lack of other means of information. Such students need people capable of nurturing talent.

I was lucky that my teacher in eighth class motivated me constantly. Even after I went higher he guided me. Without his help, I would not have made it to where I am.

The crucial part for me when I heard this interview was the sentence, "No one in my circle dreamed big." It helped me understand why the young people whom I had interviewed earlier in villages of Rajasthan and Karnataka generally had such low career aspirations. It's because no one in their social network has made it big in the past, and no one in their immediate circle is dreaming of bigger achievements.

Contrast this with the situations of children growing up in professional middle-class families, who have a ready-made network of high-achieving family friends and uncles and cousins. That's how parents' education makes a big difference – by producing a better learning environment at home, and by embedding young people within a context in which bountiful flows of career information are taken for granted.

Other children, whose parents are not so well educated, grow up in a very different situation. Such children are cut off from networks providing information about careers, and they are deprived of connections with people who can serve as role models and can give them a leg up at critical moments. When they see no examples in their immediate vicinity other than schoolteachers, *jawaans*, linesmen, and constables (in villages) – or auto-rickshaw drivers, security guards, and masons (in urban slums) – it becomes difficult for young people to conceive of a wider range of career pathways. Children growing up in these circumstances end up with much lower levels of what the anthropologist Arjun Appadurai has referred to as the "capacity to aspire."[34] Lack of achievement in the past limits achievement in the future by placing narrow bounds on the range of visible career alternatives.

Lack of information narrows their lines of sight, resulting in a myopic view of possibilities. The same points – about the absence of better role models, shortage of information about better career choices, and lack of motivation and guidance, leading to a diminished sense of self-worth – were emphasized by every outlier whom I interviewed.

In common, too, outliers spoke glowingly about the role played by a chance outsider – a cousin in Shivana's case, another relative in the case of Varun, Venkata's uncle, and Suraj's teacher – who happened to come along at the right moment, motivating these individuals and providing them with useful information and career guidance. Such chance outsiders played a critical role in the life story of every outlier. They feature as well in accounts by other scholars who have investigated instances of individual success in the face of adversity.[35] Where there is no institutional support available to plug the gaps that exist in knowledge, exposure, guidance, and motivation, talents do not get connected with opportunities, except when fortuitously helped by good samaritans. Mentorship is an essential aspect of promoting individuals' life chances in a low-information society, resonating with the argument by Amartya Sen about a broader range of capabilities.[36]

Society cannot, however, bank on the dim chance that some such helpful outsider will arise by chance to assist every latent talent growing up in a situation of disadvantage. More reliable and predictable means of providing career information and guidance will have to be developed.

The institutional provision of information is a very important part of a bottom-up development strategy. Investing in information provision is critical, I believe, for generating greater social mobility leading to higher national achievement – but not only for that reason. Information is important as well for making democracy more truly democratic, and for forging a social compact, helping Indians learn more about each other and uniting them in a shared vision of the nation's future. Lack of information is a highly neglected aspect, requiring a separate discussion, which I take up in the following chapter.

One other factor, financial difficulty, was also revealed to be a significant obstacle. I am inclined to give less attention to this factor, not because it isn't important, but because it has been given the most play in the past and is also the easiest to offer. Politicians are quick to seize on this particular intervention: it's the kind of snap-of-the-fingers "solution" they prefer, not wishing to get caught up in longer-term reform battles. But financial assistance isn't a complete remedy. In fact, it can end up accomplishing very little – unless the other obstacles are tackled simultaneously. Let's look at the first important factor that was identified by the outliers – the low quality of school education.

Unequal and Low-Quality Education

Some of the best educational institutions in the world, turning out top-quality artists, designers, engineers, and business managers, are in India – and so are some of the worst institutions. The highly unequal learning environments that prevail in a wide variety of educational facilities get reflected in a wide array of educational outcomes. India's children achieve the highest test scores in the world, while also coming in at the bottom of international rankings. The trouble is that the latter group of low scorers is very large, while the former group of high scorers is tiny in comparison. The results of standardized tests conducted in a wide variety of countries show that for every 10 children who achieved the highest test scores in the United States there were 4 such children in India, which is reassuring – but for every 10 children who *failed* the test in the United States, there were more than 200 children who failed the test in India, a dismal outcome.[37]

Apart from a handful of exceptional private schools, and another handful of exceptional public schools,[38] the quality of education in India is poor, and instead of improving, it has become worse in recent years. Results from the Annual Status of Education (ASER) reports, compiled after testing nearly half-a-million students, show that an alarming proportion of students enrolled in the fifth standard could not read even at a second-standard level, with this share increasing from 46 percent of all students in 2010 to 53 percent in 2014. The proportion of third-standard students who could not solve simple two-digit subtraction problems increased from 63 percent to 75 percent over the same four-year period.[39] Staying in school for more years adds relatively little value: the gains in learning are very small in the kinds of schools attended by the majority.[40]

The official response to the growing concern about gaps in education has come by way of providing additional inputs.[41] Primary schools have been set up by the government in even the most remote places. Where before there were no schools, today nearly 100 percent of villages have a primary school within a distance of 2 km, and nearly 80 percent have a middle school within the same distance. Enrollment at schools has consequently increased vastly. More than 95 percent of all children between the ages of 6 and 14 years are enrolled at schools, and the difference between boys' and girls' attendance is diminishing. These are vast improvements on an earlier generation, a commendable achievement for the nation since achieving independence.[42]

However, the need to make improvements in the quality of learning has not been given the same level of attention. What exists today by way of the educational infrastructure in the countryside is much better than what existed before, but better than nothing is nowhere near good enough – certainly not in this age of globalization, where the accretion of cognitive skills matters more than ever for multiple valued individual and societal outcomes.[43]

The kinds of schools that the children of the poorer majority attend continue to deliver, by and large, a poor-quality education, which is leading up to a potentially disastrous situation. A student acquiring education hopes to gain an economic advantage, but when she or he ends up learning very little, the hope is belied, and education itself can be called into question.

Raju and Bhura Ram, my walking companions in the village, exemplify this kind of situation. What they know is impressive. But what they learn at school does not augur well for a bright future. Nine-year-old Raju can neither spell his name nor read the simplest sentences. Fourteen-year-old Bhura Ram can multiply (but not divide) numbers.

Their parents are unable to help in this regard. When these parents were young, there were no schools within a practical distance. Across large parts of India, schools have been set up only in the past few decades, as a result of which many students are first-generation learners.

In such circumstances, teachers and schools should ideally take on a greater share of the responsibility, but in general, students are not getting what they need from their schools and their teachers. Most teachers in government schools have permanent, formal-sector jobs and they are paid decent salaries – far more than what teachers in private schools are paid in the majority of cases.[44] Surveys show, however, that between 15 and 25 percent of government schoolteachers are missing from their posts on any given day.[45] Teachers complain that they are often deputed for other tasks – such as supervising elections, conducting the national population or livestock censuses, helping compile reports and assisting in their supervisors' offices – and that's what accounts for their absences from the classroom. It's a knotty problem that urgently needs to be resolved, whatever the underlying reasons.

But it's not only or primarily a matter of missing teachers. The problems of school education are multiple and complex.

The elements that make for a good school – well-trained and well-motivated teachers, a well-designed curriculum that is flexible and can be adapted to particular circumstances, an environment of innovation and learning with high quality standards, effective supervision, invested parents, well-performing alumni – are missing from a majority of schools in India.

India's school teachers are less well trained than those of other countries. Anurag Behar, CEO of the Azim Premji Foundation, which has made education reform the focus of its efforts, informed me, with only a touch of hyperbole, that in India "we have the least prepared teachers in the entire world." With a twelfth-standard education, followed by a diploma earned in just eighteen months, a person can qualify to become a schoolteacher. Compare that with the situation in Finland or South Korea, he added, where it takes five to six years after high school to train as a teacher, and that, too, in a well-governed system with higher quality standards that are tightly regulated.[46] The situation isn't remedied by in-service training. Very few teachers in India gain a higher qualification after being recruited.[47] A senior official of the education ministry in New Delhi affirmed that, in 2012, when a teacher eligibility test was conducted, only 2.5 percent of all existing teachers managed to score passing marks. Presented with the problem of low-quality teacher training, the government of India appointed a high-level committee.[48]

Teachers in India are also poorly motivated – in the vast majority of schools, both public and private. More dedicated teachers are not given higher rewards than those who neglect their duties. Pay increases are achieved on the basis of seniority. Other rewards that public school teachers care for – postings and promotions – are centrally determined in the state capital, and these rewards rarely reflect the effort put in by a teacher or the results achieved by her students. Inspections by departmental supervisors are sporadic, cursory, and focused on incidental inputs that happen to have high priority at the moment (such as constructing toilets at the time of writing). In the majority of private schools, too, except for a tiny number of elite institutions, the teachers are poorly trained, poorly motivated, and given little freedom of action.

One NGO leader, who has invested a lifetime in the cause of school education, explained to me how "there is a sense of despair among teachers, a lack of agency and purpose and autonomy."[49] Governance by centralized fiat leaves hardly any room for enterprise and innovation in the classroom. Teaching to a centrally determined curriculum is deemed more important than nurturing individuals' separate capacities. Textbooks designed with elite children in mind are pitched at an unrealistic level for other children. I have seen Raju and Bhura Ram struggling mightily with their Hindi textbooks, full of abstruse words and complex sentences that even I, for all my love of the language, find hard to follow.[50]

But that's not all. Involvement and oversight by parents is almost entirely missing. There's hardly any occasion when parents and teachers meet one another and join hands in a common purpose. Taking note of this situation, the Right-to-Education (RTE) Act, introduced in 2009, required that consultative bodies be constituted. As a consequence, school management committees or village education committees were set up in many places, but in a helter-skelter, check-the-box fashion – without any shared commitment to the cause and with little seriousness of purpose. Exceptions apart, these committees rarely meet, nor do they have a mandate that is widely known and respected. Parents who have been nominated to such committees are often entirely unaware of their appointments.[51]

Informing these people about their rights and their duties, and ensuring their deeper engagement, is among the important remaining tasks of reforming school education. Equally important is the need to change attitudes and values and reallocating authority within the system.

Innovations in the Classroom

Dealing with each of the different elements of reform is not going to be quick or easy, but it is essential. India can't keep producing millions who attend schools but who end up learning very little.

Individually, parents have been fashioning their own remedies. Many have exercised what the economist, Albert Hirschman, described as the exit option, leaving the public system in large numbers, since the other option, voice, has been rendered ineffective.[52] From just under 19 percent in 2006, the share of rural children in private schools increased steadily to reach 31 percent in 2014. In urban areas, the share of children in private schools increased earlier and faster. In 2009, it was already at 58 percent, and since then it has risen further.[53]

Parents' motivations for sending their children to private schools are complex, however, reflecting not just a quest for higher-quality learning but also a desire to differentiate their children from others. Embedded as they are in India's segmented society, many parents see a distinct advantage in sending their children to study in an environment resembling that of urban "convent" schools where, along with learning the English language, children can learn how to dress, behave, and conduct themselves in the manner of upper-class, city-bred, English-speaking people. Much of this imbibing of mannerisms is only by way of outward appearance. In the searing heat of the Indian summer, I have seen young rural children incongruously dressed in uniforms that have neckties and stiff collars.

Privatization, without effective monitoring and regulation, has produced a broad range of schools, offering education at various price points and with widely varying outcomes.[54] It's not clear that privatization will resolve the quality problem in beyond-5-km villages, where it is felt most acutely. The private schools that I have visited in rural areas are of an indifferent quality; some among them are no more than "extractive money-making machines with modest educational offerings."[55]

Boosting the trend toward greater privatization through the use of school vouchers is not to be recommended – not, at least, until mechanisms are in place to enforce quality standards and ensure the availability of a viable range of choices to remote villages and poorer children. That's going to be hard to achieve – and even so, going by experiences in other countries, it might well constitute an incomplete and wasteful solution, one that exacerbates, instead of mitigating, educational inequality.[56] Several questions of a practical nature also need to be considered: Will the taxpayer have to pay twice over for the same service, once for government-run schools (where teachers have permanent tenure and fixed salaries), and once again for the voucher system? If the government system is to be entirely abandoned, then what will become of the huge public investments made over the years in buildings, equipment, textbooks, and training? From whence will come the millions of trained school teachers to staff the expansion in the voucher-based private system? Will the same government schoolteachers be reemployed in private schools? But if that's going to be the case, then shouldn't an effort be made first to improve what these teachers are able to achieve in their current positions?

Reforming the public system is both necessary and feasible. Other countries have well-functioning public school systems. Finland's school system, consistently counted among the best in the world, is entirely public: everyone attends a state school in Finland. Among developing countries, Brazil has taken impressive initiatives, adopting a sustained and incremental strategy for reforming its public school system.[57] The public education system in India can also be renovated, provided that there is a will to rock the boat and prepare for a long effort in order to achieve lasting improvements.

The essential problem, as I see it, is one of poor governance. A basic prerequisite of effective governance is to connect responsibility with authority – and authority with information. At present, those who are best informed about what is happening in a school – teachers, schoolchildren, and their parents – have hardly any say in governing the system. And those who have the authority that the system provides – departmental supervisors – rarely have the information necessary for making responsible decisions. Because they sit so far apart, authority is not effectively exercised, responsibility is evaded, and information becomes a wasted resource.

Pulling everything up to a centralized level of decision making is hardly the best way to deal with these problems. It's too slow, and it requires processing an overwhelming amount of information, with a lot that is important getting lost in transmission. System-wide reform will be best facilitated by investing in a process that enables problems and opportunities to be detected early, and responses to be fashioned through a process of continuous innovation.

Because the best available information about service quality exists at the point of delivery, authority for school management has to be decentralized to committees composed of teachers, parents, and students. The experience of school reforms in other countries shows how local school autonomy coupled with strong accountability systems, including well-informed and deeply engaged parents, has helped transform public education systems, leading to vast improvements in learning outcomes.[58] Parents who care about the education of their children – the vast majority, including those who are themselves little educated – will not easily let go of this opportunity, especially if they are well informed about their new roles and responsibilities and effectively engaged in decision making.

Computer-aided learning can help with all of these efforts, but it cannot substitute for the human element. Technological fixes – like One Laptop per Child or Hole-in-the-Wall computers – cannot fix the multifarious problems of school education, although they can help considerably, especially when accompanied by other reform elements. Analyzing these examples and many others, and learning, too, from his own often failed experiments with tech-driven solutions, Kentaro Toyama, a self-professed techno-optimist who worked for many years at developing high-tech solutions for low-quality education and other problems in India, concluded that "throwing gadgets at social problems isn't effective because it's one among many elements of a lasting solution. It's schools that work hard to maintain a strong learning culture, whose faculty and parents make important decisions together, and that put their educational goals first in making technology decisions (rather than the other way around) – that technology's power amplifies."[59] Some of the best examples of computer-aided techniques in service of higher quality education have come from organizations that have put the classroom experience at the center of the process and that have stimulated the teachers' creativity and the students' motivation.[60]

Education is not and cannot be an assembly-line process. It's more than just throwing facts at people and getting through the textbooks. Education involves discussion and dialog and creative thinking.

A greater focus on the classroom experience, accompanied by a greater delegation of authority to teachers and parents, has been an important component of educational reforms that have been successful. In Finland, teachers have the role of innovators in the classroom. There's no standard formula for success. Each teacher has the authority and the freedom to be creative. Parents partner with teachers and oversee their efforts.[61]

What is currently a highly centralized and top-down system in India needs to give way to another, in which teachers are innovative in the classroom and parents are involved as co–decision makers. Some noteworthy smaller-scale innovations developed by pioneering state governments and NGOs provide indication of the larger potential of such a course of action.[62] These and other commendable efforts should serve as starting points in a broader process of policy innovation. A system of graduated policy experiments – trying out promising alternatives at a few grassroots-level locations before progressively scaling up the ones with the best results – will be more effective than big-bang remedies implemented all at once across the nation. There is no magic bullet. Errors and missteps are inevitable. A learning process approach, focused on incremental and continuous improvements, building from the grassroots upward, needs to be initiated.

Raising the Low Glass Ceiling: Investing in Role Model Development

Raising the level and improving the quality of education is an essential requirement. In parallel, faith in education has to be restored through the achievement of greater upward mobility.

Otherwise, a backlash against education is waiting to happen. In the past three decades, there has been a rapid rise in school education, as new schools were opened up by state governments, and as parents increasingly felt it important to invest in education. The rising tide of education in rural India is largely composed of first-generation learners, in whom much parental hope has been invested. Lately, however, parents have begun to question the worth of education. Given what they have seen of the achievements of the first lot of school-goers, they will no longer blindly invest in education. Mere exhortations and aphorisms are no longer sufficient. Until some young people from their neighborhood receive visible benefits in the form of good jobs with higher salaries and better prospects, the newfound faith in education could very well falter, leading to a reversal of the recent gains in school enrollments.

Increasing social mobility is essential to forestall this backlash, and also to make better use of India's vast human potential. The country's "demographic (or youth) dividend" – its rising proportion of employment-age people – is correctly regarded as a national asset. This asset needs to be put to the best use by matching each individual's talent with a commensurate opportunity.

A program of skills development is being promoted by the Indian government, which aims to provide vocational education to millions of school leavers, with the objective of enhancing their employment prospects in industry.[63] Sterling work is being done to further this objective by a number of organizations, including the NGO Kherwadi

Social Welfare Organization;[64] the nonprofit organization B-Able;[65] and many corporations, among whom Café Coffee Day's efforts are exemplary.[66] These initiatives can go a long way, especially if jobs of these kinds are concurrently created in the requisite numbers.

But poorer youth are suited not only for becoming mechanics, electricians, and waiters. Many have a greater capacity that needs to be separately nurtured.

Talent development is a task separate from skill development, and it requires a different vehicle. When someone from a village becomes an electrician, it's certainly a positive outcome, but when someone becomes an engineer or Olympic athlete or business executive or IAS official, going beyond a middling status, then the positive effects, direct and indirect, are qualitatively superior.

Not every person from poorer sections of society will be able to take the routes leading up to higher achievement, but that doesn't make the suggestion less relevant or less applicable. In traditional poverty reduction, the effort is pitched at the achievement of some minimum level by the average individual. But the prospects of the more capable should not be constrained by what is possible for the mass or the average. Enabling the more talented to rise high is equally the task of a just and high-achieving society. Alongside measures that help people surmount poverty, other measures for talent development need to be assembled.

Helping even one or two individuals from a remote village or urban slum to reach a higher-status position acts as a crucial stimulus, raising hopes and generating energy among others. Communities that gain the confidence that their sons and daughters have a real chance of becoming engineers, MBAs, and senior government officials will shed the hopelessness their prior experiences have generated. They will feel more connected with the national mainstream. Energized by the new faith in their sons' and daughters' prospects for upward mobility, they will become more proactive, no longer helplessly accepting low-quality teaching and absentee teachers. Quality improvements mandated from the top down will become more powerful when complemented by such bottom-up efforts.

There is a great deal to be gained, directly and indirectly, by investing in a program of role model development. The national census of 2011 counted 640,000 villages in India, of which roughly 400,000 are beyond-5-km villages, where the gap between talent and opportunity has been most acutely experienced. There are also just over 100,000 urban slum settlements.

Developing one or more superior role models in this total of about 500,000 locations is not an insuperable task, especially if a longer-term view is taken, and if the effort is supported by corporate enterprises, NGOs, government agencies, universities, and concerned individuals. On a tiny scale, in my village, I am working with a small group of young people. One of these young men is studying to be an engineer. Another, who is younger, is still looking at different options, which I help him explore by arranging visits to different workplaces and facilitating discussions with people who have pursued diverse careers. Already, just a few years into this effort, I am seeing signs of a shift in other young people's motivations. They are staying longer in school, and they are actively considering better careers. Of greater scope and value are the initiatives being taken by a group of newer organizations, which are enabling large numbers of talented youth from poorer communities to strive for and achieve better careers. In diverse ways, these organizations have been dealing with the obstacles identified in our examination of outlier interviews – including the paucity of career-related information, the absence of better role models, and the lack of enabling facilities, such as libraries, mentors, and counseling centers. I expand on their roles in the following chapter, but it's fitting to cite from a few among their mission statements. Commonly, they believe, as one organization puts it, that

> Talent knows no boundaries. It is everywhere. All one needs is to spot talent and nurture it to let it blossom.[67]

A number of related interventions are required for this purpose. Investing in information flows and working on changing attitudes and beliefs is as important as improving the quality of education or providing college loans and other kinds of financial assistance.

> Money is not the sole issue facing kids belonging to poor rural families. Their parents are illiterate. They need handholding.
> There is a big gap between what the students know and learn, and what the industry expects from them. To help these kids, it is very important to address other issues also.[68]

> We aim to provide a nurturing environment for children and youth from marginalized communities to transform their passion into gainful employment through career guidance, life skill development, and mentorship.[69]

The next chapter takes up a discussion of these "soft factors," which, despite being fundamental in importance, are most often overlooked in policy discussions.[70]

6 ATTITUDES, EXPERIENCES, AND INFORMATION

Why does the poorer majority have to attend schools of a poor quality that leave them ill prepared for the modern economy? Why do women in India find it harder to achieve higher education and tread the better career pathways? Why do so many spend their whole lives working, only to end up with no provision for retirement? Why do Scheduled Castes and Scheduled Tribes face discrimination in hiring? Why has India's official poverty line been set far below that of other countries in comparable situations?

A number of factors – population growth, the legacy of colonial rule, and competing policy priorities – have played a part, no doubt, in producing these outcomes. But no explanation is complete or compelling without taking into account attitudes, beliefs, and values.

These "soft" factors matter as much as other factors,[1] such as plan formulations and budget allocations. In fact, soft factors have a prior part in the explanation: plans and budgets reveal preferences that are, in turn, derived from beliefs and values that dominate policy discussions. Rural schools in the public system are bare-bones affairs – two rooms, a blackboard, a couple of teachers for all of five grades, nothing much by way of extracurricular activities, and usually no library – not because the money can't be reallocated, but because planners' priorities reflect particular values. Dalits,[2] women, and people from rural areas face a low glass ceiling, not because they're less hardworking or less capable, but because many people are mired in belief systems that view these individuals in a certain fashion. Domestic servants aren't given pension benefits, not because these people have another way of dealing with old age, but because their needs aren't regarded as equal. When a *mazdoor* is seriously injured at work, the employer feels all right about sending her home without paying compensation.

Laws have been enacted to deal with some among these situations, but they remain statements of intent: on the books, but with little bite or practical value. That's because the corresponding norms and beliefs haven't changed, and laws that don't accord with norms and beliefs are rarely respected, even by many responsible for law enforcement.[3]

The realization that the application of laws gets refracted through the prism of norms and values came to me first when, as a college student, I traveled on a scholarship to the UK, and lived for a while in a village a short train ride from London. Late at night, after reveling with other young people in the big city, I took the last train back to the village. Walking to my apartment, in the dark and deserted street, I saw a speeding car screech to a halt when a traffic light turned from green to amber. I shook my head in disbelief. The driver must be deranged, I thought. For if it were India, even during the day, few would stop for a red light when there were no police and no traffic. It's the same traffic signal in intent and construction, and the same laws and penalties apply in both countries, but in one case the driver considers it right to come to a halt, and in the other case he doesn't. It's not that one society is more uniformly civil or law abiding;[4] people in India go beyond the law in being considerate and civil, showing respect to elders as a matter of course and extending hospitality to perfect strangers. The more important point is about the constellation of norms and taken-for-granted forms of behavior, which steer people in one direction or another. Where I live in India, one calculates whether to stop for a red light; where I live in the United States, it's one of many taken-for-granted behaviors.

The beliefs that guide taken-for-granted behaviors in different societies have wider implications, influencing a variety of economic outcomes. Societies answer key questions differently, depending on which beliefs and values take hold: How much is the right amount of assistance to give to poorer people? Who are the deserving and the undeserving poor? How much inequality can be tolerated? Who is one of us, and who isn't? The attitudes, beliefs, and values that prevail in a country are reflected in its poverty line, its minimum wage level, and the relative generosity of its social welfare programs. None of these development outcomes can be fully understood without referring to attitudes and values. The attitudes and values that have come to prevail in India's segmented society uphold forms of behavior that deny a fair opportunity to large numbers of its people. Instead of being seen as secondary or tangential, soft factors are more appropriately regarded as a central part of the agenda for growth and development.

Attitudes, Beliefs, and Values

Public choices get skewed in situations where biased attitudes have an overbearing influence on the policy process. A variety of examples lend support to this statement.

Consider a likely answer to the pair of questions: Why is the quality of education in elite private schools so much higher than the quality of education in public schools attended by the poorer majority? And why, simultaneously, does the opposite happen at the college level: why are so many of the highest-ranked colleges and universities in the public sector, including the Indian Institutes of Management and the Indian Institutes of Technology?

It can't be put down to inefficiencies in the government sector, for that would explain the first outcome without explaining the second. Nor can it be attributed to lack of resources, for money is fungible and can be moved between schools and colleges.

A more persuasive explanation makes reference to attitudes and values. It helps to begin with a short extract from an infamous "minute" or policy document written in 1835 by Thomas Macaulay, then a member of the governing council of the colonial government led by the East India Company – a minute to which William Bentinck, the Governor General, gave his "entire concurrence." This document, which was to lay the foundations for India's education policies, gave expression to a set of beliefs that were widely shared at the time by British officials and a small but growing group of upper-middle-class Indians.

> We have to educate a people who cannot at present be educated
> by means of their mother-tongue. We must teach them some
> foreign language ... We must at present do our best to form a
> class who may be interpreters between us and the millions whom
> we govern – a class of persons Indian in blood and color, but

English in tastes, in opinions, in morals and in intellect . . . to render them by degrees fit vehicles for conveying knowledge to the great mass of the population.[5]

Modern education institutions that were set up to give effect to these beliefs and values were narrowly focused on urban locations and elite education. Colleges and high schools were established in the bigger cities, but many villages did not have a primary school until decades after national independence.[6] A small class of people – urban, middle class, English-speaking, and college educated; "Indian in blood and color, but English in tastes and opinions" – came into being that amassed considerable cultural and intellectual resources, acquiring disproportionate economic weight and policy influence.[7]

One might have thought that this colonial-era policy – which tilted education expenses toward elites and away from the general public – would have been reversed once an independent and democratic government had been established. On the contrary, the bias in educational expenditures has persisted well into the seventh decade of a democratic government. India continues to spend ten times as much per student at the college level compared to what it spends on primary-level students. In advanced industrial economies and in other fast-growing developing countries, the ratio between what is spent on college-level and primary-level students is no more than two times on average, indicating that the public exchequer is five times as bountiful for India's college students – despite the fact that children from richer and big-city homes capture the largest share of college admissions.[8]

Why have India's planners thought it appropriate to persist with such a skewed set of educational policies? Attitudes and beliefs have central explanatory value.

"Members of the Indian middle class conceptualize a distinction between the children of the poor and their own children," explained the political scientist, Myron Weiner. "A distinction is made between children as 'hands' and children as 'minds'; that is, between the child who must be taught to 'work' and the child who must be taught to 'learn,' the acquisition of manual skills as distinctive from cognitive skills." The policies that have resulted from these attitudes have "enabled the middle class to send their children to separate private (but government-aided) schools, while the lower classes send their children to underfunded, under-equipped municipal and village schools."[9] The latter group of students, the majority, emerges ill prepared to compete successfully for places in the highest-ranked colleges and universities.

Beliefs and values have given shape to policies that result in producing highly unequal educational outcomes. Other outcomes that derive from values and attitudes handicap other parts of the country's population. Women are held back because of attitudes and beliefs about appropriate social roles that can be rigidly gender-specific.[10] There is little empathy for people of distant and culturally different regions, sometimes leading to pogrom-like assaults on their properties and persons.[11]

An egregious example consists of the social and economic handicaps that Dalits experience on account of negative stereotyping. Even as the role of caste in society and politics has changed – with a "democratic upsurge" elevating the former untouchables[12] – attitudes and beliefs continue to uphold the differential treatment of people believed to be unequal.[13] Studies show that, on the whole, Dalits' social and political circumstances have improved to some extent, especially in some parts of the country,[14] but the chances of significant economic successes remain low on account of widespread discrimination in hiring.[15]

Yet another example relates to the behaviors and attitudes many urban elites exhibit toward poorer members of society. There are those who would consider a poor person to be morally inferior because, they might argue, would not a morally upright person have made his way out of poverty through working hard and abjuring bad habits? The facts of the case may point to the opposite conclusion – that despite trying hard, many are overtaken by adverse events – but where blind beliefs prevail, the facts of the matter are given little importance. Demeaning attitudes toward poorer people are passed down from generation to generation, unthinkingly adopted and frequently touted. "Heaping humiliation upon geography" is how an urban sociologist describes the treatment of slum dwellers by their posher neighbors.[16]

Attitudes matter, not only on the side of elites, but also on the parts of poorer people. Dinesh, a young man from my village, completed high school and was hired to be an x-ray technician at a private hospital. He is paid 5,000 rupees monthly. Another young man, Ragho, who also completed high school, was hired to be a library assistant at a private business college. He is paid slightly less, 4,500 rupees monthly. Ragho and Dinesh could have made more money by working as *mazdoors*, who can make more than 200 rupees daily. But attitudes and values have influenced their choices. To become a *mazdoor* after completing high school is widely seen as a comedown. The pool of graduates willing to work for a pittance in an office has vastly expanded.[17]

Another development that cannot be satisfactorily explained without reference to values and attitudes has to do with the growing divide in the economic prospects of those who are fluent in English and others who aren't, but who may, otherwise, be equally meritorious. In diverse walks of life, English speakers have an advantage, even among engineers recruited to fill back-office positions.

Why does being able to function in the English language, to read and write fluently and speak without a distinct accent, matter so much for career achievement in a country where English is but one of many languages? Partly, no doubt, it's because globalization has made English a universal language of business. But partly, it's a question, not so much of the utility of the language, but of the accompanying markers of family background and social status. "Command over the English language represents both a form of cultural capital as well as a structural marker of middle class identity . . . The possession of such language skills can be transformed into social and economic capital in the labor market . . . English is not merely a skill that the new middle class can use . . . It is constitutive of this group's *identity*."[18]

It would be good, of course, if everyone could learn to speak English well – then everyone would have the same opportunities – but as of 2012, only 5 percent of rural (and 22 percent of urban) children, 8–11 years old, could read even a single word written in English.[19] The beliefs that underlie the preference for English, together with attitudes and values that limit the educational opportunities of poorer children, have resulted in creating a situation wherein large numbers of talented and hardworking children confront multiple handicaps to upward mobility. It's part of a larger system of beliefs and values that limit poorer and rural people's prospects.

In the mainstream media, and in the public discourse more generally, there has been a change of focus – away from the concerns and lifestyles of the rural and poorer parts and toward the richer and more Westernized parts of the country. "Living in India," writes Mark Tully, longtime BBC station chief in New Delhi, "I can almost sense the enormous pressure . . . to conform to the Western secular, materialist way of life. Many of the influential elite in India can't see that there is any alternative . . . In their eyes, you are either in favor of Western culture, or you are some antediluvian romantic."[20] One gets a sense of the values and attitudes that are prevalent by examining how much space a country's newspapers devote to different topics. I conducted such a study with the help of two research assistants, and we looked at six newspapers – two national English dailies; two published in a local language in a state capital; and two published in a district capital, also in the local language. We assessed the relative emphasis these newspapers place on different topics by arranging all printed matter into fourteen separate categories of published items. Apart from advertisements, which covered between 16 percent and 51 percent of the newsprint in different papers, the largest amount of space was taken up by two categories of items: sports (which covered between 5 and 12.5 percent of the newsprint in different papers) and politics and administration (between 7 and 21 percent of the space). The smallest amount of space was given by newspapers to the category "poverty and social welfare" – no more than 1 percent, on average, of all printed matter, falling to 0.12 percent in the case of one publication.[21]

Newspaper readers are commonly un-interested in reports about poor people and social welfare programs. They are equally uninterested in news from outside big cities: the coverage of rural areas is paltry.[22] Living in a posh neighborhood in a big city, and getting one's information from newspapers and primetime TV, one could quite easily come to believe that the country is composed entirely of its richest one percent.[23] The gaze of the state and of power holders has turned away from poorer people and rural areas. The village has receded from the national imagination.[24] Among rural elites and politicians elected from rural constituencies, there is a rush toward big cities. That's where their children go to study and live, where their futures are imagined.[25]

The attitudes and beliefs that have accelerated these changes in national priorities have led to other demands, some of which can seem pushy and undemocratic. These beliefs reflect a disparaging image of poorer rural people, in whose habits and behaviors, customs and institutions, the argument goes, city elites have a legitimate right to enforce remedial changes.

One example of such pushy demands is provided by a law enacted in 2015, separately but almost simultaneously by two state governments, Rajasthan and Haryana. It disqualified specific groups of rural citizens from contesting *panchayat* elections, including those who had fallen behind on loan repayments to banks, whose electricity bills were in arrears, who did not have a functional lavatory in their home – and who lacked a certain threshold of educational qualifications (high school for men, and middle school for women and Dalits). Interestingly, no similar stipulations were laid down for urban voters and city-based electoral candidates.[26]

What purpose is being served by the educational requirement, one might ask? Not the promotion of higher education, for if that were the case, then the requirement would have been applied prospectively – to come into effect eight or ten years *after* the law was introduced. Such a forward-looking law would have had a beneficial effect, helping tilt the decision for those whose educational choices were still in the offing. But that's not how the law was framed. It came into effect immediately, penalizing the people whose educational choices were made as many as twenty or thirty years in the past. Many among these individuals cannot be faulted for not going to school; there were no schools in many parts of rural India until quite recently. In Haryana, no more than 14 percent of males and 24 percent of females had the requisite educational qualification when the law was enacted; in the other state, Rajasthan, the degree of exclusion was higher.[27]

The image of the rural that gave shape to these laws was stamped with a deep lack of knowledge, especially the law related to lavatories. Consider what should have been a prior question: *Why* do some village homes not have indoor toilets? One answer could be that rural people are backward, ignorant, and slow to realize the obvious health benefits. Alternatively, it could be that there's no piped water supply, and that buckets and jars of water need to be hauled in from several kilometers. The facts on the ground lend more support to the second explanation. Houses in villages where a piped water supply is available are more than three times as likely to have personal toilets.[28] There seems to be an orderly progression: when there's more piped water supply, there will be more indoor plumbing and toilets. Where there isn't any piped supply, however, a toilet can be a wasteful investment. Toilets built in such villages remain unused or have become cesspools of infection, because there isn't running water to clean them.[29] The attitudes that found expression in these laws were rooted, however, in the first impression: that rural India is backward and ignorant and needs to be hectored into building toilets – no matter what the ground situation.

Such attitudes and beliefs are at the heart of why the two thirds of the population that lives in rural India gets much less than its fair share of media attention. That's not how it used to be; in the late-1960s, *Jai Jawaan, Jai Kisaan*, was the country's slogan, given voice by a popular Prime Minister, hailing soldiers' and farmers' contributions to the nation.

Attitudes toward the rural population have changed considerably since then, not only in India, but also in other countries. Poorer and rural people are becoming invisible to the elites, not an important part of the imagined future of the nation.[30] Such a change of focus may be easier to accommodate in countries such as Chile or Venezuela, which for a long time have been more than three-quarters urban. But India is different: in larger part, rural and agrarian. In India, these shifting attitudes and priorities bode poorly for a large part of the population.

The countryside is becoming harder to govern in consequence. "Every little incident in a small town or rural area now assumes big proportions," the chief secretary of a state government, the highest-ranking civil servant, told me when I met him in his office in early 2016. "There's a great deal of frustration, and people are on the lookout for occasions when they can give voice to their sense of being left behind by the progress they see others achieving."[31] Other officials with equally distinguished careers in public service expressed a similar appreciation of unfolding events.[32]

Without reforming attitudes and exposing blind beliefs to the light of reason, it is going be difficult to reverse policy biases and to provide a level playing field to every citizen. It's not an easy task, but it's not insurmountable.

In some part, people's beliefs are strategic and self-serving, but in another part they're the result of information gaps and lack of experience. Enhancing information flows and helping engender a richer set of experiences will help buttress other tasks of development.

Experiences

Experiences can reshape attitudes and shake up long-held beliefs. The effects in each case will depend on the type of experience.

Part of the problem of India's many-layered society is that people's activities, and hence their experiences, tend to be narrowly confined to interactions with other people of the same social layer. A person from one layer of society rarely has an opportunity to experience the lived realities of people who belong to other social layers. Bounded lives lead to hidebound beliefs, reproducing prejudice and reinforcing social segmentation.

Fostering a wider set of experiences can help reform attitudes and expose beliefs to the light of facts and reason. One example of a development organization that quite deliberately uses experience as a tool for changing values and reforming belief structures comes from the work of Pramod Kulkarni and his colleagues at Sathi.[33] At the time I met Kulkarni, in the summer of 2015, this organization was working yearly with more than 4,000 runaway children. There are many such children in India, but very little is known among the general public about their circumstances. Ill-informed beliefs put it down to desperate poverty or broken households, whereas the truth is different and simpler.

"We started in Raichur railway station, where we saw seven or eight children running around. We thought they needed motivation and direction. Over the next three years, we put 30 such children, the older ones, into jobs in a friend's business. But half of them ran away within six months." No crime was committed, he quickly inserted. "We looked for these children, and we found that most hard returned to their original homes (which, contrary to what we had expected, were not dysfunctional). So why had they run away from their parents' homes? Sometimes because of deviant company, but mostly for some small precipitating reason – such as the father beating the son for not doing homework.

"Once a child runs away it becomes progressively difficult to go back," he added. "When you run away, you want to go back, but every additional day you spend away from home, the harder it becomes to explain your absence. Such children congregate at railway stations. After one year of being a runaway, a child has traveled on trains across the length and breadth of the country."

"Many of our earlier beliefs were proved incorrect," Kulkarni continued, "and we have now become more pro-active. We learned that a child is more in need of roots than of security and money. We catch children as soon as they reach the railway station, and we endeavor to reunite them with their parents."

The big experiential moment comes in a ceremony that the organization regularly arranges, where runaway children and their parents are reunited with one another. A great deal of naked emotion is on display. Sobbing parents and children cling to each other as if they will never again be physically separated. Witnessing these scenes is enough to churn the insides of a stoic; I couldn't get more than halfway through a recorded version. Reunification ceremonies are, however, a central part of the organization's mobilization strategy, and they serve as its main communications platform. The experience, Kulkarni believes, serves as a morale booster for staffers, reinforcing their commitments to the organization's mission. It's good as well for the children and their parents, who see others overcome by the same emotions.

Potential donors, senior government officials, journalists, and others are invited, indeed pressed, to participate in the monthly reunification ceremony. They emerge with a better understanding of the prevalence of the phenomenon, of its underlying causes, and of appropriate and inappropriate interventions.

Other examples show how experiences can be deliberately engendered that help people rid themselves of blind beliefs and biased values. Studies show, for instance, how adjusting the social mix within schools and neighborhoods has boosted the performance of disadvantaged students without negative effects on the performance of other students.[34] One study recorded the impacts of a policy change, introduced in 2007, which required elite private schools in Delhi to recruit 20 percent of their students from among poorer sections. These schools, many of which were built on lands leased from the Delhi government, had undertaken to admit such students, but until the government stepped in actively, school administrators had been dragging their feet, implementing this provision in a laggardly fashion. Immediately, the experience of bringing richer and poorer students together in the same classroom led to a few ugly scenes. Slum children were stigmatized and discriminated against, in multiple ways being made to feel small and unwanted.[35] Over a longer period, however, the learning and the experiences that accrued were of a very different nature. A few years after the policy came into effect, a careful study found that "having poor classmates makes wealthy students more prosocial and generous. They become more likely to volunteer for a charity at school, more generous toward both rich and poor students . . . Having poor classmates makes wealthy children discriminate less against poor children . . . and more willing to socialize with poor children outside school."[36]

Those who get to know people who are not like themselves become more able to shed the stereotypes they've been handed.[37]

Research shows how Hindus and Muslims are less likely to be violent toward each other in those cities and neighborhoods where organizations have existed that have brought them together in regular face-to-face interactions.[38]

Misconceptions become fewer when people have the opportunity to learn more about each other. Conversely, narrower and more segmented experiences reinforce prejudice and deepen attitudinal divisions.[39] Where there's little contact between rural and urban, between richer and poorer – where each individual remains confined to his or her own social layer – there, stereotypes harden.

Very few among those who live in big cities have any direct experience of life in a beyond-5-km village. The unknown and the unfamiliar rural tends to get projected in images of backwardness and caste conflict and filth and illnesses. The 600,000 villages of India aren't alike, however. They differ considerably, some being dens of distrust while others are havens of social capital. There are cleaner and dirtier villages, peaceful and violent ones, some with great harmony and collective spirit and others with deep rifts and long-lasting enmities.[40] One could have picked, thus, from a number of images, but a negative image – born of inexperience and lack of knowledge – has dominated the urban imagination.

Changing these images is necessary. Otherwise, it can become a vicious cycle. Attitudes and beliefs that portray villages as backward help produce policies that lean toward city-centric development. Villages fall farther behind, reinforcing the negative image.

Breaking this cycle is necessary for equalizing opportunity and repairing the broken ladder. Along with experiential learning, the spread of information can help.

Information

"I believed that it was the right thing to do," Vasundhara told me, "and it would make an important difference to these children's progress."

She was telling me about the work she has been doing with young adults in her village, helping them plan for higher education and to consider a wider range of career options. We were sitting in a coffee shop in Bengaluru, close to her workplace in a ritzy district. A demure young woman in her mid-thirties, Vasundhara was dressed conservatively in a loose kurta and baggy trousers. Her steely gaze gave me a window into the determination that lurked just below the mild-mannered surface.

"They have no clear career plan," she told me. "Not like the big city kids, you know, who after doing X, are aware that they have to do Y, then do Z, and so on... These big-city kids are aware of the paths that lead from high school to a good career. Young people in my village know nothing of this; they have no means to get this help for themselves. I assist them by collecting and sharing useful information. So far, I have helped four children in my village."

Vasundhara's own life story is unusual and illustrative. She grew up in a village in northern Karnataka. Economic conditions were tight in her family, and she faced additional hurdles on account of being a woman. She succeeded nevertheless in becoming a software engineer. She works for one of the most highly regarded companies in Bengaluru.

How was she able to make this impressive leap? She narrated the following experience.

"I studied in the school in my village until Class 5, that is, elementary school. Then I went to the neighboring village where my grandparents lived. I studied there until I finished Class 7. That would have been the end of my studies, but one of my teachers recommended to my father to send me to an urban high school." This teacher had detected that Vasundhara was especially talented. In multiple ways, not least through guidance, motivation, and information provision, he helped her raise her sights and achieve her ambitions.

"He went and obtained the official application form and he actually processed the entire application. He was the one who initially informed my father about the possibility of getting a fully paid scholarship to a good school in the city, and then he continued to urge us on. With his guidance, I wrote an examination meant to pull in the talent among rural children." She performed very well at this competitive examination. "And then I went to attend a public school in a big city. That's where I completed my high school."

"Initially, when I got that admission, my parents were reluctant. But my schoolteacher continued to be helpful. He told my parents that it would be safe for me there, because he has relatives who live in this city (who could look after me)."

After graduating from high school, she won another fellowship and attended a well-regarded engineering college, ending up with a high-paying job in the software industry. She lives in a big city now and comes to the village for a few days each month to work with young people.

My heart filled with gladness upon hearing her story. I wished there could be a thousand replications.

Unfortunately, these stories are only too rare. There are very few layer-climbing individuals like Vasundhara, and very many who work in poorly paid and insecure positions, even after getting higher education.

Contrast Vasundhara's story with that of Leela, a talented and hardworking young woman who grew up in a slum in Bengaluru. She ended up becoming a low-paid assistant in a private pathology laboratory.

Both belong to a Scheduled Caste, both grew up in relatively poor families, and both are highly capable individuals, but one was able to reach a high point on the career ladder and keeps rising higher; the other is stuck in a low-paid dead-end position. The critical difference was made by the timely provision of information and guidance – about different and better career options, about the required preparation, about the financial assistance that could be obtained, and most of all, about having faith in oneself and belief in one's abilities. Vasundhara's schoolteacher provided these critical inputs, but no well-informed individual came around to help Leela, and as a result, her line of sight was restricted.

More broadly, studies have found how the benefits of education are considerably reduced in information-poor contexts.[41] Conversely, other studies show how the provision of timely and reliable information adds considerable value to the career prospects of talented young people. One such study, undertaken in the United States, showed how low-income students who received easy-to-understand packets of information about college costs and the college application process were much more likely to apply for, and be accepted to, selective colleges than others in similar circumstances who were not provided with this information. After entering elite colleges, the well-informed low-income students performed at the same standard as their better-off peers – showing how a vast potential exists that can be activated through information provision.[42]

Some notable initial steps have been taken in India. A number of organizations have come up that are engaged in promoting the social mobility prospects of talented but poorer children. Their founders believe that:

> There are many bright kids with great potential who belong to families from below poverty threshold ... but due to lack of right guidance and awareness, they lose out on relevant future career prospects.[43]

Acting on such beliefs, these organizations have developed programs that reach out to poorer children and give them a leg up by working on diverse soft factors. Their interventions include different combinations of information provision, supplementary education, building self-confidence, providing motivation, and enabling access to superior role models.

Implemented so far on a fairly small scale and mostly in urban centers, these programs are, in diverse ways, helping extend the aspirational horizons of poorer young men and women. I came to learn about a cross-section of such organizations and program outcomes.[44] They work in diverse ways to promote social mobility, some aiming at the top jobs and working with the best-prepared individuals; other organizations, with a different philosophy of action, direct their efforts, instead, toward a larger cross-section of the poorer population.

Overall, I was able to distinguish among four broadly different modes of engagement:

> *Broad-based soft factor interventions*, including Prerana, Vidyaposhak, Mumbai Smiles, and Udaan India Foundation.[45]
> *Top-level entrance examination preparation*, including Super 30, Avanti Fellows, and CSRL.[46]
> *Mentoring, role models, and life-skills training*, including Dream a Dream, Make a Difference, Friends of Children, Bright Future India, Vazhai, the Green Batti Project, Bhumi, Mentor Together, Mentor Me India, Manzil, and ACH Bejobbed Foundation.[47]
> *Forging critical linkages*, including Aspiring Minds, Bharat Calling, Lead Trust, and Institutional Excellence Forum.[48]

The first type of organization focuses diffusely on improving career preparation, but without singling out any particular career for specific preparation. Some among these organizations work only with more meritorious students, as evaluated by the organization's entrance examination, but many open their doors to all comers from poorer households.

The second type, of which Super 30 is the first mover and the one whose model of action is widely emulated, helps a selected group of students gain admission to highly ranked institutes, particularly top-level engineering colleges. The third type complements the efforts of the first two types by working more diffusely and among a broader population. These organizations are focused on developing mentoring relations, which help raise self-worth and foster higher career aspirations by providing guidance and information.

Organizations of the fourth type focus on the linkage task, helping students connect with colleges and with employers. By providing students with information about various colleges, by helping fill out admission forms, and guiding college preparation, these organizations help nontraditional college-goers through what can otherwise be a daunting transition. Aspiring Minds fills a particular niche, enabling high-performing students from lower-ranked colleges to connect with higher-paying employers.

Apart from these organizations, there are others that help fill a specific gap – for instance, English E-Teach, which prepares and distributes DVDs to government schools in urban and rural Maharashtra, additionally fielding a team of facilitators who guide and motivate teachers and students.[49] There are also a vast number of organizations that are helping to identify and groom sports talent, in hopes of helping India overcome its past famine of Olympic medals.[50]

No specific corporate form dominates among any type of organization. Stellar actions have been performed by nonprofits and for-profit organizations, together with those working with a model of cross-subsidization.[51] Organizations established by government officials have contributed to this effort, as have others directed by religious motivations. The scope exists for broad-based actions.

The problem to tackle "is not only economic poverty but also social poverty – the absence of social support systems and the sociocultural atmosphere."[52] That's where information, guidance, and motivation can make a significant difference.

Institutions that provide information, engender experiences, and work broadly on soft factors are required – not only to promote social mobility, a critical task, but also to support other objectives of democracy and development, and more generally, to generate better national understanding and societal consensus. Information is often a key missing element of the broader development process.

Filling information gaps can also help improve electoral outcomes. The knowledge that voters need in order to assess the respective merits of different candidates is frequently not available. In such situations, voters are more likely to make decisions on the basis of caste or religion or party loyalties, or something fleeting and frivolous, such as cash handouts or liquor. Studies show how providing information of different kinds – about competing candidates and their track records, about incumbents' performance, about the procedures involved in getting one's vote registered, and about the importance of doing one's civic duty – has helped deepen democratic engagement in diverse parts of India.

Voters update their beliefs in response to new information. An initiative undertaken at the time of the 2008 state legislature elections in Delhi showed how better-informed voters tend to make better choices.[53]

Faith in democracy, political efficacy, and participation in various acts of democratic governance are all at a higher level among individuals who are better informed. The level to which a person is educated matters for these outcomes. But the number of different information sources she consults matters in addition to her education level.[54]

Education matters a great deal, but information plays a separate and equally important part in making democracy work more effectively in diverse contexts.[55] The state enacts law after law – there is a plethora of pro-poor legislation in India – but the state does not make the effort to inform citizens about the law's provisions. The protections, opportunities, and benefits of democracy are not availed of by many because they lack the requisite information. Misdeeds go unreported, because the public does not know how misdeeds are legally defined and reported in practice.

The enactment of rights such as the right to work or the right to education does not automatically result in people realizing that right; this happens only when the right becomes widely known and when information about feasible legal remedies becomes publicly available.[56] If an individual does not know what democratic rights she has, or what needs to be done in order to have those rights enforced, then for all practical purposes these rights do not exist for her.

Enhancing information availability on a regular and reliable basis is necessary to establish faith in democracy and to enhance people's engagements with democratic processes.[57] Decentralization, too, is made more effective by information provision. Various examples attest to the beneficial association that exists between information and decentralization. For instance, village education committees and parent–teacher associations have been mandated in several states, but most villagers, including those appointed as office-bearers in these committees, know very little about the rules that apply and about the rights and duties of committee members. No one has thought to brief these members about their roles and responsibilities. As result, the members are inactive and the committees are ineffective. Some states have taken the matter of information provisions more seriously than others. Karnataka, for instance, has invested more heavily in generating community awareness and disseminating information. In the process, Karnataka has achieved better learning outcomes than, for instance, Uttar Pradesh or Madhya Pradesh, states in which "committee members are unaware of their roles, meetings are rarely held and parent-teacher associations are not involved in school decisions."[58]

For promoting democracy, for raising social mobility, for making decentralization more powerful and effective, and for other related objectives, the provision of information has to be considered a fundamental service fulfilling a basic need, equivalent in some ways to health care and education. In fact, information is a prior requirement; the quality of education and of health care both improve in contexts where information is provided freely, widely, and more reliably than at present.[59] Information institutions that are accessible and effective need to be established.

A National Project

Influential analyses of the pathways taken by more and less successful nations have found that a broad social consensus is an important part of what makes for sustained economic development. Where there is no social consensus and no solidarity, distributive fights predominate, and the state itself becomes the zone for vicious zero-sum contests.[60]

Developing agreements on goals and procedures that are broadly respected by all is necessary for realizing a shared national vision. But where stereotypes rule, and attitudes have hardened, it becomes difficult to have a meaningful conversation. In such situations, reforming values, attitudes and beliefs is very important. Experiences and information will help.

No formulaic solutions can, or should, be recommended. Monitored experimentation is necessary in order to understand what works better – and under what circumstances.

Internships for city kids in villages (and for village kids in cities) can be usefully examined in this context. Children growing up in comfortable circumstances need to be given opportunities to spend time with poorer children, appreciating their circumstances and potentials better – conversely, poorer children need to be exposed to the everyday lives of richer people. Like the students in the elite Delhi classrooms whose attitudes have changed for the better after studying alongside a group of slum children, carefully organized internships can help develop more accurate and complete mental images.

I have learned for myself, while running a summer program on behalf of my university, how such experiences can change attitudes and help align people's beliefs with the facts of the situation. We bring college students from big cities in India and from the United States, assigning mixed teams of students to village locations. The teams come into town to attend classes, and then return to live in villagers' homes for extended periods. They speak to a wide spectrum of village residents, inquiring into a variety of economic and social conditions.

Each year, I have seen how students' beliefs about poverty have fundamentally changed and how their attitudes toward rural people and the less educated have been transformed through these experiences. Here are some samples of the written feedback that students turned in at the end of the program: "I have learned that poverty is only one part of person's existence; it doesn't dominate all aspects of her thinking and yearning"; "There is joy, and love, and dignity, and self-respect; there is intelligence and humor among poorer people"; "To say that someone's work is unskilled or less skilled doesn't imply that just anyone can do it" – and so on, reflecting a newly acquired respect and understanding. On their parts, too, villagers have been able to update their ill-formed beliefs about big, bad Mumbai and faraway America. Hosting big-city and foreign individuals has helped them see more clearly: that the Mumbai-wallah isn't a dishonest guy; the girl from America is as principled as the one next door.[61]

It would, though, be a more complete experience if villagers, too, could come to live for a while in the big city. Investigations undertaken among migrant groups have, in fact, found that "greater social and spatial exposure is a catalyst for citizen action."[62] Such individuals' self-confidence, their capacity to aspire, and their attitudes toward people of other caste groups and regions have changed for the better.[63] These experiences have also helped them realize how urban ways of living can be sensibly and usefully applied in rural contexts. That seems to be the more promising way, compared with legislation or administrative fiat, for propagating the benefits of indoor plumbing and other changes in lifestyle.

Spending a month or two in the summer, not fancy free but with a well-thought-out project, will help these interns learn specific skills while acquiring valuable experiences. Village kids coming to cities could learn the skills, for instance, of map reading, taking the metro, and learning to work with high-speed computers. They will come to know more about pathways leading to fast-track careers. At the other end, city kids coming to villages would acquire other skills, including how to navigate by the stars and how to tell apart flora and fauna, providing a boost to the nation's efforts to conserve biodiversity. Most of all, they would learn to appreciate the other families who live in India.

Experiences of meeting people from different regions of India will help generate a greater sense of community. Inductees to India's elite civil services are sent off on a month-long India tour. Young adults in schools and colleges should also be given such an opportunity, if only once in their lifetime, if only for a week, and if only to visit a single place at the other end of the country.

Another initiative worth considering, which is being implemented to good effect in some provinces in China, involves exchanges of teachers and students between rural and elite-urban schools, with benefits of different kinds accruing to both types of students.[64] Not least among these benefits is the greater understanding that city and village students acquire about each other.

Other institutions, encouraging intermingling of different kinds, will help serve a similar purpose. Interfaith councils with regular meetings, particularly in cities with a history of religious or caste-based strife, can help generate positive experiences, diluting biased attitudes and exposing bigoted beliefs to the light of facts and reason.

As attitudes start to change, investments must be made in creating a network of information centers. Why can't smart kids in slums and beyond-5-km villages have access to newspapers, libraries, career counselors, role models, and mentors as a matter of course, and not, as it so often turns out, as an exception? When people refer to the current period as the "information age," they usually conceive of computers, smartphones, and other modes of digital communication. The range and utility of these modes of information provision are growing day by day. But information in other forms can also have powerful effects – particularly where computers and smartphones are out of reach financially, or where the erratic electricity supply makes their use unreliable and intermittent.

Libraries can make an important difference, providing information in multiple formats, digital and printed. Public libraries began to be widespread in England and the United States as early as the seventeenth century, well before these countries became prosperous. In India, even today, few villages or urban slums have libraries. As a recently recruited software engineer, who grew up poor in a village, told me:

> Even extra reading books, libraries . . . they don't have that in my
> place. In my native place there is not a single library . . . Even
> today it is not there. At that time [when I was studying in school]
> I was very interested in novels, fiction but I couldn't get that stuff.
> Whenever I found somebody had books, I used to go and read.
> But everybody can't do that. If you had a good library, then at
> least you would know that things like this are there in the world.
> You would be going there to read and try to understand. In
> Bangalore, you get that. For my son, actually, there is a small
> library for kids. I can go and pick up stuff which he can read. I
> couldn't do that in my place. I still can't do that in small places.

A few years ago, I set up a small library in my village home with books donated by friends whose children had outgrown these volumes. Many village children have become regular patrons. Their enthusiastic response shows that there is much to be gained by investing, in information provision – using contextually relevant means and materials. On a larger scale, the NGO Room to Read has been installing functional libraries, complete with student-led oversight and management committees. Like other novel initiatives, this organization has groped its way in the dark initially; as new learning was gained, operating procedures have been adjusted.[65]

Similar ventures are required for developing other types of information institutions – such as career centers, voter information institutes, centers for generating and authorizing simple versions of laws, civics textbooks in schools, rating agencies that evaluate public facilities, interfaith councils, and many others. Little is known except that information is important; the jury is still out on the best means of provision. Experiments of different kinds are ongoing. Realizing the importance of information, donor agencies have invested in projects where information provision is a central intervention.[66]

Well-regarded information initiatives, including Citizen Report Cards and the Right-to-Information Act, have been launched in India.[67] These initiatives have made significant inroads in helping overcome the constraints that ordinary citizens routinely experience.

More needs to be done to make the provision of information a bigger part of serving the everyday needs of ordinary citizens. Laws and legal processes need to be simplified. Everyday versions of more complex laws, containing the gist of the most important provisions, must be compiled and made widely available. Disseminating this knowledge in schools will help with this objective. Young people growing up will learn about their rights and those of others, about the legitimate remedies that are available, and about their responsibilities as citizens. Of course, generating new experiences along with generating and disseminating helpful information is only one part of a larger package of initiatives. Citizens must be able to act on the information they acquire, and state officials must be sympathetic and responsive while being effective and enterprising.[68]

7 DEMOCRACY AT THE DOORSTEP

At a day-long workshop organized by a public interest group in the capital city of a northern state, speaker after speaker castigated the government for its substandard provision of medical services. Some invitees spoke out against the current health policy; others railed against the quality of service in public hospitals; a third group, denouncing the behaviors of medical staff, cited instances of callousness, disrespect, and corruption.

At the end of the day, however, when a statement of action points was put together, the group drafted a memorandum declaring that the state should do *more*: budgets for rural hospitals should be increased, staffing levels should be raised, and better equipment should be made available. Decrying the performance of the state led to demands, ironically, for expanding the size and scope of the state's activities, but incongruous behavior of this kind isn't uncommon.[1]

The state is, after all, the only agency that provides on a large scale the kinds of services that citizens, especially poorer ones, consider most important. In education and in health care, in electricity and water supply, in roads and sanitation, the state has discharged, and will continue to undertake, critically important functions. Private organizations and civil society actors can and should play larger roles, but their activities will not make the state redundant. Questions of regulation and oversight will remain: if some entity other than the state is charged with providing a public service, then who is responsible for overseeing this other entity? Any organization that makes the rules or oversees their implementation acquires state-like qualities, in essence becoming a part of the state.[2]

The state cannot be wished away. The state will remain. It is important to examine how the state machinery at multiple levels can be made more accountable and more effective.

Because of the relatively high pay scales they offer, and because of the security and prestige associated with a government job, public bureaucracies in India are able to recruit very capable individuals.[3] And yet most citizens receive poor-quality services, and interactions with the government are exercises in frustration.

Where does the slippage occur between high-quality recruits and low-quality service provision? Four elements help construct an explanation:

- The tiered state
- A distant state with opaque processes
- The administrative stretch
- A policy tilt toward urban areas and dollar-economy people

Each element forms an important part of the explanation for poor-quality governance, and each element needs to be suitably addressed for developing effective solutions. I present these explanations and recommendations later in this chapter after briefly introducing the four elements here.

The first element – the tiered state – is a product of how state formation occurred in India. As in other former colonies, the structure of the state inherited by the independent government was constructed from the top down. The chain of governance – which connects the highest levels in New Delhi and state capitals, through intermediate levels (district towns and *taluka* headquarters), to the lowest-level officials – was stretched out over a long distance and thin on the ground.[4] The processes that were followed within this top-down structure were highly centralized, and little authority was given to officials in the lower tiers of the administrative structure.

A segmented society found reflection in a stratified state, with higher and lower layers of public administration, staffed by people who came from different social layers, which had the result of restricting communications, engendering distrust between higher and lower officials, and imposing a centralizing will. Such a system was good for maintaining a particular kind of order, keeping the natives at bay, but it was not designed to be responsive to their needs or to elicit the involvement of the general public. Commenting on the system as it operated in the early part of the twentieth century, the economic historian R. C. Dutt observed:

> It is somewhat remarkable that no British administrator seriously endeavoured to improve the police and general administration of the country by accepting the cooperation of the people themselves and their village communities.[5]

The separation of governance from the public was compounded by the second element of the explanation: a distant state with opaque procedures has operated in India. The task of state construction was left incomplete, with the chain of governance ending before reaching rural habitations, where a majority of the people lived.[6] As a consequence, government offices remained distant for most people, described in the following terms by a British colonial official:

> In England, justice goes to the people; in India, the people come to justice. An aggrieved person might have to travel any distance up to 50 miles over a road-less country. A police matter, again, involved a journey to the station, perhaps ten miles off. Trials involved much hanging about, many journeys to and fro, and a constant spending of money. The common person had to find his way to this strange tribunal in an unknown land as best he could, in charge of the police, whose tender mercies he dreaded.[7]

Despite the advent of democracy and national independence, the Indian state has remained tiered and distant, and the processes of the state remain hierarchical, compartmentalized, insular and upward-looking. Even today, the state remains at a considerable distance, both physically and cognitively, from ordinary citizens. People from beyond-5-km villages, who constitute nearly half of the country's population, have to travel great distances in order to undertake routine dealings with police stations and courts, *taluka* and *tehsil* headquarters, high schools and colleges, electricity and water supply officials. But it's not only they for whom contacting the state is, more often than not, costly, uncertain, and exasperating. For slum dwellers and other poorer city residents, too, "the state can and often does appear a sovereign entity set apart from society."[8] Contacting the state is a formidable enterprise for ordinary people like Keshu, Chandru, Jaitram, and Leela, for whom the workings of the state remain mysterious, and whose encounters with public officials quite often have the nature of supplications. Reporting a nonperforming schoolteacher is a daunting task where the supervisory official is located at a great distance and where a parent–teacher association does not exist, where there is no school board or town council (or these bodies are largely symbolic), and where newspapers rarely report everyday grassroots experiences.

In such circumstances, it becomes difficult to realize one's rights as a democratic citizen. Those who are able to gain privileged access acquire extraordinary influence. Unequal democracy gets reflected in the unequal treatment of citizens in different social layers.

The third element – administrative stretch – has added to the turmoil of governance. In the wake of globalized growth, the spectrum of the world's population has come to be represented in India – including a sizeable number of those who are among the richest in the world and the largest number of those who are among the poorest in the world – visualized in the streamgraph of Figure 1.1 (in Chapter 1). Speaking simultaneously to their diverse concerns has made the state take on an ever larger manifest of duties, requiring the pursuit simultaneously of rich-country tasks, such as building modern airports and high-technology research centers, along with poor-country tasks, such as constructing one-room schoolhouses and basic toilets. Such a wide range of objectives, all requiring concurrent attention, is enough to overwhelm the capacity even of a well-coordinated state apparatus. It has led to a skewed set of outcomes in India. Dollar-economy concerns, more readily addressed through policy reforms carried out by the highest tiers of the state, are easier to handle within this structure. Rupee-economy concerns, more heavily dependent on grassroots implementation, are turned over to the weakest, least motivated, most distrusted, and least modernized parts of the administrative apparatus. Not surprisingly, it is poorer people's concerns that are the least well addressed in this situation.

Why is Indian democracy, so excellent in other ways, not able to rid itself of these problems of distance and unequal treatment? Why are rupee-economy concerns not given higher priority? Why are poorer people not more closely involved in everyday governance?

The answer to these questions has to do with how democracy works in practice as different from theory, the fourth element of explanation. One might think of democracy as involving multiple acts of free choice, but in fact voters have a constrained set of choices. Political parties preselect the candidates for elections, in effect acting as the gatekeepers to electoral democracy. That's a fact of life in all democracies, made worse in India, where most political parties are not internally democratic. Like the state, political parties in India are organized in a tiered and hierarchical manner. There are no meaningful internal party elections; top-level party officials decide who their candidates should be for national elections. Parties' candidate choices have progressively reduced the representation of poorer and rural people in Parliament. Together with changes in ideology at the top levels of parties, their selection of candidates has accentuated the tilt in public policy toward urban areas and dollar-economy people.

Rebuilding the state is essential for bringing the benefits of democracy closer to people at the grassroots. Decentralization is an important part of what is necessary, but it should not be seen as an end in itself. Instituting multiple forums for informed and empowered decision-making at the grassroots level is better visualized as the first step in a longer-term reform process.

The discussion that follows draws its evidence from India, but the argument has broader implications. Other postcolonial developing countries also have tiered states infused with top-down processes. These states, too, are distant from ordinary people. Favoring higher-ups at the expense of local discretion and responsiveness, these states, too, need rebuilding in a phased reform process. Each country will have to design institutions that fit better with its particular context, but the process of institutional innovation and the learnings that accrue from it can be shared. I will return to this theme after expanding on the four elements of the explanation in the Indian case.

The Tiered State: Top-down Processes in a Bottom-heavy Structure

Government ministries and departments in India are organized in a tiered fashion. Separate cadres of public employees are recruited to different tiers of state bureaucracies. Most experience little upward

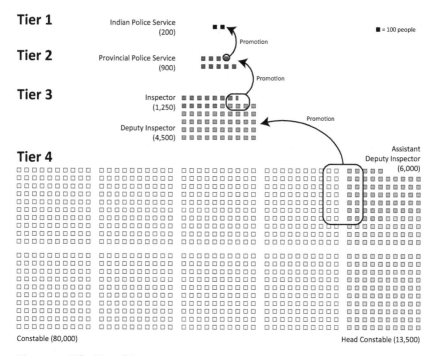

Figure 7.1 The Tiered State.

mobility, remaining within the same tier to which they were recruited through their entire period of government service.

Consider the case of the police, organized in most states within a four-tier hierarchy. Figure 7.1, which graphs this hierarchy, is based on data obtained from one state's police department. A man or woman starting a career in the lowest tier (joining as police constable) has little chance of rising to the next higher tier and becoming an inspector, and no chance at all of rising to become the department's top official, the director general. No director general in service was recruited as constable. Most constables serve out their thirty years and retire in the same position. Toward the end of their careers, a handful are promoted within the same tier, becoming head constables or assistant deputy inspectors. An even tinier number are elevated to the next higher tier, retiring as deputy inspectors. A similarly tiny rate of movement across tiers is observed at other levels of the police hierarchy. Between the top tier (staffed by the elite Indian Police Service) and the bottom tier (constables), there are two other tiers in which new recruits start out, respectively, as deputy inspectors (also called sub-inspectors) and deputy superintendents. From each of these tiers a few individuals are able to make it to the next higher tier. The rare few who climb past two or more tiers become legends in their departments.

The police department is not special in this regard. Other departments of government, more closely involved in development enterprises – agriculture, animal husbandry, forestry, education, and health – are similarly stratified, with very little movement of people up the tiered hierarchy.[9]

Such a tiered system of public administration was inherited by independent India from its British colonial rulers, with elements traceable to Mughal and earlier administrations. Its highest tier was manned by British men and successful Indian imitators. People educated in India, but in the medium of English, entered the second tier, followed by others who were educated in the local languages. The lowest tier was staffed by lower-social-class and less well-educated individuals.[10]

In essential respects, the structure of the public bureaucracy remains as it was, even as the tasks of governance have become vastly different. In Britain itself, the older structure was reformed by flattening the tiers and ushering in a single-entry system of recruitment. In its police force, almost everyone joins as constable; the top official has the designation of chief constable.[11] Not so in India, where separate recruitments are still made to each of the four tiers, characterized by large differences in authority and status.[12]

The tiered state – with its top-down but bottom-heavy structure – has the effect of producing unwieldy and unbalanced governance. "When crafting policy, there is a need to be realistic about the system within which we will work," cautioned a former chief adviser to the Indian government.[13] But realism is given short shrift, as policy and implementation are widely separated within the tiered state. Those who design policies have no personal experience of implementation, having only served in top-tier positions, whereas those who are charged with implementation have no place at the policy-making table.

Communications and information flows are severely constricted. Lower-level officials do not usually have the gumption to call top bosses to offer ideas or obtain clarification, and top bosses rarely bother to get reports and updates directly from the lowest-tier field officials. If the social situation were different – for instance, if they were to meet in the evening at the same social clubs – communications would become easier and the work of government would become more effective. But in practice, there's little intermingling in what Jawaharlal Nehru once referred to as the "caste system in our civil services."[14]

Another adverse consequence of the tiered state takes the form of over-centralization. While paying lip service to the diversity of India, top-tier officials end up producing a succession of highly centralized programs. There are national- and state-level programs of poverty reduction, but no district- or *taluka*-specific, far less city- or village-centric, initiatives are supported. Other government programs – of health care, of development assistance, of promoting alternative technologies – also tend to be centrally designed in New Delhi or a state capital. These are minutely detailed and implemented in a standardized manner across the country or across entire states, nine of which have populations larger than France or the United Kingdom.

Centralization has some benefits. The uniform application of accounting procedures helps curb corruption to some extent, and uniformity also implies equivalence across jurisdictions.

But centralization, pushed beyond a point, imposes a levy on motivation and creativity, and ultimately on program outcomes. Authority needs to be distributed in some rational manner along the institutional chain – in proportion, first, to the amount of job-related information available at various points, and second, to the relative importance of standardized versus localized solutions. Some actions of the state, such as currency management or foreign relations, by their very nature, have to be undertaken in a centralized fashion. But for other enterprises – rural development, for example, or primary and secondary education – the variance in ground conditions is more important. That's where the central plan needs to be modified locally, incorporating what management experts have referred to as loose-tight programs of action.[15] Used to thinking in aggregate terms, however – a district, a state, the nation – and having served always in higher positions, few senior officials have much idea about the nitty-gritty of grassroots implementation. Acknowledging that context matters, that the person on the spot is best positioned to identify the utility (or otherwise) of particular interventions, could result in diminishing senior officials' perceptions about their own positions. It would also require trusting in the capacities and the motivations of subordinate officials. Because of their segregated experiences, however, senior officers tend to have little trust in the probity and effectiveness of lower-tier officials.

That's a pity, not only because street-level bureaucrats, like senior officials themselves, are recruited through stiff competition among vast pools of capable individuals, but also because lower-tier officials, the service providers and program implementers, constitute the largest and most visible part of the government apparatus. They are the ones whom most citizens meet on an everyday basis – the postman, the *patwari* or *talathi*, the forest guard, the policeman, the schoolteacher, the electricity lineman. For most people, that is the face of the government. Schoolteachers teach, not deputy directors of education. Nurses inoculate babies, not assistant secretaries in the medical department.

India's street-level bureaucrats (or grassroots or field-level officials – I am using these terms interchangeably) are a demotivated lot, however, which makes it difficult to get things done in the manner intended – and more difficult still to foster creativity and generate innovations at the grassroots level. A number of factors have resulted in producing a situation in which the largest part of the state machinery is disheartened.

Motivation is a prime casualty in situations where career advancement seems virtually impossible. Joy in one's job is further limited when the directives one is given appear irrelevant to the situation at hand or when these directives are too many and too confusing, which is often. In a revealing account of the Indian state at the grassroots, focusing on departments in charge of welfare provision, anthropologist Akhil Gupta argued that "the overt goal of helping the poor is subverted by the very procedures of the bureaucracy," which has resulted in confused and arbitrary actions. Such arbitrariness, he maintains, "is not itself arbitrary; rather, it is systematically produced by the very mechanisms" of government bureaucracies.[16] Segmentation and centralization have worked together to produce a situation in which a dispirited and overworked grassroots bureaucracy recognizes the futility, locally, of standardized programs sent down the pipeline. Gupta narrates the following conversation with a block development officer whom he calls Malik, occupying a lower-tier office between the district and the grassroots levels:

> Targets were applied to the whole state, ignoring the fact of disparate conditions. Malik complained that the people who set targets had little experience in or knowledge of rural areas. People like him who had extensive experiences in rural India were not

consulted either about the design of programs or about
reasonable targets. Instead, orders were simply sent from above.[17]

Dispirited public officials continue to carry on; unlike 90 percent of the country's workforce, public officials have secure jobs, with relatively high salaries. The weakening of other and nobler motivations – climbing the career ladder, making a difference to society – is an important part, however, of what goes into the making of large-scale corruption.

A strange kind of accountability link has lately arisen that further skews the incentives of field-level officials. Senior politicians have grown accustomed to making claims and holding officials to account, allegedly expressing the "desire" of their constituents – but without holding any genuinely public consultations. They exercise this newly acquired power by asking for the transfers of allegedly nonperforming officials.

An entire "desire economy" has arisen in many states, in which cash and favors are given in exchange for preferred postings. A field-level veterinary surgeon, who has spent more than twenty-five years working for the government, told me, for instance:

> Transfers and postings are decided entirely on the wishes of the MLA [the elected member of the state legislative assembly]. If he and his people are happy with you then you won't be replaced by some other officer. You keep them happy by giving top priority to the tasks they assign. People come to them and make requests, and they call you demanding some intervention. I get to their cases immediately, ignoring others.

The official was frank in admitting that he did not respond with the same alacrity to the instructions sent down by his departmental superiors. Senior officers, he explained, don't count for much anymore when it comes to the critical matter of transfers and postings (which are the incentives that really matter, given that few lower-tier officials expect to achieve seniority through promotion). "That's a big change from when I began service," the official added. "In the 1990s, transfers were determined entirely by the department's senior officers. If you needed a transfer, you put in an application and appeared before the director of the department. Things started going downhill around 2000, when it became the unwritten rule that there would be no transfers, except upon the MLA's desire."

Ideally, in order to effect coordination and fix responsibility, a supervisory official should have the authority to transfer and discipline her subordinate officials. But in the tiered structure, the power to determine transfers and postings was arrogated to the top tier, and then – in an effort to purchase their allegiance and to shore up a weak ruling party – the power to ask for the transfer of officials was first shared with, and later handed over to, MLAs and party organizations. The top-down and hierarchical allocation of authority in the tiered state made it possible to give such extra-constitutional powers.

The lines of supervision in state bureaucracies have become blurred as multiple vectors of influence have started to operate. The cognitive distance between different tiers of the state bureaucracy has increased, adding to the overall mismanagement and confusion. Another field official, a junior engineer, who retired from government service in 2015, informed me:

> We don't have a calendar of activities for the entire year. We get directive after directive from headquarters, many of which are entirely unexpected. We work on an ad hoc basis under a lot of pressure. There's little that's being done to maintain a high quality of work. It's all about targets and keeping the politicians happy. Government services, no doubt, still provide the greatest job security, but there's no advancement, only blockage, which leads to frustration. Our senior officers are no longer shielding us from spurious complaints that can result in punishment postings and disciplinary action. Our working situation has become riskier. I am glad I was able to make an escape without having to suffer a blemish upon my career.

Confused, not clearly directed or effectively supervised, nor encouraged or motivated, at risk always of being transferred or charge-sheeted, field-level officials plod on – a well-paid but ill-used army, amply provisioned by the Indian taxpayer.[18] The seeming futility of what they are required to do and the poor results they frequently encounter has engendered a culture of defeatism: it's safer to not go the extra mile when the downside risks are large, and on the upside, there's little chance of moving up the tiers.[19]

Tasks requiring judgment and the exercise of discretion on the ground cannot be performed well unless the front-line service providers are well trained, highly motivated, and empowered to make decisions – unless they are clearly accountable and the system is designed to look out for the interests of diverse publics. The tiered state makes each of these conditions hard to achieve. It is relatively good at performing multiple repetitive tasks, codified and with little deviation, such as conducting elections or administering polio vaccines – and quite ineffective at doing things that require local creativity and working in coordination with ordinary people.

Improving the working conditions of street-level bureaucrats – enabling these individuals to be creative and self-respecting while also being responsible and responsive – is an essential part of the administrative reforms required. Reforms at higher links in the chain of governance are necessary, but reforms at the grassroots are more essential. That's where the policy rubber meets the road, where a central intention gets transformed into manifold local outcomes.

None of the foregoing discussion should be read to imply that lower-tier officials are invariably more sinned against than sinning. There is evidence to show frequent absences from duty stations, especially in beyond-5-km villages,[20] and experiences of ill treatment at the hands of service providers are common. How to convey a sense of menace, particularly to poorer people, is a trait learned early by a police constable. But it's not just the police. Other departments of the government have their own ways of making ordinary people feel miserable.[21]

Both outcomes – demotivated grassroots officials and their lack of respect for the general public – are traceable in large part to the same design weakness in the system: institutional forums do not exist that can energize street-level bureaucrats while empowering ordinary citizens.

Ad hoc means of enforcing accountability, such as the "desire" system, operate because investments were not made in creating more robust forums for involving the general public. The citizens' right to hold public officials to account has been pocketed by particular individuals, because ordinary citizens have no viable avenues for gaining access to the official system.[22]

Along with the task of making street-level bureaucrats more efficacious and creative – and in addition to providing them with better chances for career advancement – it is necessary to have forums that, simultaneously, make it possible for ordinary people to more effectively demand accountability from their newly empowered local officials. Strengthening village *panchayats* and municipal councils is an important part of this task, but it isn't all that is required.

A Distant and Mediated State

In the absence of such opportunities, how have citizens been dealing with situations of low-quality public services and unresponsive officials? The answer depends on who is asked the question.

Dollar-economy people and others who can afford private provision have largely exited the public system. How public-sector service providers behave is of less concern to those who have become accustomed to hiring their own security guard, drilling their own borewells, installing their own generators, sending their children to private schools, and visiting only private hospitals.[23]

But for others, the majority in the rupee economy, there is no realistic alternative to the regular police, to public water and electricity companies, and to the government's schools and hospitals. They cannot bypass it, they have to meet the state, and they deal with it however possible. People either forgo interacting with the state – putting off treatment until an illness has become critical, putting up with a nonperforming schoolteacher, accepting intermittent electricity supply because the local lineman tells them that it's out of his hands, and avoiding the police altogether – or they seek the help of someone who can effectively mediate their transactions with government officials.

An informal apparatus has emerged that helps connect ordinary citizens with the formal state system. In circumstances where the last link in the chain of governance institutions is weak or nonexistent, where local-level service providers are disempowered and demotivated, and where there remains a considerable distance between citizens and higher officials, mediators have arisen who take care of government dealings on behalf of ordinary people. For generations it has been the case that some "expeditor is usually involved who may not be a man with any official power, but is always someone who is familiar with the intricacies of administration."[24] Recent research affirms that "when poorer people meet local state officials, they do so with reference to their non-state networks, [including] a broader range of caste leaders, brokers, and political fixers."[25]

Who are the people who fill the mediators' roles – and how do they come to acquire these positions? Around my village, *pahunch* and *poochh* have become the currency of local politics – and those who have stocks of this currency have become the mediators of official interactions. *Pahunch* (literally, reach) – how widely an individual has influence within government offices – gives rise to *poochh* (literally, request), how often this individual receives requests from others for intervention. In turn, wider *poochh*, by increasing the number of one's followers and favor-seekers, augments one's standing before government officials and electoral candidates, enhancing *pahunch*. These terms, from Hindi, are used in the north, but the dynamics in other parts of the country are similar.[26] If he is able to help negotiate a deal with the police, helping fend off a beating in lieu of a "fine" of 5,000 rupees,[27] and if he helps alleviate the irritating and costly grit involved in gaining for oneself that which the democratic state has promised – a ration card, a housing subsidy, a college scholarship, a standpipe in one's neighborhood – then an aspiring politician becomes more popular and more respected.

People who are unable to meet the state directly – the majority – become obligated to their informal mediators and elected representatives. These positions are interchangeable. Former mediators have been elected to positions in *panchayats*, and *sarpanchas* (elected heads of *panchayats*) play the mediator's role in many cases.[28] That's because these *sarpanchas* too wish to acquire more *poochh* and *pahunch*, the currencies of local politics. The more people who come asking them for favors – a chit to the local hospital, a phone call to the block development officer or the police station – the more assuredly they can count on a bank of grateful voters.

Jaitram, the young farmer in my village, who makes ends meet by supplementing the products of his tiny farm with the *mazdoori* (wage labor) he performs in a nearby city, told me of an incident when he had to approach an official of the irrigation department. A schedule of sending water down an irrigation canal had been announced and farmers in the village had planned their crop rotations, but when the time came to release the needed water, the concerned official was not to be found – he had taken leave, and no substitute had been appointed. The canal ran dry, and the young plants began to wither. Agitated by their impending financial ruin, a group of farmers set off one day to meet with the supervisory official, whose office is located 25 km away, in the district capital. The first time they went, the supervisory official wasn't available: he had been called away to a departmental meeting in the state capital. A week later, they went again, spending more money and taking more time off their duties. This time, the official did meet with them, but he wasn't willing or able to perceive the farmers' urgency. He accepted their petition and he marked it for inquiry to his assistant, giving no assurances as to when they would open the lock and release water. It seemed clear to Jaitram that the supervisor had little idea of what went on in his jurisdiction and little control over his subordinate officials.

Piqued by the futility of their appeals and despondent about the prospect of another crop failing, Jaitram and his companions were sitting forlornly at a tea shop, awaiting the bus that would take them home, when they ran into Nanaram, a young man who runs a small grocery shop in a nearby village. Having studied up to class 10, he is known as a *naya neta* (a new leader), one of those who, over years of transacting with officials, has acquired familiarity with how to get things done in government offices.

Moved by the farmers' plight, and reckoning as well on a future advantage, Nanaram offered his help in the matter. The following day, he took Jaitram on a motorcycle trip to the district capital. Reaching the irrigation department's office, he asked to meet with the supervisory official. Once again, this official was not in his office. Nanaram addressed his staff and demanded: "What are the rules? What is the prescribed schedule of water rotation? Why are you favoring one village over another? Should I speak to the MLA and get him to speak with the minister of your department?" Cowed by Nanaram's evident knowledge of how the system worked and his access to higher-ups, the staff scurried to make telephone contact with the supervisory official. Nanaram repeated his combination of threats and entreaties, and the official felt impelled to take immediate action. Instructing one of his junior officials to go to the site and take up the vacant position, he directed him to forthwith unlock the canal and release enough water.

Jaitram was able to save his crop. He remains grateful to Nanaram for his timely and effective intervention.

I was pleased that the story had a happy ending, but peeved by the sequence of events. Why were Jaitram and his fellow farmers not able to get the same official response directly – without taking recourse to Nanaram's intervention? Why had one person's word counted for much more than another's while describing the same situation? Why do people in rural India so often have to depend on mediators? And why, consequently, do they fail to get their due where mediators are unavailable, ineffective, or unwilling to render assistance?

Distance is an important part of the explanation – the supervisor's office is far from Jaitram's village – but it is not the only factor.

In cities too, where government offices are located, it is usually the case that the state is contacted with the help of mediators. Investigations conducted in the early 1980s in Chennai (then Madras) captured the typical reaction of slum residents when asked about meeting government officials: "It is of no use, we do not know exactly whom to approach. They may not let us into the office. Only if we go together with a leader we may be able to speak to an influential person."[29] Thirty years later, the same sentiment was picked up by another careful study, which found that "leaders play a key role in facilitating access to the state, particularly in recently established slum settlements and for those who are less wealthy and less well connected. Without political involvement, paperwork and applications usually 'wander' in the office for a long time and are then sent back to lower levels for reassessment."[30]

Mediation makes up the bulk of the interactions between the state and society because unmediated ways of meeting with the state aren't easily accessible. The state remains distant, both physically and cognitively; its processes are shrouded in mystery. No one has taken the trouble to inform ordinary people about the laws that govern their lives and of the means they have for defending their rights and articulating their interests. With rare exceptions, forums do not exist where citizens can meet directly with government officials on a regular basis, contributing their knowledge and ideas, volunteering their time, participating in making binding decisions and holding these officials accountable.

Last-mile institutions have not been built, and like the accountability link, the service-delivery link between citizens and their service providers operates only indirectly. While elected politicians and party officials mediate the accountability link, the service-delivery link is mediated by diverse people, many among whom have no formal position. Some among these individuals may be publicly motivated while others may be unsavory characters.[31] That's important to note, but it's beside the main point, which is that, in common, mediators like Nanaram are occasional actors. There's no assurance they will be around to render assistance when it is urgently required, and thus there is no stability or predictability in the system.

That's not the way in which strong links are built between the state and its citizens. Different and better structures need to be constructed, which are more direct, less mediated, more reliable, easier to access, and better equipped with the relevant information.

Ordinary citizens (and not just elected politicians) need to acquire greater leverage – countervailing power. They need to start meeting more often, as equals, with state officials, within forums that have clearly described powers, which meet regularly and follow procedures that are commonly known and widely respected. That's the way in which civil society can be energized and fruitful interactions engendered.[32] Not everyone has to attend these forums, and not everyone will. But knowing how things work and having the opportunity to attend, to raise concerns if things aren't going well – and to be entitled to receive timely and persuasive responses from the concerned officials – will go a long way toward making democracy more democratic and development more effective.

Administrative Stretch

The policy stretch that has accompanied globalized growth has resulted in compounding the existing difficulties of governance. The limited capacities of the tiered and distant state have been stretched in different directions. The old central ministries – agriculture, animal husbandry, water resources, law, railways, health, and education – remain, but now there are new central ministries for biotechnology, electronics and information technology, new and renewable energy, overseas Indian affairs, skills development and enterprise, and telecommunications.[33]

Each of these mandates is important, and each must command a fair share of policy attention and resources. But undertaking all of these diverse tasks simultaneously places an enormous burden on the structures of public administration.

Privatizing some parts of the administrative burden can be helpful, as can the use of enabling technology, but there's no getting away from the fact that excessive centralization makes it difficult to simultaneously perform all of the expanding tasks of public administration. In addition to sharing them with non-conventional actors, the tasks of governance need to be reallocated along the chain of public administration. Following the principle of subsidiarity, which holds that issues should be dealt with at the lowest administrative level consistent with their resolution, lower tiers should have more authority and more resources. The higher tiers should play a subsidiary (i.e., a supporting and facilitating) role, directly performing only those tasks that cannot be effectively undertaken in lower tiers. Monetary policy and foreign relations are two examples of the latter type that we had considered earlier. But for dealing with the everyday governance concerns of the majority – in matters such as law and order, conflict resolution, higher-quality schools, clinics, and water and electricity supply – a larger part of decision making is better located in the lower tiers of the administrative structure.

The central government needs to loosen the reins, giving an opportunity to others' creativity and talent. Many state governments have pioneered good programs, some of which have been extended with modifications to benefit the rest of the country.[34] In turn, state governments need to undertake the reforms that can help make field-level officials more energetic and more creative. Having motivated and engaged schoolteachers is as important as (and arguably more important than) developing a well-balanced national curriculum.

Elinor Ostrom, who won the Nobel prize in economics for her work concerned with social and economic development, introduced an important distinction between technical knowledge and situational information. Both types of knowledge – one learned from books, the other on the ground – are important in development enterprises, and each type of knowledge has a positive impact on program outcomes. The best impacts are made by initiatives that draw on both types of knowledge. By closely involving technical experts and area residents, these are able to capitalize on both streams of information. This body of work, which provides a compelling justification for public participation, at the same time provides an additional argument for subsidiarity. Ultimately, it is the field official (equipped with better technical knowledge) and the local committee (with greater situational knowledge) working together in a mutually acceptable arrangement that determines the shape of the final outcome. But if the field official has no power to alter a decision or reallocate resources, what will people achieve by engaging with him or her?[35]

Empowering field-level officials with greater discretion is necessary. At the same time, they need to be effectively supported and overseen by empowered local institutions. That will enable a larger burden of administrative tasks to be undertaken by lower-tier links in the chain of public administration. It will also enable better resolutions for the first two elements that we discussed: the tiered state and the need for mediators.

Municipalities and *panchayats* have to be strengthened, and other local institutions need to be constructed in addition. Either under the umbrella of the existing local bodies or separately, multiple local institutions corresponding to diverse socially important activities – including parent–teacher associations, hospital oversight committees, local road safety boards, and farmers' or weavers' associations – need to be set up and nurtured with purpose and energy. Each type of institution serves a different natural constituency, and each is served, in turn, by a separate government department.

Having multiple local institutions addressing diverse locally important concerns is necessary to advance the agenda of good governance. The incomplete decentralization that has been carried out in India has created a network of *panchayats* and city councils, but except in one or two states, it has not endowed these bodies either with authority for carrying out their mandates or with the requisite funds and personnel. The budgets of *panchayats* and city councils in India collectively constitute less than 5 percent of total government expenditure – five times smaller than the average share in most industrially advanced countries and many developing ones, where local governments command, on average, more than 25 percent of the government budget.[36] Matching their low resource base, local governments in India have hardly any authority to adapt and modify centrally determined programs, and far less authority for introducing innovations. For the most part, lower-level officials and local bodies remain the implementing machinery, the hands and feet, carrying out the orders of a brain located in the state or national capital – a clear violation of the subsidiarity principle.[37]

These local bodies provide few opportunities for ordinary citizens to engage with public officials and to participate in making, implementing, and overseeing decisions. So far, the only opportunity for participation that a village resident has available is to take part in a *gram sabha* (village assembly) convened by her village *panchayat*. The attendance rate at these venues is, in general, abysmally small: most village residents see these assemblies as merely symbolic, venues for rubber-stamping decisions taken behind closed doors by local coteries. A lack of information has bedeviled the likelihood of empowered participation, along with other limitations arising from the misallocation of authority and resources.[38]

Several examples show that substantial improvements are possible and beneficial. In Kerala, *panchayats* are more generously resourced and *gram sabhas* have been made more meaningful by a series of gradually instituted innovations.[39] In other countries, too, citizens are actively involved in public decision making. In cities of Brazil, every resident can potentially weigh in on discussions of civil works and the municipal budget, with an opportunity to participate in making authoritative decisions.[40]

Similarly empowered, a web of local institutions will help counterbalance the adverse effects of administrative stretching in India. Dispersing responsibility for decision making, coupled with effective support and supervision, will enable a larger number of development initiatives to be undertaken.

No ready-made templates of institutions that respond to the need are immediately available, nor will any such best-practice institutions be universally applicable. Alternative institutional designs must be evaluated for their appropriateness to diverse local conditions.

An institution is much more than a set of rules and an office. Legitimacy and effectiveness are equally important. Unless people believe in the validity of its purpose and unless they respect its processes, an institution will be ineffective. *Aankh ki sharm aur sarkar ki taakat*, was how an elderly politico friend of mine described what it takes to have an effective institution: moral force *and* formal authority.[41]

Controlled and systematically monitored experimentation is necessary for uncovering the institutional designs that work best in specific contexts. Among other forms, customary institutions need to be considered. Research in different parts of India and other countries has demonstrated their utility.[42] Skewed in some ways and erratic in others, these customary organizations, which exist outside the formal system, with no written laws, nevertheless help resolve more than 80 percent of interpersonal conflicts in many villages and urban settlements.[43] The majority of residents whom I interviewed in villages of Rajasthan and Madhya Pradesh and others interviewed in rural Tamil Nadu and Karnataka mentioned how they would prefer to take their dispute to the local council of elders and *not* to the local court or police station.[44] In Rajasthan, I heard people refer to these home-grown local bodies as *hamari* (our) as opposed to *sarkari* (the government's) *panchayats*. Other scholars who have examined customary local organizations have not, however, been equally positive in their conclusions.[45] Newspaper accounts have highlighted the monstrous judgments handed down on occasion by some traditional institutions. But these aren't the only decisions they make, and they aren't the only traditional institutions.

No form of institution always produces good results – democracy, for instance, provided the start to the careers of Hitler and Mussolini. Along with other alternative forms, traditional institutional forms need to be fairly evaluated.

No matter what form the local institution takes, information provision is a necessary reform component. The possibility of elite capture, a constant danger for decentralized initiatives, is considerably alleviated in situations where relevant information is easily and regularly available to the general public.[46] When citizens know about the program they are supposed to be overseeing and about its budget, and when they are fully informed about their rights and responsibilities, then citizen oversight is more effective.[47] The fitful efforts taken up in the past to create participatory local institutions – for instance, the mandate to set up parent–teacher associations and village education committees in Uttar Pradesh and Madhya Pradesh – have largely failed to achieve their intended purposes. In large part, that's because no prior effort was made to provide ordinary people with the associated information.[48]

The Right to Information Act, instituted in 2005, has made a good beginning in this regard by making it possible for citizens to obtain information from government departments as a matter of right and established practice. But rather than waiting for people to come and ask for information, it should be the duty of the state and its officials to inform people about the rules and programs that bear on their actions.

Grassroots institutions enabling information dissemination, public discussions, and shared decision making are additionally necessary. Such last-mile institutions are necessary for combating administrative stretch and for concluding the incomplete task of state formation. That's an important part of how advanced democracies have been able to achieve more effective governance – by investing in multiple forums for grassroots deliberations and by bringing everyday decision making closer to the people.

The Leaning Tower of Parliamentary Democracy

Independent India's long and nearly unbroken record of democratic rule marks it out as an outlier among developing countries, many of which have been ruled for years by nondemocratic governments. In India, elections are conducted on schedule. The loss of popular support has gone together with peaceful transitions of power. Hardly anyone in the country would seriously advocate a nondemocratic form of government. These are significant achievements, painstakingly built, which need to be staunchly protected.

A number of troubling questions remain, however: Why does India's democracy continue to deliver uneven outcomes? Why does a citizen continue to experience difficulties in asserting her rights and getting a fair hearing? Why have the required reforms not been carried out with seriousness? Why is the "government's fiscal and investment policy heavily oriented toward urban areas,"[49] instead of leaning more toward the two thirds who are rural?

Along with its considerable strengths, there are significant shortcomings in the practices of democratic governance. The failure to build vibrant last-mile governance institutions, important among these shortcomings, is made worse by the failure to build federated party organizations.

Paralleling the structure of the state, India's major political parties are top-down and incomplete organizations. Most lack internal democracy; many have little grassroots presence, especially in rural areas. Decision making within political parties too remains distant from, and impervious to, ordinary citizens.[50]

Because they are the gatekeepers of electoral democracy, however, party elites get to preselect the candidates who later become the people's elected representatives.[51] Nominating candidates to elections, like other aspects of decision making within India's major political parties, is not guided by transparent or democratic procedures.

The distance between the people and their elected representatives – the representation gap – has widened as a result of political parties' candidate nominations. The choices they have made have left India's parliament looking less rural, less agricultural, less grassroots-based, and less representative of the poorer majority; instead, it has become more city-based, more Westward-looking, and more elite-dominated.

Ever richer individuals are getting picked by political parties to contest parliamentary elections. India's MPs possess more than twenty times as much wealth as the average Indian family – a wider representation gap than in most democracies, including the United States, where the composition of Congress has been roundly criticized for lacking blue-collar representation. The declared net worth of the average member of parliament (MP) was 53 million rupees in 2009, which placed him or her among the top 1 percent of all Indians. The proportion of MPs who are *crorepatis* – or multimillionaires – increased from 30 percent in 2004 to 62 percent in 2014. Individuals who were MPs in 2004 and who contested elections again in 2009 increased their net worth by an average of 289 percent in the intervening five-year period, a stunning rate of growth, many times the rate of growth of national income.[52]

In other ways, too, MPs are becoming more exclusive and less representative. The share of MPs with agriculture as the primary occupation fell sharply from about 50 percent in the 12th Lok Sabha (lower house of Parliament, elected in 1998), to less than 30 percent in the 16th Lok Sabha (elected in 2014).[53] The share of party dynasts – individuals preceded in representative politics by a family member related by blood or marriage – was 30 percent in 2009, up from 20 percent five years earlier.[54] Foreshadowing a rising trend, the share of those with hereditary and "hyper-hereditary" links was larger among younger compared to older parliamentarians.[55] People untested at the grassroots are being pitchforked by parties into higher levels of electoral politics.

Like the tiered state, electoral politics follows a steep and tiered hierarchy in India. Those who start in the bottom tier of representative democracy tend to remain there; very few in top-tier positions have ever held bottom-tier electoral office. Only eighteen of 499 MPs elected to the 15th Lok Sabha (2009–14) previously held any position in a village *panchayat*, and another thirty MPs held office at the next higher level of representative democracy (*panchayat samitis* or municipal councils). Thus, in all, less than 10 percent of MPs climbed the political ladder from the bottom.[56] The rest, because of family connections or other means of privileged access, entered straightaway into the highest tiers of electoral politics. The idea that local governments would serve as schools of democracy does not appear to have found favor among the party elite.

This narrowing demographic composition of MPs has gone together with a change in their dominant ideas. MPs of the past vigorously debated agricultural development and state industrial investments, but these old lines of discussion are no longer active topics. Instead, the talk is of special economic zones, of easier labor laws, and of loosening regulations on capital. This increasing ideological support for globalized growth has brought MPs of different parties in sync with the policy preferences of corporate business, inculcating a set of beliefs that includes faith in the power of globalized growth to solve the gamut of social and economic problems, conviction that the corporate ways of doing things are better (including within government offices), and adherence to the view that Western ways and urban values are superior to traditional ways and rural societies.[57]

These ideas match well with the aspirations that elected representatives, as well as government officials, have for themselves and their children. Officials and politicians see how the city is the place that has better facilities and greater opportunities; the bigger the city, the greater the perceived advantage. One rarely hears of a politician who after being MP returns to contest a seat in the village *panchayat*. The ladder of ambition leads in the other direction. Representatives elected from rural areas move with their families to live in big cities. Aspiring to dollar-economy positions, their children attend better schools and colleges.

The gap grows between the representative and his constituents, as voters and MPs experience different realities. The distance between the dollar economy and the rupee economy gets replicated in the arena of parliamentary decision making. Political scientist Atul Kohli's thesis – that "the Indian state has basically catered to the winners in the new economy, without intervening much on behalf of those left behind"[58] – has to be viewed against the backdrop of these developments. For this reason too, top-down decision making in the tiered state and segmented polity needs to be progressively complemented by empowered forums for bottom-up decision making.

Democracy at the Doorstep

The four elements that we have discussed – the tiered state, distance and mediation, the administrative stretch, and the tilt in electoral democracy – need to be jointly addressed in a longer-term reform process. It cannot be the case that people continue living, generation after generation, with a dysfunctional state, hoping someday for a miraculous transformation.

An overhaul of its administrative machinery is required for making the state better at dealing with the concerns of ordinary citizens. Not all at once, but in carefully staged and closely monitored phases, extending over a long period, the state needs to be reconstructed.

The pathologies associated with some elements have specific cures. For instance, de-tiering the public administration is a necessary longer-term reform. As a prominent historian of the civil services in India observed, "recruiting a few young men each year to a separate service and giving them, and only them, a clear run to the top is the height of elitist administration. This meant that other administrators who did not, or could not, get into that service were forever denied access to the top positions, however able they might subsequently become. Colonial administration was in consequence highly stratified."[59] The contemporary situation is equally untenable. The situation cannot continue where a democratic and egalitarian government is internally divided into castelike strata. The public administration of the future has to make it possible for the brightest and hardest-working to build stellar careers. Over the longer term, India must aim to institute a single-entry system in its public bureaucracies. Together with an independent agency that oversees promotions and postings and administers professional performance evaluations, such a system will help inculcate a greater sense of fairness and raise the level of performance. Similarly, reforming political parties and making them more internally democratic is another element-specific initiative that can be helpful. It will help narrow the representation gap and counteract the policy tilt, though it would help to remain aware of likely side effects and adverse outcomes.[60]

There's one important reform, however, that can commonly address significant parts of the pathologies associated with each of the four elements. And that requires rebuilding the state, in stages, starting from the bottom.

Democracy becomes more real where its protections, benefits, and opportunities are available at one's doorstep – and not when accessing these benefits is excessively costly or time consuming. That's the kind of opportunity ordinary people in India have been lacking. There's need to empower lower-level links in the chain of governance and to bring decision making closer to ordinary people. They should be able to achieve more by themselves, becoming less dependent on distant representatives and unaccountable mediators.

Grassroots officials – including schoolteachers, village nurses, and junior engineers – should be endowed with greater authority and responsibility, and simultaneously, citizens should acquire greater powers of oversight and more opportunities for participation. Countervailing power in the hands of citizens is a necessary accompaniment of greater decentralization.

Empowering the street-level bureaucrat with discretion and resources will help reduce the ill effects of tiering and distance.

Administrative stretch is also better handled by reallocating authority down the chain of governance.

Allowing more discretion at the grassroots level will also serve another purpose. Few important problems of development and societal change are ever finally resolved. Each step toward a solution throws up new problems and reveals unanticipated opportunities. Even the best-designed program must be revalidated periodically, making it more relevant to emergent conditions. And each program must be grounded in the local situation, particularly those for which situational knowledge counts for more, and where rote implementation is not efficacious. That also requires a considerable amount of field-level discretion.

Given how things operate at present, however, field-level officials are widely demotivated. Feelings of discontent and demotivation have been reported as well among higher officials.[61] But while some reforms have been made at the highest levels, the task of strengthening the lowest links in the institutional chain has been left largely unattended.[62]

Instead of having their skills upgraded and their mandates broadened, field-level officials are facing replacement by technological equipment. Mirroring the trend in the private sector, where robots are replacing manned service centers, the small amount of discretion available with field-level officials is being handed over to e-service centers. Establishing such centers has become fashionable, and it is being pursued for a number of reasons.[63] However, even though such a center may be adequate for issuing routine documents, such as caste certificates and copies of land registrations, replacing people with technology will not lead to more responsive health care or more effective teaching in the classroom. There are limits to how far technology can help make systemic improvements.

Technology in the service of an empowered and motivated field official is a different matter, however. Armed with instant access to dozens of examples of local innovations – and with the ability to engage in virtual discussion with the concerned individuals – officials who have the ability (and the mandate) to innovate will embark on more fulfilling and more socially productive careers. Technology can be an important component of the overall reform, adding power to individual capabilities, instead of bypassing officials.

Unfortunately, technology has been mostly used so far in support of extending centralized direction and tightening top-down control. I spoke with an official who worked at the time as collector and district magistrate in a particular district. I had held the same position many years earlier, and a bond was established. "There are frequent videoconferences," he told me, "where we are asked to report on implementation progress; there are constant calls for digital maps with project locations." The conversations that occur in these videoconferences, he added, were in the nature of compliance reporting. There's no scope for offering renegade thoughts or suggesting innovations. Occasionally, an enterprising district collector, or more rarely, an innovative block development officer, will have the gumption to pursue a new idea, but people with the deepest and latest knowledge of conditions on the ground – teachers, extension workers, *patwaris*, police constables, and so on – a vast army – are being reduced incrementally to automatons.

That amounts to a huge waste of taxpayers' money. Why pay for thousands of people who are of no great use? Kick them out or put them to better use – those are the only alternatives. Implementing the first alternative will be impractical and wasteful. There's need for village schoolteachers and community nurses and electricity linemen and police constables. Large-scale personnel changes are the ultimate resort, but they are not necessary or helpful. The capacity exists for performing better with the same set of government employees who, at each different level, were selected from among the cream of the crop. It's their work environment that makes these people perform below capacity, producing ennui and demotivation and leading many toward corruption. There are examples from India that show how a dormant bureaucratic capacity has been successfully reawakened.[64] In other countries, too, impressive results were achieved when the task environments of middle- and lower-tier public officials were improved.[65]

More discretion and more resources – accompanied by better training – are necessary if service providers are to perform better than before. Greater power goes together, however, with greater responsibility and more transparency. Power needs to be exercised, not arbitrarily and individually, but collectively and within institutionalized forums. Providers need to be accountable to the populations they serve – in relation to both what the providers do and what they don't do. Ideally, the people who are served, who observe on a regular basis the quality of education that their children receive, and the behaviors, respectful and otherwise, of health-care providers, should have the power, collectively, to hire and fire these providers, or at least to have a say in these decisions. That kind of direct accountability link is more effective than one in which a complaint is hard to make and almost impossible to follow through. The long and indirect process of the tiered state is not effective; there's little real accountability in the system.

Investments should be made that will progressively result in creating a network of effective local institutions. Without these building blocks, the edifice of a more effective democracy and civil society will remain incomplete and disconnected. Other reforms will follow once the foundation is in place. Higher-level links in the chain of governance have to be refitted to accommodate the changes that occur at the grassroots.

Not all of this can happen in one stroke, nor should any single institutional form be pushed on all local jurisdictions. Solutions that work cannot be thought up full-blown in an office. They need to be tested in different ground conditions.

A process of trial-and-monitoring, discussed in the next chapter, will enable the country to build the required institutions in stages. There's no way of knowing in advance which institutional designs will work better in a particular context. That knowledge needs to be generated after carefully evaluating experiences, giving alternative designs a fair chance to be proven.[66]

It's not necessary, and it may be foolhardy, to look for a single best national solution. Such a quest is itself the product of a top-down mode of thinking and analysis. Taking a bottom-up view, one recognizes that the ground situation is variable, and the quest for solutions can lead in different directions. An alchemist-like search for a universal solvent has proven to be ineffective. Locally grounded process innovation is necessary; there are no viable shortcuts, no easy solutions.

Other developing countries have also inherited states that suffer from many of the same pathologies.[67] Too often, political scientists refer to them as weak states, but in fact these are (or can relatively rapidly become) strong states, given the right incentives together with a reallocation of authority. Presently organized in favor of top-down hierarchy at the expense of local discretion and responsiveness, these states too can gain by investing in processes of bottom-up innovation.

8 LOOKING AHEAD: GROWING THE ECONOMY – AND DEVELOPING INDIVIDUALS

In the seventy years since national independence, a great deal of progress has been made in the country. Unprecedented macroeconomic stability, faster highways and newer airports, a growing economy, increased clout and visibility in international forums – these are considerable achievements, painstakingly put together, which have to be acknowledged and consolidated.

The forces associated with these achievements have helped many individuals soar upward, but for many others, these forces have not produced ever-improving standards of living. There are signs of improvement everywhere – cell phones, electricity, roads, and school buildings – but still, the forces that operated have not enabled the achievement of significant upward mobility for millions of Indians. People from poorer homes and rural areas, no matter how smart or hardworking, have rarely made it into higher-paying positions. Commendable macroeconomic growth has occurred, but without substantially improving many individuals' micro-situations. Millions are vulnerable to falling into acute poverty, and these downward tugs have not subsided. The chances of a downfall remain large for too many, and their prospects for upward mobility aren't exciting.

Take Keshu, for instance, the first person in my village to obtain a high school diploma. He worked hard at his lessons, and after graduating, Keshu looked for a job befitting his higher educational status. But no better jobs came around, and Keshu found work as a day laborer. He makes 7,000 rupees a month, the same as others who stopped going to school much earlier.

Growth in the country has not been directly and proportionately experienced by every individual. For some, the gains were large; for others, they have been minimal.

What has mattered in each case is the microclimate experienced by the individual – her quality of preparation, support systems, level of self-confidence, and flows of guidance and information. Leela, a young woman who grew up in a Bengaluru slum, achieved excellent grades all the way through high school. She had set her heart on becoming a doctor, but ended up becoming a low-paid laboratory assistant. Her family did not have the money to pay for coaching classes that help individuals prepare for the entrance examination. Two subsidized coaching programs for less advantaged kids are run by NGOs in her city, but neither Leela nor anyone in her circle knew of their existence.

Deficient in some elements, unwholesome microclimates crush and obscure the talents of many individuals. In addition to promoting faster economic growth, something purposive needs to be done to support microclimate improvements. It's not rocket science, nor is it hugely expensive.

Two sets of development strategies are required in tandem: a macro strategy to grow the national economy, and a micro strategy to promote individual development. There is a symbiotic and cyclical relationship between aggregate growth and an individual's development. Opportunities for individual development increase when there is faster economic growth in the country; conversely, growth is given a boost when, across the board, individuals start producing more. The best long-term results have been achieved by countries that have nurtured this symbiotic relationship.[1] India has not been able to keep the two parts in balance. Its macro strategies have been relatively well developed and well managed, but its micro strategies have been ineffective.

The Microclimates of Development

Developing better micro strategies can be broadly defined as improving the vectors impinging on a person's life chances by reducing the downward pull of vulnerability, and strengthening the upward impetus. Understanding what kind of strategies to devise is assisted by taking a worm's-eye, rather than a bird's-eye, view of grassroots developments. Gross similarities across sites are emphasized when bird's-eye views are taken from a great distance. But such panoramas miss out on the specifics of sites, and these details can be very important.

Consider the case of two neighboring villages of Andhra Pradesh that I visited when I was studying household movements into and out of poverty. In one village, I found that the share of households in poverty had fallen by 40 percent during the preceding ten-year period. In the neighboring village, however, the rate of poverty had *increased* by almost the same proportion, 40 percent, over the same period. I learned how these opposite trends had come into being. In the first village, which sits atop a bluff abutting a seasonal river, an enterprising villager started experimenting with lift irrigation. Raising water from an underground aquifer, using a series of pipes and a diesel engine, he was able to double his production. Other farmers began to follow his example. Incomes rose, and over the years, many families climbed out of poverty in this village.

In the second village, however, the situation was very different. Located on the bank of the same river, this village has a more favorable location. A business concern, seeking assured supplies of water, set up a factory in this village that produced a certain type of industrial chemical. Immediately, the villagers found employment close to their homes, and there were signs of prosperity. In a few years, however, the positive results were overtaken by a saga of adverse events. First, their cattle started to die in large numbers. Then the goats and the sheep started dying. Later, many people fell ill with weak bones. Large numbers were admitted to hospital. Huge expenses were incurred, and many died. Many families were pushed into poverty. Their water sources had become severely polluted, and these effects persist, as I learned from a later visit.[2]

Big effects are produced in people's lives by their different microclimates and local situations.[3] But local-level factors tend to be rendered invisible when planning occurs at a great distance.

A standardized program of action sent from the top down may be relevant for dealing with the local factors that operate in a subset of villages – and largely irrelevant for other villages' situations. A country shouldn't be looking to only introduce standardized solutions. Local opportunities, such as the potential for lift irrigation, need to be seized on, and local threats, such as the water poisoning, need to be countered. A worm's-eye view is necessary for this purpose.

Taking a worm's-eye view also helps uncover why large, inanimate forces such as growth, education, urbanization, globalization, and technological advancement – sometimes regarded as the cures for the problems of development – have effects that can cut both ways and vary widely across locations. Sometimes a large force is of little consequence, and in some instances, there have been reversals.

Take education, for instance, which hasn't delivered the kind of high rewards that were implicit in the promise of educating first-generation learners. Parents who were mostly unlettered sent their children to a place they did not know, believing that it would be the ladder to a well-paid job and out of hard labor. That expectation has been widely belied. Keshu became a *mazdoor* after completing high school. His younger brother and sister decided to drop out of school much earlier. What good would it do to remain in school? What was the point in repeating their older brother's experience?

The enthusiasm with which unlettered parents sent their children to schools has started to wane in many villages. Seeing the first generation of school attendees receiving slim pickings has had a dampening effect on others' motivations. Something purposive is required to rejuvenate the national project of education. Making better national policies is important, but it isn't all that is necessary; large forces can have little effect where microclimates aren't supportive.

Similarly, another large force, urbanization, hasn't substantially increased people's chances of upward mobility. A stratification of slums has emerged, kept in place by assortative residential choices. The better off live in better-off slums. Poorer people live in blue-polygon settlements. Hardly anyone moves from a worse to a better address. Families have lived in the same slum home for multiple generations. Young slum dwellers follow their parents and neighbors into low-income informal occupations.

Diverse elements in their microclimates diminish the upward mobility prospects of millions of individuals. Chandru, a teenager whom I met in a remote village of Andhra Pradesh, is proficient in mathematics, but his parents simply would not believe that his desire to become an engineer was practically possible for someone in their situation. No one from their village or circle of acquaintances had ever become an engineer. No one knew the steps that lead from a school in the village to an engineering career. Where none has achieved a secure and high-paying career before, the paths ahead of others are very unclear. Diverse elements combine to produce a low-mobility situation. In addition to poor-quality preparation and lack of information, the absence of role models is a deterrent to individuals' ambitions.

Millions are forced by their unwholesome microclimates to become *mazdoors*, among whom there are many who, given a fair chance, can become inventors and entrepreneurs. Nurturing talent wherever it may be found – in the home of a rich man or a poor woman, in remote villages or in metro towns – is the task of the future. At present, the country is making poor use of its vast pool of human potential.

Recognizing this need, many individuals have been paying for the education of their maid's son or driver's daughter. Charitable contributions enable other poorer children to attend better schools. Organizations have sprung up that work on improving other elements of individuals' microclimates. With the help of mentorship, career guidance exam preparation, and other means, these organizations help bridge the gap between ability and achievement.[4]

Initiatives such as these need to be multiplied. No matter where in India she grows up, a child must have an equal chance of a better future. Philanthropic efforts can only go a certain distance. In order to extend this right to the largest number of children, there is a need to make improvements in the system. Although they are widely broken, public systems cannot be abandoned; they have to be rejuvenated. Once again, it is a proposition that is not too expensive and not too complicated.

Quality Standards in Public Systems

Increasing the budgetary allocation to education and health is very important. Equally, there's a need to engender greater effectiveness within the system. Several examples testify to the need for inculcating higher quality standards, suggesting that it is not a shortage of money that holds service quality back; it is the acceptance of low quality standards within the public system. For instance, the educations that Keshu and Leela received were of a poor quality, not because their schoolteachers were paid poorly. Teacher salaries in the public system have been raised many times, and are much higher than most schools in the private system. But even as salaries went up, the quality of learning deteriorated. What's needed is not so much to raise salaries yet again as it is to improve the effectiveness of the system. Similarly, on the medical side, it's a matter of making quality improvements more than adding resources or legislation. Chunnilal, a farmer in my village, had an accident at a stone quarry, losing his left leg and ultimately his livelihood, not because there aren't mine safety laws or because he couldn't get free medical attention. These laws exist, and free medical care is available, but the laws aren't implemented faithfully, and hospital staff are frequently callous and careless.

Everyday institutional failures of these kinds mar the life prospects of many individuals. Building more schools and dispensaries is important, but it is equally important to attend to the finer aspects of institutional failure.

As things stand, the state simply does not have the machinery to observe and record the quality of service performance at the grassroots. The presence of the state does not extend into beyond-5-km villages and blue-polygon slums – that's the way the state has been constructed. But there's no one other than its employees whom the state trusts to observe and report on performance quality. The result is that the state has no means to keep itself informed about quality standards.

Instead of remedying this lapse, government agencies have widely adopted a bean-counting approach to monitoring and program evaluation. They count what they can count, adding up the numbers of school buildings constructed and scrutinizing attendance records. These markers of progress are considered carefully, and the quality of the service is given less attention.

Instilling higher quality standards will require making reforms in the structures and processes of governance at the grassroots. Those who are located at the point of delivery have the best information about the quality of performance. But ordinary people have been left out in the cold by the existing system. Notable examples apart, ordinary people have no involvement in public decisions. They have no place at the table where quality concerns can be debated. The systems of everyday governance keep ordinary people at a considerable distance. Half-hearted attempts to set up parent–teacher councils in Uttar Pradesh and other states of India constitute a string of missed opportunities.

The distancing of ordinary people dilutes quality concerns; it has also had an adverse effect on incentives. If they have a stellar schoolteacher, parents and students can't raise the teacher's pay; if they have a slacker, they can't levy a deduction. A wide separation arises between performance quality and rewards in the system, another reason why the system is broken.

To make the connections stronger between incentives and performance standards, networks of local institutions bringing together service providers and ordinary people are required. Ordinary people have to be involved in the tasks of monitoring and enforcing quality standards. Examples from across the world show how effective partnerships have substantially improved the quality of government performance.[5]

In India, however, installing a network of local institutions is a task that was started but left uncompleted. *Panchayats* were set up, but they remain toothless creatures, unable in most states to uphold quality standards, because they have neither the authority nor the resources. The span of supervision – the range of disparate tasks that the *panchayats* oversee – is too vast for any one organization. Even as the *panchayats* are given greater powers and more resources, newer local organizations must be constituted.

The search is not for a sweeping institutional reform that can, right from the start, be implemented in every location across the country. The knowledge gaps are large, and specific institutional forms are not known that will be effective in diverse situations. There is no particular merit to seeking a common solution. Different types of institutions – cooperatives, limited-liability companies, voluntary societies, and others – can fill the same need, depending on the context. The worth of any type in particular should not be assumed; it has to be demonstrated. Institutions are effective when people have faith in them, are willing to contribute time and other resources, and commit to abide by the collective decision. These ends are best achieved when ordinary people play a part in designing and maintaining the institutions of local governance.[6]

Innovating Institutions

How does one go about launching a different mode of development assistance and setting up a process of institutional innovation? There are more than 4,000 statutory towns and half a million villages in

India. There are also other, equally daunting complications. Information is essential for effective participation, but who will take on the responsibility of equipping ordinary people with information? How will it be ensured that local elites do not subvert the operations of local institutions?

There are no ready answers to these operational questions. This does not mean that the mission is impossible. Answers will have to be incrementally fashioned through a sequential process of learning and adaptation. It helps to be humble, starting out small, not intending to make a difference in the first instance to all of 100,000 schools or dispensaries.

An incremental approach, scaling up in stages, will help produce solutions that are more abiding and effective. Start out on a small scale, implementing previously tested models and promising alternatives. Assess these alternatives in carefully monitored experiments that are carried out initially in only a few villages and urban localities. Proposals that work well in these smaller jurisdictions, delivering good results over the first three to five years, should, in the next stage of the process, be offered for adaptation to the next larger jurisdiction (development blocks or city wards). Progressively, after successive stages of testing, evaluation, and adaptation, alternative solutions will emerge that can, with greater assurance, be offered for use across the country.[7]

The urge to rapidly extend a local innovation, scaling it up helter-skelter to the national level, has to be resisted. Trying to telescope the process will have deleterious consequences. An infant must learn to stand before she learns how to walk, then run, then do a marathon. Jumping immediately to the national level will be wasteful. Moving with deliberation and persistence will help develop more useful solutions.

Proceeding from the bottom up in this manner will help uncover a menu of alternatives. Diverse alternatives will work better in different situations; the idea shouldn't be to start look immediately for a single national solution.

Many smaller-scale examples show how the first stage in this process of institutional innovation can be initiated. Consider, first, an example from the health-care sector. Improving the institutions of health care is of great importance; far too many people fall deeply into poverty because of illnesses, accidents, and the high cost of medical attention.

No large-scale remedy is available, however, that can solve all of the nation's health-care problems. A number of smaller-scale initiatives show, however, that high-quality health-care services can be provided at low cost to poorer families.

I heard about one of these inspiring NGOs when I was waiting at a bus stop one morning in a distant village in the northern state of Rajasthan. As happens so often in these remote locations, the bus was late in coming, and to pass the time I struck up a conversation with a young couple. I had assumed, wrongly as it turned out, that the couple lived in the village and were going to the city on some errand.

"What is taking you to the city?" I inquired. "Are you going to see a movie or to buy provisions?"

"We do not live in this village," the man corrected me. "We live in the city. We came just for the day to this village."

"Do you have relatives here?"

"Her sister's in-laws live in the next village," he said. But that wasn't the main reason behind their visit.

"My wife is pregnant," he added with a shy smile. "It will be our first child, and we are being extra careful."

They had been coming every month to see the doctor in the village dispensary, which surprised me greatly, for when someone in these villages is in need of qualified medical care, he or she usually goes in the opposite direction – to the city.

"Why did you come to a village dispensary, so far from home," I inquired, "instead of going to a city hospital, where there are more facilities?"

The wife spoke up for the first time. "The quality of care is much better here," she stressed. "There's an NGO that runs the dispensary in this village. Their doctor is very good. She is always in attendance. Their nurses are attentive, and they treat us with respect. It will be safer and better to deliver in this dispensary."

Intrigued, I came back as soon as I could to spend time at the village dispensary. I saw an orderly outfit being run with professionalism and quiet urgency, providing reliable maternity services to hundreds of families. I learned that this NGO has dotted a larger area with other clinics and dispensaries that are equally effective.[8]

Other initiatives, undertaken by diverse organizations including state governments, foundations, and NGOs, also provide inspiring examples. Positive changes are not only possible, these examples show that they can be achieved by a variety of actors.[9]

In other sectors, too, including education and information provision, there are shining examples of how effective service delivery has been achieved as a result of participatory institutional innovation. In each case, an innovative organization has, over time, developed a process involving people centrally in managing the machinery of finding solutions. Their mission statements speak of this central intention. One such organization aims to "create a system of health care which builds on a continuing and mutually enriching dialogue with the people it serves";[10] another acts out its belief that "involving the communities themselves, especially those poor and marginalized, in deciding the needs and defining the parameters" is the proper way of building a better health-care system.[11] These small-scale examples can serve as the grist for a larger process of institutional innovation.

Innovating in stages, this process will help develop a menu of institutional options, thereby saving money for the nation. Failures are part of any process of innovation, and learning from failures is as important as learning from successes. However, failures also represent a wasted investment and so must be minimized in order to save public resources. The problem with top-down initiatives, introduced with a big bang across the country, is that they fail simultaneously in tens of thousands of villages.[12] That amount of public waste is neither useful nor necessary. Failures should be detected and weeded out on a smaller scale, at an early stage of the development process. The bottom-up method of sequential development, by weeding out failures early, will make more effective use of public resources.

Continuous monitoring and evaluation is necessary for ensuring that the system works in the manner intended. It is not only outcomes that have to be evaluated, but also the processes that have led to these outcomes. *What* should be done is important to ascertain. *How* it is to be done is another important, and often missing, part of the learning process.

A strong central capacity is necessary for maintaining integrity in the bottom-up process of innovation. A number of functions are better performed in a centralized fashion – evaluating trials in a professional and transparent manner; coordinating the efforts of diverse agencies; monitoring the course of progress through different stages of the process; and most important, disseminating the results and analyzing outcomes. This should not merely be the task of a government bureaucracy or a group of academics. Combining expertise from diverse walks of life will better uncover different facets of the process.

For too long, an anemic system of governance has suppressed ordinary people's life chances. Throwing the existing system out root and branch will be wasteful and could easily become chaotic. Building the institutions of governance back in stages, following a carefully monitored process, represents a surer way to a more productive society.

Staying on the Road

It will be a long and winding road, but there are no better ways of resolving the problems. There are no magic bullets around; no prefabricated solutions. It will help to move forward in small steps that are taken with deliberation. It is necessary to be persistent and to stay on the road – not moving in large fits and bursts never brought to completion.

I was reminded of the need for deliberation and persistence when I went to live in my village in January 2017, two months after the announcement of demonetization. On November 8, 2016, Prime Minister Modi had taken to the airwaves to announce a strong move for curbing the flow of black money (tied to tax evasion). His government had decided to "demonetize" banknotes of two specified values. The existing 500-rupee and 1,000-rupee notes would become worthless on December 30, 2016. People could either exchange these old notes for the new 2,000-rupee and 500-rupee notes that the government would issue, or they could deposit these notes into their bank accounts. A single bank account was permitted to be deposited with cash worth no more than 250,000 rupees – larger deposits would invite the probing eyes of the tax authority. Individuals who had hoarded larger amounts of cash would lose the excess amount. That would destroy stashes of black money across the board – or so it was contemplated.

Enterprising people found innovative ways to beat the government at its game. More than 95 percent of the old banknotes made their ways into banks before the year was out. Employers paid their workers for months ahead of time. Robust informal exchanges came up that traded the old notes at a discount. Thousands of bank accounts of laborers and small farmers that had held zero balances for months and years were suddenly filled to the limit of 250,000 rupees, below the line of sight of the tax authority.

It wasn't clear how the demonetization move had destroyed the black market. People awaited the government's next move.

Meanwhile, life carried on, but not without significant disruptions. Some poorer people were largely unaffected, but many more had a hard time from the beginning. Week after week, as people lined up for hours in front of bank branches and banks ran out of cash, the market collapsed. People stopped buying things and employers started letting go of employees.

Bigger businesses with larger inventories and greater access to sources of finance held on for a longer time, but many smaller businesses were falling apart. Take Hiralal, for instance, a man of about fifty years, who had a masonry business in my village. He built and repaired drystone walls, generating enough work to employ four assistants. But after demonetization, "banks were letting account holders withdraw only 10,000 rupees monthly. People held on to that money for making essential expenditures. People were putting off any expenditures that they could put off. There was no one who wanted to build a wall in the near future."

For more than two months, Hiralal told me, when I met with him in late January, he had received no commissions, and his team of workers, once united, had scattered.

I asked why he wasn't accepting payment by check, instead of just sitting around and waiting for a return to business as normal.

"But how can I do that?" Hiralal asked in consternation.

I asked if he had a bank account, and Hiralal fished out a bank passbook. In the months prior to demonetization, the government had run a campaign to open bank accounts for unbanked people. Millions of new bank accounts had been registered. But even as he had acquired a bank account, Hiralal hadn't acquired knowledge about the benefits of banking. No one had informed him about how to write or deposit checks, or how to take out a loan to run his business operations. Persistence was missing from the project of bringing banking to the poor, which ended once the numbers of new accounts had been totaled and reported. If the project had been run with a longer time horizon and greater persistence, the benefits of banking could have been brought home to Hiralal and other previously unbanked people.

Undertaking demonetization after people had become familiar with banking would have produced less pain and greater overall benefit. But persistence is a frequent casualty in a world of quick-fire campaigns and top-down imaginations – where the intent, so often, is not to develop, but to give away things in the name of development.

Development isn't, however, about giving away a set of things; what's required is to provide opportunities so that people can develop. A robust micro strategy for developing individuals in diverse microclimates is necessary for this purpose. Giving shape to these strategies is the need of the day. There's much to be gained from investing in a bottom-up innovation process.

Other High-variance Societies

Similar situations are being experienced across a wide swath of the developing world, especially in countries where, as in India, a large part of the population lives in rural areas. More than half the world's population lives in such largely agrarian countries, which have, to varying degrees, opened themselves up to global flows of goods, services, and investments. Relatively little is known, however, about how growth in this era of globalization will affect the fortunes of different people in these countries.

Signs point to the emergence of high-variance societies. The architecture of global inequality is changing. The old distinction between the First and Third Worlds has eroded. The world's richest and poorest are found, not on different continents as before, but more and more within the same country. Gated communities in Bengaluru and Lima, Nairobi and Kampala, private-island resorts near Manila – all have First-World amenities. But deep into the countryside, Third World pockets persist, and these are the places that have seen the least improvement.

In multiple ways, the prospects of people in rural areas are inferior to those of city people. Poverty is more widespread in rural areas. Eleven percent of city residents are poor in Ghana, but more than three times as many rural residents, 39 percent, live in poverty. In Zambia, Ecuador, Vietnam, and Cambodia, for example, the poverty rate is *three times* higher in rural areas.[13]

Years of urban bias, during the colonial era and after, led to the concentration of investments in national and provincial capitals. Rural areas were underprovisioned in terms of infrastructure and public services. The following examples are illustrative: More than 95 percent of the urban population in Ethiopia has access to safe drinking water – less than half the share (42 percent) of the rural population. More than 60 percent of city residents in India have access to improved sanitation, but only 25 percent of village residents. More than 60 percent of the urban population finished secondary school in Pakistan, compared to 30 percent of the rural population. Less than half of all rural students in sub-Saharan countries reached the expected competency levels, compared to more than 75 percent of urban students.[14]

The wide gap between urban and rural has grown wider in this era of globalization. Infrastructure and services have flowed into "the largest cities," the World Bank reports, "those where governments, the middle-classes, opinion-makers and airports are disproportionately located."[15]

Growing inequalities are on the minds of policy makers worldwide, their fissiparous effects for societies ever more apparent. Different dimensions of the inequality problem have gained traction in diverse countries. In countries with large agrarian populations, the rising spatial inequality between urban and rural areas is giving rise to a volatile situation.

What needs to be done to fix the emergent situation is not clearly known. No ready-made solutions are available. Following in the footsteps of the West is not a good idea. The situation today is very different from what it was 50 or 100 years ago. Automated processes of production, world-connecting technologies, and the changed architecture of the global economy have made it necessary for countries to hew different paths of economic development. They will not do well to borrow institutions and programs wholesale from other countries. Such a cookie-cutter approach to development has been widely discredited. Institutions that perform well in France are different from those that perform well in Germany, and both are different from the institutions that work well in Japan, the United States, and other countries. Each country has its own set of institutions, based on what works and what fits with its circumstances and sensibilities.[16]

Instituting processes of national innovation, rather than waiting to imitate a good idea from some other country, is perhaps the most important lesson of economic history. Processes of innovating institutions, similar to the one outlined for India, are required in other countries. These projects of national development can become opportunities for mutual learning.

Countries can choose to adopt various goals for guiding their national development projects. Three principles, however, need to be protected, which are simultaneously valued ends and necessary devices:

- First – the provision of a minimum living standard for all, adjusted to a country's changing circumstances
- Second – an equal chance of upward mobility for everyone's son or daughter
- Third – accessible forums for expressing governance concerns and overseeing quality standards in service delivery

Recognizing the first principle, a minimum living standard has been institutionalized in many richer countries. Among developing nations, China has been guaranteeing a minimum living standard. It has been implementing a number of related programs, including *Dibao*, one reason why hardly anybody in China is now found at the bottom of the world's income distribution.[17] Other developing countries too should work toward upholding minimum living standards.

A number of efforts are required for realizing this principle. Improving health care and reducing large-scale informality are primary among these efforts. It should be humanly possible to pay for a loved one's medical treatment without having to lose one's shirt in the process. Having papers for one's property and a contract for one's job are equally essential for living with dignity and security.

In line with the second principle, individuals should have better opportunities so that they can rise to positions commensurate with their capabilities. There's greater need than before to focus on higher-quality education and invest in efforts to promote upward mobility.

Technological advances and global value chains have made it necessary for producers worldwide to work with the latest technology. Compared to the era of assembly-line manufacturing, the newer techniques require a smaller number of workers with higher qualifications. More and more in the years to come, the better types of employment will require specialized qualifications. Talent development and higher-quality education are critical for making progress in today's extremely competitive global economy. Putting individuals and their diverse capacities at the center of development is necessary for building the future's most productive societies.

The third principle, of democratic governance at people's doorsteps, will help realize in practice the promise that has made the idea of democracy appear attractive. If the teachers at her daughter's school are not showing up or if they are shirking their duties, an individual should be able to have the situation rectified – quickly, assuredly, and without being out-of-pocket. This principle is widely violated, diminishing people's experiences of everyday democracy and vitiating their microclimates. Much more needs to be learned about how to fix these building blocks of development and democracy.

The view that I have presented of India is intended to be a contribution to an ongoing discussion of diverse perspectives and alternative pathways of development. The solutions to today's development problems aren't fully known, nor can they be lifted from another country's history. Institutional innovation on an extensive scale is required for generating the missing knowledge. Implementing untested ideas from the top down or testing the same ideas in a ground-up process – these are the choices. I'd opt, on balance, for the slower but surer method, realizing, as I grow older, that there are no magic bullets, and that resolving the hardest problems takes the longest.

NOTES

Chapter 1 The Dollar Economy and the Rupee Economy

1. In some parts of India, drivers and conductors of public buses turn a blind eye toward children who travel to school without purchasing tickets. They believe that by doing so they are playing a part that helps with a social effort. A song that is popular in Keshu's area laments the fate of a girl whose parents unknowingly arranged for her to marry an illiterate: "Such a laughable occurrence! In this day and age!" Young girls, learning this song, come to believe in its lyrics.

2. In investigations that I conducted in different states using the Stages-of-Progress methodology, I found commonly that immediately after becoming capable of meeting their food needs, families aim to spend their next rupee on children's education. The high priority that education has come to have in families' expenditure decisions is also a feature in other countries. See Krishna (2010) for these results and the underlying methodology. See also World Bank (2011a). It is noteworthy that even where no school fees need to be paid, sending a child to school is hardly costless to the family. See National Sample Survey Office (NSSO, 2008) for an estimate of the costs incurred by families at the primary, secondary, and college levels.

3. Drèze and Sen (2013: 287).

4. The economists Jagdish Bhagwati and Arvind Panagariya are among the best known proponents of such a view, which they have expressed, among their other writings, in a 2013 book. A useful review of this book and the one by Drèze and Sen, referred to above, is provided by Pankaj Mishra (2013).

5. On the whole, the professional middle classes in the largest cities have been the main proponents of civil society activities. Chatterjee (2004) differentiates between what he calls "civil" and "political" societies in India. The former,

populated principally by English-educated and Western-oriented elites in cities, involves itself in mounting concerted and claim-making civic actions, while the latter, the domain of the poor and the rural majority, negotiates its claims, mostly those of a survival nature, in atomized fashion, using ad hoc and often underground methods. Jayal (2013: 195–96) draws a very similar conclusion about the thinness of civil society actions in India, as do Harris (2006) and Jha et al. (2007).

6. Aspects other than money, which bring joy in people's lives, include family, close friends, the beauty and bounty of nature, community bonds, and social occasions. For a lucid exposition of this proposition in a group of Indian villages, see Bhrigupati Singh (2015).

7. The same villages that performed well in economic development programs also performed better for civic peace and democratic engagement. Villages that performed poorly in any one domain also performed poorly in both others. Krishna (2002) presents these results.

8. This all-too-brief examination glosses over finer details, which have been admirably presented, together with the policy debates of the day by, for example, Bhagwati and Desai (1970), Chibber (2003), Khilnani (1997), Panagariya (2008), and Rudolph and Rudolph (1987).

9. Four Indian citizens feature among the sixty-two wealthiest people globally, who own half the world's combined wealth. See www.oxfam.org/en/ pressroom/pressreleases/2016-01-18/62-people-own-same-half-world-reveals-oxfam-davos-report and www.dnaindia.com/money/report-out-of-62-four-indians-wealth-equal-to-50-of-world-s-poorest-people-2167406. Accessed on April 4, 2016.

10. For personal computer ownership, see www.nationmaster.com/country-info/ stats/Media/Personal-computers/Per-capita; for credit card possession, http://databank.worldbank.org/data/reports.aspx?source=global-findex-(global-financial-inclusion-database; for internet usage, http://data.un.org .proxy.lib.duke.edu/Data.aspx?q=internet+users&d=WDI&f=Indicator_Code %3aIT.NET.USER.P2.; for motor vehicles, www.oica.net/category/ vehicles-in-use/; for international tourism, World Tourism Organization. 2015. "World Tourism Data." 8 April 2015. http://data.un.org.proxy.lib.duke .edu/DocumentData.aspx?id=371 (All accessed on July 4, 2015). Verification and additional data were derived by consulting different nationally representative data sets for India.

11. These data are drawn from the India Human Development Survey (IHDS) undertaken between 2011 and 2012 by the National Council for Applied Economic Research (NCAER), a well-known applied economics research institution in India, in collaboration with the University of Maryland. See http://ihds.info/ for more details. A different analysis, using data on monthly expenditures (instead of incomes), produced a very similar percentage

distribution. Using NSSO data of 2009–10 for monthly per-capita expenditure (MPCE), we found, for instance, that 22 percent in urban areas and 43 percent in rural areas had MPCEs below 1,000 rupees. I thank Devendra Bajpai for help with this examination.

12. World Bank (2011a: 4).

13. "India's Staggering Wealth Gap in Five Charts," *The Hindu*, December 8, 2014. www.thehindu.com/data/indias-staggering-wealth-gap-in-five-charts/article6672115.ece. Also see Banerjee and Piketty (2005), Gandhi and Walton (2012), Jayadev et al. (2011), and OECD (2011).

14. See Azam (2012), Azam and Blom (2008), Cain et al. (2010), Chamarbagwala (2006), Kijima (2006), Mohanty (2006), Sarkar and Mehta (2010), Tilak (2007), and World Bank (2011a).

15. Azam and Blom (2008) and NSSO (2008).

16. See, especially, NCEUS (2007, 2009), but also Dougherty (2008), Kannan and Raveendran (2009), and Unni and Raveendran (2007).

17. See Naipaul (1977).

18. For education see ASER (2011), Chavan (2013), Das and Zajonc (2010), and Muralidharan (2013). The health situation is presented in Baru et al. (2010); Dilip and Duggal (2002); Hammer, Aiyar, and Samji (2007); Joe (2014); and Nagaraj (2013). For nutrition, see Deaton and Drèze (2009).

19. Roger Cohen, "Inequality, Indian Style," *New York Times*, December 19, 2013.

20. In general, the width of the streamgraph at any point from left to right represents the share of that country's population belonging to the corresponding point on the horizontal axis.

21. Summary measures of inequality, e.g., the Gini coefficient of income, indicate that inequality is lower in India as compared to many other countries. Measured at 33.9 for India, the Gini coefficient of income is lower than that of Brazil (52.9) and Zambia (57.5) – see http://hdr.undp.org/en/content/income-gini-coefficient (accessed on April 4, 2016). However, the Gini and other summary measures do not adequately reflect the full range of difference – the wide gap in lifestyles at the extremes of the wealth distribution – which needs to be depicted separately, particularly because it is this range of difference that severely complicates the tasks of governance. A similar spread of lifestyles is being witnessed in some other countries, notably South Africa and Indonesia, and others that also have largely agrarian populations.

22. See, for instance, Wu and Treiman (2007); Wang, Piesse, and Weaver (2011); and Xie and Zhou (2014).

23. Comparing India with China and other countries, Bardhan (2010: 132), concluded that India "is fast becoming one of the worst countries in terms of

opportunities for upward mobility." Other analyses, reviewed in Chapter 5, have produced the same conclusion.

24. *Ek Bharat, Shreshtha Bharat; Sabka Saath, Sabka Vikas.* BJP Election Manifesto 2014. Accessed on October 10, 2015 at www.bjp.org/images/pdf_ 2014/full_manifesto_english_07.04.2014.pdf.

25. See http://inc.in/images/Pages/English%20Manifesto%20for%20Web.pdf. Accessed on October 10, 2015.

26. An emergent literature discusses how many of today's developing countries have to undertake what these authors regarded to be "compressed development." See, for instance, Whittaker et al. (2010), who observe how "with compressed development the role of the state remains crucial, but it has become more complex and difficult than in the past," because it has to take account simultaneously of so many more dimensions. See also Howell (2006).

27. Sassen (2001: 3)

28. Porter (2000: 32). See also Florida (2003, 2008) and Moretti (2012), whose analyses support a similar conclusion about the large and growing influence of big cities.

29. For these and related estimates, see Bhagat (2014), Breman (2013), Deshingkar and Akter (2009), NSSO (2010b), Srivastava and Sasikumar (2003), and Thachil (2016).

30. The website of the Census of India has these figures: censusindia.gov.in. At these rates, according to the economist, Arvind Panagariya (2011: 159), appointed in 2015 to head India's new-look planning commission, "it will be another 50 years before urbanization reaches even 40 percent."

31. Weiner (1990: 7).

32. See, for instance, Deshpande (2011), Deshpande and Newman (2007), Deshpande and Palshikar (2008), Deshpande and Yadav (2006), Thorat and Attewell (2007), and Thorat and Dubey (2012).

33. See Shrivastava and Kothari (2012: 167). The pejorative Hindi term, *ganwaar* (literally, village resident but used in scorn and derogation, like the English terms, rube or yokel), is synonymous in many urbanites' minds with backward and uncultured. I have heard similarly disparaging terms in other developing countries.

34. A description of how the term *hurry slowly* came into modern conversation is provided at www.psychologytoday.com/blog/everyday-recovery/201005/ i-have-learned-hurry-slowly. Accessed on November 15, 2016.

35. A growing literature attests to this point. See, for instance, Brynjolfsson and McAfee (2014) and Carr (2014). For the declining shares of labor in national income, see Karabarbounis and Neiman (2013). For distributional consequences more generally, see Goldberg and Pavcnik (2007), Milanovic (2005), and OECD (2010b).

36. Bourguignon (2015: 3–4).
37. Mosse (2010: 1165).
38. See, for instance, Berg and Ostry (2011); Ranis, Stewart, and Ramirez (2000); Rodrik (2002); and Wilkinson and Pickett (2009).

Chapter 2 Beyond-5-km Villages: Where the Lights Aren't Shining Brightly

1. The average figure of 2 hectares for the entire country is a useful approximation (NCEUS 2007: 120). These calculations obviously vary, depending on the quality of land, where it is situated, and what kinds of complementary inputs are applied (quality seed, fertilizer, agronomic techniques, careful management, and so on). The 2-hectare cutoff is a handy tool, though, which like the poverty line (discussed in Chapter 4), helps separate farm families who can make a reasonable living off the land from other farm families who cannot.

2. See, Lerche (2010); Reddy and Mishra (2009); Rawal (2008); and Sen and Bhatia (2004).

3. More broadly, as Chhibber and Verma (2014) contend, those who receive government handouts do not, by and large, end up voting for the ruling party.

4. Most villages have been in existence for generations, as evidenced by the land record, archaeological evidence, and oral histories. There are very few villages from which large numbers of families have entirely disappeared. The numbers coming into towns are large, but the numbers remaining behind are larger by an order of magnitude, as I found in villages of the five states where I conducted grassroots studies. Other investigations have come to similar conclusions. For instance, Breman (1996: 37), a close observer of developments in rural Gujarat, observed that he had "seldom come across cases of households who left in their entirety to seek a new life elsewhere." For Tamil Nadu, Djurfeldt et al. (2008) report a similar finding. Similar results – showing a clear difference between individuals' and households' migration patterns – have been reported as well for other communities and countries (Banerjee and Duflo, 2006). We will take up the issue of rural-to-urban migration in more detail in the following chapter.

5. In this part of India as in many others, a daughter's share of the inheritance is customarily paid in advance in the form of dowry – a combination usually of jewelry, appliances, furniture, and cash – that is given by the bride's parents to the couple and her in-laws. Legally, daughters are supposed to have an equal share in the land, and dowry has been outlawed. But practice lags behind the intent of such laws, which were intended in the first place not to recognize and formalize common beliefs and practices but to engender a transformative effect.

6. Thachil (2014a) has mapped these *chowks* in New Delhi and Lucknow. Various NGOs, including *Aajeevika Bureau*, have mapped *nakas* and *chowks* in other cities.

7. Data from two nationally representative surveys, IHDS2 and DLHS3, were used for this part of the analysis. IHDS2, or the second round of the India Human Development Survey, was undertaken by the National Council for Applied Economic Research (NCAER) in coordination with the University of Maryland, is representative of rural areas of 16 major states. These multi-dimensional surveys, conducted in 2004–05, encompass a wide range of human development and poverty-related issues. District-Level Household and Facility Surveys (DLHS) were launched by the Government of India in 1996–1997 and conducted by the Mumbai-based Indian Institute for Population Sciences (IIPS). The third such survey (DLHS-3) was conducted from 2007 to 2008. It provides information related to 720,320 households from 28 States and 6 Union Territories of India.

8. I use the terms "town" and "city" interchangeably, following the Census of India (2001), which adopted the following criteria for defining towns (urban areas): "(a) All statutory places with a municipality, corporation, cantonment board or notified town area committee, etc. or (b) A place satisfying the following three criteria simultaneously: i) a minimum population of 5,000; ii) at least 75 percent of the male working population engaged in nonagricultural pursuits; and iii) a density of population of at least 400 per sq. km. (1,000 per sq. mile)."

9. Shukla (2010). In addition, poverty continues to be lowest in the largest cities and highest in small towns and rural areas (Kundu and Sarangi, 2007).

10. Clearly, 5 km is an average figure, and some of the biggest towns, such as Delhi or Bangalore or Mumbai, may cast their beneficial shadows over a wider area, whereas smaller towns, often only just larger than villages, may have more circumscribed radial effects. While the 5-km divide is robust on average, one has to be wary when interpreting these results in relation to any particular city or village. Distance remains, however, the best available measure for assessing a location's relative remoteness, with data provided in diverse databases, including IHDS and DLHS. Similar conclusions based on analyses of distance are reported by Das, Ghate, and Robinson (2015); Kundu, Pradhan, and Subramanian (2002); and World Bank (2011a).

11. See, for instance, Basant and Sen (2014); and Krishna (2013c); and NSSO (2010a: 18). More broadly, as World Bank (2001) finds, distance and transportation concerns impede girls' education.

12. Author surveys in 40 villages of Karnataka and Rajasthan (Krishna, 2013c).

13. Krishna and Ananthpur (2013). Other studies have corroborated this inference, showing how the gaps are growing. See Baru et al. (2010); and

UN-Habitat State of Urban Youth: Report 2010/11 (accessed on January 16, 2015, at mirror.unhabitat.org/pmss/getElectronicVersion.aspx? nr=2928&alt=1).

14. I can understand why it may be appropriate to locate the larger and more specialized facilities in closer and more centrally located villages, but what puzzles me is why a disproportionate number of even the simpler facilities, such as dispensaries, are located closer to cities. See also Hammer, Iyer, and Samji (2006) and Singh et al. (2011), who report similar conclusions.

15. See Kaufmann, Kraay, and Zoido-Lobatón (1999) and Kaufmann, Kraay, and Mastruzzi (2008). I left out one of their dimensions, related to the ease of doing business, which, in the context of these villages, was not as relevant.

16. See Krishna and Schober (2014). We used distance to taluka (or tehsil) HQ as a proxy for distance to nearest town for this analysis, considering that these variables are closely correlated.

17. In the case of teachers, these proportions are, respectively, 7 percent and 3.5 percent; and in the case of medical staff, they are 5 percent and 1.4 percent. (Author calculations from IHDS2.) See also Krishna and Schober (2014), which expands on the point about differences in the quality of governance. Notably, some recent studies have found an increase in the incidence and intensity of villagers contacting their local government (or *panchayat*) officials. See, for instance, Kruks-Wisner (2015) and Bussell (n.d.). The majority of these contacts are confined to within-village transactions for which *panchayats* have been empowered, such as the grant of assistance from welfare programs of the government. The scope of panchayats' jurisdiction and their range of authority remain highly restricted (Bardhan and Mookherjee, 2006; Manor, 2010). And panchayat officials rarely enable villagers to transcend village boundaries and make contact with higher levels of government. The increasing contact with panchayats, while welcome, still does not affect the overall gradient of governance.

18. See Ian Johnson, "China Releases Plan to Incorporate Farmers into Cities," *New York Times*, March 18, 2014. The national plan to which this article refers calls for deliberately moving, by force if necessary, an additional 100 million people into China's cities by 2020. It relies upon enlarging "the state's role in deciding who should move from rural land and where they should live."

19. The share of students attending public schools has steadily decreased. From just under 19 percent in 2006, the share of rural children in private schools increased to 31 percent in 2014. In urban areas, the share of children in private schools increased earlier and faster. In 2009, it was at 58 percent. See Desai et al. (2009) and Wadhwa (2014). See Baru et al. (2010) and Hammer, Aiyar, and Samji (2007) for comparable information regarding government hospitals and clinics.

20. Land reforms undertaken soon after national independence contributed to the breaking up of large land holdings, but the total amount of "surplus" land that was transferred was quite small in relation to total land ownership. See, on this point, Appu (1996); Bandyopadhyay (1986); Ladejinsky (1972).

21. A claim has been made, for instance, by Rawal (2008) that large tracts of land are available for redistribution. A closer look shows, however, that much of this claimed surplus land is located in the deserts of Rajasthan.

22. World Bank (2006).

23. The government of the time also assisted farmers by manipulating the prices at which the government-owned Food Corporation of India undertook to purchase the most important farm products, particularly wheat and rice, thereby influencing terms of trade in favor of agriculture. But this remedy benefited those farmers who had large surpluses to sell, the 5 percent, and not so much the majority, whose produce was barely sufficient for home consumption. For an elaboration of the ways in which this grand bargain with powerful farmers was achieved and how it worked in practice, see Rudolph and Rudolph (1987) and Varshney (1995).

24. Charan Singh, a prominent rural leader and Prime Minister of India between July 1979 and January 1980, makes such a claim in his 1981 book. Analysts examining public investments made during this time found that the thrust of government programs was in areas especially favored by large tracts of plain agricultural land and water availability – the original green revolution areas – with much less attention being given to hilly and stony lands with smaller and more isolated farms, areas that have much greater need and thus greater call on public resources.

25. See Balakrishnan (2010); Chand and Parappurathu (2012); Fan et al. (2005); GOI (2007); Jha (2007: 13); NCEUS (2007: 142); Kumar and Mittal (2006); Ramachandran and Rawal (2009); Reddy and Mishra (2009); and Sriram (2014). For the China case, see Hu et al. (2012).

26. GOI (2007: 30).

27. See World Bank (2006: 6, 102). Another illuminating analysis is provided by Kannan and Sundaram (2011).

28. See Damodaran (2012); S. Singh (2010; 2012); World Bank (2006); and World Bank (2011a). The Gini coefficient of land ownership, one measure of inequality that ranges from zero (indicating perfect equality with equal shares for all) to one (perfect inequality, with all land owned by just one person), increased from 0.67 in 1983 to 0.73 in 2005, showing a considerable widening of difference.

29. Deb (2011: 127).

30. Dev (2005).

31. Calculated at the base prices prevailing in 1993–94, the average daily earnings in 2005 for agricultural labor were Rs. 28 per day for males and Rs.

19 per day for females. Wages for nonagricultural labor were a little higher: Rs. 40 per day for males and Rs. 26 for females. People with salaried and professional jobs made on average Rs. 101 per day, nearly four times as much as agricultural laborers (Unni and Raveendran, 2007). See also Srivastava and Singh (2006).

32. NCEUS (2007: 133) emphasizes that "There are no social security measures to provide risk coverage . . . no laws to ensure they work under suitable conditions and are not subject to health hazards," a government commission observes. "There is no fixity of working hours, no compliance to minimum wages . . . whatever laws are in place suffer from poor implementation and enforcement."

33. These numbers are provided in the next chapter.

34. See Eswaran et al. (2009); Kotwal et al. (2011); Lahiri-Dutta and Samanta (2013); and Paris et al. (2005).

35. Burra (2005) cites the results of a survey organized by the Indian government in rural areas of six states, which found that more than 10 percent of girls and boys in the age group 6–14 years spend 2–3 hours daily in herding and grazing domestic animals. Another 14 percent of girls of this age group were engaged in collecting fuelwood, fodder, and drinking water.

36. In 2004, a young person from the top expenditure quintile was more than 10 times as likely to complete high school and go on to college compared to a person of the same age group from the two bottom quintiles. This ratio has increased significantly since the early 1980s, indicating growing educational inequalities (Azam and Blom, 2008; NSSO, 2008).

37. Jeffrey (2010: 66, 70). While Jeffrey's rich farmers are in the north of India, richer farmers in the southern part of the country have exercised the same options. See Harriss-White and Janakaranjan (2004); and Lerche, Shah, and Harriss-White (2013).

38. See Eswaran et al. (2009); Lanjouw and Murgai (2009); and World Bank (2011a: 133), which states that regular (or salaried) "non-farm employment is regressively distributed across the rural population: the richer you are, the more likely you are to enjoy such employment."

39. Damodaran (2008).

40. For instance, during the period between 1993 and 2005, average real incomes fell in beyond-5-km villages, with the steepest declines in income experienced by the poorest. See Krishna and Bajpai (2011). Also see Chakravarty and Dand (2006); Sen and Himanshu (2004); and World Bank (2011a).

41. According to the Socio-Economic and Caste Census undertaken by the government in 2011, in nearly 75 percent of rural households, the main earning family member makes less than Rs. 5,000 per month. Similar findings have resulted from other recent surveys, including the India Human Development Survey of 2011–12.

42. See Amaresh Dubey and Reeve Vanneman, "An Inclusive Growth Policy," *The Hindu*, April 5, 2014. Relative prices moved during this period in favor of agriculture, reversing the prior decline. Rainfall was good for consecutive years. Yields increased in particular regions. Public investments have remained low, however, especially in beyond-5-km villages, and the decline of public research and extension institutions has continued unabated. See Balaji and Pal (2014); Hnatkovska, Lahiri, and Paul (2013); Ghani, Kerr, and O'Connell (2013); Lall and Chakravarty (2005); and World Bank (2011a). An illuminating example of a village transformed by the ribbon growth accompanying highway building is provided by the journalist, Akash Kapur (2013). For a contrasting account of a village in the interior, see Ramachandran (2010).

43. Breman (2003: 30). Also see Deb (2011); and Vaidyanathan (2014).

44. While some analysts consider that farmer suicides, increasing in numbers, are a consequence of the agrarian crisis described in the preceding section, others believe that the reasons are more complex. See, for instance, Gruere and Sengupta (2011); Mohanty (2011); Reddy and Mishra (2009); and Sainath (2009, 2010).

45. See Basu and Das (2013); Guerin, D'Espallier, and Venkatasubramanian (2012); Kennedy (2014); Sundar (2006); and Pandita (2011) on these movements, alternatively known as Naxalite or Maoist movements.

46. See, for instance, www.thehindu.com/news/national/naxalism-biggest-threat-to-internal-security-manmohan/article436781.ece and www.dnaindia.com/india/report-we-must-root-out-naxal-menace-build-on-our-successes-manmohan-singh-1923622. Accessed on February 2, 2014.

47. Government of India, Ministry of Home Affairs, Annual Report 2008–09, p. 15. Accessed on January 8, 2015 at http://mha.nic.in/hindi/sites/upload_files/mhahindi/files/pdf/AR%28E%290809.pdf. Another experts' report commissioned by the government makes similar points (GOI 2008). Research findings by independent scholars uphold a similar view, for instance, Gomes (2015), and Kennedy (2014), who finds that in areas of India where these movements are the strongest, the presence of democracy and the development state are the weakest.

48. More than 90 percent in Naxalite-affected states, such as Andhra Pradesh, Bihar, Chhattisgarh, Jharkhand, Odisha, and West Bengal, live in beyond-5-km villages, compared to 60 percent in rural parts of other Indian states.

49. NSSO (2008); Azam and Blom (2008).

50. Undertaking a study of rural migrant settlements in Mumbai, Svati Shah (2014: 42) notes that, although in an earlier period, a boom in textile manufacturing and other labor-intensive operations created "access to the possibility of a more stable sustainable livelihood in the city . . . By the

mid-1990s, Mumbai's industrial sector had stalled, leaving ever fewer formal sector jobs ... Rural migrants who had hoped to work in the textile mills, as well as those who had been laid off, responded by trying to secure livelihoods through the far more insecure day wage labor market. Day wage labor markets form at *nakas* throughout Mumbai and constitute the most visible aspect of the city's vast informal economic sectors." Close investigations in other cities have found similarly. See, for example, Agarwala (2008); Mitra (2006); NCEUS (2007); Thachil (2014a); and Vijay (2005).

51. Gandhi, whose worldview kept evolving, did not modify this demand in later life although he acknowledged the need for "reconstructing" the village and transforming its character in certain ways, including making it more democratic and egalitarian in its internal functioning, a need stridently emphasized by another prominent thinker, Babasaheb Ambedkar. See Jodhka (2002) for an excellent brief examination of different views about the village and its place in modern India as expressed, respectively, by Gandhi, Nehru, and Ambedkar. President A. P. J. Abdul Kalam proposed the ideas that led to the government program Provision of Urban Amenities to Rural Areas (PURA), which was a tepid and half-baked response to Kalam's original ideas.

52. The report, by Fan, Chan-Kang, and Mukherjee (2005: 14), makes a similar comparison for China, finding a similar urban bias.

53. See World Bank (2006). See also the reports available at www.nasscom.in/future-outlook; and www.knowledgecommission.gov.in.

54. See Whang (1981). There are, of course, other factors – including its legacy of Japanese colonialism (Kohli 2004) and a favorable Cold-War international regime (Cumings, 1984) – that account for South Korea's success story, but what it made of these favorable circumstances is a separate matter of prudent policy preferences.

55. A useful beginning was made with the budget allocations announced by the BJP government in 2016. It would be important to extend these initiatives and make them more encompassing.

56. Kerala, Karnataka, and Maharashtra are ahead of other states in this respect. See the ranking of states done by the Indian Institute of Public Administration (Alok, 2013).

57. At all three levels of the *panchayat* institutions, there is a high level of dependence on fiscal transfers from the state and central governments, with village *panchayats* raising, on average, 11.3 percent of all revenues internally, and intermediate (or block-level) and district *panchayats* raising, respectively, only 0.4 percent and 1.6 percent from internal revenues. The share of internally generated revenues varies across states, ranging from 37 percent in MP and Maharashtra to less than 5 percent (for all three levels) in HP,

Manipur, Odisha, Rajasthan, Uttarakhand, and UP. See Babu (2009) and Center for Policy Research (2014).

58. Esman and Uphoff (1984) make the general case for local organizations in rural and urban development. I have more to say on the question of *panchayats* and other local organizations in Chapter 7, which is centrally concerned with issues of governance. For supporting viewpoints on the limited efficacy of *panchayats* in the current setup, see, for instance, Bardhan and Mookherjee (2006) and Manor (2010). For contrary viewpoints, see Bussell (n.d.) and Kruks-Wisner (2015).

59. See, for instance, Chandrasekhar and Ghosh (2002); Dougherty (2008); Joshi (2010); Kannan and Raveendran (2009); and NCEUS (2007, 2009).

60. See Milly (1999); Findlay and Wellisz (1993); Page (1994); and Whang (1981). In South Korea, the Samuel Undong program, which made up fully half of all government investments during the 1970s, helped create physical and communication infrastructure, linking rural residents with the urban centers of growth, and fostering a new spirit of confidence and connectedness.

61. Special Economic Zones (or SEZs) have been located in rural areas, but their effects on the rural population have varied greatly. Some of these zones have had exclusionary effects, shutting out rather than pulling in the rural masses. See Levien (2015).

62. See Brulhart and Sbergami (2009); Ezcurra and Rodriguez-Pose (2013); and Kanbur and Venables (2007) for an overview of these trends in developing countries. Among commentaries that review how these trends have operated in India, see Binswanger-Mkhize (2013); Chandrasekhar and Ghosh (2002); Dev and Ravi (2007); Dubey, Gangopadhyay, and Wadhwa (2001); Kotwal et al. (2011); Kundu and Sarangi (2007); Sarkar and Mehta (2010); Topalova (2008); Vaidyanathan (2014); Vakulabharanam (2010); Weisskopf (2011); World Bank (2011a); and Zacharias and Vakulabharanam (2011). "The urban elite, constituting about 10 percent of the total population in the country, has monopolized almost the entire relative gains," conclude Vakulabharanam and Motiram (2012: 47).

63. Florida (2008: 19). Studies that have uncovered similar trends in India include Dubey, Gangopadhyay, and Wadhwa (2001); Kundu and Sarangi (2007); and World Bank (2011a).

64. The contemporary discussion of metropolitan bias builds on earlier expositions of urban bias, for instance, by Bates (1981) and Lipton (1977).

65. See, for instance, a story in the *New York Times* (August 8, 2016), which highlights the role of rural-urban differences in explaining this country's ongoing political crisis. www.nytimes.com/2016/08/09/world/asia/thailand-junta-constitution-opposition.html. Accessed on September 15, 2016.

Chapter 3 Up and Down in the City

1. See Ferré, Ferreira, and Lanjouw (2012); Florida (2008); Moretti (2012); Porter (2000); and Sassen (2001). Works that have uncovered a similar trend in India include Dubey, Gangopadhyay, and Wadhwa (2001); Kundu and Sarangi (2007); and World Bank (2011a).

2. See, for instance, Frankenhoff (1967); Glaeser (2011); and World Bank (2009).

3. Some projections show that cities will grow to accommodate more than half of the country's population by mid-century. That's a huge change, implying a doubling of the absolute size of the urban population. Instead of waiting for the inevitable bulge, proponents contend that the country must invest aggressively in developing its cities. A high-level committee constituted by the Indian government observed, for instance, that cities "are the reservoirs of skills, capital and knowledge. They are the centers of innovation and creativity. They are the generators of resources for national and state exchequers" (GOI, 2011). See also the report of the McKinsey Global Institute, which projects the urban population to grow to 590 million by 2030 (McKinsey Global Institute, 2010). Other commentaries illuminating such contentions include Gooptu (2011) and World Bank (2006, 2011a).

4. In contrast, the population of France increased over the same period (between 1951 and 2001) from 42 to 60 million and that of England increased from 39 to 53 million.

5. See Tumbe (2012); Chopra (2014). See also De Haan (2002); Gardner and Osella (2004); and Alpa Shah (2006).

6. A number of grassroots studies attest to the same trend. See, for instance, De Haan (2002); De Haan and Rogaly (2002); Deshingkar and Start (2003); Khandelwal and Gilbert (2007); Mosse et al. (2002); Paris et al. (2005); Rodgers and Rodgers (2011); Rogaly et al. (2002); Sah and Shah (2005); and Shah (2014).

7. These figures, for 2010, were obtained from the World Bank website, http://data.worldbank.org/indicator/SP.URB.TOTL.IN.ZS.

8. It is difficult to measure precisely the number of short-term rural-to-urban migrants in any given year. But scholars agree widely that the definition adopted by the Census of India has led to a skewed representation of internal migrants (because it includes all women who moved to their husband's place of residence after marriage) as well as a huge underestimation of their likely numbers (because short-term migrants tend to be missed, being enumerated in their "usual" place of residence, i.e., at the family home in the village). According to the national census of 2011, 22 percent of urban residents were internal migrants, in the sense that they were not born in or had not previously lived in the city where they currently live but have moved to make

this place their present residence. This number is almost certainly an underestimate, however, because of the reasons recounted above. The National Sample Survey Organization (NSSO), particularly in its 55th and 64th rounds, used a different definition and provided a different estimate of these numbers. It regarded as short-term migrants all individuals who stayed away from their usual place of residence for a period of 1 month or more but less than 6 months during the previous 365 days (for employment or in search of employment). By missing out on shorter- and longer-duration migrants and because of the methods employed to identify migrants, this effort, too, has produced an underestimate, even though it recorded that in 2008 as many as 35 percent of urban residents were internal migrants. Independent estimates have recorded a higher number. See, for instance, Singh, D. P. (2009); Srivastava (2011); Bhagat (2014); Breman (2013); and Deshingkar and Akhter (2009).

9. As defined by one analyst, "the informal sector consists of economic units that produce goods and services legally, but engage in operations that are not registered or regulated by fiscal, labor, health and tax laws. Thus the primary difference between informal and formal workers is that the latter are protected and regulated under state law while the former are not" (Agarwala, 2008: 376). Informal workers are of different kinds, including employees in informal enterprises; informal employees in formal enterprises; the self-employed; and contractors who work for formal or informal enterprises through subcontractors. These are the types of workers whose numbers have increased the most. See, for instance, Dasgupta (2003); Joshi (2010); Kapoor (2014); NCEUS (2007, 2009); Sanyal and Bhattacharya (2009); and Unni and Raveendran (2007).

10. A number of examples attest to such a view, including the notorious one-way flyover on the way to the international airport in New Delhi (see Sharma, 2015); knee-jerk responses to outbreaks to health epidemics (Amrith, 2009; and Dasgupta, 2005); and the manner in which slum housing has been built and allocated (Kamath, 2012).

11. A term coined by Jan Breman (2003).

12. A survey undertaken between 2009 and 2011 with a sample frame spanning 20 of the country's 28 states found that 16 percent of women migrants and 18 percent of men were medium-term migrants (who had come to the city for a period of up to a few years); 20 percent of migrating women and 23 percent of migrating men were circular migrants (who lived in the city for more than four months but less than one year); 9 percent of both men and women migrants were short-term seasonal migrants (spending the major part of the working year in the village); while 6 percent of the women and 7% of the men were day migrants. The authors of the survey concluded that "Only 42% of women migrants and 36% of males are long-term migrants; in other

words, 58% of female labour migration and even more of male labour migration appears to be of a temporary nature" (Mazumdar, Neetha, and Agnihotri 2013: 56).

13. On this notion of rural cosmopolitanism, see Gidwani and Sivaramakrishnan (2004). Others have characterized internal migrants as "in-between" people, suggesting three senses in which the term is applicable: the typical internal migrant is in between rural and urban, rich and poor, children and the aged. See Young and Jeffrey (2012).

14. For descriptions of circumstances faced by migrant laborers, their risky journeys to and fro, the exploitative roles of labor contractors and other middlemen, and the very limited prospects for social mobility, see, for instance, Breman (2003); Joshi and Khandelwal (2009); Sundari (2005); Vijay (2005); Majumdar (2015); Guerrin, Venkatasubramaniam, and Kumar (2015); and Picherit (2014).

15. Although plastic sheets are available in multiple colors, those colored blue are most commonly available in some cities. In other cities, including Delhi and Patna, I have come across similar settlements covered with gray or black plastic sheets (or with straw roofs). But the distinctive blue pattern found, for instance, in Bengaluru and Mumbai makes it easy and compelling to identify such settlements. To see four such blue-polygon slums for yourself, enter the following geo-coordinates into Google Earth or Google Maps (which has a satellite view option). It will drop a pin right in the middle of four clearly visible blue polygons, within each of which one can clearly see the small, densely packed blue-tented houses. (Be careful, though: some of these settlements may have disappeared; there is a tendency for blue polygons to be transitory.)

Nallurhalli	12°58'12.18"N, 77°44'15.36"E
Pramod Nagar/Layout	12°55'59.78"N, 77°31'36.98"E
Thobarahalli	12°57'12.42"N, 77°43'6.72"E
Uttarahalli lake	12°54'25.76"N, 77°32'20.93"E

16. Examinations of satellite images coupled by on-the-ground verification in other cities, including Patna and Jaipur, also show how this class of urban settlements has grown rapidly, both in the center of the city and its periphery.

17. A survey undertaken in Bengaluru in 2014 found that blue-polygon men earned a little under 300 rupees a day, with women earning less, closer to 200 rupees, even when undertaking the same kind of employment.

18. A general pattern we observed, which other slum studies also show, is that the poorer a settlement, the greater tends to be the proportion of SC and ST residents. In eight of the eighteen blue-polygon slums that we studied intensively, SCs constituted 100 percent of the residents.

19. For a photo narrative about one blue-polygon settlement and vignettes about some of its residents, see the website http://urbanindiastories.com/projects/namma-mane-our-home-srinivasa-colony/. A more complete analysis is provided in Krishna, Sriram, and Prakash (2014).

20. In addition, as Mander (2012: 81–2) points out, these rural poor do not have access to the kinds of community supports and environmental resources (such as forage and especially firewood) that many rural poor are able to garner without expending money.

21. In blue polygon slums of Bengaluru, I found that more than three-quarters (77 percent) of all household members aged 14 years or older had no formal education. More young people of school-going ages were out of school than were attending schools regularly (Krishna, Sriram, and Prakash, 2014). Reed (2014) documents the educational failures of children left behind in villages by migrants.

22. See also Breman (1996, 2013); Jeffrey, Jeffery, and Jeffery (2004); and Jeffrey (2010).

23. For these and related points about the segment of the Indian population that migrates internally becoming blue-polygon residents, see, for instance, Korra (2011); Subbaraman et al. (2012); Geetha and Swaminathan (1996); Khasnabis and Chatterjee (2007); and Sundar and Sharma (2002).

24. Svati Shah (2014: 33), whose study of a blue-polygon slum and of the lives of its inhabitants, both in the city (Mumbai) and in the native village, paints these circumstances in vivid detail, observes how "Mumbai was part of a circular itinerary, in which people came and went seasonally. And yet, while living conditions were contingent on the duration that people had been living in the city, all lived in conditions of precarity with respect to basic municipal services, including access to water, stable housing, and steady income. This precarity informed negotiations for economic survival that included sexual commerce." Shah found a number of blue-polygon women, especially single heads of households, soliciting for sex work at labor *nakas*. Similar conclusions have been reported as well by Subbaraman et al. (2012) for Chennai; Nijman (2006) for Mumbai; and Roy, Hulme, and Jahan (2013) for Dhaka.

25. The national census of 2001 for the first time separately assessed the slum population in a few cities of India, and the census of 2011 extended this task to other cities. For these purposes, slums were defined to constitute three separate categories: "(i) All areas in a town or city notified as 'Slum' by a state or local government;(ii) All areas recognized as 'Slum' by a state or local government, which may have not been formally notified; (iii) 'A compact area of at least 300 population or about 60–70 households of poorly built congested tenements, in unhygienic environment usually with inadequate infrastructure and lacking in proper sanitary and drinking water facilities.'"

While slums of Categories (i) and (ii) exist on official records, Category (iii) slums – neither notified nor recognized – are harder to pin down and enumerate. Census estimates of both 2001 and 2011 have largely missed these types of settlements, as evidenced by the fact that, in 2011, an unbelievably larger share (81 percent) of recorded slum dwellings had bathrooms; 93 percent were of permanent (*pukka*) or semipermanent construction; 74 percent had piped water connections; 53 percent of slum residents had bank accounts; and 51 percent used LPG for cooking. Many states reported no slums at all, which is also unrealistic. See Bhan and Jana (2013) and GOI (2010b).

Different estimates of the slum population are provided by NSSO because, instead of the Census' threshold number of 60–70 households, it uses a different definition of the third category, counting as slums even such settlements that have a minimum of 20 households (NSSO 2003, 2009). Further, NSSO has changed its definition several times over the previous decades, revising the minimum number from 50 to 25 to the current definition of 20 households. The estimates provided by Census and NSSO consequently differ, but both agencies' statistics are underestimates. See http:// mospi.nic.in/Mospi_New/upload/concepts_golden.pdf; http:// indiasanitationportal.org/18551. Accessed on March 14, 2016.

26. "State-sponsored slum policies," as Appadurai (2002: 21) points out, "have an abstract slum population as their target, and no knowledge of its concrete, human components."

27. Some exceptionally fine accounts of life in the lowest layers of big-city society include Boo (2012); Faleiro (2012); Mehta (2005); Roberts (2005); and Sethi (2013). Among independent scholars' studies, see, for instance, Harriss (2006), and Mitra (2006) for Delhi; Weinstein (2014) for Mumbai; Benjamin (2000), Benjamin and Bhuvaneswari (2001), Heitzman (2004), Nair (2005); and Schenk (2001) for Bengaluru; Khasnabis and Chatterjee (2007) for Kolkata; Mahadevia (2010) and Unni and Rani (2007) for Ahmedabad; and Amis and Kumar (2000) for Vishakhapatnam.

28. With the help of a methodology that combines satellite image analysis with detailed household surveys, M. S. Sriram, Erik Wibbels, and I, working together with a team of students, plotted the slums of Bengaluru, discerning five different categories, examples of which can be seen at the website: www .urbanindiastories.com. Emily Rains helped us extend these inquiries into Jaipur and Patna. Initial results are provided by Krishna, Rains and Wibbels (2016).

29. A total of 33,510 slums were identified by official data collecting agencies, of which 41% were notified and 59% were non-notified. See http://pib.nic.in/ newsite/PrintRelease.aspx?relid=102108 (accessed on April 6, 2016). The number of non-notified slums is clearly underestimated here, because lower-category slums, especially blue-polygon ones, have been missed.

30. De Soto (2000) shows the benefits that can be gained by investing in a campaign of giving titles to all property. Such a policy is hard to implement, however, without giving rise to a huge amount of speculation and land-grabbing, in places where the habitation record is patchy and outdated.

31. The year 2000 is as far back as publicly available Google Earth images enable comparisons. I worked together with a group of students, more technologically capable than I, to undertake these image comparisons. I thank, especially, Grady Lenkin and Saumya Jain. These investigations have continued, considering an expanding sample of slum settlements. The full results were not available at the time of writing but are being updated regularly at the website: www.urbanindiastories.com.

32. See, for instance, Bapat (2009); Kit, Lüdeke, and Reckien (2013); and Mitra (2006). For a larger perspective, see Fox (2014).

33. Krishna (2013a) presents this evidence.

34. For instance, a study of slum households in Mumbai found that "more than four-fifths had been staying in these slums for over 10 years…41 percent were daily workers, most employed as cleaners of roads and sweepers, and over one-third were in service, mostly as maids, helpers and drivers" (Bhatia and Chatterjee, 2010: 24). Following slum households over the period 1973–1992, Ramachandran and Subramanian (2001: 72) similarly found how, despite the passage of nearly 20 years, "the nature of employment of the slum population did not appear to have undergone any positive change." Mitra (2010: 1388), studying four Indian cities – Jaipur, Ludhiana, Mathura, and Ujjain – found that the probability of experiencing upward mobility is not significantly higher among longer-duration migrants. More poignantly, Katherine Boo (2009: 27) describes the circumstances of one individual in a Mumbai slum who was able to make greater economic progress than other slum children: "In Gautam Nagar, there was a single boy who could reasonably pass as a scholar. His name was Prakash…now cramming for a board exam that might secure him a scholarship to management school…But Prakash's father had gone to college, too…Relative to other boys in Gautam Nagar, he was privileged." The circumstances of the small minority who are able to make it big are usually quite special, as we will see later (in Chapter 5).

35. Bapat (2009: 19).

36. Sarkar and Mehta (2010: 47).

37. See Goldberg and Pavcnik (2007) for the general case. For India, see Azam (2012); Chamarbagwala (2006); Vasudeva Dutta (2006); Kijima (2006); Mohanty (2006); and Pieters (2010).

38. Correspondingly, the share of agriculture fell from 51 percent (in 1951) to a mere 14 percent (in 2011). The share of manufacturing and mining, which had increased between 1951 and 1981, a result of centrally planned

industrialization, remained nearly unchanged over the next 30-year period. For these sectoral shares, see the Government of India website https://data .gov.in/catalog/gdp-india-and-major-sectors-economy-share-each-sector-gdp-and-growth-rate-gdp-and-other#web_catalog_tabs_block_10.

39. See NCEUS (2007, 2009).

40. See Gothoskar (2013); Sunita Kumar (2015); Sharma and Kunduri (2015); and Wadhawan (2013). By providing domestic servants, street vendors, and construction laborers with cheap housing options, slums tend to subsidize the lifestyles of people in higher social layers, "lubricating and driving urban growth and also keep it manageable and relatively inexpensive" (Mukhopadhyay 2006: 879).

41. Author calculations from employment data provided by NSSO surveys of 1993–94 and 2004–5. These estimates are likely to understate the true numbers of such low-paid workers, because of the large incidence of informality. (In counterpoint, the number of "cultivators," i.e., agriculturists, went up from 88 to 107 million.)

42. See, for instance, Dougherty (2008); NCEUS (2007, 2009); Pieters (2010); Joshi (2010).

43. "Among nearly 22 million manufacturing sector workers, 32 percent are homeworkers," NCEUS (2007: 58). See also Vasudeva Dutta (2006); Mazumdar and Sarkar (2009); Sanyal and Bhattacharya (2009); Kannan and Raveendran (2009); and Unni and Raveendran (2007).

44. Brynjolfsson and McAfee (2014: 135). The same point is made by other analysts of technology trends. See, for instance, Carr (2014). A report in the *Economist* notes how the spread of technology globally "has created a growing reservoir of less-skilled labor while simultaneously expanding the range of tasks that can be automated" ("The privileged few: To those that have shall be given," *Economist*, October 4, 2014). These trends will deepen, a report from the Boston Consulting Group predicts, and countries with a greater number of robotic programmers and high-tech infrastructure will become more attractive to manufacturers than other countries with large reserves of cheaper but less-skilled and less-educated labor (www .bcgperspectives.com/content/articles/business_unit_strategy_innovation_ rise_of_robotics/). Another article in the *Economist*, referring to newly established manufacturing operations in India, notes how "most of the value added is in a few big sophisticated firms that prefer using machines to humans... What manufacturing FDI [foreign direct investment] India does attract tends to be high-end – for instance, Volkswagen has a smart €570 million plant full of robots" ("Wasting Time," *Economist*, May 11, 2013).

45. On this question of employability, related to the generally poor quality of college education in much of India, see Aspiring Minds (2016); and Farrell et al. (2005) – cited by Kotwal, Ramaswami, and Wadhwa (2011).

46. In Chapter 5, which deals in more detail with matters related to education, I expand on this point, advancing an explanation.

47. See Gruber and Kosack (2014); and Kosack (2012, 2014). See also Kochhar et al. (2006), who count India's "lopsided" educational investments among the policy legacies holding back faster and more equitable growth in this country.

48. See Milly (1999); Kohli (2004).

49. For a classic exposition of this point, see Keynes (1936). For a lucid contemporary discussion, see Atkinson (2015).

50. See, for instance, Alesina and Glaeser (2004); Benabou and Tirole (2006); and Gilens (2000).

51. Harris-White (2003: 34).

52. For instance, the historian Douglas Haynes (2012) has documented how business practices in parts of western India were consecutively adjusted to take account of changing labor laws and enforcement regimes, ending up with large-scale informalization of labor.

53. See, for instance, Stiglitz (2013).

54. See, for instance, Atkinson (2015); Birdsall (2006); Esping-Anderson (1990); and Rueda, Wibbels, and Altamarino (n.d.).

55. Barnes, Das, and Pratap (2015) show how the provisions of the Contract Labor (Abolition and Regulation) Act 1970 have been progressively weakened, both by implementation failures and by recent legislative changes. Also see Kapoor (2014); Rajasekhar (2008); and Roychowdhury (2005).

56. Though caste itself was not immutable – people crossed over caste lines regularly – until the caste system was codified in official records by the colonial administration. See Dirks (2001).

57. Gooptu (2001: 4, 14).

58. Young slum dwellers are often brutally beaten by policemen, not out in the open but within the confines of a police station – a practice rendered vividly in all its bestiality and meanness by Katherine Boo (2012). Other careful observers, working with the same substratum of big-city residents, have also recorded similar incidents, for instance, Sethi (2013). Other accounts, in a more traditionally scholarly vein, include Sunita Kumar (2015) and CHRI (2005).

59. More than 70 percent of the nearly 1,500 households in 14 notified slums that I surveyed in Bengaluru possess official papers establishing ownership of the land on which their homes were built. Yet, hardly any among these households was assisted by institutional finance for the purpose of home building or home improvement. Nearly 45 percent of the total amount they spent for these purposes was paid for from out of personal savings, another 21 percent was paid from loans provided by family and friends, and 28 percent was obtained from private moneylenders – making for a total of 94

percent. Less than 6 percent of the total amount paid for home ownership was obtained from institutional sources of any kind (including government agencies, NGOs, employers, and banks). See Krishna (2013).

60. This survey, the *Human Development Profile of India – II*, covering more than 50,000 households, was administered by the Indian National Council for Applied Economic Research (NCAER) in 2004–05.

61. See the illuminating discussion on this point by Auerbach (2016) and by Auerbach and Thachil (2016).

62. Manor (1993: 10). Similarly, Bhatia and Chatterjee (2010) document the financial exclusion of slum dwellers in Mumbai, the financial capital of the nation. Other notable references on the same point include Benjamin (2000), who refers to slum dwellers as people embedded in "local economies," low-cost manufacturing and service operations catering to other low-income residents in a narrow adjoining area.

63. Many Indian cities were designed to have these different parts – a smaller planned part consisting of the civil lines and cantonment areas, and a larger and messier part that grew helter-skelter and was meant to house lesser individuals. "The cantonments and the British residential areas, with spacious roads and grounds . . . privileged with machinery to assure good sanitation conditions . . . were segregated from Indian areas" (Dasgupta 2005: 5160). For similar accounts of divided cities in post-colonial Africa, see Fox (2014) and Njoh (2004).

64. A phenomenon that urban theorist Ananya Roy (2009) refers to as "splintered urbanism."

65. "Key structures of the world economy are necessarily situated in global cities," as the urban sociologist Saskia Sassen (2001: 3) has noted.

66. Diverse examinations have highlighted this aspect. Kanbur and Venables (2007) presents the general case, along with Ferré, Ferreira, and Lanjouw (2012). Fan, Chan-Kang, and Mukherjee (2005); Wang, Piesse and Weaver (2011); and Zhang and Zhang (2003) show such a trend has been operating within China. That a similar situation has developed in areas as diverse and geographically spread out as Eastern Europe, Vietnam, Peru, Latin America, and sub-Saharan Africa is shown, respectively, by Forster, Jesuit, and Smeeding (2005); Jensen and Tarp (2005); Escobal and Torrero (2005); Chomitz, Buys, and Thomas (2005); and Christiaensen, Demery, and Paternostro (2005). Examinations within India show how "states with high urbanization and modern industrialization seem to show a rather poor record in poverty reduction" (Kannan and Raveendran, 2011: 62).

67. As Deshingkar and Farrington (2009: 10) observe, migration to a city "starts from a differentiated situation. The social class of a migrant already predicts for what type of work the migrant has been qualified, equipped, or not, with education/skills and other forms of capital. The outcome of migration leads to further inequality in the sense that the most successful are able to

further improve their economic and social status ... while in the lower echelons of the work hierarchy migration rarely results in structural improvement."

68. One survey concluded that "life in slums might constitute a form of poverty trap for a majority of their residents" (Marx, Stoker, and Suri, 2013: 188). Other overviews have come to similar conclusions (e.g., Fox, 2014; and Mitlin and Satterthwaite, 2012).

69. For the initial case about regionally spread performance hubs see, for instance, Herrigel (1996) and Locke (1995). For the contemporary relationship between global value chains and diverse regional competencies, see Buciuni and Finotto (2016); Gereffi (2012); Pietrobelli and Rabellotti (2011); and World Bank (2009).

70. Particularly if the initial energy invested in this initiative is sustained for at least a couple of decades, and particularly if it permeates the entire administrative machinery (not remaining a gleam in the eye only of top officials), this initiative might deliver the required impacts of making smaller cities more attractive to potential investors. See their mission statement at the website http://smartcities.gov.in/writereaddata/smartcityguidelines.pdf (Accessed on August 18, 2016).

71. Aajeevika Bureau, Babajobs, Janarth, LabourNet, Lokadrushti, PRAYAS Center for Labor Research and Action, and SETU are included among NGOs whose efforts in these areas have been favorably noted. See the website: www.migrationpolicy.org/article/internal-labor-migration-india-raises-integration-challenges-migrants (accessed on April 12, 2016).

72. One measure of how well integrated the different parts of a city government are can be gained by observing how often the roads in your neighborhood get dug up during the course of any given year for repairing or installing water, gas and sewage lines, electricity and internet cables, and so on. Ideally, it shouldn't happen more than once every two or three years, but in practice it's more ad hoc and frustratingly frequent.

73. A technical group constituted by the central government estimated, for instance, "that the total shortage of dwelling units in urban areas in 2007 was 24.71 million, climbing at the rate of 360,000 units per annum, of which 98% pertains to the urban poor" (Ministry of Housing and Urban Poverty Alleviation, Government of India, Strategy Paper, 10th February 2011). Accessed on December 2, 2015, at www.mhupa.gov.in/writereaddata/UploadFile/MHUPA-STRATEGY_PAPER.pdf.

Chapter 4 Preventing Future Poverty

1. See, for instance, Bhagwati and Panagariya (2013); Bhalla (2002); Panagariya (2008); and Virmani (2006).

2. See, especially, Reddy and Pogge (2002) and Wade (2004).

3. In India, these surveys, run every five or ten years by the National Sample Survey Organization, an outfit of the central government, include a list of more than 350 disparate items. Trained investigators go down this list of items – "How much rice did you consume over the last thirty days? In kilograms? In rupees?" How much wheat? How much on salt and potatoes? The list goes on to include thirty-three kinds of vegetables and eighteen types of fruit, along with toddy, country liquor, beer, foreign liquor, marijuana, and airfare. Incomes are not typically used for these assessments, because most poor people do not have fixed or regular incomes, as we will see in the next section. Between 250,000 and 500,000 households are surveyed each time poverty is estimated in India. But India has a vast population of more than 1 billion people. In Uganda, a country of about 40 million people, only 5,000 households are surveyed for the purpose of estimating the extent of poverty in the country.

4. This necessarily short discussion of poverty measurement is shorn of conceptual and statistical nuances, which interested readers can find in other books and articles. See, for instance, Deaton and Kozel (2005); Deaton and Tarozzi (2005); Himanshu and Sen (2014); Krishna (2010); Mehta et al. (2011); Ravallion (2011); Subramanian (2010); and Vakulabharanam and Motiram (2012). For discussions about the official poverty statistics of India, see also Bhalla (2002); Deaton and Drèze (2002); Dev and Ravi (2008); Palmer-Jones and Sen (2001); Saith (2005); Sundaram and Tendulkar (2003a and 2003b); and World Bank (2011a and 2011b).

5. The important discussion on multidimensional poverty measures has provided greater insight into the role played by public goods in making the conditions of poverty better. See, for instance, Alkire and Seth (2015), and the ongoing work of the Oxford Poverty and Human Development Initiative (OPHI). Accessed on August 9, 2016 at www.ophi.org.uk/policy/multidimensional-poverty-index/. See also Deaton and Drèze (2009), a set of findings that began the debate about whether and how nutrition levels have been falling even as the national economy was growing.

6. For a discussion of these and other issues that tend to complicate the tasks of poverty measurement, see, for example, Chaudhuri and Ravallion (1994); Datt and Ravallion (2002); Deaton (2000); Kakwani and Son (2006); Karshenas (2003); Krishna (2010); Lanjouw (1998); Lok-Desallien (1999); Reddy (2008); Schelzig (2001); and Wade (2004).

7. Lanjouw (1998: 4).

8. For instance, when the period of recall was changed in surveys – asking about people's consumption expenditures over a period of one week instead of one month – the estimate of India's poverty rate changed a great deal. See Sen and Himanshu (2004) and Visaria (1999). Changing the list of consumption items or their price schedules similarly affects these calculations sharply.

9. Respectively, Himanshu (2006); Dev and Ravi (2008); and Patnaik (2007).

10. See www.merriam-webster.com/dictionary/poverty.

11. See Ravallion (2010). Because many things are cheaper in India than in the United States, particularly food and personal services (think haircuts), the PPP exchange rate is derived by multiplying the official exchange rate by a correction factor, which was 0.3 at the time of writing. In 2016, when the official exchange rate was about 66 rupees to a dollar, a PPP dollar was thus worth about 20 rupees. There are, of course, disputes about which particular goods and services should go into making cost-of-living comparisons across dissimilar countries. See in this regard Reddy and Pogge (2002) and Wade (2004). In 2015, the World Bank changed its poverty lines, in large part because of the availability of new PPP information. Because of price changes in the intervening period, the old $1.25 poverty line was deemed equivalent to $1.90, while the old $2 line was reset at $3.10. See www-wds.worldbank.org/external/default/WDSContentServer/WDSP/IB/2015/10/03/090224b08311e963/1_0/Rendered/PDF/Aoglobalocountooandoinitialoresults.pdf

12. The basis for setting the poverty line in India has been frequently adjusted, a response both to statistical differences about the underlying judgment calls and the thumb rules that were used earlier and to political compulsions. (The lower the poverty line is set, the fewer people will be declared to be living in poverty.) This spate of revisions has led a prominent scholar to comment that "official concern with poverty in India has tended to focus heavily, if not exclusively, on the definition of the poverty line and on estimating poverty incidence and its trends," and not so much on finding more effective mechanisms for its reduction (Vaidyanathan 2001). The most recent official commission at the time of writing – chaired by C. Rangarajan – http://planningcommission.nic.in/reports/genrep/pov_repo707.pdf – introduced yet another set of revisions. See Rangarajan et al. (2014); and Rangarajan and Dev (2015). See also GOI (2009).

13. Kannan and Raveendran (2011). The official commission found 77 percent of the population living in poverty, with these numbers increasing from 732 million in 1994 to 811 million in 2000 to 836 million in 2005 (NCEUS, 2007).

14. Evidence about this lack of connection is provided by, among others, Himanshu and Sen (2014); Kannan and Raveendran (2011); and Krishna and Shariff (2011). Sinha (2005) makes a compelling case for why local and regional factors have acquired additional importance in the post-globalization period in India. More generally, the claim that national growth reduces the national stock of poverty is based on cross-country comparisons – and not on tracking these effects through intermediate links down to the level of individuals. This methodology has been challenged, however, on grounds of

statistical validity, econometric method, and causal logic. See, for instance, Lipton (1997); Reddy and Pogge (2002); Rodrik (2002); Rodrik and Rodríguez (2001); Sachs (2005); Srinivasan (2004); and Wade (2004). A long chain of events links growth at the aggregate national level with poverty reduction at the level of families and individuals, and how these effects operate at each of these links remains mired in uncertainty, because the evidence is missing or controversial.

15. A circular logic can be detected: A belief that aggregate growth is all that matters has led to the development of a methodology of collecting poverty statistics. Because the samples that are constructed are representative of a state or the nation, but not of particular localities or subregions, the data can be analyzed to examine the worth *only* of state-level and of aggregate-level influences.

16. Berner (1997: 170) illuminates the situation in the Philippines. For a wider perspective, see Banerjee and Duflo (2006) as well as Sinha and Lipton (1999).

17. See Chambers (1997) and Chambers, Longhurst, and Pacey (1981). How the individuals affected by risks and fluctuations manage their money flows is analyzed by Collins, Morduch, Rutherford, and Ruthven (2009).

18. In order to deal with such situations, scholars distinguish between "structural" and "stochastic" poverty. The structural poor are those who live below the poverty line through the year. The stochastic poor are on average above the poverty line, but in particular months their incomes and expenditures dip, falling below the poverty threshold. See Carter and May (2001) and Carter and Barrett (2006). A parallel distinction has been drawn between "chronic" and transitory (or temporary) poverty. See Addison, Hulme and Kanbur (2009); Hulme and Shepherd (2003); and CPRC (2005).

19. Official agencies measure poverty as a stock. By looking at households' consumption expenses during a particular week or month, they derive an estimate of the total number in poverty. Flows of poverty are not separately examined, which results in hiding from view the millions who fluctuate in and out of poverty (and the millions of others who fall into chronic poverty).

20. See Gaiha and Deolalikar (1993); Gaiha and Imai (2004); Shah and Sah (2003); and Singh and Binswanger (1993). The reported numbers remained large even where the official poverty line was employed for the calculation.

21. Higher poverty rates continue to prevail among SCs and STs. In terms of various social indicators, SCs are assessed to be 10 years behind trends in the rest of the population, and STs are assessed to be another 10 years behind SCs (World Bank, 2011a: 227). Female-headed households are also disproportionately poverty stricken. In investigations undertaken in Gujarat villages, for instance, Krishna et al. (2005) found more than 90 percent of such households in poverty. A nuanced analysis of the interplay of these factors is provided by Iyer, Sen, and George (2007).

22. For some notable examples, see Kapur, Babu, and Prasad (2014).

23. Studies of poverty flows undertaken in India include Attwood (1979); Dercon, Krishnan, and Krutikova (2013); Guerin, D'Espallier, and Venkatasubramaniam (2012); Jodha (1988); Krishna and Lecy (2008); Mehta and Shah (2003); Shah and Sah (2003); Walker and Ryan (1990); and the ones referred to in Table 4.1 below. Studies of poverty dynamics undertaken in other countries include Aliber (2003); Baulch (2012); Dercon (2005); Deininger and Okidi (2003); Haddad and Ahmed (2003); Krishna (2010); and Sen (2003).

24. The rows of this table, reading from top to bottom, relate respectively to the following studies: Krishna (2004); Krishna et al. (2005); Krishna (2006); Hatlebakk (2014); Bhide and Mehta (2003); Dhamija and Bhide (2009); and Krishna and Shariff (2011).

25. See, respectively, Bhide and Mehta (2003); Dhamija and Bhide (2009); and Krishna and Shariff (2011).

26. Examining trends in two consecutive time periods helped establish these rates of rebound – of people who fell into poverty in the first time period, only to bounce back during the second time period. See Krishna (2010).

27. Japan and South Korea in addition to the Scandinavian countries are examples among richer nations. Cuba, Costa Rica, and Colombia, not known for being rich countries, have also adopted poverty-prevention and poverty-reduction measures in parallel, and these countries also have relatively low rates of poverty.

28. For an accounting of these results in rural Rajasthan, Andhra Pradesh, and Gujarat see, respectively, Krishna (2004, 2006) and Krishna et al. (2005). Krishna (2013) finds similar trends operating in urban locations. Subsequent studies undertaken in different locations have helped uphold the primacy of ill health and high costs of medical treatment. See Narayan, Pritchett, and Kapoor (2009); and Kumar (2015).

29. See Krishna (2004, 2007a) and Krishna et al. (2004, 2005). Regression analyses support the same findings (Krishna, 2006). A World Bank study uncovered similar results (Narayan, Pritchett, and Kapoor, 2009). More broadly, across a swath of countries, an earlier focus on the so-called culture of poverty, emphasized originally in the US context, has been largely discredited.

30. See Krishna (2010).

31. See Garg and Karan (2005); Gupta and Mitra (2004); and World Bank (2011b).

32. See, for example, Baru et al. (2010); Das et al. (2012); Das Gupta (2005); Das Gupta and Muraleedharan (2014); Duggal (2005); Hammer, Aiyar, and Samji (2006, 2007); Joe (2014); Subramanian et al. (2006); and World Bank (2006). According to a report in the *Times of India* on March 6, 2013, India

is in the "health care hall of shame," having among the highest burden of diseases and injuries and among the lowest public expenditures on health care. Health indicators in fast-growing states are no better than in poorer and slower-growing parts of the country. Mahadevia (2000: 3200–3) observes, for instance, that "In spite of rapid economic growth . . . the diseases of poverty remain widespread . . . Despite its relatively richer status, the state of Gujarat spends less on healthcare than the average for other Indian states . . . the urban-rural difference is very high in Gujarat . . . dependence on private healthcare is quite high, even among the lower expenditure classes and in rural areas."

33. Whitehead, Dahlgren, and Evans (2001: 833). See also Gupta and Mitra (2004).

34. See the related discussion in Chapter 3. My investigations in rural Gujarat showed that less than one third of all households who escaped poverty were able to secure formal employment. A very large part of this number was accounted for by a one-time mass recruitment of school teachers (Krishna et al., 2005). Industrial growth in Andhra Pradesh has also not resulted in making formal jobs a viable pathway out of poverty for all but a small number of individuals. The 12 villages that I studied in Nalgonda district of this state are located close to a cluster of privately owned cement plants. But less than 10 percent of all households who escaped poverty in any of these villages were benefited by a formal job in any of these undertakings. Those local residents who did find work in the cement industry were most often hired by intermediaries and contractors (and not directly by the cement factories), and they were paid, for years on end, on a day-to-day basis, with no benefits and no security of tenure (Krishna, 2006). It's worth noting, too, that the kinds of precarious and low-paid jobs that poorer individuals coming into cities tend to get are by no means easy to enter. Not everyone can come to a city and immediately acquire such a position. An uncle, a cousin, a fellow villager, or some other preexisting connection usually facilitates the initial entry, providing an introduction to likely employers and vouching for the bona fides of the new entrant. See, for instance, Dhillon, Iversen, and Torsvik (2014); and Munshi and Rosenzweig (2006).

35. On this point, see, for instance, Dev and Ravi (2007); Krishna and Shariff (2011); Krishna and Bajpai (2011); and Singh, Bhandari, Chen, and Khare (2003).

36. Some among India's most noted development programs were introduced initially by state governments. MGNREGA, the employment guarantee program, was tried and tested first in Maharashtra; important parts of National Rural Health Mission were scaled up from programs of the Gujarat government; the National Rural Livelihoods Mission traces its origins to an

earlier program in Andhra Pradesh; and the older IRDP programs had their genesis in Rajasthan.

37. For a more complete description of these and other national programs, see Asian Development Bank (2012) and World Bank (2011b). Some programs implemented by particular states are also noteworthy. We look at some examples in Chapter 7.

38. Several studies have found that these errors and the resulting leakages can be very large. See, for instance, Besley, Pande, and Rao (2012); Khera (2011); Panda (2015); and Saxena (2009). Jalan and Murgai (2008) calculate that between 30 and 75 percent of poor households in different states have been so misclassified.

39. This is the approach taken, for example, by the giant Bangladeshi NGO, BRAC, in its much acclaimed and critically evaluated program, "Challenging the Frontiers of Rural Poverty: Targeting the Ultra-Poor," better known by its acronym, CFPR/TUP.

40. MNREGA promises up to 100 days of paid employment per household per year. In practice, participating households worked for an average of 43 days during financial year 2011–12, the latest one for which confirmed figures were available at the time of writing. The total amount paid on wages during this year was Rs. 243 billion, against a total of 2,188 million person-days worked, making for an average daily wage rate of Rs. 111. The average MNREGA-employed household was thus paid a total of Rs. 4,773 during the year (43 days × Rs. 111/day). Dividing this amount among five members of the average household, and dividing further by 365 days, results in an incremental daily amount of Rs. 2.60 per person per day – a sum that is hardly substantial. (The figures were obtained from the official program website: http://nrega.nic.in/netnrega/writereaddata/Circulars/Report_People_Eng_jan_2014.pdf) See also, Desai, Vashishtha, and Joshi. (2015) and Ravallion (2016). The indirect benefits of MNREGA can be substantial, including making the statutory minimum wage less of a fiction and more of a reality, and by reducing the gender gap in wage payments.

41. The jury is out on the question of whether the assets built with MNREGA funds have a lasting utility. On the one hand, there is widespread anecdotal evidence that these assets are mostly of indifferent quality on account of factors including poor project selection; an erosion of work ethic (because laborers have come to realize they will be paid regardless of how hard they work); inadequate numbers of supervisory staff; and an overweening focus on employment generation, often at the expense of project quality. See, for instance, Chopra (2014); Murgai, Ravallion, and Van de Walle (2015); and Zimmerman (2013). Journalist Edward Luce (2006: 202) has also noted how the program "promises no investment in upgrading the skills of the people it

is designed to help." Engineers with whom I spoke in different states spoke of how these reasons have come to be common in practice. A contrary view is represented by Narayanan (2016).

42. Few households, less than 10 percent in any of the rural or urban regions I studied, had received any such programmatic assistance, and few among them succeeded in escaping poverty. It is possible that people are more willing to speak glowingly of their own roles, and they will minimize the role played by outside assistance, but most households that escaped poverty had, in fact, received no direct government assistance, and indirect forms of assistance – such as electricity, water supply, roads, and schools – were available as well to other households, who remained persistently poor or became poor. This result, which I reported from my first study, in Rajasthan, India (Krishna, 2003a, 2004), I found to be valid as well in the other regions (see Krishna, 2006, and Krishna et al., 2005). Subsequently, a World Bank team extended this finding to other regions in India (Narayan, Pritchett, and Kapoor, 2009). Not coincidentally, an evaluation by the Asian Development Bank concluded that India's antipoverty measures are more in the nature of isolated "schemes rather than long-term strategic programs" (ADB, 2012: 39).

43. A PPP dollar equated to roughly 20 rupees at the time of writing. See the earlier discussion and the references listed therein for a discussion of PPP calculations.

44. Economists speak of the poverty-reducing elasticity of economic growth: by how many percentage points does poverty get cut as a result of a 1 percent increase in the growth rate? This elasticity varies across time and between countries. Those who have measured this elasticity find that it is lower in India compared to other countries, including China and Brazil, that have followed a different strategy of economic development. See Ravallion (2011); also Kotwal et al. (2011) and World Bank (2011a). The connection between growth, urbanization, and poverty reduction has also become weaker. "States with high urbanization and modern industrialization seem to show a rather poor record in poverty reduction" (Kannan and Raveendran, 2011: 62).

45. See EQUITAP (2005) and www.who.int/whr/2000/en. Also see Reid (2009) for a comparison among the health systems of richer countries, which comes to a similar conclusion.

46. See Das Gupta and Muraleedharan (2014); Gupta and Chowdhury (2014); and Rao and Choudhury (2012). Amrith (2009) provides a historical analysis, rooted in colonialism, intended to explain the continuing low priority given in public expenditures to preventive health care.

47. A World Bank team attributes the slide in public-sector health care to widespread governance failures, including inadequate competence of staff; inadequate effort by the providers; discourteous behavior; and bribes and

illegal payments (Hammer, Aiyar, and Samji, 2006, 2007). Das et al. (2012) present startling evidence on the points about inadequate competence and lackadaisical effort on the parts of public health care providers – outcomes they found to be much more pronounced in public rather than private health care settings.

48. See Baru et al. (2010); Dilip and Duggal (2002); Drèze and Sen (2013); Gupta and Mitra (2004); Hammer, Aiyar, and Samji (2006); Joe (2014); and Sen, Iyer, and George (2002).

49. Rights-based initiatives, such as the Right to Education, Right to Health, and the Right to Information, have been advocated, and some have been brought into being as a means for empowering ordinary people, especially poorer ones. But even once these rights have been enacted, getting them realized requires information provision and the scaffolding of supportive organizations at the local level; otherwise, the rights might, like other pro-poor legislation, remain largely on the record. See Joshi (2009).

50. Such methods have been developed and are freely available. One such method, the Stages-of-Progress, which I have helped develop, can be freely downloaded from the website: https://sites.duke.edu/krishna/poverty/stages-of-progress/. Krishna (2010) details how this method has been used to good effect by NGOs, donor agencies, and academics and recommends a network of strategically located poverty-monitoring stations, which can help keep track of local threats and opportunities on a regular basis. Recent technological developments suggest other alternatives for tracking poverty in real time amid diverse locations. See, for instance, Blumenstock, Cadamuro, and On (2015); and Jean et al. (2016).

51. Appadurai (2002: 28), whose description of the lives of urban poor in Mumbai is revealing of the precariousness of existence.

Chapter 5   A Deep Pool of Talent

1. Among studies undertaken in rural areas, see, for instance, Datta et al. (2014); Djurfeldt et al. (2008); Reddy and Swaminathan (2014); and Wadley (1994). Urban studies that have produced parallel findings include Bapat (2009); Bhatia and Chatterjee (2010); Dewit (2001); Mitra (2010); Mukhopadhyay (2006); and Ramachandran and Subramanian (2001).

2. See Brunori, Ferreira, and Peragine (2013).

3. Clark (2014) deployed an innovative method, using data on surnames as a means of tracking these father–son connections. He studied three particular occupations in the case of India – physicians (and medical students), judges, and police sergeants, using data largely drawn from Bengal.

4. See, for instance, Motiram and Singh (2012); Kumar et al. (2002a and 2002b); Majumder (2010); and Reddy (2015).

5. Schoolteachers employed in regular positions in the government sector can earn up to 7 or 8 times as much as teachers in private schools, whose positions are also less secure, being mostly informal.

6. I have, though, interviewed such children wherever I have met them – in the homes of friends and colleagues, at workshops, and so on – and invariably, their answers have been qualitatively different.

7. Esping-Andersen (2005: 149). See also Bjorklund, Eriksson, and Jantii (2010).

8. See, for instance, Holden (2006) and Diamond (2000).

9. Jawaharlal Nehru, Letter to Chief Ministers, June 27, 1961, cited in Shourie (2006: x).

10. For data on number of patents filed by country and trends over time, see http://data.worldbank.org/indicator/IP.PAT.RESD. For the number of research papers, see http://academia.stackexchange.com/questions/18767/ research-publications-per-capita. For new businesses registered, see http:// data.worldbank.org/indicator/IC.BUS.NREG. All of these numbers have been divided by the concerned country's population as given for the relevant year by the World Bank.

11. For instance, it could be said that India does not have a sports culture, that most parents do not encourage children to take up a sport as a career, or that learning by rote, as practiced in India, does not encourage research, or that new businesses are hindered by low risk-taking abilities. There is, however, hardly any evidence in support of any of these assertions, nor does any of them travel across domains to explain widespread poor performance.

12. Nilekani (2008: 22–3), a co-founder of Infosys, a leading player in the global software industry.

13. See, for instance, Azam and Bhatt (2012); Desai and Kulkarni (2008); Gang, Sen, and Yun (2012); Hnatkovska, Lahiri, and Paul (2013); and Jalan and Murgai (2008).

14. Gladwell (2008).

15. A rush for admission to engineering colleges has followed the rapid rise of the software industry. Whereas in the early 1980s, there were only about 100 engineering colleges admitting fewer than 25,000 students each year, the number of engineering colleges reached nearly 1,600 by 2010, collectively admitting more than 500,000 students each year. Similarly, in the years after economic liberalization, "enrolling in an MBA program, particularly at an elite school, has become the equivalent of taking an elevator to the executive suite" (Bolshaw, L. "Push to Help Women find the Keys to the C-suite." *Financial Times*, November 21, 2011. Retrieved from www.ft.com/cms/s/2/ 23b91ca8-0ee0-11e1-b585-00144feabdco.html#axzz1fAbUCUcd). More than 100,000 students now start MBA programs each year, to cater to whom more than 100 new business schools have been established annually since the mid-1990s. Not all of the individuals who enter these institutions will end up

getting high-paying jobs; getting a college degree does not guarantee high-paid employment (Jeffrey et al., 2004; Jeffrey, 2010). But *not* getting a college degree almost certainly ensures against higher upward mobility. Getting into a good college is thus a first or gateway step, a necessary condition.

16. Newspaper reports highlight the highly competitive nature of entrance examinations to government services. See, for instance, http://articles .economictimes.indiatimes.com/2009-03-25/news/28435314_1_civil-services-private-sector-aspirants.

17. I must thank, especially, Varun Aggarwal, Aishwarya Ratan, Ankur Sarin, S. Sadagopan, the Director and faculty of the Lal Bahadur Shastri National Academy of Administration, Mussoorie, and the directors of two state academies for facilitating these interviews.

18. These assignments into quality tiers were made after employing a number of criteria, including educational qualifications of faculty, employment prospects of graduates, students' average test scores, and the rankings provided by popular publications. See Krishna (2013b, 2014) for the full set of results.

19. Krishna (2014) presents these results, finding that in addition to Class 10 board examination scores, other factors, examined later, also matter.

20. See, for instance, Fuller and Narasimhan (2006, 2007); Krishna and Brihmadesam (2006); and Upadhya (2007).

21. Subroto Bagchi (2013) selected more than fifty new entrepreneurs to profile in his book and TV show, covering a range of activities and locations. Only two among these fifty-plus entrepreneurs, just 4 percent, were from a rural area. Bagchi expressed surprise when I made this fact known to him, underlining once again the care his team had taken in selecting these entrepreneurs.

22. The full report of the Sachar committee can be downloaded from http:// minorityaffairs.gov.in/sachar (accessed on April 10, 2016). See also Jamil (2014), an insightful analysis of how such exclusion operates in practice.

23. In 1975, women constituted an infinitesimally small proportion (0.68 percent) of engineering graduates. This proportion has risen over the years, but it was still only 8.74 percent in 1988 (Parikh and Sukhatme, 2004). The higher civil services have also traditionally been a male preserve. Among all IAS officials serving at the beginning of 1985, no more than 8 percent were women. (See the report titled "Social Background of Officers in the Indian Administrative Service," by Santosh Goyal, accessed on May 3, 2013, at http://isidev.nic.in/pdf/santosh1.pdf.) The greater entry in recent years by women into the professions is a wider phenomenon, picked up as well by other studies. See, for instance, Patel and Parmentier (2005) and Kelkar et al. (2002). A newspaper account related to the increasing number of women commercial pilots can be seen at http://articles.economictimes.indiatimes .com/2015-07-06/news/64143205_1_air-india-female-pilot-cent (accessed on August 10, 2015).

24. A similar conclusion is reported, for instance, by Chanana (2007) and Emran and Shilpi (2015).

25. These proportions were computed from the India Human Development Survey, 2004–5.

26. These percentages were also computed for 2005, the time when these young people were in high school. See NCERT (2005).

27. See, for instance, ASER (2014); Desai et al. (2009); Goyal and Pande (2012); and Mukerji and Walton (2013).

28. Badminton champion Saina Nehwal's father, Dr. Harvir Singh, was a former university badminton champion, while her mother, Usha Nehwal, was former state badminton champion of Haryana. Tennis star Leander Paes's father, Vece Paes, was a midfielder in the bronze medal–winning Indian field hockey team at the 1972 Munich Olympics, while his mother, Jennifer, captained the Indian team in the 1980 Asian basketball championship. Archery star Laishram Bombayla Devi's mother, M. Jamini Devi, is a state archery coach, while her father Manglem Singh is a state handball coach. Many other Indian Olympians have parents, siblings, or close relatives who participated earlier at high levels in sports, teaching the future Olympians about the pathways involved and the ways to get the facilities and training. These include archers Rahul Banerjee and Tarundeep Rai; track-and-field stars Gurmeet Singh, Mayookha Johny, and Sahana Kumari; boxers Devendra Singh and Shiva Thapa; shooter Heena Sidhu; wrestlers Sushil Kumar and Geeta Phogat; and hockey players Sandeep Singh, Sardar Singh, Birendra Lakra, Manpreet Singh, Gurvinder Singh Chandi, Shivendra Singh, Danish Mujtaba, and Tushar Khandker.

29. Including Somdev Devvarman, Ranjan Sodhi, Abhinav Bindra, Rohan Bopanna, Shagun Chowdhury, Sania Mirza, and Mahesh Bhupati.

30. Including Basanta Bahadur and Ram Singh Yadav (Army); Sanjeev Rajput (Navy); Krishna Poonia, Joydeep Karmakar, Sahana Kumari, Ignace Tirkey, Manpreet Singh, and Gurvinder Singh Chandi (Indian Railways); Ashwini Ponnappa and Vishnu Vardhan (ONGC); Tushar Kahdkar, S. V. Sunil, Manpreet Singh, and Birendra Lakra (BPCL); P. Sreejesh, Dharmvir Singh, Kothaljit Singh, S. K. Uttappa, and V. R. Raghunath (Indian Oil Corporation); Vikas Krishan Yadav (Electricity Board); Bharat Chetri (Canara Bank); Sardar Singh and Gurbej Singh (Punjab Police); and Sandeep Singh (Haryana Police). See also the article about India's hockey players at https://in.news.yahoo.com/ why-members-indian-men-hockey-183841499.html. A number of deserving athletes from backgrounds of poverty have been given places by the military and other public undertakings, including the rower Dattu Bhokanal (www .bbc.com/news/world-asia-india-36185307). The point, however, is that these athletes first needed to reach a certain level of prowess before the military or

other undertakings could take notice. And getting to that threshold level requires an exceptional level of talent, luck, and perseverance.

31. I did see the inspiring feature film based on the life story of Mary Kom, but I regret that I wasn't able to interview any Olympians in person. I thank Mamta Shekhawat for undertaking this painstaking analysis of Olympics team members. While she was able to research the backgrounds of most members of India's 83-strong team for the 2012 London Olympics, the backgrounds of a few athletes proved harder for us to track down. We had started looking at the backgrounds of the 2016 Rio Olympics squad at the time of this writing.

32. The study of social mobility is still in its infancy in India and other developing countries. Even in the West, where social mobility has been studied for a longer time, "the transmission of economic success across generations remains something of a black box," with the available theories explaining no more than one-quarter of the observed variation in earnings (Bowles, Gintis, and Groves, 2005: 3).

33. See www.huffingtonpost.in/2016/06/15/rajasthan-mnrega-workers-son-cracks-iit-but-doesnt-know-how-he/ (accessed on September 6, 2016).

34. Better-off individuals, who regularly see their siblings and cousins and neighbors and friends rising to high positions, grow up developing "a more complex experience of the relationship between a wide range of ends and means . . . and a bigger stock of available experiences." In contrast, poorer people "have a more brittle horizon of aspiration and a thinner, weaker sense of pathways" leading upward (Appadurai, 2004: 68–70).

35. More often than not, the exemplary Dalit entrepreneurs interviewed by Kapur et al. (2014) were assisted at crucial junctures by such chance outsiders. With few exceptions, they had parents with formal jobs and obtained their educations in city schools, going on to study in colleges. Similarly, the "kids" who made it big from humble origins in Putnam's small hometown in Ohio, USA, were almost invariably benefited with advice, guidance or financial help by an outsider who stepped in at the right moment (Putnam, 2015).

36. Amartya Sen (1999) expands on the relationships among freedom, opportunities, and capabilities, which he places at the center of the development process.

37. Das and Zajonc (2010). In general, India fares poorly in such international comparisons. See, for instance, OECD (2009), which reports that the one time India did agree to take part in a widely recognized international testing program, the Program for International Student Assessment (PISA), in 2009, it came in second-to-last among all participating countries. In other assessments, too, India features near the bottom of the world table, lower

than countries at similar levels of per-capita income. See Muralidharan (2013) and Muralidharan and Zieleniak (2013).

38. The government system also includes *Navodaya Vidyalas*, one in each district, established as a new-generation unit of learning, and *Sainik School* and *Kendriya Vidyalayas*, both of which are a cut above the rest of the system. Some of the outliers whom I met were educated in such schools.

39. The well-regarded reports of ASER can be obtained at the website of this organization: www.asercentre.org. One other result is also worth mentioning. The percentage of students in the eighth standard who could not read even a simple sentence in English increased from 40 percent in 2009 to 53 percent in 2014 – even as larger numbers of English teachers were being recruited.

40. The proportion of 3rd-standard students who could not solve the same simple problems two years later, while studying in the 5th standard increased from 29 percent to 46 percent between 2010 and 2014.

41. *Sarva Shiksha Abhiyan* (SSA, or education-for-all campaign) and the more recent Right to Education (RTE) Act, presently the principal vehicles of national educational reform, have made greater impacts on such inputs and smaller impacts on learning quality and school governance. See, for instance, ASER (2014); Joshi (2009); Mukerji and Walton (2013); and Muralidharan (2013).

42. NSSO (2008) provides these figures, which are supported by the findings of other examinations. See also GOI (2004, 2013).

43. See, for instance, Barro (1997); Brynjolfson and McAfee (2014); and Hanushek and Woessmann (2008).

44. The two government schoolteachers in my village earn in excess of 30,000 rupees each month, not counting the health care benefits and pension contributions provided by the government. Teachers in private schools in adjoining villages earn much less, no more than 5,000 rupees in many cases. In general, contract (i.e., temporary) teachers in government schools as well as teachers in many private schools (apart from a few elite ones) are paid about one-fifth as much as the permanent cadre of government school teachers. The "market-clearing" wage for such teachers is too low in many cases to make for a decent livelihood, the kind one would want to see one's children's teachers living. See, for instance, Anurag Behar, "Education in India: Getting Back to Basics," *Mint*, October 16, 2013. Accessed at www.livemint.com/Opinion/pXeoEb1olcquHfQJou81bM/Education-in-India-getting-back-to-basics.html on November 16, 2015.

45. ASER (2014) has the low figure of 15 percent. The higher figure is reported by Kremer et al. (2004) and Chaudhury et al. (2006). Journalist Rahul Pandita (2011: 122), in an insightful account of his long sojourn in Naxalite-held areas of central India, provides a wryly amusing vignette: "Vanessa, a French journalist who is with us, is keen to know whether there is

a school nearby and if a teacher ever takes classes there ... Dolu laughs. 'Guruji [the teacher], he comes every year on 15 August, unfurls the national flag, and that is it. We never see him again!'"

46. In India, where the number of private teacher training colleges has exploded in response to the expansion of the school system, increasing from about 1,600 in 1994 to more than 16,000 in 2011, regulation and quality control are almost nonexistent. Individuals who emerge from these institutions are poorly prepared, yet they are recruited to be teachers. Comparatively few acquire higher qualifications after being recruited. (Interview with Anurag Behar, Bangalore, June 18, 2015.)

47. In Canada, Behar told me, more than 2,000 teachers gain a master's- or PhD-level education each year, becoming teacher educators and curriculum developers and staffing the higher levels of education administration, but in India this number is minuscule – no more than 300 every year out of a much larger pool of individuals. Sinha (2013: 36) places a similar emphasis.

48. Chaired by Justice Verma, this committee's report, which stresses some of the points listed here, can be viewed at http://mhrd.gov.in/sites/upload_files/ mhrd/files/document-reports/JVC%20Vol%201.pdf (accessed on November 16, 2015).

49. He also mentioned that "there are schools where teachers are treated well and where they have a self-image and feel a responsibility to themselves and to the parents to deliver a good education." But those, he claimed, are the exceptions. "In general, in our system, the responsibility is only to fool the scouting eye of the central officer, who feels he/she knows what to do and must enforce what he/she thinks needs to be done without even having been to the schools, leave alone interacting with children." Personal e-mail communication with Hridaykant (Hardy) Dewan.

50. On these and related points, see, for instance, Banerjee and Duflo (2012); Chavan (2013); Desai et al. (2009); Kingdon and Muzammil (2013); Mukerji and Walton (2013); Pritchett and Beatty (2012); Pritchett and Murgai (2006); and World Bank (2011b).

51. See, for instance, Jensen (2010); Pandey, Goyal, and Sundararaman (2008a and 2008b); and Pritchett and Pande (2006). Two students of mine, Elizabeth Hannah and Kendal Swanson, who undertook field investigations in different parts of rural India, returned with the same conclusion about parents not being aware of their positions or roles, including those who held offices in SMCs. Sunisha Ahuja, who for many years headed up the NGO, Room to Read, which gave her a chance to visit hundreds of rural schools, informed me: "We haven't really given our schools much autonomy or powers to take initiatives ... There is no real shared decision making." (Author interview with Sunisha Ahuja, October 2, 2015.)

52. Hirschman (1970).

53. In addition to these expenses, parents of about one quarter of all schoolchildren paid privately for extra tuition. See Desai et al. (2009) and Wadhwa (2014): http://img.asercentre.org/docs/Publications/ASER %20Reports/ASER%202014/Articles/wilimawadhwa.pdf.

54. See, for instance, Goyal and Pande (2012); Hill et al. (2011); Karopady (2014); Mukerji and Walton (2013); and Wadhwa (2014).

55. Drèze and Sen (2013: 137).

56. Studies undertaken in different countries show how a separate and unequal system, the apartheid in education, became further entrenched after the introduction of a voucher system. See Ladd (2003). For grassroots-level examinations of the inequities resulting from creeping privatization in India, see Hill, Samson, and Dasgupta (2011) and Karopady (2014).

57. Starting in 1995, a series of reforms were carried out in Brazil that focused on decentralizing school management to local jurisdictions while raising and enforcing quality standards; improving teacher training and encouraging local innovations; reducing school costs for poorer children; and equalizing funding levels in schools across the nation. See Bruns et al. (2012) for an examination of reforms carried out in Brazil.

58. Along with Bruns et al. (2012) for Brazil, see Chen (2014) for an account of school reforms in China. The broader case is made by Hanushek and Woesmann (2008) and by Kremer, Miguel, and Thornton (2009). Also see Pritchett and Pande (2006) for a similar recommendation in the case of India.

59. In other cases, he adds, the technology interventions results in the familiar litany of computer equipment gathering dust, or stored in locked cupboards, or used only to play games, or fried by erratic power surges – fads more than aids to learning, quick fixes that have largely failed to deliver (Toyama, 2015: 20, 121). See also Cristia et al. (2012).

60. Eric Savage, who has insider knowledge of these and other initiatives, pointed me to the following organizations, whose websites I checked out independently: Edutel (www.edutel.in/); Hippocampus (www.hippocampus .org); InOpen Technologies (www.business-standard.com/article/ management/inopen-technologies-computer-science-programme-to-be-offered-in-all-tata-classedge-schools-114101100168_1.html); and Zaya (www.zaya.in/).

61. Highly trained individuals compete to become schoolteachers in Finland: it has become a prestigious occupation. See the report by the OECD on "Finland: Slow and Steady Reform for Consistently High Results." Accessed on March 31, 2016, at www.oecd.org/pisa/pisaproducts/46581035.pdf. Brazil's decentralization reforms have also given greater freedom and authority to teachers while bringing parents in to partner with teachers and school administrators and to oversee the system. Enrollments have increased

and test scores have improved after these decentralization reforms were implemented (Bruns et al., 2012).

62. Among states in India, Himachal Pradesh has given a greater stake to its teachers and parents; its public schools perform better than those of other states (Mangla, 2014). Among the work of notable NGOs, see, for instance, that of the MV Foundation (http://mvfindia.in/); Akanksha Foundation (www.akanksha.org/); Eklavya (www.eklavya.in); Digantar (www.digantar .org); Educate Girls (www.educategirls.in/); Vikramshila (www.vikramshila .org); Pratyaya EduResearch Lab (www.pratyayaeduresearchlab.org); Pragat Shikshan Sansthan (www.pragatshikshansanstha.org); Samavesh (www .samavesh.org/); Muskaan (www.muskaan.org/); Pratham (www.pratham .org); Avehi Abacus (http://avehiabacus.org/); Katha (www.katha.org); Navnirmiti (www.navnirmiti.org/); Jodo Gyan (http://jodogyan.org/); Azim Premji Foundation (www.azimpremjifoundation.org/); Teacher Foundation (www.teacherfoundation.org/); Stir Education (www.stireducation.org/); and Vidya Bhawan (www.vidyabhawan.org/).

63. The mission statement of the national policy on skill development is available at the website of the newly formed central Ministry for Skill Development and Entrepreneurship: www.skilldevelopment.gov.in/assets/images/Skill %20India/policy%20booklet-%20Final.pdf.

64. I spoke with Mrinalini Kher, the honorary secretary and trustee of this organization, and I was impressed with their initiatives. For more information, see www.yuvaparivartan.org/.

65. Sushil Ramola, the managing director of this organization, told me how they are focusing their efforts on rural youth, many of whom have dropped out of school after grades 4, 6, 8, or 10, and whom they are training in a number of trades, including as security guards, rural opticians, for retail trade, and for the hospitality industry. Basic English-language skills and knowledge of computers are part of every training program. Ambitiously, the organization aims to train 1 million individuals over the next ten years.

66. N. Balachander, Group Director for Human Resources, told me about the vocational training centers that this company has been running for several years, where rural youth are recruited and trained to become waiters and baristas. Teaming up with the government's initiative, this effort has been scaled up recently, spawning several larger initiatives, including the Centurion University, which works among youth of deep rural Odisha.

67. www.super30.org.

68. Interview with N. Venkatesan, CEO, Vidyaposhak – www.vidyaposhak.ngo.

69. www.brightfutureindia.org.

70. Scholars, however, have often found that "soft factor" are a central part of the explanation. See, for instance, Bourdieu (1986); Heckman (2011); and Ray (2006).

Chapter 6 Attitudes, Experiences, and Information

1. I employ this term, expanding on the discussion of "soft skills" by Heckman (2011) and of "cultural capital" by Bourdieu (1986), to connote a set of cognitive factors, including attitudes, beliefs, mores, norms, self-esteem, and information about how things work in practice.

2. Dalit, literally "oppressed" in Sanskrit, is term often applied to caste groups formerly deemed to be untouchable and thus outside the pale of Hindu society.

3. Consider, for instance, the laws about child labor, gender-neutral inheritance, minimum wages, and workplace safety regulations, among the many that are rarely enforced and widely disregarded.

4. In counterpoint to the law about traffic signals, consider mandatory speed limits, a regulation routinely flouted by drivers in the UK and the United States.

5. Extracted on March 2, 2016 from "Minute by the Hon'ble T. B. Macaulay, dated the 2nd February 1835," www.columbia.edu/itc/mealac/pritchett/00generallinks/macaulay/txt_minute_education_1835.html.

6. It was mostly in the decades following the 1980s when vast expansion of the rural school network was undertaken; before then, only a minority of Indian villagers had access to schools. Except in a few native states, mostly notably Travancore and Cochin, which later became the state of Kerala, rural education was mostly neglected. Nearly one-quarter of all schools in UP and Odisha; 30 percent in Rajasthan; nearly 50 percent in Bihar and Tripura; and 70 percent in Jharkhand and Jammu and Kashmir have been established since 2002. See www.dise.in/Downloads/Publications/Publications%202011-12/Elementary%20Education%20in%20Rural%20India.pdf. (Accessed on September 15, 2015.)

7. This influence has been passed down across generations. The greatest share of India's new post-globalization middle class is constituted by the descendants of the earlier college-educated government officials. See Fernandes (2006).

8. In 1983, the children of the richest 20 percent were eight times as likely to attend colleges compared to the children of the poorest 20 percent; by 2004, this disproportion had grown to fourteen times and was still increasing (Azam and Blom, 2008). Because elites' children attend higher-quality private schools, they are much better prepared to secure places in top-ranked colleges than are poorer children attending lower-quality public schools. See Gruber and Kosack (2014) for a fuller explanation of how elite ideas and power resources account for the "tertiary tilt" in the education budgets of India and other developing countries.

9. Weiner (1990: 188–9).

10. See, for instance, Agarwal (1994); Banerjee and Raju (2009); Chanana (2007); Drèze and Sen (1995); and Kabeer (2005).

11. Two examples, both current at the time of writing, consisted of attacks on northerners in cities of Maharashtra, including Mumbai and Pune, and assaults on northeasterners in Bengaluru. See, respectively, https://en .wikipedia.org/wiki/2008_attacks_on_Uttar_Pradeshi_and_Bihari_migrants_ in_Maharashtra and www.thehindu.com/news/national/karnataka/ after-rumours-northeast-people-flee-bangalore/article3776549.ece. (Accessed on February 12, 2016.)

12. See, on this point, Jaffrelot (2003); Yadav (2000); and Krishna (2008). See also Mayer (1997) and Manor (2010), who find that caste today represents difference more than hierarchy.

13. A nationwide study undertaken in 2012 inquired, among other things, about respondents' attitudes toward Dalits. A large fraction of respondents expressed responses suggesting strong biases. More than 40,000 individuals were surveyed using a battery of questions, two of which are especially relevant to this discussion. The first survey question asked respondents about whether they would be comfortable if a low-caste person were to enter their kitchen and use their cooking utensils; the second asked about their level of comfort with inter-caste dining. Cited by Ahuja (2016). But see Kapur et al. (2010) for other evidence indicating that these differences and prejudices are receding; and Chauchard's (2014) finding that reservations in *Gram Panchayat* positions have led to changes in attitudes and beliefs with the same consequences.

14. See, for example, Banerjee and Somanathan (2007); and Witsoe (2013).

15. See, for instance, Ajit, Donker, and Saxena (2012); Deshpande and Newman (2007); Deshpande (2011); Deshpande and Yadav (2006); and Thorat and Attewell (2007).

16. Priyam (2016). Another egregious example is given by Rahul Chandran – www.livemint.com/Sundayapp/RcM4ibkXQV1fP3L7JlHTfL/Class-divide-in-a-gated-community.html. (Accessed on December 13, 2016.)

17. Such attitudes and values have added to the problems that bedevil the national objective of skills development, according to Sushil Ramola, whose organization, B-ABLE, has been making great strides in realizing this objective. Also see Higham and Shah (2013) for an insightful exploration of how attitudes belittling manual labor and traditional lifestyles have become part of the mindset of a new generation.

18. The examination of these values of the middle class by Fernandes (2006:69) is complemented by other analyses, including Fernandes and Heller (2006); Ganguly-Scrase and Scrase (2009); Rajagopal (1999); Sheth (1999); and Verma (1998). Emphasizing the point about the English language, historian Ramachandra Guha (2008: 764) notes how "the language of the colonizers has, in independent India become the language of power and prestige, the language of individual as well as social advancement."

19. Based on data from the India Human Development Survey, 2011–12, undertaken by the University of Maryland and the National Council for Applied Economic Research, New Delhi (www.ihds.info).

20. Tully (2007: 122).

21. This study, which I supervised, was undertaken over January and February of 2013 and separately from mid-March through mid-July 2014 by two research assistants. They read through and then coded (assigning to one of fourteen different categories) each of the different news items published in every paper. Similar results were reported by a separate study undertaken by Mudgal (2011).

22. Mudgal (2011: 92) found that newspapers assign "only a minuscule proportion – no more than 2 percent – of their total coverage to rural India's issues, crises and anxieties."

23. More expansively, Drèze and Sen (2013: 268) note how a "comparatively small group of the relatively privileged seem to have created a social universe of their own."

24. Sociologist Dipankar Gupta's (2005) account of the disappearing Indian village is better seen as a metaphorical reference to its disappearance from the discourse of urban influential. Not everyone agrees, though, with the preference for the urban – for instance, the journalist Akash Kapur (2012: 273–4) writes, "After more than seven years in the country, I knew that India's future – like its present – was a lot more complicated than the postcard version offered by the cities. I found the countryside more real and more honest."

25. See, for instance, the article ("A bad boom") in the *Economist* of March 15, 2014.

26. Commenting on these provisions, the historian Mukul Kesavan observed, "In a poor country like India the educated and the debt-free are, by definition, better off than those who are not educated or have debt. To designate the first as exemplary, or credit them with superior moral will, is to imply that the others are feckless and unwilling to improve themselves. In fact, those others are simply poor. And to limit the poor's access to office is to say that they deserve to vote but only for their betters." ("India's Move against the Poor," *New York Times*, January 14, 2016).

27. Census 2011 data provide these numbers. See www.censusindia.gov.in/ 2011census/C-series/C08.html (accessed on February 23, 2016).

28. Author calculations from India Human Development Survey, 2011–12.

29. There's much more to sanitation than simply building a toilet, which is better seen as one part of a complex and integrated sanitation system. See Deepak Sanan, "Swacch Bharat Mission: Another Futile Toilet Chase?" www.downtoearth.org.in/blog/swachh-bharat-mission-another-futile-toilet-chase-55758 (accessed on October 16, 2016).

30. Or as Gilman (2014) puts it, "citizenship no longer signifies the liberal ideal of an identical package of rights for all, but instead means very different things depending on where individuals are in physical and social space." See also Mosse (2010).

31. Meeting with Chief Secretary, January 19, 2016.

32. A senior official from a state in the eastern part of country, referring to V. S. Naipaul's third book on India, spoke to me about the rise of a "million mutinies" in the rural parts of his state and about frustrated expectations among educated rural youth, who have come to form, in his view, a tinderbox of discontent.

33. See www.thebetterindia.com/11219/sathi-ngo-runaway-children-railway-platforms-india/ (accessed on July 1, 2015).

34. See, for instance, Causa and Chapuis (2009) and OECD (2010b). Studying the longer-term effects of an experiment that offered randomly selected families living in high-poverty housing projects assistance to move to lower-poverty neighborhoods, Chetty et al. (2016) found that it had significantly improved college attendance rates and earnings for the low-income children who had moved with their families.

35. Sarin and Gupta (2014).

36. Rao (2013).

37. A series of investigations undertaken in different countries have been reaffirming this conclusion, including Burns, Corno, and La Ferrara (2015) in the context of contact between black and white students in South Africa. Boisjoly et al. (2006: 1891) similarly find that "white students who are randomly assigned African-American roommates are significantly more likely to endorse affirmative action and have personal contacts with members of other ethnic groups after their first year."

38. Varshney (2002). In another context, Barnhardt (2009) came to a similar conclusion after investigating religiously mixed neighborhoods in public housing.

39. Summarizing a body of related research, Pettigrew and Tropp (2006: 751) conclude that "intergroup contact typically reduces intergroup prejudice." Wilkinson (2004) has a similar finding regarding inter-group violence.

40. Several studies have exposed differences between villages within a contiguous region, probing for the causes that underlie these differences. See, for instance, Krishna (2002) and Wade (1994).

41. See, for instance, Jeffrey, Jeffery, and Jeffery (2004) and Munshi and Rosenzweig (2006).

42. See Hoxby and Turner (2013).

43. http://achbejobbedfoundation.com/ourWork.php (accessed on August 15, 2016).

44. Swapnil Agarwal, who was at that time an MBA student at IIM-Ahmedabad, assisted me in this research effort. Our search into information providing organizations was limited, ironically, by lack of information. There is no existing directory or established association of such organizations. We had to rely on a number of makeshift methods, ultimately restricting our search to organizations that have a web presence. Within this shortlist, our examination was further restricted to organizations that responded favorably to our requests for interviews. Because of these limitations, we have likely missed out on a number of stellar organizations. More details are provided in Krishna and Agarwal (2016).

45. Respectively, Preranamerit.org; Vidyaposhak.ngo; Mumbaismiles.org; and Udaanindiafoundation.org.

46. Respectively, Super30.org; Avantifellows.org; and Csrl.in.

47. Respectively, Dreamadream.org; Makeadiff.in; Friendsofchildrentrust.org; Brightfutureindia.org; Vazhai.org; Thegreenbattiproject.in; Bhumi.org .in/lakshya; MentorTogether.org; Mentormeindia.org; and Achbejobbedfoundation.com.

48. Respectively, Aspiringminds.com; Bharatcalling.in; Leadtrust.in; and Iefglobal.org.

49. E-teachenglish.org.

50. Notable examples include RJS Boxing club, Bihar; Hockey Village India; One thousand hockey legs; Citizens group; Stick for India; Bangalore Sports School Foundation; Slum Soccer; Sparky Football; My Angels Academy; Project Play; Yuwa India; Special Olympics Bharat; Aditya Mehta Foundation; and Yatna.

51. By charging higher-income students for its IIT entrance exam coaching program, Super 30, for instance, is able to provide the same program free of cost to low-income students.

52. www.yuvaparivartan.org.

53. Prior to these elections, newspapers containing report cards on politicians were distributed in a random sample of slum settlements. Compared to other neighborhoods, those in which people had been given this information experienced higher voter turnout and fewer incidences of vote buying, and they gave a higher share of their vote to more qualified candidates. "If this information had reached the entire jurisdiction," the authors of the study concluded, "electoral outcomes would have changed [for the better] in the two closest elections" (Banerjee et al., 2011). Pande (2011) separately emphasizes the point about voters' beliefs changing as a result of information provision.

54. See Keefer and Khemani (2005) and Krishna (2006, 2008).

55. Bratton (2008) and Bratton and Mattes (2001) demonstrate the importance of education and information for democracy in an African context. Finkel

(2002), Hiskey and Seligson (2003), and UNDP (2004) do the same for different Latin American contexts.

56. See Fox (2015), Jayal (2013), and Joshi (2009).

57. "For democratic structures to endure – and to be worthy of endurance – they must listen to their citizens' voices and engage their participation," asserts Diamond (2008: 39), a longtime scholar of democracy. "They must tolerate their protests, protect their freedoms, and respond to their needs." None of this is possible without the free flow of information. See also Lijphart (1997).

58. See Pandey et al. (2008a and 2008b). The authors of these studies organized information campaigns in villages of UP and MP. As part of the campaign, community members in each state were made aware of their rights and responsibilities. The results of this campaign were quite impressive. Community oversight increased considerably, and there were visible improvements in the provision of school uniforms, meals, and stipends to students. Most notably, test scores went up – in reading, writing, and mathematics. Evidence from other countries also upholds the positive effects of information provision on school performance. For example, Reinikka and Svensson (2004) show how a newspaper campaign initiated by the Ugandan government increased the ability of schools and parents to monitor officials' handling of a large school grant program.

59. More effective resolutions for the medical poverty trap can be developed, for instance, by providing households with information about common diseases, about their symptoms and early-stage remedies, about sound hygiene practices, about the appropriate costs for various treatments, and about the reputations of health-care providers in their vicinity. See, for instance, Hammer, Aiyar, and Samji (2006) and Krishna (2004). The broader point is made by Kosack and Fung (2014). Reviewing the results of recent accountability and transparency initiatives supported by international donors, they find that information helps enrich service provision. The kinds of information that are most beneficial are those that are clearly understandable and salient to citizens; that illuminate problems in inputs and processes, not merely ranking performance; and that suggest a clear course of action.

60. See North, Summerhill, and Weingast (2000) and North, Wallis, and Weingast (2012). A similar case for broad-based and inclusive public institutions is made by Acemoglu, Johnson, and Robinson (2006) and Acemoglu and Robinson (2012). Singh (2015) advances a persuasive case for how varying degrees of solidarity have affected social welfare outcomes in states of India.

61. These interactions needed to be coordinated and preceded by training. In the summer program that I've helped set up, we run orientation programs for village host families, who learn what to expect from and how to cater to big-city kids and Westerners. At the other end, we orient students about village norms and customs and what to expect and what not to. A brief

description of the program is available at the websites http://iimu.ac.in/
programs/summer-school/about-the-program.html and https://sanford
.duke.edu/academics/special-programs/india-summer-program-for-
international-development-leaders.

62. Kruks-Wisner (n.d.), a claim supported as well by Brule's (2015)
investigations.

63. As Thachil (2014a) also found in his investigations among migrant men in
Lucknow and Delhi.

64. See, for instance, the government instruction of Anhui province, available at
the website: www.ahedu.gov.cn/upload2009/20121125295466676423_1.doc;
or the policy of an elite high school affiliated with Yunnan Normal University
(www.ynsdfz.net/InfoDetails.aspx?infoid=3136). I thank Harry Chen for
translating both documents from the Chinese.

65. Telephone interview with Sunisha Ahuja, October 2, 2015. One can learn
more about the programs being implemented by this organization at its
website: www.roomtoread.org/OurPrograms.

66. See Fox (2015) and Kosack and Fung (2014) for reviews of some of the most
important initiatives.

67. Citizens' report cards, pioneered by Samuel Paul and the Public Affairs
Centre in Bengaluru, demonstrate how information can help enforce
accountability by putting public pressure on service providers. A description
of this initiative is given at www.citizenreportcard.com/. An early evaluation,
reporting mixed results, is provided at http://siteresources.worldbank.org/
INTEMPOWERMENT/Resources/14832_Bangalore-web.pdf. India's Right
to Information Act was put into effect in 2005 in response to demands by
civil society activists and smaller-scale demonstrations of success, especially
by the activist group and people's movement *Mazdoor Kisan Shakti Sangh*
(MKSS; www.mkssindia.org/). As explained on the government website,
www.righttoinformation.gov.in/, the Act "mandates timely response to
citizen requests for government information." (Accessed on April 17, 2016.)

68. As Fox (2015) puts it in a review article, it is unrealistic to assume that
information that is not linked to credible pathways to change and assisted by
simultaneous reforms in governance structures and processes will make a
lasting impression.

Chapter 7 Democracy at the Doorstep

1. Chandhoke (2005) shows how citizens continue to have high expectations of
the state even after important state functions were delegated to civil society
organizations.

2. As Michael Mann (1984: 195) writes, arguing for the necessity of the state,
"Only three alternative bases for order exist, force, exchange, and custom,

and none of these is sufficient in the long-run. At some point new exigencies arise for which custom is inadequate; at some point to bargain about everything in exchange relations is inefficient and disintegrating; while force alone . . . will soon 'deflate'. In the long run, normally taken for granted, but enforceable, rules are necessary to bind together strangers or semi-strangers." This body of rules and the associated enforcement mechanisms underlie what is commonly regarded as the state. And any organization performing these functions is part of the state.

3. The ratio of those who apply to those who are admitted continues to remain hefty, with no more than 1 in nearly 500 applicants making it into the elite Indian Administrative Service. Even for recruitments to lower levels of the state administration, more than 200 applicants commonly apply for every advertised position. In a country where more than 90 percent of jobs are informal, a tenured (permanent) job with the government is highly sought after. See, for example, http://articles.economictimes.indiatimes.com/ 2009-03-25/news/28435314_1_civil-services-private-sector-aspirants. Pay scales have risen consistently, making government jobs – such as those of teachers – more highly paid than comparable jobs in the private sector.

4. Public administration at lower levels is organized in districts, subdivisions, and *talukas* (also called *tahsils*), of which the first and third units have the greatest historical and contemporary importance (Morris-Jones, 1967; Potter, 1996). At the time of writing, India was divided into 642 districts, further divided into *tahsils* or *talukas*, which functioned in colonial times as the basic units of land administration and revenue collection. Development Blocks, with block development officers (BDOs) as their chief executives, have been added on more recently, many coterminous with *tahsils* and *talukas*.

5. Dutt (1903: 196), cited in Mookherjee (2004: 19).

6. Leading some observers to refer to the Indian system as a "thin state." See Kaviraj (1997) and Chatterjee (1997).

7. Carstairs (1912: 12–13).

8. Fuller and Harriss (2000: 23).

9. In the same Indian state, the forest department makes recruitments at five separate levels – forest guard, forester, ranger, the State Forest Service, and the Indian Forest Service. On average, 200 individuals are recruited each year to the post of forest guard, of whom a few rise to the level of forester in the concluding years of their service. Hardly any forest guard rises to ranger, and none to the State Forest Service. The agriculture department recruits at three different levels – agricultural supervisor, assistant agriculture officer, and agriculture officer. The distinction between officer and supervisor is maintained by regulating promotions in such a manner that hardly anyone recruited as supervisor rises to become officer. Newer and more technically specialized departments of government tend to be less tiered in nature, though

even here the class distinction is maintained between what are known as fourth-class staff (the cleaners, fetchers, and bundle lifters), clerical staff, and officers.

10. For two accounts written by former police officers whose more detailed arguments similarly trace this lineage to the colonial origin, see Dhillon (2005) and Verma (2005).

11. See ACPO (2012).

12. For a fascinating account of how constables and other front-line police personnel cope with the situational imperatives that emerge from working within such a structure, see Jauregui (2016), who makes explicit how various pulls and pressures, some formal and others of an informal nature, result in "provisionalizing" the statutory authority of street-level bureaucrats in India. She also presents for another Indian state (Uttar Pradesh) a chart that depicts a bureaucratic ladder very similar to the one depicted in Figure 7.1.

13. Basu (2010: 25).

14. Cited in Godbole (2014: 7).

15. The term is used to refer to structures and processes and management that give more discretion to cutting-edge functionaries, coupled, of course, with more effective process oversight and performance monitoring. See, for instance, Peters and Waterman (1982). In the context of bureaucratic organizations with grassroots development responsibilities, a similar argument is made by Pritchett and Woolcock (2004).

16. Gupta (2012: 23–4). This work builds on Gupta's illuminating earlier examination of the grassroots bureaucracy (Gupta, 1998).

17. Gupta (2012: 48).

18. With the implementation of successive reports of federal Pay Commissions, "India has moved toward a high-wage civil service . . . even among equivalent jobs the public sector [wage] exceeds the private" (World Bank 2006: 42).

19. Some state governments raise the salaries of their employees after a certain number of years, even though there is no elevation to the next higher position. Such pay increases are given to all who have the same number of years of service, high performers as well as low performers, all except those who have a criminal case or a departmental inquiry against them.

20. See, for instance, Chaudhury et al. (2006). The likelihood of absenteeism is greater in beyond-5-km villages, because the quality and availability of educational and medical facilities, as well as other kinds of infrastructure, are poorer in remoter locations (see Chapter 2), because of which few government officials are willing to bring up their children in such places. See, for instance, Harriss-White (2003).

21. Here's one documented example. Political scientists Amit Ahuja and Pradeep Chhibber (2012: 399) found that poorer participants in the focus groups they

organized "reported frequently being treated with disrespect and summarily dismissed when they interacted with state officials. One poor citizen said 'When big people enter a government office, the official stands up. When poor people go in, no one ever asks them to sit.' The poor also complained of intimidation and coercion at the hands of the state's functionaries ... they had no control over the teachers in their schools; they were openly intimidated in police stations; they faced rampant neglect in health centers; and in district offices, their petitions got put on the back burner."

22. Other kinds of exclusionary local practices have also arisen. One example consists of what the scholar Barbara Harriss-White (2003: 241) has called "the intermediate classes" – loose coalitions of small-scale capitalists, agrarian and local agribusiness elites, and local officials who collude to derive benefits from the state for themselves, because the public at large is denied information and access.

23. Corbridge et al. (2005) use the term "elite revolts" to refer, inter alia, to this class of behavior.

24. Weiner (1963: 123).

25. Corbridge et al. (2005: 108).

26. The following investigations have also reported extensively on the nature of mediation in different regions of India: Reddy and Haragopal (1985) for Andhra Pradesh, Krishna (2002, 2003b) for Rajasthan and Madhya Pradesh, and Mitra (1992) for Gujarat and Odisha. Manor (2000) indicates how such roles are widespread in other states, including Uttar Pradesh and Karnataka. Chandra (2000) documents how similar concerns in other areas led to the rise of Dalit parties. Chhibber (1999) refers more broadly to the absence of grassroots political organizations in large parts of India, giving rise to the need for mediators. For a broader examination of mediation in other contexts, see Kitschelt (2000).

27. Being able to lord it over the local police station is an announcement of a politician's arrival. For an insightful depiction, see Brass (1997). Interestingly, as Jauregui (2013) points out, police officers are themselves implicated in circuits of "provisional" authority – ambiguous roles, not clearly legitimized practices and the need constantly to "make do" in situations of resource shortages and overlapping and conflicting lines of authority.

28. See Kruks-Wisner (2015, n.d.), Bussell (n.d.), and Krishna (in press). Their offices require them to discharge a number of specified duties: registering births, deaths, and marriages; undertaking local construction works; overseeing subsidized grain distribution to poorer households; and so on. But some *sarpanchas* go above and beyond the specified duties. For political or commercial or social service motivations – more likely, some mix of the three – *sarpanchas* become involved in being mediators with agencies of the

government – like the electricity company or public sector banks – with which they have no official or formal connection.

29. De Witt (1986) cited in Blomkvist (1988).

30. Auerbach (2016: 115, 117). Similar observations have been recorded by other slum studies, including Harriss (2005); Jha, Rao, and Woolcock (2007); and Krishna (2013a).

31. There is disagreement among scholars about how to regard the activities of these local intermediaries. Should they be seen as performing a needed social service, or are they more appropriately seen as touts and brokers who make their living gouging desperate individuals. See, for instance, Levien (2015).

32. An example of the benefits of this kind of linkage is provided by Mahajan (2016).

33. I recognize that some of these areas of work – education and health – are state subjects per India's constitution, but still there are federal ministries in both areas, and they have huge budgets that dwarf, while feeding into, the budgets of individual state governments.

34. Many of India's most noted development programs were brought into being by state governments. MGNREGA, the rural employment guarantee program, was tried and tested first in Maharashtra. Important parts of the National Rural Health Mission were scaled up from earlier projects in Gujarat, and the National Rural Livelihoods Mission traces its origins to Andhra Pradesh. Other promising innovations in health and education are currently under way in other states. In the health sector, Rajasthan and Tamil Nadu have introduced schemes ensuring better availability in government hospitals and clinics of medicines free of cost, especially helping the poorer sections. Tamil Nadu is on the way to developing integrated online patient records. Bihar has revitalized its district hospitals using novel public–private partnership arrangements.

35. See Ostrom, Schroeder, and Wynne (1993). Other examinations of successful and unsuccessful development initiatives have similarly found value in empowered local forums bringing together office holders and citizens. See, for example, Fung (2004); Fung and Wright (2003); Grindle (2007); Tendler (1997); and Uphoff, Esman, and Krishna (1998).

36. Rising to more than 40 percent in countries such as Denmark and Finland (World Bank, 2006). The average figure of 5 percent masks wide differences across states of India, in one of which, Kerala, 40 percent of all state finances are handled by *gram panchayats* (Rao and Sanyal, 2010).

37. "Panchayat resources are dominated," a World Bank report (2006: 57–59) asserts, "by earmarked transfers designed by higher levels of government. Even the micro-allocation of the resources is determined by guidelines prepared by the state and central governments. PRIs [Panchayati Raaj

Institutions] are given functions but have little or no effective control over the people expected to carry them out." See also Bardhan and Mookherjee (2006), Heller (2001), and Manor (2010).

38. See, for instance, Rao and Sanyal (2010) and Manor (2010).

39. See, for instance, Isaac and Heller (2003).

40. See Abers (2000) and Baiocchi (2005).

41. For academic expositions of these views, see, for instance, Di Maggio and Powell (1983), Friedland and Alford (1991), Scott (1987), and Swidler (1986). In the context of developing countries, see, particularly, Scott (1985, 1990).

42. See, for instance, Azari and Smith (2012), Baldwin (2016), and Helmke and Levitsky (2004).

43. See Krishna (2003b).

44. Ananthpur (2007).

45. See, for instance, Galanter (1989).

46. As Mark Schneider and Nilanjan Sircar's field investigations in eighty-four gram panchayats conclude, the "suspicion of elite capture . . . is exaggerated and fails to consider contextual characteristics that encourage progressive targeting." Local politicians in the Indian villages they studied are constrained to abide by a local moral economy, both because these villages are high-information contexts and because politicians, after finishing their terms, have to continue living with the same norms and amid the same people. Working paper, accessed on October 10, 2016, at markaschneider .com/research.

47. See, in this regard, Afridi and Iversen (2014), Khera (2016), and Ravallion (2016).

48. See, for instance, Pandey, Goyal, and Sundararaman (2008a and 2008b).

49. As we saw earlier in Chapter 2. See Fan, Chan-Kang, and Mukherjee (2005: 14).

50. "Most of these political formations, which serve as instruments of democratization of society are themselves completely undemocratic in their organizational set-up" (Yadav, 1996: 100). See also Kohli (1987, 1990), Krishna (2002), Mehta (1997), and Yadav (1999).

51. As Schumpeter (1950: 285) stated, "Democracy means only that people have the opportunity of accepting or refusing the men who are to rule them." Democracies have dealt in different ways with this shortcoming.

52. See, for instance, the report titled "Analysis of Criminal and Financial Details of MPs of 15th Lok Sabha (2009)," compiled by the Association for Democratic Reforms. Accessed on October 7, 2014, at http://adrindia.org/ files/High%20level%20criminal,%20financial%20&%20educational %20analysis%20LS%202009.pdf. Wealth figures for individual MPs can also be accessed at http://india60.com/mps/wealth. Congressmen in the

United States are fourteen times wealthier than the average US household. See
www.usnews.com/news/blogs/data-mine/2014/01/09/let-them-eat-
cake-members-of-congress-14-times-more-wealthy-than-average-american.
(Accessed on October 7, 2014.) Even with this lower ratio, the representation
gap is large in the United States. Carnes (2013) provides a trenchant
examination.

53. This 30 percent figure is still an overestimate. Being described as an
agriculturist has a positive cachet: many who have never tilled a field or
milked a cow nonetheless list "agriculturist" as their primary profession.
Correcting partially for the likely overstatement, we arrived at a lower figure
of 23 percent, exactly equal to the share of MPs whose principal occupation
was business. This set of results, as well as some of the earlier ones, is from a
study by Ajit Phadnis, using data carefully compiled by him from diverse
sources, which he conducted in regular discussions with me when he was a
visiting postdoctoral fellow at Duke University.

54. See Chandra (2016).

55. French (2011). He considers individuals with multiple links to government
influentials – such as the daughter of a senior MP who is also the
daughter-in-law of a former maharaja and the wife of a senior civil servant –
as hyper-hereditary.

56. This information was compiled by two research assistants working under my
direction from individual bio-profiles provided in the official listing of MPs,
available online at http://loksabha.nic.in/. Only 499 of a total of 543
members listed this information.

57. On this point about the convergence of ideology between MPs of different
parties and corporate business interests, see Basu (2008), Mooij (2005), Sinha
(2010), and especially Kohli (2012). Chatterjee (2011: 24) considers that
policy elites have come under the "moral–political sway of the bourgeoisie."
For a more complete exposition of this thesis, see Chatterjee (2004).

58. Kohli (2012: 13).

59. Potter (1996: 34). Also see Gilmour (2005), Kolsky (2010), and Mason
(1985).

60. Holding primary elections, as in the United States, is one way to go; other
long-standing democracies provide different examples. But new problems
might follow such solutions, as they almost invariably do; in the United
States, primary elections, which parties hold to select candidates, have been
held responsible, together with "gerrymandered" electoral districts, for
pushing parties and candidates into extreme positions. See, for instance,
Zakaria (2003).

61. According to a survey carried out by the Indian government among top-tier
officials, those belonging to the elite all-India services – which include the IAS,
IPS, and foreign service – more than 70 percent felt that the training they

received was not relevant to the job they were doing; no more than 16 percent agreed or strongly agreed that the appraisal system used to judge their performance had been effective; only 22 percent felt that their seniors were capable ("most of the time" or "all of the time") of taking tough decisions and speaking up when needed; but as many as 72 percent agreed or strongly agreed that "corrupt civil servants manage to get plum postings" (GOI, 2010a). The survey had a low response rate (26 percent), which brings into question some of the results, but support is provided as well by a number of illuminating studies, some of them personal narratives, which have examined in considerable depth the contexts in which higher-level officials function.

62. See, for example, Das (2010, 2013, especially Chapter 9), Godbole (2014), Potter (1996), and Subramanian (2004).

63. Some of these reasons are public-oriented, but others are implicated in opportunities for corruption that arise when large orders for technological devices and services are placed for an entire state by senior public officials. See Bussell (2012).

64. See, for instance, Mathew and Moore (2011) and Witsoe (2013).

65. For instance, Finland, discussed in the next chapter, and South Korea and Sri Lanka.

66. The need for such a staged process of institutional development can be inferred from the work of scholars, including Bardhan (2002), Rodrik (2007), North (1990), and North, Wallis, and Weingast (2012). By following a process of this kind, China has been successfully rebuilding its public health-care system in stages. See www.worldbank.org/en/results/2015/04/02/reform-innovation-for-better-rural-health-services-in-china (accessed on July 29, 2015). Also see Zhao (2006) and Xu et al. (2003).

67. See, for instance, Boone (2003), Cammett and Maclean (2011), Davidson (1993), Maclean (2011), and Mamdani (1996).

Chapter 8 Looking Ahead: Growing the Economy – and Developing Individuals

1. These are the countries that could sustain high rates of macroeconomic growth without raising inequality to alarming levels. Ranis, Stewart, and Ramirez (2000) present this argument by comparing the growth paths of different countries over long periods of time. Milly (1999) and In-Joung (1981) present studies of twinned strategies in the contexts, respectively, of Japan and South Korea. See also the lucid discussion by Barrientos (2013) about the logic of social development.

2. Oral histories compiled by a doctor friend of mine associated the symptoms with those of a fluorosis sufferer's.

3. Other examples of a similar kind are related in Krishna (2010).

4. See Chapter 6 for some examples of such organizations.

5. See, for instance, the examinations by Abers (2000) and Baiocchi (2005) of participatory budgeting in cities of Brazil. A larger variety of cases is examined by Fox (2015), Fung (2004), and Krishna, Uphoff, and Esman (1997).

6. For the seminal work in this regard, see Ostrom (1990). See also Ostrom, Schroeder, and Wynne (1993).

7. Andrews, Pritchett, and Woolcock (2012), and separately Easterly (2006), persuasively argue the case for taking such a learning process approach to institution- and program-building. An earlier expression of the learning process approach to development is Korten (1980).

8. Because of the quality of its work, this NGO, Arth, which has its head office in Udaipur, later won the prestigious MacArthur Award (www.arth.in). Accessed on August 27, 2015.

9. Diverse actors have made notable contributions. Among state governments, Rajasthan and Tamil Nadu introduced programs ensuring the better availability of medicines free of cost, helping especially the poorer sections; and Bihar revitalized its district hospitals using novel public–private partnership arrangements. Organizations affiliated with the BJP have also stepped in to provide rudimentary medical care (and basic education) in remote rural regions and urban slums. Because of the urgency of the need, people living in these areas have responded very positively to these overtures, according to a scholar who has studied these trends (Thachil, 2014b). Corporate social responsibility (CSR) organizations have made a series of notable contributions.

10. Jan Swasthya Sahyog, an organization that works in Chhattisgarh (www .jssbilaspur.org/about/vision.php). Accessed on August 27, 2015.

11. Comprehensive Rural Health Project, or CRHP, an organization that works in Maharashtra (www.jamkhed.org/approach/our_approach). Accessed on August 27, 2015.

12. Performance has been far from uniform in the big-bang programs that have been implemented: some worked well in Bihar but failed to make an impact in UP; others worked well in Rajasthan but performed poorly in Tamil Nadu. There are several examples of program evaluations that uphold the conclusion about patchy outcomes. Basu and Sen (2015) and Ravallion (2016) make the case in respect of MGNREGA, the rural employment guarantee scheme. Krishna and Shariff (2011) consider a more general case, finding that no program has had a positive impact on poverty reduction all across India; in each state, some ventures had a positive influence while others didn't make much of an impact.

13. See Population Reference Bureau (2015) for these percentages in these and many other countries.

14. See World Bank (2013).
15. Ferré, Ferreira, and Lanjouw (2012: 353–4). Also see Brunori, Ferreira, and Peragine (2013).
16. On the broader point of institutional diversity, see, for instance, Acemoglu, Johnson, and Robinson (2006); Acemoglu and Robinson (2012); Andrews (2010); Hall and Soskice (2001); North (1990); North, Wallis, and Weingast (2012); Przeworski (2004); and Rodrik (2007). In the specific area of health care, Reid (2009) shows how national institutions of health care are different in important respects and how each of them delivers good results in separate contexts.
17. For an overview of the Dibao program, originally introduced in urban areas, and at a later stage extended to rural areas, see www.ilo.org/dyn/ilossi/ ssimain.viewScheme?p_lang=en&p_scheme_id=919&p_geoaid=156. Some problems have, of course, been encountered in the process of institutionalization and scaling up. See, for instance, the analysis by a World Bank team: https://openknowledge.worldbank.org/handle/10986/8831. Both websites were accessed on December 14, 2016.

BIBLIOGRAPHY

Abers, Rebecca Neaera. *Inventing Local Democracy: Grassroots Politics in Brazil*. Boulder, CO: Lynne Rienner, 2000.

Acemoglu, Daron, and James A. Robinson. *Why Nations Fail: The Origins of Power, Prosperity, and Poverty*. New York, NY: Crown Business, 2012.

Acemoglu, Daron, Simon Johnson, and James Robinson. "Understanding Prosperity and Poverty: Geography, Institutions, and the Reversal of Fortune." In *Understanding Poverty*, edited by Abhijit Banerjee, Roland Benabou, and Dilip Mookherjee, 19–35. Oxford, UK: Oxford University Press, 2006.

ACPO. *Policing in the UK: A Brief Guide*. London, UK: Association of Chief Police Officers, 2012. Accessed April 20, 2016. http://wyp-unison.org.uk/assets/2410%20-%20ACPO%20-%20Policing%20in%20the%20UK.pdf.

Addison, Anthony, David Hulme, and Ravi Kanbur. "Poverty Dynamics: Measurement and Understanding from an Interdisciplinary Perspective." In *Poverty Dynamics: Interdisciplinary Perspectives*, edited by Addison, Hulme, and Kanbur, 3–28. Oxford, UK: Oxford University Press, 2009.

Adiga, Aravind. *The White Tiger*. New Delhi, India: Harper Collins, 2008.

Afridi, Farzana, and Vegard Iversen. "Social Audits and MGNREGA Delivery: Lessons from Andhra Pradesh." In *India Policy Forum 2013–14*, 297–330. New Delhi, India: Sage, 2014.

Agarwal, Bina. *A Field of One's Own: Gender and Land Rights in South Asia*. Cambridge, UK: Cambridge University Press, 1994.

Agarwala, Rina. "Reshaping the Social Contract: Emerging Relations between the State and Informal Labor in India." *Theory and Society* 37, no. 4 (2008): 375–408.

Aggarwal, Aradhna. "New Insights into the Relationship between Employment and Economic Growth in India." Working paper 002, Wadhwani Foundation Policy Research Centre, New Delhi, 2014.

Ahuja, Amit. *Mobilizing the Marginalized: Dalit Politics in India.* Manuscript, Department of Political Science, University of California, Santa Barbara, 2016.

Ahuja, Amit, and Pradeep Chhibber. "Why the Poor Vote in India: 'If I Don't Vote, I Am Dead to the State.'" *Studies in Comparative International Development* 47 (2012): 389–410.

Ajit, Dayanandan, Han Donker, and Ravi Saxena. "Corporate Boards in India: Blocked by Caste?" *Economic and Political Weekly* 47, no. 31 (2012): 39–43.

Alesina, Alberto, and Edward L. Glaeser. *Fighting Poverty in the US and Europe: A World of Difference.* Oxford, UK: Oxford University Press, 2004.

Aliber, Michael. "Chronic Poverty in South Africa: Incidence, Causes and Policies." *World Development* 31, no. 3 (2003), 473–90.

Alkire, Sabina, and Suman Seth. "Multidimensional Poverty Reduction in India between 1999 and 2006: Where and How?" *World Development* (72) (2015): 93–108.

Alok, Vishwa Nath. "Strengthening of Panchayats in India: Comparing Devolution across States, Empirical Assessment 2012–13." New Delhi, India: Indian Institute of Public Administration, 2013. Accessed November 16, 2015. www.iipa.org.in/upload/panchayat_devolution_index_report_2012-13.pdf.

Amis, Philip, and Sashi Kumar. "Urban Economic Growth, Infrastructure, and Poverty in India: Lessons from Visakhapatnam." *Environment and Urbanization* 12, no. 1 (2000): 185–96.

Amrith, Sunil S. "Health in India since Independence." Working paper 79, Brooks World Poverty Institute, University of Manchester, 2009.

Ananthpur, Kripa. "Rivalry or Synergy? Formal and Informal Local Governance in Rural India." *Development and Change* 38, no. 3 (2007): 401–21.

Andrews, Matt. "Good Government Means Different Things in Different Countries." *Governance* 23, no. 1 (2010): 7–35.

Andrews, Matt, Lant Pritchett, and Michael Woolcock. "Escaping Credibility Traps through Problem-Driven Iterative Adaptation (PDIA)." Working paper 299, Center for Global Development, 2012. Accessed March 14, 2016. www.cgdev.org/publication/escaping-capability-traps-through-problem-driven-iterative-adaptation-pdia-working-paper.

Appadurai, Arjun. "Deep Democracy: Urban Governmentality and the Horizon of Politics." *Urban Culture* 14, no. 1 (2002): 21–47.

Appadurai, Arjun. "The Capacity to Aspire: Culture and the Terms of Recognition." In *Culture and Public Action: A Cross-Disciplinary Dialogue on Development Policy*, edited by Vijayendra Rao and Michael Walton, 59–84. Palo Alto, CA: Stanford University Press, 2004.

Appu, Putenveetil S. *Land Reforms in India: A Survey of Policy, Legislation, and Implementation*. New Delhi, India: Vikas, 1996.

Arimah, Ben C. "The Face of Urban Poverty: Explaining the Prevalence of Slums in Developing Countries." In *Urbanization and Development: Multidisciplinary Perspectives*, edited by Beall, Jo, Basudeb Guha-Khasnobis, and Ravi Kanbur. New York, NY: Oxford University Press, 2010.

ASER. *Annual Status of Education Report (Rural) 2011*. New Delhi, India: ASER Center, 2012. Accessed September 24, 2016. http://img .asercentre.org/docs/Publications/ASER%20Reports/ASER_2011/aser_ 2011_report_8.2.12.pdf.

ASER. *Annual Status of Education Report, 2014: Main Findings*. ASER, 2015. Accessed September 16, 2016. img.asercentre.org/docs/Publications/ASER %20Reports/ASER%202014/National%20PPTs/aser2014indiaenglish .pdf.

Asian Development Bank. *India: Updating and Improving the Social Protection Index*. Project Number 44152. Manila, Philippines: Asian Development Bank, 2012.

Aspiring Minds. *National Employability Report – Engineers: Annual Report, 2016*. Aspiring Minds, 2016. Accessed September 14, 2016. www.aspiringminds.com/sites/default/files/National%20Employability %20Report%20-%20Engineers%20Annual%20Report%202016.pdf.

Atkinson, Anthony B. *Inequality: What Can Be Done?* Cambridge, MA: Harvard University Press, 2015.

Attwood, Donald W. "Why Some of the Poor Get Richer: Economic Change and Mobility in Rural West India." *Current Anthropology* 20, no. 3 (1979): 495–516.

Auerbach, Adam M. "Clients and Communities: The Political Economy of Party Network Organization and Development in India's Urban Slums." *World Politics* 68, no. 1 (2016): 111–48.

Auerbach, Adam, and Tariq Thachil. "Who do Brokers Serve? Experimental Evidence from Informal Leaders in India's Slums." Paper presented at the Annual Meeting of the American Political Science Association, 2016.

Azam, Mehtabul. "Changes in Wage Structure in Urban India, 1983–2004: A Quantile Regression Decomposition." *World Development* 40, no. 6 (2012): 1135–50.

Azam, Mehtabul, and Vipul Bhatt (2012). "Like Father, Like Son? Intergenerational Education Mobility in India," IZA Discussion Paper 6549,

IZA, Bonn, Germany, 2012. Accessed April 23, 2013. http://ftp.iza.org/ dp6549.pdf.

Azam, Mehtabul, and Andreas Blom. "Progress in Participation in Tertiary Education in India from 1983 to 2004." World Bank Policy Research Working Paper 4793, World Bank, 2008.

Azari, Julia, and Jennifer Smith. "Unwritten Rules: Informal Institutions in Established Democracies." *Perspectives on Politics* 10, no. 1 (2012): 37–55.

Babu, M. Devendra. "Fiscal Empowerment of Panchayats in India: Real or Rhetoric?" Working paper 229, Institute for Social and Economic Change, Bangalore, 2009.

Bagchi, Subroto. *Zen Garden: Conversations with Pathmakers.* New Delhi, India: Penguin Books, 2013.

Baiocchi, Gianpaolo. *Militants and Citizens: Local Democracy on a Global Stage in Porto Alegre.* Stanford, CA: Stanford University Press, 2005.

Balaji, S. J., and Suresh Pal. "Agricultural Productivity Growth: Is There Regional Convergence?" *Economic and Political Weekly* 49, no. 52 (2014): 74–80.

Balakrishnan, Pulapre. *Economic Growth in India: History and Prospects.* New Delhi, India: Oxford University Press, 2010.

Baldwin, Kate. *The Paradox of Traditional Chiefs in Democratic Africa.* New York, NY: Cambridge University Press, 2016.

Bandyopadhyay, Debasis. "Land Reforms in India: An Analysis." *Economic and Political Weekly* 21, no. 25–26 (1986): A50–6.

Banerjee, Abhijit, and Esther Duflo. "The Economic Lives of the Poor." Working paper 135, Bureau for Research and Economic Analysis of Development, 2006.

Banerjee, Abhijit, and Esther Duflo. *Poor Economics: A Radical Rethinking of the Way to Fight Global Poverty.* New York, NY: Public Affairs, 2012.

Banerjee, Abhijit, and Thomas Piketty. "Top Ten Indian Incomes, 1922–2000." *World Bank Economic Review* 19, no. 1 (2005): 1–20.

Banerjee, Abhijit, and Rohini Somanathan. "The Political Economy of Public Goods: Some Evidence from India." *Journal of Development Economics* 82, no. 2 (2007): 287–314.

Banerjee, Abhijit V., Selvan Kumar, Rohini Pande, and Felix Su. "Do Informed Voters Make Better Choices? Experimental Evidence from Urban India." Working paper, 2011. Accessed May 14, 2014. www.povertyactionlab .org/node/2764.

Banerjee, Arpita, and Saraswati Raju. "Gendered Mobility: Women Migrants and Work in Urban India." *Economic and Political Weekly* 44, no. 28 (2009): 115–23.

Banga, Rashmi. "Critical Issues in India's Service-Led Growth." Working paper 171, Indian Council for Research on International Economic Relations, New Delhi, 2005.

Bapat, Meera. "Poverty Lines and Lives of the Poor: Under-estimation of Urban Poverty – the Case of India." Working paper. International Institute of Environment and Development, London, 2009.

Bardhan, Pranab. "Decentralization of Governance and Development." *Journal of Economic Perspectives* 16, no. 4 (2002): 185–205.

Bardhan, Pranab. *Awakening Giants: Feet of Clay*. Princeton, NJ: Princeton University Press, 2010.

Bardhan, Pranab, and Dilip Mookherjee. "The Rise of Local Governments: An Overview." In *Decentralization and Local Governance in Developing Countries,* edited by Bardhan and Mookherjee, 1–52. Cambridge, MA: MIT Press, 2006.

Barnes, Tom, Krishna Shekhar Lal Das, and Surendra Pratap. "Labour Contractors and Global Production Networks: The Case of India's Auto Supply Chain." *Journal of Development Studies* 51, no. 4 (2015): 355–69.

Barnhardt, Sharon. "Near and Dear? Evaluating the Impact of Neighbor Diversity on Inter-religious Attitudes." Working paper, Harvard Kennedy School of Government, Harvard University, 2009.

Barrientos, Armando. *Social Assistance in Developing Countries*. Cambridge, UK: Cambridge University Press, 2013.

Barro, Robert. *Determinants of Economic Growth*. Cambridge, MA: MIT Press, 1997.

Baru, Rama, Arnab Acharya, Sanghmitra Acharya, A. K. Shivakumar, and K. Nagaraj. "Inequities in Access to Health Services in India: Caste, Class and Region." *Economic and Political Weekly* 45, no. 38 (2010): 49–58.

Basant, Rakesh and Gitanjali Sen. "Parental Education as a Criterion for Affirmative Action in Higher Education." *World Development* 64, no. C (2014): 803–14.

Basu, Deepankar, and Debarshi Das. "The Maoist Movement in India: Some Political Economy Considerations." *Journal of Agrarian Change* 13, no. 3 (2013): 365–81.

Basu, Kaushik. "The Enigma of India's Arrival: A Review of Arvind Virmani's Propelling India: From Socialist Stagnation to Global Power." *Journal of Economic Literature,* 46, no. 2 (2008): 396–406.

Basu, Kaushik. "Micro-foundations of Inclusive Growth." In *Economic Survey, 2009–10,* 21–36. New Delhi, India: Government of India, 2010.

Basu, P., and Kunal Sen. "Welfare Implications of India's Employment Guarantee Programme with a Wage Payment Delay." Discussion paper 9454, IZA, Bonn, Germany, 2015. Accessed December 1, 2016. http://ftp.iza.org/dp9454.pdf.

Bates, Robert. *Markets and States in Tropical Africa: The Political Basis of Agricultural Policies.* Berkeley: University of California Press, 1981.

Baulch, Bob. *Why Poverty Persists: Poverty Dynamics in Asia and Africa.* London, UK: Edward Elgar, 2012.

Benabou, Roland, and Efe A. Ok. "Social Mobility and the Demand for Redistribution: The POUM Hypothesis." *Quarterly Journal of Economics* 116, no. 2 (2001): 447–87.

Benabou, Roland, and Jean Tirole. "Belief in a Just World and Redistributive Politics." *Quarterly Journal of Economics* 121, no. 2 (2006): 699–746.

Benjamin, Dwayne, Loren Brandt, and John Giles. "The Evolution of Income Inequality in Rural China." *Economic Development and Cultural Change* 53, no. 4 (2005): 769–824.

Benjamin, Solomon. "Governance, Economic Settings, and Poverty in Bangalore." *Environment and Urbanization* 12, no. 1 (2000): 35–56.

Benjamin, Solomon, and R. Bhuvaneswari. "Democracy, Inclusive Governance and Poverty in Bangalore." Working paper 26, University of Birmingham, UK, 2001. Accessed November 16, 2011. http://casumm.files. wordpress.com/2011/02/democracy-poverty-and-goverance-in-bangalore. pdf.

Berg, Andrew, and Jonathan Ostry. "Inequality and Unsustainable Growth: Two Sides of the Same Coin?" Staff Discussion Note SDN/11/08, IMF, 2011. Accessed May 15, 2015. www.imf.org/external/pubs/ft/sdn/2011/ sdn1108.pdf.

Berner, Erhard. "Opportunities and Insecurities: Globalisation, Localities and the Struggle for Urban Land in Manila." *European Journal of Development Research* 9, no. 1 (1997): 167–82.

Besley, Timothy J., and Robin Burgess. "Can Labour Regulation Hinder Economic Performance? Evidence from India." *Quarterly Journal of Economics* 119, no. 1 (2004): 91–134.

Besley, Timothy J., Rohini Pande, and Vijayendra Rao. "Just Rewards? Local Politics and Public Resource Allocation in South India." *World Bank Economic Review* 26, no. 2 (2012): 191–216.

Béteille, Andre. *Caste, Class and Power: Changing Patterns of Stratification in a Tanjore Village.* Delhi, India: Oxford University Press, 1996.

Bhagat, Ram B. "World Migration Report 2015: Urban Migration Trends, Challenges and Opportunities in India." Background paper, International Organization for Migration, 2014. Accessed November 26, 2016. www.solutionexchange-un-gen-gym.net/wp-content/uploads/2016/01/ WMR-2015-Background-Paper-RBhagat.pdf.

Bhagwati, Jagdish, and Padma Desai. *India: Planning for Industrialization.* New York, NY: Oxford University Press, 1970.

Bhagwati, Jagdish, and Arvind Panagariya. *Why Growth Matters: How Economic Growth in India Reduced Poverty and the Lessons for Other Developing Countries*. New York, NY: Public Affairs, 2013.

Bhalla, Surjit S. *Imagine There's No Country: Poverty, Inequality and Growth in an Era of Globalization*. Washington, DC: Institute for International Economics, 2002.

Bhan, Gautam, and Arindam Jana. "Of Slums or Poverty: Notes of Caution from Census 2011." *Economic and Political Weekly* 48, no. 18 (2013): 13–6.

Bhatia, Navin, and Arnav Chatterjee. "Financial Inclusion in Slums of Mumbai." *Economic and Political Weekly* 45, no. 42 (2010): 23–6.

Bhattacharjea, Aditya. "Labour Market Regulation and Industrial Performance in India: A Critical Review of the Empirical Evidence." *Indian Journal of Labour Economics* 39, no. 2 (2006): 211–32.

Bhide, Shashanka, and Aasha K. Mehta. "Chronic Poverty in Rural India, An Analysis Using Panel Data: Issues and Findings." Paper presented at the International Conference on Staying Poor: Chronic Poverty and Development Policy, Manchester, April 7–9, 2003. http://idpm.man.ac.uk/cprc/Conference/conferencepapers/Bhide%20and%20Mehta%2023.02.03.pdf.

Binswanger-Mkhize, Hans P. "The Stunted Structural Transformation of the Indian Economy: Agriculture, Manufacturing and the Rural Non-farm Sector." *Economic and Political Weekly* 48, no. 26–27 (2013): 5–13.

Birdsall, Nancy. "Stormy Days on an Open Field: Asymmetries in the Global Economy." Working paper 81, Center for Global Development, Washington, DC, 2006. Accessed August 5, 2011. www.cgdev.org.

Bjorklund, Anders, Karin Eriksson, and Markus Jantii. "IQ and Family Background: Are Associations Strong or Weak?" *B. E. Journal of Economic Analysis and Policy* 10, no. 1 (2010): 1–12.

Blomkvist, Hans. "The Soft State: Housing Reform and State Capacity in Urban India." PhD thesis, Department of Government, Uppsala University, Sweden, 1988.

Blumenstock, Joshua, Gabriel Cadamuro, and Robert On. "Predicting Poverty and Wealth from Mobile Phone Metadata." *Science* 350, no. 6264 (2015): 1073–6.

Boisjoly, Johanne, Greg J. Duncan, Michael Kremer, Dan M. Levy, and Jacque Eccles. "Empathy or Antipathy? The Impact of Diversity." *American Economic Review* 96, no. 5 (2006): 1890–905.

Boo, Katherine. "Opening Night." *New Yorker*, February 23, 2009, 22–9.

Boo, Katherine. *Behind the Beautiful Forevers: Life, Death and Hope in a Mumbai Undercity*. New York, NY: Random House, 2012.

Boone, Catherine. *Political Topographies of the African State: Territorial Authority and Institutional Choice*. New York, NY: Cambridge University Press, 2003.

Bourdieu, Pierre. "The Forms of Capital." In *Handbook of Theory: Research for the Sociology of Education*, edited by J. G. Richardson, 241–58. New York, NY: Greenwood Press, 1986.

Bourguignon, Francois. *The Globalization of Inequality*. Princeton, NJ: Princeton University Press, 2015.

Bowles, Samuel, Herbert Gintis, and Melissa Osborne Groves. "Introduction." In *Unequal Chances: Family Background and Economic Success*, edited by Samuel Bowles, Herbert Gintis, and Melissa Osborne Groves, 1–22. Princeton, NJ: Princeton University Press, 2005.

Brass, Paul. *Theft of an Idol: Text and Context in the Representation of Political Violence*. Princeton, NJ: Princeton University Press, 1997.

Bratton, Michael. "Poor People and Democratic Citizenship in Africa." In *Poverty, Participation, and Democracy: A Global Perspective*, edited by Anirudh Krishna, 28–64. New York, NY: Cambridge University Press, 2008.

Bratton, Michael, and Robert Mattes. "Support for Democracy in Africa: Intrinsic or Instrumental?" *British Journal of Political Science* 31, no. 3 (2001): 447–74.

Breman, Jan. *Footloose Labour: Working in India's Informal Economy*. Cambridge, UK: Cambridge University Press, 1996.

Breman, Jan. *The Labouring Poor in India: Patterns of Exploitation, Subordination, and Exclusion*. New Delhi, India: Oxford University Press, 2003.

Breman, Jan. *At Work in the Informal Economy of India: A Perspective from the Bottom Up*. New Delhi, India: Oxford University Press, 2013.

Brule, Rachel. "Accountability in Rural India: Local Government and Social Equality." *Asian Survey* 55, no. 5 (2015): 909–41.

Brulhart, Marius, and Federica Sbergami. "Agglomeration and Growth: Cross-country Evidence." *Journal of Urban Economics* 65, no. 1 (2009): 48–63.

Brunori, Paolo, Francisco H. G. Ferreira, and Vito Peragine. "Inequality of Opportunity, Income Inequality, and Economic Mobility: Some International Comparisons." World Bank Policy Research Working Paper 6304, Washington, DC: World Bank, 2013.

Bruns, Barbara, David Evans, and Javier Luque. "Chapter 1: Brazilian Education 1995–2010, Transformation." *Achieving World-Class Education in Brazil: The Next Agenda*. Washington, DC: The World Bank, 2012.

Brynjolfsson, Erik, and Andrew McAfee. *The Second Machine Age: Work, Progress, and Prosperity in a Time of Brilliant Technologies*. New York, NY: W. W. Norton, 2014.

Buciuni, Giulio, and Vladi Finotto. "Innovation in Global Value Chains: Colocation of Production and Development in Italian Low-Tech Industries." *Regional Studies* 50, no. 12 (2016): 2010–23. doi: 10.1080/00343404.2015.1115010.

Burns, Justine, Lucia Corno, and Eliana La Ferrara. "Does Interaction Affect Racial Prejudice and Cooperation? Evidence from Randomly Assigned Peers in South Africa." 2015. Unpublished manuscript. Accessed September 9, 2016. www.ne.su.se/polopoly_fs/1.226646.1425460291!/menu/standard/file/BurnsCornoLaFerrara_BREAD.pdf.

Burra, Neera. "Crusading for Children in India's Informal Economy." *Economic and Political Weekly* 40, no. 49 (2005): 5199–208.

Bussell, Jennifer. *Corruption and Reform in India: Public Services in the Digital Age.* New York, NY: Cambridge University Press, 2012.

Bussell, Jennifer. n.d. "Clients or Constituents? Citizens, Intermediaries, and Distributive Politics in India." Working paper, Department of Political Science, University of California, Berkeley.

Cain, J. Salcedo, Rana Hasan, Rhoda Magsombol, and Ajay Tandon. "Accounting for Inequality in India: Evidence from Household Expenditures." *World Development* 38, no. 3 (2010): 282–97.

Cammett, Melanie, and Lauren Maclean. "Introduction: The Political Consequences of Non-state Social Welfare in the Global South." *Studies in Comparative International Development* 46, no. 1 (2011): 1–21.

Carnes, Nicholas. *White-Collar Government: The Hidden Role of Class in Economic Policy Making.* Chicago, IL: University of Chicago Press, 2013.

Carr, Nicholas. *The Glass Cage: Automation and Us.* New York, NY: W. W. Norton, 2014.

Carstairs, Robert. *The Little World of an Indian District Officer.* London, UK: Macmillan, 1912.

Carter, Michael R., and Christopher B. Barrett. "The Economics of Poverty Traps and Persistent Poverty: An Asset-Based Approach." *Journal of Development Studies* 42, no. 2 (2006): 178–99.

Carter, Michael R., and Julian May. "One Kind of Freedom: Poverty Dynamics in Post-apartheid South Africa." *World Development* 29, no. 12 (2001): 1987–2006.

Causa, Orsetta, and Catherine Chapuis. "Equity in Student Achievement across OECD Countries." Working paper 78, Department of Economics. Paris: Organisation for Economic Co-operation and Development, 2009.

Center for Policy Research. "Rural Local Body Core Functions and Finances: A Study for the Fourteenth Finance Commission." New Delhi, India: Centre for Policy Research, 2014. Accessed November 16, 2015. http://cprindia.org/sites/default/files/Rural%20Local%20Body%20core%20functions%20and%20finances.pdf.

Chakravarty, Sujoy, and Sejal A. Dand. "Food Insecurity in Gujarat: A Study of Two Rural Populations." *Economic and Political Weekly* 41, no. 22 (2006): 2248–58.

Chamarbagwala, Rubiana. "Economic Liberalization and Wage Inequality in India." *World Development* 34, no. 12 (2006): 1997–2015.

Chambers, Robert. *Whose Reality Counts? Putting the First Last.* London, UK: Intermediary Technology Publications, 1997.

Chambers, Robert, R. Longhurst, and A. Pacey. *Seasonal Dimensions to Rural Poverty.* London, UK: Frances Pinter, 1981.

Chanana, Karuna. "Globalisation, Higher Education and Gender: Changing Subject Choices of Indian Women Students." *Economic and Political Weekly* 42, no. 7 (2007): 590–8.

Chand, Ramesh, and Shinoj Parappurathu. "Temporal and Spatial Variations in Agricultural Growth and Its Determinants." *Economic and Political Weekly* 47, no. 26–27 (2012): 55–64.

Chandhoke, Neera. "'Seeing' the State in India." *Economic and Political Weekly* 40, no. 11 (2005): 1033–39.

Chandra, Kanchan. "The Transformation of Ethnic Politics in India: The Decline of the Congress and the Rise of the Bahujan Samaj Party in Hoshiarpur." *Journal of Asian Studies* 59, no. 1 (2000): 26–61.

Chandra, Kanchan. "Democratic Dynasties: State, Party and Political Families in India." In *Democratic Dynasties: State, Party and Political Families in India*, edited by Chandra. New York, NY: Cambridge University Press, 2016.

Chandrasekhar, C. P., and Jayati Ghosh. *The Market That Failed: A Decade of Neoliberal Economic Reforms in India.* New Delhi, India: LeftWord Books, 2002.

Chatterjee, Partha. "Introduction: A Political History of Independent India." In *State and Politics in India*, edited by P. Chatterjee, 1–39. Delhi, India: Oxford University Press, 1997.

Chatterjee, Partha. *Politics of the Governed: Reflections on Popular Politics in Most of the World.* New York, NY: Columbia University Press, 2004.

Chatterjee, Partha. "Democracy and Economic Transformation in India." In *Understanding India's New Political Economy: A Great Transformation?* edited by Sanjay Ruparelia, Sanjay Reddy, John Harriss, and Stuart Corbridge, 17–39. New York, NY: Routledge, 2011.

Chauchard, Simon. "Can Descriptive Representation Change Beliefs about a Stigmatized Group? Evidence from Rural India." *American Political Science Review* 108, no. 2 (2014): 403–22.

Chaudhuri, Shubham, and Martin Ravallion. "How Well Do Static Indicators Identify the Chronic Poor?" *Journal of Public Economics* 53 (1994): 367–94.

Chaudhuri, Shubham, and Martin Ravallion. (2007). "Partially Awakened Giants: Uneven Growth in India and China." In *Dancing with Giants: China, India, and the Global Economy*, edited by Leonard Alan Winters and Shahid Yusuf, 175–210. Washington, DC: World Bank, 2007.

Chaudhury, Nazmul, Jeffrey Hammer, Michael Kremer, Karthik Muralidharan, and F. Halsey Rogers. "Missing in Action: Teacher and Health Worker Absence in Developing Countries." *Journal of Economic Perspectives* 20, no. 1 (2006): 91–116.

Chavan, Madhav. "Old Challenges for a New Generation." In *Annual Status of Education Report 2013*, 1–4. New Delhi, India: ASER Center, 2014.

Chen, Keijie. "Urban-biased Social Policies and Urban-Rural Divide in China." Master's thesis, Sanford School of Public Policy, Duke University, Durham, NC, USA, 2014.

Chetty, Raj, Nathaniel Hendren, and Lawrence Katz. "The Effects of Exposure to Better Neighborhoods on Children: New Evidence from the Moving to Opportunity Project." *American Economic Review* 106, no. 4 (2016): 855–902.

Chhibber, Pradeep. *Democracy without Associations: Transformation of the Party System and Social Cleavage in India*. New Delhi, India: Vistaar Publications, 1999.

Chhibber, Pradeep, and Rahul Verma. "The BJP's 2014 'Modi Wave': An Ideological Consolidation of the Right." *Economic and Political Weekly* 49, no. 39 (2014): 50–6.

Chibber, Vivek. *Locked in Place: State-Building and Late Industrialization in India*. Princeton, NJ: Princeton University Press, 2003.

Chomitz, Kenneth M., Piet Buys, and Timothy S. Thomas. "Quantifying the Rural-Urban Gradient in Latin America and the Caribbean." World Bank Policy Research Working Paper 3634. Washington, DC: World Bank, 2005.

Chopra, Deepta. "'They Don't Want to Work' versus 'They Don't Want to Provide Work': Seeking Explanations for the Decline of MGNREGA in Rajasthan." Effective States and Inclusive Development Working Paper 31, Manchester, UK: University of Manchester, 2014.

Chopra, Radhika. "Maps of Experience: Narratives of Migration in an Indian Village." *Economic and Political Weekly* 30, no. 49 (1995): 3156–62.

CHRI. *Police Accountability: Too Important to Neglect, Too Urgent to Delay*. New Delhi, India: Commonwealth Human Rights Initiative, 2005. Accessed April 20, 2016. www.humanrightsinitiative.org/publications/chogm/chogm_2005/chogm_2005_full_report.pdf.

Christiaensen, Luc, Lionel Demery, and Stefano Paternostro. "Reforms, Remoteness, and Risk in Africa: Understanding Inequality and Poverty during the 1990s." In *Spatial Inequality and Development*, edited by Ravi Kanbur and Anthony J. Venables, 209–36. Oxford, UK: Oxford University Press, 2005.

Clark, Gregory. *The Son Also Rises: Surnames and the History of Social Mobility*. Princeton, NJ: Princeton University Press, 2014.

Collins, Daryl, Jonathan Morduch, Stuart Rutherford, and Orlanda Ruthven. *Portfolios of the Poor: How the World's Poor Live on $2 a Day*. Princeton, NJ: Princeton University Press, 2009.

Corbridge, S., G. Williams, M. Srivastava, and R. Veron. *Seeing the State: Governance and Governmentality in India*. New York, NY: Cambridge University Press, 2005.

Corbridge, Stuart, and John Harriss. *Reinventing India: Economic Liberalization, Hindu Nationalism, and Popular Democracy*. Cambridge, UK: Polity Press, 2000.

CPRC. *The Chronic Poverty Report 2004–05*. Manchester, UK: Chronic Poverty Research Centre, 2005.

Cristia, Julian, Pablo Ibarran, Santiago Cueto, Ana Santiago, and Eugenio Severin. "Technology and Child Development: Evidence from One Laptop per Child Program." Working paper 304, Inter-American Development Bank, 2012. Accessed September 16, 2016. www.iadb.org/en/research-and-data/publication-details,3169.html?pub_id=IDB-WP-304.

Crook, Richard, and James Manor. *Democracy and Decentralization in South Asia and West Africa: Participation, Accountability and Performance*. Cambridge, UK: Cambridge University Press, 1998.

Cumings, Bruce. "The Origins and Development of the Northeast Asian Political Economy: Industrial Sectors, Product Cycles, and Political Consequences." *International Organization*, 38, no. 1 (1984): 1–40.

Damodaran, Harish. *India's New Capitalists: Caste, Business and Industry in a Modern Nation*. Ranikhet, India: Permanent Black, 2008.

Damodaran, Harish. "The Untold Farm Rebound Story." *India Seminar* (2012). Accessed October 16, 2015. www.india-seminar.com/2013/641/641_harish_damodaran.htm.

Dandekar, Vishnu M., and Nilakantha Rath. "Poverty in India." *Economic and Political Weekly* 6, no. 2 (1971).

Das, Jishnu, and Tristan Zajonc. "India Shining and Bharat Drowning: Comparing Two Indian States to the Worldwide Distribution in Mathematics Achievement." *Journal of Development Economics* 92, no. 2 (2010): 175–87.

Das, Jishnu, Alaka Holla, Veena Das, Manoj Mohanan, Diana Tabak, and Brian Chan. "In Urban and Rural India, a Standardized Patient Study Showed Low Levels of Provider Training and Huge Quality Gaps." *Health Affairs* 31, no. 12 (2012): 2774–84.

Das, S. K. *Building a World-class Civil Service for Twenty-first Century India.* New Delhi, India: Oxford University Press, 2010.

Das, S. K. *The Civil Services in India.* New Delhi, India: Oxford University Press, 2013.

Das, Samarjit, Chetan Ghate, and Peter E. Robinson. "Remoteness, Urbanization and India's Unbalanced Growth." *World Development* 66 (2015): 572–87.

Dasgupta, Monica. "Public Health in India: Dangerous Neglect." *Economic and Political Weekly* 40, no. 49 (2005): 5159–65.

Dasgupta, Monica, and V. R. Muraleedharan. "Universal Health Coverage: Reform of the Government System Better Than Quality Health Insurance." *Economic and Political Weekly* 49, no. 35 (2014): 29–32.

Dasgupta, Sukti. "Structural and Behavioural Characteristics of Informal Service Employment: Evidence from a Survey in New Delhi." *Journal of Development Studies* 39, no. 3 (2003): 51–80.

Datt, Gaurav, and Martin Ravallion. "Is India's Economic Growth Leaving the Poor Behind?" *Journal of Economic Perspectives* 16, no. 3 (2002): 89–108.

Datta, Amrita, Gerry Rodgers, Janine Rodgers, and B. K. N. Singh. "Contrasts in Development in Bihar: A Tale of Two Villages." *Journal of Development Studies* 50, no. 9 (2014): 1197–208.

Davidson, Basil. *The Black Man's Burden: Africa and the Curse of the Nation-State.* New York: Three Rivers Press, 1993.

De Haan, Arjan. "Migration and Livelihoods in Comparative Perspective: A Case Study of Bihar, India." *Journal of Development Studies* 38, no. 5 (2002): 115–42.

De Haan, Arjan. "Rural-Urban Migration and Poverty: The Case of India." *IDS Bulletin* 28, no. 2 (1997): 35–47.

De Haan, Arjan, and Ben Rogaly. "Introduction: Migrant Workers and Their Role in Rural Change." In *Labour Mobility and Rural Society*, edited by Arjan De Haan and Ben Rogaly, 1–14. New York, NY: Frank Cass, 2002.

De Soto, Hernando. *The Mystery of Capital: Why Capitalism Triumphs in the West and Fails Everywhere Else.* New York, NY: Basic Books, 2000.

De Witt, Joop. "Slum Dwellers, Slum Leaders, and the Government Apparatus." Urban Research Working Paper 8, Amsterdam: Institute of Cultural Anthropology, 1986.

Deaton, Angus. "Counting the World's Poor: Problems and Possible Solutions." 2000. Accessed October 21, 2016. www.princeton.edu/rpds/papers/pdfs/deaton_worlds_poor.pdf.

Deaton, Angus, and Jean Drèze. "Poverty and Inequality in India: A Re-examination." *Economic and Political Weekly* 37, no. 36 (2002): 3729–48.

Deaton, Angus, and Jean Drèze. "Food and Nutrition in India, Facts and Interpretation." *Economic and Political Weekly* 44, no. 7 (2009): 42–65.

Deaton, Angus, and Valerie Kozel. "Data and Dogma: The Great Indian Poverty Debate." *World Bank Research Observer* 20, no. 2 (2005): 177–99.

Deaton, Angus, and Alessandro Tarozzi. "Prices and Poverty in India." In *The Great Indian Poverty Debate*, edited by Angus Deaton and Valerie Kozel, 381–411. New Delhi, India: Macmillan, 2005.

Deb, Siddhartha. *The Beautiful and the Damned: A Portrait of the New India.* New York, NY: Faber & Faber, 2011.

Deininger, Klaus, and John Okidi. "Growth and Poverty Reduction in Uganda, 1992–2000: Panel Data Evidence." *Development Policy Review* 21, no. 4 (2003): 481–509.

Dercon, Stefan. *Insurance against Poverty.* Oxford, UK: Oxford University Press, 2005.

Dercon, Stefan, Pramila Krishnan, and Sofya Krutikova. "Changing Living Standards in Southern Indian Villages 1975–2006: Revisiting the ICRISAT Village Level Studies." *Journal of Development Studies* 49, no. 12 (2013): 1676–93.

Desai, Sonalde, and Veena Kulkarni. "Changing Educational Inequalities in India in the Context of Affirmative Action." *Demography* 45, no. 2 (2008): 245–70.

Desai, Sonalde, Amaresh Dubey, Reeve Vanneman, and Rukmini Banerji. "Private Schooling in India: A New Landscape." *India Policy Forum* 5:1–58. New Delhi, India: Sage, 2009.

Desai, Sonalde, Prem Vashishtha, and Omkar Joshi. *Mahatma Gandhi National Rural Employment Guarantee Act: A Catalyst for Rural Transformation.* New Delhi, India: National Council of Applied Economic Research, 2015.

Deshingkar, Priya, and Daniel Start. "Seasonal Migration for Livelihoods in India: Coping, Accumulation and Exclusion." Working paper 220, Overseas Development Institute, 2003.

Deshingkar, Priya, and Shaheen Akter. "Migration and Human Development in India." Human Development Research Paper 2009/13. New York, NY: United Nations Development Programme, 2009.

Deshingkar, Priya, and John Farrington. "A Framework for Understanding Circular Migration." In *Circular Migration and Multilocational Livelihood Strategies in Rural India*, edited by Priya Deshingkar and John Farrington, 1–36. New Delhi, India: Oxford University Press, 2009.

Deshpande, Ashwini. *Grammar of Caste: Economic Discrimination in Contemporary India.* New Delhi, India: Oxford University Press, 2011.

Deshpande, Ashwini, and Katherine Newman. "Where the Path Leads: The Role of Caste in Post-university Employment Expectations." *Economic and Political Weekly* 42, no. 41 (2007): 4133–40.

Deshpande, Rajeshwari, and Suhas Palshikar. "Occupational Mobility: How Much Does Caste Matter?" *Economic and Political Weekly* 43, no. 34 (2008): 61–70.

Deshpande, Satish. "Exclusive Inequalities: Merit, Caste and Discrimination in Indian Higher Education Today." *Economic and Political Weekly* 41, no. 24 (2006): 2438–44.

Deshpande, Satish, and Yogendra Yadav. "Redesigning Affirmative Action: Castes and Benefits in Higher Education." *Economic and Political Weekly* 41, no. 24 (2006): 2419–24.

Deuchar, Andrew. "All Dressed Up with Nowhere to Go: Transitions to (Un)Employment for Lower Middle Class Young Men." *Economic and Political Weekly* 49, no. 17 (2014): 104–11.

Dev, Mahendra. "Agriculture and Rural Employment in the Budget." *Economic and Political Weekly* 40, no. 14 (2005): 1410–3.

Dev, Mahendra, and C. Ravi. "Poverty and Inequality: All-India and States, 1983–2005." *Economic and Political Weekly* 42, no. 6 (2007): 509–21.

Dev, Mahendra, and C. Ravi. "Revising Estimates of Poverty." *Economic and Political Weekly* 43, no. 10 (2008): 8–10.

Dewit, Michael. "Slum Perceptions and Cognitions." In *Living in India's Slums: A Case Study of Bangalore*, edited by H. Schenk, 79–112. New Delhi, India: Manohar Publishers, 2001.

Dhamija, Nidhi, and Shashanka Bhide. "Dynamics of Chronic Poverty: Variations in Factors Influencing Entry and Exit of Chronic Poor." CPRC-IIPA Working Paper 38. Indian Institute of Public Administration, New Delhi Chronic Poverty Research Centre, 2009. Accessed May 7, 2015. www.chronicpoverty.org/uploads/publication_files2/CPRC-IIPA%2039-new.pdf.

Dhillon, Amrita, Vegard Iversen, and Gaute Torsvik. "Employee Referral, Social Proximity, and Worker Discipline." Working paper, 2014. Accessed June 2, 2015. https://manchester.academia.edu/VegardIversen.

Dhillon, Kirpal. *Police and Politics in India: Colonial Concepts, Democratic Compulsions: Indian Police, 1947–2002*. New Delhi, India: Manohar, 2005.

Diamond, Jared. *Guns, Germs and Steel: The Fates of Human Societies*. New York, NY: Norton, 2000.

Diamond, Larry. "The Democratic Rollback: The Resurgence of the Predatory State." *Foreign Affairs* 87, no. 2 (2008): 36–48.

Dilip, T. R., and Ravi Duggal. "Incidence of Non-Fatal Health Outcomes and Debt in Urban India." Working paper, Centre for Enquiry into Health and Allied Themes (CEHAT), Mumbai, India, 2002.

DiMaggio, P. J., and W. W. Powell. "The Iron Cage Revisited: Institutional Iso-morphism and Collective Rationality in Organizational Fields." *American Sociological Review* 48, no. 2 (1983): 147–60.

DiMaggio, Paul. "Cultural Capital and School Success." *American Sociological Review* 47, no. 2 (1982): 189–201.

Dirks, Nicholas B. *Castes of Mind: Colonialism and the Making of Modern India*. Princeton, NJ: Princeton University Press, 2001.

Djurfeldt, Göran, Venkatesh Athreya, N. Jayakumar, et al. "Agrarian Change and Social Mobility in Tamil Nadu." Working paper, Department of Sociology, Lund University, Sweden, 2008.

Dollar, David, and Aart Kraay. "Growth Is Good for the Poor." *Journal of Economic Growth* 7, no. 3 (2000): 195–225.

Dougherty, Sean. "Labour Regulation and Employment Dynamics at the State Level in India." Working papers 264, Department of Economics. Paris: Organisation for Economic Co-operation and Development, 2008.

Drèze, Jean, and Amartya Sen. *India: Economic Development and Social Opportunity*. New Delhi, India: Oxford University Press, 1995.

Drèze, Jean, and Amartya Sen. *An Uncertain Glory: India and Its Contradictions*. Princeton, NJ: Princeton University Press, 2013.

Dubey, Amaresh, Shubhashis Gangopadhyay, and Wilima Wadhwa. "Occupational Structure and Incidence of Poverty in Indian Towns of Different Sizes." *Review of Development Economics* 5, no. 1 (2001): 49–59.

Duggal, Ravi. "Public Expenditures, Investment and Financing under the Shadow of the Growing Private Sector." In *Review of Healthcare in India*, edited by Leena Gangolli, Ravi Duggal, and Abhay Shukla, 225–46. Mumbai, India: CEHAT, 2005.

Dumont, Louis. *Homo Hierarchicus: An Essay on the Caste System*. Chicago, IL: University of Chicago Press, 1970.

Dutt, Romesh C. *Economic History of India*. New York, NY: Burt Franklin, 1903.

Easterly, William. *The White Man's Burden: Why the West's Efforts to Aid the Rest Have Done So Much Ill and So Little Good*. New York, NY: Penguin Press, 2006.

Emran, Shahe M., and Forhad Shilpi. "Gender, Geography, and Generations: Intergenerational Educational Mobility in Post-reform India." *World Development* 72 (2015): 362–80.

Equitap. "Paying Out-of-Pocket for Health Care in Asia: Catastrophic and Poverty Impact." Working paper 2, Equitap, 2005. Available at www.equitap.org. Accessed November 2, 2016. www.equitap.org/publications/docs/EquitapWP15.pdf.

Escobal, Javier, and Maximo Torrero. "Adverse Geography and Differences in Welfare in Peru." In *Spatial Inequality and Development*, edited by Ravi

Kanbur and Anthony J. Venables, 77–122. Oxford, UK: Oxford University Press, 2005.

Esman, Milton J., and Norman T. Uphoff. *Local Organizations: Intermediaries in Rural Development*. Ithaca, NY: Cornell University Press, 1984.

Esping-Andersen, Gosta. *The Three Worlds of Welfare Capitalism*. Princeton, NJ: Princeton University Press, 1990.

Esping-Andersen, Gosta. "Education and Equal Life-Chances: Investing in Children." In *Social Policy and Economic Development in the Nordic Countries*, edited by O. Kangas and J. Palme, 147–63. New York, NY: Palgrave Macmillan, 2005.

Eswaran, Mukesh, Ashok Kotwal, Bharat Ramaswami, and Wilima Wadhwa. "Sectoral Labour Flows and Agricultural Wages in India, 1983–2004: Has Growth Trickled Down?" *Economic and Political Weekly* 44, no. 2 (2009): 46–55.

Ezcurra, Roberto, and Andres Rodrigues-Pose. "Does Economic Globalization Affect Regional Inequality? A Cross-country Analysis." *World Development* 52, no. C (2013): 92–103.

Faguet, Jean-Paul. *Decentralization and Popular Democracy: Governance from Below in Bolivia*. Ann Arbor: University of Michigan Press, 2012.

Faleiro, Sonia. *Beautiful Things: Inside the Secret World of Bombay's Dance Bars*. New York, NY: Black Cat, 2012.

Fan, Shenggen, Connie Chen-Kang, and Anit Mukherjee. (2005). "Rural and Urban Dynamics and Poverty: Evidence from China and India." Discussion paper 196, Food Consumption and Nutrition Division. Washington, DC: International Food Policy Research Institute, 2005.

Farrell, Diana, Martha Laboissiere, Jaeson Rosenfeld, Sascha Sturze, and Fusayo Umezawa. *The Emerging Global Market: Part II – The Supply of Offshore Talent in Services*. New York, NY: McKinsey Global Institute, 2005.

Fernandes, Leela. "Restructuring the New Middle Class in Liberalizing India." *Comparative Studies of South Asia, Africa and the Middle East*, 20, no. 1–2 (2000): 88–112.

Fernandes, Leela. *India's New Middle Class: Democratic Politics in an Era of Economic Reform*. Minneapolis: University of Minnesota Press, 2006.

Fernandes, Leela, and Patrick Heller. "Hegemonic Aspirations: New Middle Class Politics and India's Democracy in Comparative Perspective." *Critical Asian Studies* 38, no. 4 (2006): 495–522.

Ferré, Celine, Francisco H. G. Ferreira, and Peter Lanjouw. "Is There a Metropolitan Bias? The Relationship between Poverty and City Size in a Selection of Developing Countries." *World Bank Economic Review* 26, no. 3 (2012): 351–82.

Findlay, Ronald, and Stanislaw Wellisz. "Hong Kong." In *Five Small Open Economies*, edited by Ronald Findlay and Stainslaw Wellisz, 16–92. New York, NY: Oxford University Press, 1993.

Finkel, Steven E. "Civic Education and the Mobilization of Political Participation in Developing Democracies." *Journal of Politics* 64, no. 4 (2002): 994–1020.

Florida, Richard. "Cities and the Creative Class." *City and Community* 2, no. 1 (2003): 3–19.

Florida, Richard. *Who's Your City? How the Creative Economy Is Making Where to Live the Most Important Decision in Your Life*. New York, NY: Basic Books, 2008.

Forster, Michael, David Jesuit, and Timothy Smeeding. "Regional Poverty and Income Inequality in Central and Eastern Europe: Evidence from the Luxembourg Income Study." In *Spatial Inequality and Development*, edited by Ravi Kanbur and Anthony J. Venables, 311–47. Oxford, UK: Oxford University Press, 2005.

Fox, Jonathan A. "Social Accountability: What Does the Evidence Really Say?" *World Development* 72 (2015): 346–61.

Fox, Sean. "The Political Economy of Slums: Theory and Evidence from Sub-Saharan Africa." *World Development* 54 (2014): 191–203.

Frankenhoff, Charles A. "Elements of an Economic Model for Slums in a Developing Economy." *Economic Development and Cultural Change* 16, no. 1 (1967): 27–36.

French, Patrick. *India: A Portrait*. London, UK: Penguin, 2011.

Friedland, R., and R. R. Alford. "Bringing Society Back In: Symbols, Practices and Institutional Contradictions." In *The New Institutionalism in Organizational Analysis*, edited by W. W. Powell and P. J. DiMaggio, 232–66. Chicago, IL: University of Chicago Press, 1991.

Friedman, Thomas L. *The World Is Flat: A Brief History of the Twenty-first Century*. New York, NY: Farrar, Straus and Giroux, 2005.

Fuller, Chris J., and John Harriss. "For an Anthropology of the Modern Indian State." *The Everyday State and Society in Modern India*, edited by Chris J. Fuller and V. Benei, 1–30. New Delhi, India: Social Science Press, 2000.

Fuller, Chris J., and Haripriya Narasimhan. "Engineering Colleges, 'Exposure,' and Information Technology Professionals in Tamil Nadu." *Economic and Political Weekly* 41, no. 3 (2006): 258–62.

Fuller, Chris J., and Haripriya Narasimhan. "Information Technology Professionals and the New-rich Middle-class in Chennai (Madras)." *Modern Asian Studies* 41, no. 1 (2007): 121–50.

Fung, Archon. *Empowered Participation: Reinventing Urban Democracy*. Princeton, NJ: Princeton University Press, 2004.

Fung, Archon, and Erik Olin Wright, eds. *Deepening Democracy: Institutional Innovations in Empowered Participatory Governance*. New York, NY: Verso, 2003.

Gaiha, Raghav, and Anil Deolalikar. "Persistent, Expected and Innate Poverty: Estimates for Semi-arid Rural South India." *Cambridge Journal of Economics* 17, no. 4 (1993): 409–21.

Gaiha, Raghav, and Katsushi Imai. "Vulnerability, Persistence of Poverty, and Shocks: Estimates for Semi-arid Rural India." *Oxford Economic Studies* 32, no. 2 (2004): 261–81.

Galanter, Marc. *Law and Society in Modern India*. Delhi, India: Oxford University Press, 1989.

Gandhi, Aditi, and Michael Walton. "Where Do India's Billionaires Get Their Wealth?" *Economic and Political Weekly* (October 6, 2012): 10–14.

Gang, Ira N., Kunal Sen, and Myeong-Su Yun. "Is Caste Destiny? Occupational Diversification among Dalits in Rural India." Working paper 162, Brooks World Poverty Institute, Manchester, UK, 2012.

Ganguly-Scrase, Ruchira, and Timothy J. Scrase. *Globalization and the Middle Classes in India: The Social and Cultural Impact of Neoliberal Reforms*. New York, NY: Routledge, 2009.

Gardner, Katy, and Filippo Osella. "Migration, Modernity and Social Transformation in South Asia: An Introduction." In *Migration, Modernity and Social Transformation in South Asia*, edited by Filippo Osella and Katy Gardner, xi–xlviii. New Delhi, India: Sage, 2004.

Garg, Charu C., and Anup K. Karan. "Health and Millennium Development Goal 1: Reducing Out-of-Pocket Expenditures to Reduce Income Poverty – Evidence from India." Equitap Project Working Paper 15, 2005. Accessed May 14, 2014. www.equitap.org.

Geetha, S., and Madhura Swaminathan. "Nutritional Status of Slum Children in Mumbai: A Socio-economic Survey." *Economic and Political Weekly* (April 6, 1996): 896–900.

Gereffi, Gary. "Global Value Chains in a Post-Washington Consensus World: Shifting Governance Structures, Trade Patterns and Development Prospects." *Review of International Political Economy* 21, no. 1 (2012): 9–37.

Ghani, Ejaz, William R. Kerr, and Stephen D. O'Connell. "Input Usage and Productivity in Indian Manufacturing Plants." PREM Policy Research Working Paper 6656, Washington, DC: World Bank, 2013.

Gidwani, Vinay, and Kalyanakrishnan Sivaramakrishnan. "Migration and Rural Cosmopolitanism in India." In *Circular Migration, Modernity and Social Transformation in South Asia*, edited by Filippo Osella and Katy Gardner, 339–67. New Delhi, India: Sage, 2004.

Gilens, Martin. *Why Americans Hate Welfare: Race, Media, and the Politics of Antipoverty Policy*. Chicago, IL: University of Chicago Press, 2000.

Gilman, Nils. "The Twin Insurgency." *American Interest* 9, no. 6 (2014): 3–11. Accessed December 14, 2015. www.the-american-interest.com/2014/06/15/the-twin-insurgency.

Gilmour, David. *The Ruling Caste: Imperial Lives in the Victorian Raj*. New York, NY: Farrar, Straus and Giroux, 2005.

Giridhardass, Anand. *India Calling: An Intimate Portrait of a Nation's Remaking*. New York, NY: Times Books, 2011.

Gladwell, Malcolm. *Outliers: The Story of Success*. New York, NY: Little, Brown and Company, 2008.

Glaeser, Edward. *Triumph of the City*. New York, NY: Penguin, 2011.

Godbole, Madhav. *Good Governance: Never on India's Radar*. New Delhi, India: Rupa, 2014.

GOI. "Educational Statistics at a Glance." New Delhi, India: Ministry of Human Resource Development, Bureau of Planning, Monitoring and Statistics, Government of India, 2004. Accessed May 4, 2016. http://mhrd.gov.in/sites/upload_files/mhrd/files/statistics/EAG2014.pdf.

GOI. *Report of the Expert Group on Agricultural Indebtedness*. New Delhi, India: Ministry of Finance, Government of India, 2007.

GOI. *Development Challenges in Extremist Affected Areas: Report of an Expert Group to Planning Commission*. New Delhi, India: Planning Commission, Government of India, 2008.

GOI. *Report of the Expert Group to Review the Methodology for Estimation of Poverty*. New Delhi, India: Planning Commission, Government of India, 2009.

GOI. *Civil Services Survey: A Report*. New Delhi, India: Ministry of Personnel, Public Grievances, and Pensions, Department of Administrative Reforms and Public Grievances, Government of India, 2010a.

GOI. *Report of the Committee on Slum Statistics/Census*. New Delhi, India: Ministry of Housing and Urban Poverty Alleviation, Government of India, 2010b. Accessed January 19, 2016. http://mhupa.gov.in/W_new/Slum_Report_NBO.pdf.

GOI. *Report on Employment and Unemployment Survey (2009–10)*. Chandigarh: Labour Bureau, Ministry of Labour and Employment, Government of India, 2010c.

GOI. *Strategy Paper*. New Delhi, India: Ministry of Housing and Urban Poverty Alleviation, Government of India, 2011. Accessed December 2, 2015. www.mhupa.gov.in/writereaddata/UploadFile/MHUPA-STRATEGY_PAPER.pdf

GOI. *All India Survey on Higher Education (2011–12 (Provisional))*. New Delhi, India: Department of Higher Education, Ministry of Human Resource Development, Government of India, 2013. Accessed May 4, 2016. http://mhrd.gov.in/sites/upload_files/mhrd/files/statistics/AISHE2011-12P_1.pdf.

Goldberg, Pinelopi Koujianou, and Nina Pavcnik (2007). "Distributional Effects of Globalization in Developing Countries." *Journal of Economic Literature* 45, no. 1 (2007): 39–82.

Gomes, Joseph Flavian. "The Political Economy of the Maoist Conflict in India: An Empirical Analysis." *World Development* 68 (2015): 96–123.

Gooptu, Nandini. *The Politics of the Urban Poor in Early Twentieth-century India*. New York, NY: Cambridge University Press, 2001.

Gooptu, Nandini. "Economic Liberalization, Urban Politics and the Poor." In *Understanding India's New Political Economy: A Great Transformation?*, edited by Sanjay Ruparelia, Sanjay Reddy, John Harriss, and Stuart Corbridge, 35–48. New York, NY: Routledge, 2011.

Gothoskar, Sujata. "The Plight of Domestic Workers: Confluence of Gender, Class, and Caste Hierarchies." *Economic and Political Weekly* 48, no. 22 (2013): 63–75.

Goyal, Sangeeta, and Priyanka Pandey. "How Do Government and Private Schools Differ?" *Economic and Political Weekly* 47, no. 22 (2012): 67–76.

Grindle, Merilee. *Going Local: Decentralization, Democratization, and the Promise of Good Governance*. Princeton, NJ: Princeton University Press, 2007.

Gruber, Lloyd, and Stephen Kosack. "The Tertiary Tilt: Education and Inequality in the Developing World." *World Development* (54) (2014): 253–72.

Gruère, Guillaume, and Debdatta Sengupta. "Bt Cotton and Farmer Suicides in India: An Evidence-based Assessment." *Journal of Development Studies* 47, no. 2 (2011): 316–37.

Guerin, Isabelle, Bert D'Espallier, and Govindan Venkatasubramanian. "Debt in Rural South India: Fragmentation, Social Regulation and Discrimination." *Journal of Development Studies* 49, no. 9 (2012): 1155–71.

Guerrin, Isabelle, G. Venkatasubramaniam, and S. Kumar. "Debt Bondage and the Tricks of Capital." *Economic and Political Weekly* 50, no. 26–27 (2015): 11–8.

Guha, Ramachandra. *India after Gandhi: The History of the World's Largest Democracy*. New York: Harper Perennial, 2008.

Gupta, Akhil. *Postcolonial Developments: Agriculture in the Making of Modern India*. Durham, NC: Duke University Press, 1998.

Gupta, Akhil. *Red Tape: Bureaucracy, Structural Violence, and Poverty in India*. Durham, NC: Duke University Press, 2012.

Gupta, Dipankar. "Whither the Indian Village: Culture and Agriculture in 'Rural' India." *Economic and Political Weekly* 40, no. 8 (2005): 751–8.

Gupta, Indrani, and Samik Chowdhury. "Public Financing for Health Coverage in India: Who Spends, Who Benefits and at What Cost?" *Economic and Political Weekly* 49, no. 35 (2014): 59–63.

Gupta, Indrani, and Arup Mitra. "Economic Growth, Health and Poverty: An Exploratory Study for India." *Development Policy Review* 22, no. 2 (2004): 193–206.

Gutmann, Amy, and Dennis Thompson. *Why Deliberative Democracy?* Princeton, NJ: Princeton University Press, 2004.

Haddad, Lawrence, and Akhter Ahmed. "Chronic and Transitory Poverty: Evidence from Egypt, 1997–99." *World Development* 31, no. 1 (2003): 71–85.

Hall, Peter A., and David Soskice, eds. *Varieties of Capitalism: The Institutional Foundations of Comparative Advantage*. Oxford, UK: Oxford University Press, 2001.

Hammer, Jeffrey, Yamini Aiyar, and Salimah Samji. "Bottom's Up: To the Role of Panchayati Raj Institutions in Health and Health Services." Social Development Paper 98, South Asia Series, World Bank, Washington, DC, 2006.

Hammer, Jeffrey, Yamini Aiyar, and Salimah Samji. "Understanding Government Failure in Public Health Services." *Economic and Political Weekly* 42, no. 40 (2007): 4049–57.

Hanushek, Eric A, and Ludger Woessmann. "The Role of Cognitive Skills in Economic Development." *Journal of Economic Literature* 46, no. 3 (2008): 607–68.

Harriss, John. "Political Participation, Representation, and the Urban Poor: Findings from Research in Delhi." *Economic and Political Weekly* 40, no. 11 (2005): 1041–54.

Harriss, John. "Middle-Class Activism and the Politics of the Informal Working Class." *Critical Asian Studies*, 38, no. 4 (2006): 445–65.

Harris-White, Barbara. *India Working: Essays on Society and Economy*. Cambridge, UK: Cambridge University Press, 2003.

Harris-White, Barbara, and S. Janakaranjan, eds. *Rural India Facing the 21st Century: Essays on Long Term Village Change and Recent Development Policy*. London, UK: Anthem Press, 2004.

Hatlebakk, Magnus. "Poverty Dynamics in Rural Orissa: Transitions in Assets and Occupations over Generations." *Journal of Development Studies* 50, no. 6 (2014): 877–93.

Haynes, Douglas E. *Small Town Capitalism in Western India: Artisans, Merchants, and the Making of the Informal Economy 1870–1960*. New York, NY: Cambridge University Press, 2012.

Heckman, James. "The American Family in Black and White: A Post-racial Strategy for Improving Skills to Promote Equality." *Daedalus*, 140, no. 2 (2011): 70–89.

Heitzman, James. *Network City: Planning the Information Society in Bangalore*. New Delhi, India: Oxford University Press, 2004.

Heller, Patrick. "Moving the State: The Politics of Democratic Decentralization in Kerala, South Africa, and Porto Alegre." *Politics and Society* 29, no. 1 (2001): 131–63.

Heller, Patrick, and Vijayendra Rao. "Deliberation and Development." In *Deliberation and Development*, edited by Patrick Heller and Vijayendra Rao, pp. 1–26. Washington, DC: World Bank, 2004.

Helmke, Gretchen, and Steven Levitsky. "Informal Institutions and Comparative Politics: A Research Agenda." *Perspectives on Politics* 2, no. 4 (2004): 725–40.

Herrigel, Gary. *Industrial Constructions: The Sources of German Industrial Power*. New York, NY: Cambridge University Press, 1996.

Higham, Rob, and Alpa Shah. "Conservative Force or Contradictory Resource? Education and Affirmative Action in Jharkhand, India." *Compare: A Journal of Comparative and International Education* 43, no. 6 (2013): 718–39.

Hill, Elizabeth, Meera Samson, and Shyamasree Dasgupta. "Expanding the School Market in India: Parental Choice and the Reproduction of Social Inequality." *Economic and Political Weekly* 46, no. 35 (2011): 98–105.

Himanshu, and Kunal Sen. "Revisiting the Great Indian Poverty Debate: Measurement, Patterns, and Determinants." Working paper 203, Brooks World Policy Institute, 2014.

Himanshu. "Recent Trends in Poverty and Inequality: Some Preliminary Results." *Economic and Political Weekly* 42, no. 6 (2006): 497–508.

Hirschman, Albert. *Exit, Voice and Loyalty: Responses to Declines in Firms, Organizations and States*. Cambridge, MA: Harvard University Press, 1970.

Hiskey, Jonathan T., and Mitchell A. Seligson. "Pitfalls of Power to the People: Decentralization, Local Government Performance, and System Support in Bolivia." *Studies in Comparative International Development* 37, no. 4 (2003): 64–88.

Hnatkovska, Viktoria, Amartya Lahiri, and Sourabh B. Paul. "Breaking the Caste Barrier: Intergenerational Mobility in India." *Journal of Human Resources* 48, no. 2 (2013): 435–73.

Holden, Constance. "Hunter-Gatherers Grasp Geometry." *Science* 311, no. 5759 (2006): 317.

Howell, Jude. "Reflections on the Chinese State." *Development and Change* 37, no. 2 (2006): 273–97.

Hoxby, Caroline, and Sarah Turner. "Expanding College Opportunities for High-Achieving, Low-Income Students." SIEPR Discussion Paper 12–014, Stanford University, California, 2013. Accessed May 8, 2013. http://siepr.stanford.edu/?q=/system/files/shared/pubs/papers/12-014paper.pdf.

Hu, Ruifa, Jikun Huang, and Kevin Z. Chen. "The Public Agriculture Extension System in China: Development and Reform." Center for Chinese Agricultural Policy (CCAP), Chinese Academy of Sciences, 2012. Accessed October 22, 2016. www.syngentafoundation.org/__temp/HU_HUANG_CHEN_AG_EXTN_CHINA_DEVELOPMENT_REFORM.pdf.

Hulme, David, and Andrew Shepherd. "Conceptualizing Chronic Poverty." *World Development* 31, no. 3 (2003): 403–24.

ILO. *Decent Work and the Informal Economy*. Geneva: International Labour Office, 2002. Accessed September 15, 2016. www.ilo.org/public/english/standards/relm/ilc/ilc90/pdf/rep-vi.pdf.

ILO. *Statistical Update on Employment in the Informal Economy*. Geneva: International Labour Office, 2012. Accessed November 1, 2015. laborsta.ilo.org/informal_economy_E.html.

In-Joung, Whang. *Management of Rural Change in Korea: The Saemaul Undong*. Honolulu: University of Hawaii Press, 1981.

Isaac, T. M., and Patrick Heller. "Democracy and Development: Decentralized Planning in Kerala." In *Deepening Democracy: Institutional Innovations in Empowered Participatory Governance*, edited by Archon Fung and Erik Olin Wright, 77–110. London: Verso, 2003.

Iyer, Aditi, Gita Sen, and Asha George. "The Dynamics of Gender and Class in Access to Health Care: Evidence from Rural Karnataka, India." *International Journal of Health Services* 37, no. 3 (2007): 537–54.

Jaffrelot, Christophe. *India's Silent Revolution: The Rise of the Low Castes in North Indian Politics*. New Delhi, India: Permanent Black, 2003.

Jalan, Jyotsna, and Rinku Murgai. "Inter-generational Mobility in Education in India." Paper presented at the Fourth Annual Conference on "Economic Growth and Development," Indian Statistical Institute, Delhi, December 17–18, 2008. Accessed April 23, 2013. www.isid.ac.in/~pu/conference/dec_08_conf/.../RinkuMurgai.doc.

Jamil, Ghazala. "The Capitalist Logic of Spatial Segregation: A Study of Muslims in Delhi." *Economic and Political Weekly* 49, no. 3 (2014): 52–8.

Jauregui, Beatrice. "Beatings, Beacons, and Big Men: Police Disempowerment and Delegitimation in India." *Law and Social Inquiry* 38, no. 3 (2013): 643–69.

Jauregui, Beatrice. *Provisional Authority: Police, Order, and Security in India*. Chicago, IL: University of Chicago Press, 2016.

Jayadev, Arjun, Sripad Motiram, and Vamsi Vakulabharanam. "Patterns of Wealth Disparities in India." In *Understanding India's New Political Economy: A Great Transformation?*, edited by Sanjay Ruparelia, Sanjay Reddy, John Harriss, and Stuart Corbridge, 81–100. New York, NY: Routledge, 2011.

Jayal, Niraja Gopal. *Citizenship and Its Discontents: An Indian History*. New Delhi, India: Permanent Black, 2013.

Jean, Neal, Marshall Burke, Michael Xie, W. Matthew Davis, David B. Lobell, and Stefano Ermon. "Combining Satellite Imagery and Machine Learning to Predict Poverty." *Science* 353, no. 6301 (2016): 790–4.

Jeffrey, Craig. *Timepass: Youth, Class, and the Politics of Waiting in India*. Stanford, CA: Stanford University Press, 2010.

Jeffrey, Craig, Roger Jeffery, and Patricia Jeffery. "Degrees without Freedom: The Impact of Formal Education on Dalit Young Men in North India." *Development and Change* 35, no. 5 (2004): 963–86.

Jensen, Henning, and Finn Tarp. "Trade Liberalization and Spatial Inequality: A Methodological Innovation in a Vietnamese Perspective." *Review of Development Economics* 9, no. 1 (2005): 69–86.

Jensen, Robert. "The (Perceived) Returns to Education and the Demand for Schooling." *Quarterly Journal of Economics* 125, no. 2 (2010): 515–48.

Jha, Praveen. "Some Aspects of the Well-being of India's Agricultural Labour in the Context of Contemporary Agrarian Crisis." *Indian Journal of Labour Economics* 49, no. 4 (2007): 741–64.

Jha, Saumitra, Vijayendra Rao, and Michael Woolcock. "Governance in the Gullies: Democratic Responsiveness and Leadership in Delhi's Slums." *World Development* 35, no. 2 (2007): 230–46.

Jodha, Narpat S. "Poverty Debate in India: A Minority View." *Economic and Political Weekly* 23, no. 45–47 (1988): 2421–8.

Jodhka, Surinder S. "Nation and Village." *Economic and Political Weekly* 37, no. 32 (August 2002).

Jodhka, Surinder S. "Changing Face of Rural India." *Economic and Political Weekly* 49, no. 14 (2014): 28–31.

Joe, William. "Distressed Financing of Household Out-of-Pocket Health Care Payments in India: Incidence and Correlates." *Health Policy and Planning* 30, no. 6 (2014): 728–41.

Johnson, Ian. "China Releases Plan to Incorporate Farmers into Cities." *New York Times International*. March 18, 2014.

Joshi, Anuradha. "Do Rights Work? Law, Activism, and the Employment Guarantee Scheme." *World Development* 38, no. 4 (2009): 620–30.

Joshi, Bharati, and Rajiv Khandelwal. "Circular Migration Streams from Southern Rajasthan." In *Circular Migration and Multilocal Livelihood Strategies*, edited by Priya Deshingkar and John Farrington, 118–38. New Delhi, India: Oxford University Press, 2009.

Joshi, Vijay. "Economic Resurgence, Lopsided Reform, and Jobless Growth." In *Diversity and Change in Modern India: Economic, Social and Political*

Approaches, edited by Anthony Heath and Roger Jeffery, 73–106. Oxford, UK: Oxford University Press, 2010.

Joshi, Vijay. *India's Long Road: The Search for Prosperity*. New Delhi, India: Penguin, 2016.

Kabeer, Naila. "Gender Equality and Women's Empowerment: A Critical Analysis of the Third Millennium Development Goal." *Gender and Development* 13, no. 1 (2005): 13–24.

Kakwani, Nanak, and Hyun H. Son. "New Global Poverty Counts." Working paper 29, International Poverty Centre, United Nations Development Programme, 2006. Accessed October 21, 2016. www.ipc-undp.org/pub/IPCWorkingPaper29.pdf.

Kamath, Lalitha. "New Policy Paradigms and Actual Practices om Slum Housing." *Economic and Political Weekly* 47, no. 47 (2012): 76–86.

Kanbur, Ravi, and Anthony J. Venables, eds. *Spatial Inequality and Development*. Oxford, UK: Oxford University Press, 2005.

Kanbur, Ravi, and Anthony J. Venables. "Spatial Disparities and Economic Development." In *Global Inequality: Patterns and Explanations*, edited by David Held and Ayse Kaya, 204–15. Cambridge, UK: Polity Press, 2007.

Kannan, Elumalai, and Sujata Sundaram. "Analysis of Trends in India's Agricultural Growth." Working paper 276, Institute for Social and Economic Change, 2011.

Kannan, K. P., and G. Raveendran. "Growth *sans* Employment: A Quarter Century of Jobless Growth in India's Organised Manufacturing." *Economic and Political Weekly* 44, no. 10 (2009): 80–91.

Kannan, K. P., and G. Raveendran. "India's Common People: The Regional Profile." *Economic and Political Weekly* 46, no. 38 (2011): 60–73.

Kapoor, Radhika. "Creating 'Good Jobs': Assessing the Labour Market Regulation Debate." *Economic and Political Weekly* 49, no. 46 (2014): 16–8.

Kapur, Akash. *India Becoming: A Portrait of Life in Modern India*. New York, NY: Penguin, 2012.

Kapur, Akash. "Rush: What Happens When a Big Road Meets a Small Village." *New Yorker*, October 14, 2013, starting page 59.

Kapur, Devesh, Chandra Bhan Prasad, Lant Pritchett, and D. Shyam Babu. "Rethinking Inequality: Dalits in Uttar Pradesh in the Market Reform Era." *Economic and Political Weekly* 45, no. 35 (2010): 39–49.

Kapur, Devesh, D. Shyam Babu, and Chandra Bhan Prasad. *Defying the Odds: The Rise of Dalit Entrepreneurs*. New Delhi, India: Vintage Books, 2014.

Karabarbounis, Loukas, and Brent Neiman. "The Global Decline of the Labor Share." Working paper 19136, National Bureau of Economic Research, 2013. Accessed May 6, 2014. www.nber.org/papers/w19136.

Karlan, Dean, and Jacob Appel. *More than Good Intentions: How a New Economics Is Helping Solve Global Poverty*. New York, NY: Dutton, 2011.

Karopady, D. D. "Does School Choice Help Rural Children from Disadvantaged Sections? Evidence from Longitudinal Research in Andhra Pradesh." *Economic and Political Weekly* 49, no. 51 (2014): 46–53.

Karshenas, Massoud. "Global Poverty: National Account Based versus Survey Based Estimates." *Development and Change* 34, no. 4 (2003): 683–712.

Kaufmann, Daniel, Aart Kraay, and P. Zoido-Lobatón. "Governance Matters." World Bank Policy Research Working Paper 2196, World Bank, Washington, DC, 1999.

Kaufmann, Daniel, Aart Kraay, and Massimo Mastruzzi. "Governance Matters VII: Aggregate and Individual Governance Indicators 1996–2007." World Bank Policy Research Working Paper 4654, World Bank, Washington, DC, 2008. Accessed April 14, 2015. http://info.worldbank.org/governance/wgi/pdf/GovernanceMattersVII.pdf.

Kaviraj, Sudipta. "Introduction." In *Politics in India,* edited by S. Kaviraj, 1–36. New Delhi, India: Oxford University Press, 1997.

Keefer, Philip, and Stuti Khemani. "Democracy, Public Expenditures, and the Poor: Understanding Political Incentives for Providing Public Services." *World Bank Research Observer* 20, no. 1 (2005): 1–27.

Kelkar, Govind, Girija Shrestha, and N. Veena. "IT Industry and Women's Agency: Exploration in Bangalore and Delhi, India." *Gender, Technology and Development* 6, no. 63 (2002): 63–84.

Kennedy, Jonathan. "Gangsters or Gandhians? The Political Sociology of the Maoist Insurgency in India." *India Review* 13, no. 3 (2014): 212–34.

Keynes, John M. *The General Theory of Employment, Interest, and Money*. London, UK: Palgrave Macmillan, 1936.

Khandelwal, Rajiv, and Elon Gilbert. "Getting Set to Go: Upgrading Migration through an Innovative Educational Programme." *Journal of Education for Sustainable Development* 1, no. 1 (2007): 61–71.

Khasnabis, Ratan, and Tania Chatterjee. "Enrolling and Retaining Slum Children in Formal Schools: A Field Survey in Eastern Slums of Kolkata." *Economic and Political Weekly* 42, no. 22 (2007): 2091–9.

Khera, Ritika. "Trends in Diversion of PDS Grain." *Economic and Political Weekly* 46, no. 21 (2011): 106–14.

Khera, Ritika. "MNREGA: Technology versus Technocracy." IdeasforIndia.com, 2016. Accessed April 9, 2016. www.ideasforindia.in/article.aspx?article_id=1599.

Khilnani, Sunil. *The Idea of India*. New York, NY: Farrar, Straus and Giroux, 1997.

Kijima, Yoko. "Why Did Wage Inequality Increase? Evidence from Urban India 1983–99." *Journal of Development Economics* 81, no. 1 (2006): 97–117.

Kingdon, Geeta, and Mohd. Muzammil. "The School Governance Environment in Uttar Pradesh, India: Implications for Teacher Accountability and Effort." *Journal of Development Studies* 49, no. 2 (2013): 251–69.

Kit, Oleksandr, Matthias Lüdeke, and Diana Reckien. "Defining the Bull's Eye: Satellite Imagery-assisted Slum Population Assessment in Hyderabad, India." *Urban Geography*, 34, no. 3 (2013): 413–24.

Kitschelt, Herbert. "Linkages between Citizens and Politicians in Democratic Politics." *Comparative Political Studies* 33, no. 67 (2000): 845–79.

Kochhar, Kalpana, Utsav Kumar, Raghuram Rajan, Arvind Subramanian, and Ioannis Tokatlidis. "India's Pattern of Development: What Happened, What Follows?" *Journal of Monetary Economics* 53, no. 5 (2006): 981–1019.

Kohli, Atul. *State and Poverty in India: The Politics of Reform.* Cambridge, UK: Cambridge University Press, 1987.

Kohli, Atul. *Democracy and Discontent: India's Growing Crisis of Governability.* Cambridge, UK: Cambridge University Press, 1990.

Kohli, Atul. *State-Directed Development: Political Power and Industrialization in the Global Periphery.* Cambridge, UK: Cambridge University Press, 2004.

Kohli, Atul. *Poverty amid Plenty in the New India.* New York, NY: Cambridge University Press, 2012.

Kolsky, Elizabeth. *Colonial Justice in British India.* New York, NY: Cambridge University Press, 2010.

Korra, Vijay. "Labour Migration in Mahabubnagar: Nature and Characteristics." *Economic and Political Weekly* 46, no. 2 (2011): 67–70.

Korten, David C. "Community Organizations and Rural Development: A Learning Process Approach." *Public Administration Review* 40, no. 5 (1980): 480–511.

Kosack, Stephen. *The Education of Nations.* New York, NY: Oxford University Press, 2012.

Kosack, Stephen. "The Logic of Pro-poor Policymaking: Political Entrepreneurship and Mass Education." *British Journal of Political Science* 44, no. 2 (2014): 409–44.

Kosack, Stephen, and Archon Fung. "Does Transparency Improve Governance?" *Annual Review of Political Science* 17 (2014): 65–87.

Kothari, Rajni. *State against Democracy: In Search of Humane Governance.* Delhi, India: Ajanta, 1988.

Kotwal, Ashok, Bharat Ramaswami, and Wilima Wadhwa. "Economic Liberalization and Indian Economic Growth: What's the Evidence?" *Journal of Economic Literature* 49, no. 4 (2011): 1152–99.

Kremer, Michael, Nazmul Chaudhury, F. Hasley Rogers, Karthik Muralidharan, and Jeffrey Hammer. "Teacher Absence in India: A Snapshot." *Journal of the European Economic Association* 3, no. 2–3 (2004): 658–67.

Kremer, Michael, Edward Miguel, and Rebecca Thornton. "Incentives to Learn." *Review of Economics and Statistics* 91, no. 3 (2009): 537–56.

Krishna, Anirudh. *Active Social Capital: Tracing the Roots of Development and Democracy*. New York, NY: Columbia University Press, 2002.

Krishna, Anirudh. "Falling into Poverty: The Other Side of Poverty Reduction." *Economic and Political Weekly* 38, no. 6 (2003a).

Krishna, Anirudh. "What Is Happening to Caste? A View from Some North Indian Villages." *Journal of Asian Studies* 62, no. 4 (2003b): 1171–93.

Krishna, Anirudh. "Escaping Poverty and Becoming Poor: Who Gains, Who Loses, and Why? People's Assessments of Stability and Change in 35 North Indian Villages." *World Development* 32, no. 1 (2004): 121–36.

Krishna, Anirudh. "Poverty and Democratic Participation Reconsidered." *Comparative Politics* 38, no. 4 (2006): 439–58.

Krishna, Anirudh. "For Reducing Poverty Faster: Target Reasons before People." *World Development* 35, no. 11 (2007a): 1947–60.

Krishna, Anirudh. "How Does Social Capital Grow? A Seven-year Study of Villages in India." *Journal of Politics* 69, no. 4 (2007b): 941–56.

Krishna, Anirudh. "Do Poor People Care Less for Democracy? Testing Individual-level Assumptions with Individual-level Data from India." In *Poverty, Participation and Democracy: A Global Perspective*, edited by Anirudh Krishna, 65–93. Cambridge University Press, 2008.

Krishna, Anirudh. *One Illness Away: Why People Become Poor and How They Escape Poverty*. Oxford, UK: Oxford University Press, 2010.

Krishna, Anirudh. "Stuck in Place: Investigating Social Mobility in 14 Bangalore Slums." *Journal of Development Studies* 49, no. 7 (2013a): 1010–28.

Krishna, Anirudh. "Making It in India: Examining Social Mobility in Three Walks of Life." *Economic and Political Weekly* 48 (2013b): 38–49.

Krishna, Anirudh. "The Spatial Dimension of Inter-generational Education Achievement in Rural India." *Indian Journal of Human Developmen* 6, no. 2 (2013c): 245–66.

Krishna, Anirudh. "Examining the Structures of Opportunity and Social Mobility in India: Who Becomes an Engineer?" *Development and Change* 45, no. 1 (2014): 1–28.

Krishna, Anirudh. "Politics and Development at the Grassroots: Missing Links in the Institutional Chain." In *Oxford Handbook on the Politics of Development*, edited by Nicolas Van de Walle and Carol Lancaster (in press).

Krishna, Anirudh, and Swapnil Agarwal. "Promoting Social Mobility in India: Identifying and Examining Active and Exemplary Organizations." Working paper, Sanford School of Public Policy, Duke University, 2016.

Krishna, Anirudh, and Kripa Ananthpur. "Distance and Diseases: Spatial Health Disparities in Rural India." *Millennial Asia* 4, no. 1 (2013): 3–25.

Krishna, Anirudh, and Devendra Bajpai. "Lineal Spread and Radial Dissipation: Experiencing Growth in Rural India, 1993–2005." *Economic and Political Weekly* 46 (September 17, 2011): 44–51.

Krishna, Anirudh, and Vijay Brihmadesam. "What Does It Take to Become a Software Professional?" *Economic and Political Weekly* 41, no. 30 (2006): 3307–14.

Krishna, Anirudh, and Jesse Lecy. "The Balance of All Things: Explaining Household Poverty Dynamics in 50 Villages of Gujarat, India." *International Journal of Multiple Research Methods* 2, no. 2 (2008): 160–75.

Krishna, Anirudh, and Gregory Schober. "The Gradient of Governance: Distance and Disenchantment in Rural India." *Journal of Development Studies* 50, no. 6 (2014): 820–38.

Krishna Anirudh, and Abusaleh Shariff. "The Irrelevance of National Strategies? Rural Poverty Dynamics in States and Regions of India, 1993–2005." *World Development* 39, no. 4 (2011): 533–49.

Krishna, Anirudh, Norman Uphoff, and Milton Esman. *Reasons for Hope: Instructive Experiences in Rural Development.* West Hartford, CT: Kumarian Press, 1997.

Krishna, Anirudh, Patricia Kristjanson, Maren Radeny, and Wilson Nindo. "Escaping Poverty and Becoming Poor in Twenty Kenyan Villages." *Journal of Human Development* 5, no. 2 (2004): 211–26.

Krishna, Anirudh, Mahesh Kapila, Mahendra Porwal, and Veerpal Singh. "Why Growth is Not Enough: Household Poverty Dynamics in Northeast Gujarat, India." *Journal of Development Studies* 41, no. 7 (2005): 1163–92.

Krishna, Anirudh, M. S. Sriram, and Purnima Prakash. "Slum Types and Adaptation Strategies: Identifying Policy-Relevant Differences in Bangalore." *Environment and Urbanization* 26, no. 2 (2014): 568–85.

Krishna, Anirudh, Emily Rains, and Erik Wibbels. "Some are Slummier than Others: A Continuum of Slums and the Prognosis for Secular Improvements." Working paper, Duke University, 2016. Accessed October 27, 2016. http://urbanindiastories.com/wp-content/uploads/2014/08/Working-paper.pdf.

Kruks-Wisner, Gabrielle. "Navigating the State: Citizenship Practice and the Pursuit of Services in Rural India." Working paper, Harvard South Asia Institute, Harvard University, 2015. Accessed on November 7, 2016 at https://krukswisner.files.wordpress.com/2015/08/gkw_sai-working-paper_2015.pdf

Kruks-Wisner, Gabrielle. "Active Citizenship: Claim-Making & the Pursuit of Social Welfare in Rural India." Manuscript, n.d. Accessed October 1, 2016. https://krukswisner.files.wordpress.com/2015/08/gkw-cv_feb-2016.pdf.

Kumar, Naveen, and Suresh C. Aggarwal. "Patterns of Consumption and Poverty in Delhi Slums." *Economic and Political Weekly* 38, no. 50 (2003): 5294–300.

Kumar, Praduman, and Surabhi Mittal. "Agricultural Productivity Trends in India: Sustainability Issues." *Agricultural Economics Research Review* 19 (2006): 71–88.

Kumar, Rishi. "Issues in Poverty in Rural India." Unpublished PhD thesis. Indira Gandhi Institute of Development Research, Mumbai, India, 2008.

Kumar, Sanjay, Anthony Heath, and Oliver Heath. "Determinants of Social Mobility in India." *Economic and Political Weekly* 37, no. 29 (2002a): 2983–7.

Kumar, Sanjay, Anthony Heath, and Oliver Heath. "Changing Patterns of Social Mobility: Some Trends over Time." *Economic and Political Weekly* 37, no. 40 (2002b): 4091–6.

Kumari, Sunita. "Tribal Migrant Women as Domestic Workers in Mumbai." *Economic and Political Weekly* 50, no. 16 (2015): 84–5.

Kundu, Amitabh, and Niranjan Sarangi. "Migration, Employment Status and Poverty: An Analysis across Urban Centres." *Economic and Political Weekly* 42, no. 4 (2007): 299–307.

Kundu, A., B. K. Pradhan, and A. Subramanian. "Dichotomy or Continuum, Analysis of Impact of Urban Centres on Their Periphery." *Economic and Political Weekly* 37, no. 14 (2002): 5039–46.

Ladd, Helen. "Introduction." In *Choosing Choice: Global Trends and National Variations*, edited by David Plank and Gary Sykes, 1–23. New York, NY: Teachers' College Press, 2003.

Ladejinsky, Wolf. "Land Ceilings and Land Reforms." *Economic and Political Weekly* 7, no. 7 (1972).

Lahiri-Dutta, Kuntala, and Gopa Samanta. *Dancing with the River: People and Life on the Chars of South Asia*. New Haven, CT: Yale University Press, 2013.

Lall, Somik V., and Sanjoy Chakravorty. "Industrial Location and Spatial Inequality: Theory and Evidence from India." *Review of Development Economics* 9, no. 1 (2005): 47–68.

Lanjouw, Jean Olson. "Demystifying Poverty Lines." 1998. Accessed October 22, 2016. http://siteresources.worldbank.org/PGLP/Resources/LanjouwDemystifyingPovertyLines.pdf.

Lanjouw, Peter, and Rinku Murgai. "Poverty Decline, Agricultural Wages, and Nonfarm Employment in Rural India: 1983–2004." *Agricultural Economics*, 40, no. 2 (2009): 243–63.

Lerche, Jens. "From 'Rural Labour' to 'Classes of Labour': Class Fragmentation, Caste and Class Struggle at the Bottom of the Indian Labour Hierarchy." In *Comparative Political Economy of Development*, edited by

Barbara Harriss-White and Judith Heyer, 66–87. New York, NY: Routledge, 2010.

Lerche, Jens, Alpa Shah, and Barbara Harriss-White. "Introduction: Agrarian Questions and Left Politics in India." *Journal of Agrarian Change* 13, no. 3 (2013): 337–50.

Levien, Michael. "Social Capital as Obstacle to Development: Brokering Land, Norms, and Trust in Rural India." *World Development* 74 (2015): 77–92.

Lijphart, Arendt. "Unequal Participation: Democracy's Unresolved Dilemma." *American Political Science Review* 91, no. 1 (1997): 1–14.

Lipton, Michael. *Why Poor People Stay Poor: Urban Bias in World Development.* Cambridge, MA: Harvard University Press, 1977.

Lipton, Michael. "Editorial: Poverty – Are There Holes in the Consensus?" *World Development* 25, no. 7 (1997): 1003–7.

Locke, Richard. *Remaking the Italian Economy.* Ithaca, NY: Cornell University Press, 1995.

Lok-Dessallien, Renata. "Review of Poverty Concepts and Indicators." 1999. Accessed October 22, 2016. kambing.ui.ac.id/onnopurbo/library/library-ref-ind/ref-ind-1/application/poverty-reduction/Poverty/Review_of_Poverty_Concepts.pdf.

Luce, Edward. *In Spite of the Gods: The Strange Rise of Modern India.* London, UK: Abacus, 2006.

Maclean, Lauren. "The Paradox of State Retrenchment in Sub-Saharan Africa: The Micro-level Experience of Public Service Provision." *World Development* 39, no. 7 (2011): 1155–65.

Mahadevia, Darshini. "Health for All in Gujarat: Is It Achievable?" *Economic and Political Weekly* 35 (2000): 3193–204.

Mahadevia, Darshini. "Tenure Security and Urban Social Protection Links: India." *IDS Bulletin* 41, no. 4 (2010): 52–62.

Mahajan, Shobhit. "Waterboarding No More." *Economic and Political Weekly* 51, no. 41 (2016): 77–8.

Majumdar, Bhaskar. "Forced Migration of Labour to Brick Kilns in Uttar Pradesh – An Exploratory Analysis." *Economic and Political Weekly* 50, no. 26–27 (2015): 19–26.

Majumder, Rajarshi. "Intergenerational Mobility in Educational and Occupational Attainment: A Comparative Study of Social Classes in India." *Journal of Applied Economic Research* 4, no. 4 (2010): 463–94.

Mamdani, Mahmood. *Citizen and Subject: Contemporary Africa and the Legacy of Late Colonialism.* Princeton, NJ: Princeton University Press, 1996.

Mander, Harsh. *Ash in the Belly: India's Unfinished Battle against Hunger.* New Delhi, India: Penguin, 2012.

Mangla, Akshay. "Bureaucratic Norms and State Capacity: Implementing Primary Education in India's Himalayan Region." Working paper 14–099, Harvard Business School, Cambridge, MA, 2014.

Mann, Michael. "The Autonomous Power of the State: Its Origins, Mechanisms and Results." *European Journal of Sociology* 25, no. 2 (1984): 185–213.

Manor, James. *Power, Poverty and Poison: Disaster and Response in an Indian City*. New Delhi, India: Sage, 1993.

Manor, James. "Small-time Political Fixers in India's States." *Asian Survey* 40, no. 5 (2000): 816–35.

Manor, James. "Local Governance." In *Oxford Companion to Politics in India*, edited by Niraja Gopal Jayal and Pratap Bhanu Mehta, 61–79. New Delhi, India: Oxford University Press, 2010.

Marx, Benjamin, Thomas Stoker, and Tavneet Suri. "The Economics of Slums in the Developing World." *Journal of Economic Perspectives* 27, no. 4 (2013): 187–210.

Mason, Philip. *The Men Who Ruled India*. New Delhi, India: Rupa, 1985 [1954].

Mathew, Santhosh, and Mick Moore. "State Incapacity by Design: Understanding the Bihar Story." Working paper 366, Institute of Development Studies, Brighton, UK, 2011.

Mayer, Adrian. "Caste in an Indian Village: Change and Continuity 1954–1992." In *Caste Today*, edited by C. J. Fuller, 32–64. New Delhi, India: Oxford University Press, 1997.

Mazumdar, Dipak, and Sandip Sarkar. "The Employment Problem in India and the Phenomenon of the 'Missing Middle.'" *Indian Journal of Labor Economics* 52, no. 1 (2009): 43–56.

Mazumdar, Indrani, N. Neetha, and Indu Agnihotri. "Migration and Gender in India." *Economic and Political Weekly* 48, no. 10 (2013): 54–64.

McDowell, Christopher, and Arjan de Haan. "Migration and Sustainable Livelihoods: A Critical Review of the Literature." Working paper 65, Institute of Development Studies, Brighton, UK, 1997.

McKinsey Global Institute. "Next Big Spenders: India's Middle Class." McKinsey Global Institute, 2007a. Accessed May 2, 2014. www.mckinsey.com/insights/mgi/in_the_news/next_big_spenders_indian_middle_class.

McKinsey Global Institute. "The 'Bird of Gold': The Rise of India's Consumer Market." McKinsey Global Institute, 2007b. Accessed May 4, 2014. www.mckinsey.com/insights/asia-pacific/the_bird_of_gold.

McKinsey Global Institute. "India's Urban Awakening: Building Inclusive Cities, Sustaining Economic Growth." McKinsey Global Institute, 2010. Accessed on September 1, 2015. www.mckinsey.com/global-themes/urbanization/urban-awakening-in-india.

Mehta, Aasha Kapur, and Amita Shah. "Chronic Poverty in India: Incidence, Causes and Policies." *World Development* 31, no. 3 (2003): 491–511.

Mehta, Aasha Kapur, Andrew Shepherd, Shashanka Bhide, Amita Shah, and Anand Kumar. *India Chronic Poverty Report: Towards Solutions and New Compacts in a Dynamic Context*. New Delhi, India: Indian Institute of Public Administration, 2011.

Mehta, Pratap B. "India: Fragmentation amid Consensus." *Journal of Democracy* 8, no. 1 (1997): 56–69.

Mehta, Suketu. *Maximum City: Bombay Lost and Found*. New York, NY: Vintage, 2005.

Milanovic, Branko. *Worlds Apart: Measuring International and Global Inequality*. Princeton, NJ: Princeton University Press, 2005.

Milly, Deborah J. *Poverty, Equality, and Growth: The Politics of Economic Need in Postwar Japan*. Cambridge, MA: Harvard University Press, 1999.

Mishra, Pankaj. "Which India Matters?" *New York Review of Books* (November 21, 2013): 51–3.

Mitlin, Diana, and David Satterthwaite. "Editorial: Addressing Poverty and Inequality; New Forms of Urban Governance in Asia." *Environment and Urbanization* 24, no. 2 (2012): 395–401.

Mitra, Arup. "Labour Market Mobility of Low Income Households." *Economic and Political Weekly* 41, no. 21 (2006): 2123–30.

Mitra, Arup. "Migration, Livelihood and Well-being: Evidence from Indian City Slums." *Urban Studies* 47, no. 7 (2010): 1371–90.

Mitra, Subrata K. *Power, Protest and Participation: Local Elites and the Politics of Development in India*. New York, NY: Routledge, 1992.

Mohanty, B. B. "'We are Like the Living Dead': Farmer Suicides in Maharashtra, Western India." *Journal of Peasant Studies* 32, no. 2 (2011): 243–76.

Mohanty, Mritiunjoy. "Social Inequality, Labour Market Dynamics and Reservation." *Economic and Political Weekly* 41, no. 35 (2006): 3777–89.

Mooij, Jos. "Introduction." In *Politics of Economic Reform in India*, edited by Jos Mooij, 15–45. New Delhi, India: Sage, 2005a.

Mookherjee, Dilip. *The Crisis in Government Accountability: Essays on Governance Reform and India's Economic Performance*. New Delhi, India: Oxford University Press, 2004.

Moretti, Enrico. *The New Geography of Jobs*. New York, NY: Houghton Mifflin Harcourt, 2012.

Morris-Jones, W. H. *The Government and Politics of India*. New York, NY: Anchor Books, 1967.

Mosse, David. "A Relational Approach to Durable Poverty, Inequality and Power." *Journal of Development Studies* 46, no. 7 (2010): 1156–78.

Mosse, David, Sanjeev Gupta, Mona Mehta, et al. "Brokered Livelihoods, Labour Migration, and Development in Tribal Western India." *Journal of Development Studies* 38, no. 5 (2002): 59–88.

Motiram, Sripad, and Ashish Singh. "How Close Does the Apple Fall to the Tree? Some Evidence on Inter-generational Occupational Mobility in India." *Economic and Political Weekly* 47, no. 40 (2012): 56–65.

Mudgal, Vipul. "Rural Coverage in the Hindi and English Dailies." *Economic and Political Weekly* 46, no. 35 (2011): 92–7.

Mukerji, Shobhini, and Michael Walton. "Learning the Right Lessons: Measurement, Experimentation and the Need to Turn India's Right to Education Act Upside Down." *India Infrastructure Report 2012*, 109–26. New Delhi, India: Routledge, 2013.

Mukhopadhyay, Partha. "Whither Urban Renewal?" *Economic and Political Weekly* 41, nos. 10–11 (2006): 879–84.

Munshi, Kaivan, and Mark Rosenzweig. "Traditional Institutions Meet the Modern World: Caste, Gender and Schooling Choice in a Globalizing Economy." *American Economic Review* 96, no. 4 (2006): 1225–52.

Muralidharan, Karthik. "Priorities for Primary Education Policy in India's 12th Five-Year Plan." *NCAER-Brookings India Policy Forum.* New Delhi, India: National Council of Applied Economic Research, 2013.

Muralidharan, Karthik, and Yendrick Zeleniak. "Measuring Learning Trajectories in Developing Countries with Longitudinal Data and Item Response Theory." Working paper, Department of Economics, University of California, San Diego, 2013.

Murgai, Rinku, Martin Ravallion, and Dominique van de Walle. "Is Workfare Cost Effective against Poverty in a Poor Labor-Surplus Economy?" World Bank Policy Research Working Paper 6673, World Bank, Washington, DC, 2015.

Nagarajan, Rema. "India in Healthcare Hall of Shame: Worst Ranked among Peers, Neighbors." *Times of India*, March 5, 2013.

Naipaul, V. S. *India: A Wounded Civilization.* New Delhi, India: Vikas, 1977.

Nair, Janaki. *The Promise of the Metropolis: Bangalore's Twentieth Century.* New Delhi, India: Oxford University Press, 2005.

Narayan, Deepa, Lant Pritchett, and Soumya Kapoor. *Moving out of Poverty: Success from the Bottom Up.* New York, NY: Palgrave Macmillan, 2009.

Narayanan, Sudha. "MNREGA and its Assets." IdeasforIndia.com, 2016. Accessed April 9, 2016. www.ideasforindia.in/article.aspx?article_id=1596.

NCERT. *Seventh All-India School Education Survey.* New Delhi, India: National Council of Education Research and Training, 2005. Accessed September 11, 2014. www.ncert.nic.in/programmes/education_survey/pdfs/Schools_Physical_Ancillary_Facilities.pdf.

NCEUS. *Report on Conditions of Work and Promotion of Livelihoods in the Unorganized Sector.* New Delhi, India: National Commission for Enterprises in the Unorganized Sector, 2007.

NCEUS. *Skill Formation and Employment Assurance in the Unorganised Sector.* New Delhi, India: National Commission for Enterprises in the Unorganized Sector, 2009.

Nijman, Jan. "Mumbai's Mysterious Middle Class." *International Journal of Urban and Regional Research* 30, no. 4 (2006): 758–75.

Nilekani, Nandan. *Imagining India: Ideas for the New Century.* New Delhi, India: Penguin, 2008.

Njoh, Ambe J. "The Experience and Legacy of French Colonial Urban Planning in Sub-Saharan Africa." *Planning Perspectives* 19, no. 4 (2004): 435–54.

North, Douglass C. *Institutions, Institutional Change and Economic Performance.* Cambridge, UK: Cambridge University Press, 1990.

North, Douglass, William Summerhill, and Barry Weingast. "Order, Disorder, and Economic Change: Latin America versus North America." In *Governing for Prosperity*, edited by Bruce Bueno de Mesquita and Hilton Root, pp. 17–58. New Haven, CT: Yale University Press, 2000.

North, Douglass, John Wallis, and Barry Weingast. *Violence and Social Orders: A Conceptual Framework for Interpreting Recorded Human History.* New York, NY: Cambridge University Press, 2012.

NSSO. "Conditions of Urban Slums: Salient Features, NSS 58th Round (July–December 2002)." New Delhi, India: National Sample Survey Organization, Government of India, 2003.

NSSO. "Education in India: 2007–08. Participation and Expenditure." New Delhi, India: National Sample Survey Organization, Government of India, 2008.

NSSO. "India–Urban Slums Survey: NSS 65th Round: July 2008–June 2009." New Delhi, India: National Sample Survey Organization, Government of India, 2009.

NSSO. "Education in India: 2007–2008: Participation and Expenditure." New Delhi, India: Ministry of Statistics and Programme Implementation, Government of India, 2010a.

NSSO. "Migration in India 2007–2008." New Delhi, India: Ministry of Statistics and Programme Implementation, Government of India, 2010b. Accessed July 12, 2012. http://mospi.gov.in/nsso_4aug2008/web/nsso/reports.htm.

OECD. (2009). *PISA 2009 Results: What Students Know and Can Do, Student Performance in Reading, Mathematics, and Science.* Organisation for Economic Co-operation and Development, 2009. Accessed September 16, 2016. www.oecd.org/pisa/pisaproducts/48852548.pdf.

OECD. *Tackling Inequalities in Brazil, China, India and South Africa: The Role of Labour Market and Social Policies.* Paris: OECD Publishing, 2010a.

OECD. "A Family Affair: Intergenerational Social Mobility across OECD Countries." In *Economic Policy Reforms: Going for Growth 2010.* OECD Publishing, 2010b. Accessed August 25, 2016. www.oecd.org/dataoecd/2/7/45002641.pdf.

OECD. "Special Focus: Inequality in Emerging Economies (EES)." In *Divided We Stand: Why Inequality Keeps Rising.* OECD Publishing, 2011. Accessed August 12, 2016. www.oecd.org/els/soc/49170475.pdf.

Ostrom, Elinor. *Governing the Commons: The Evolution of Institutions for Collective Action.* New York, NY: Cambridge University Press, 1990.

Ostrom, Elinor, Larry Schroeder, and Susan Wynne. *Institutional Incentives and Sustainable Development: Infrastructure Policies in Perspective.* Boulder, CO: Westview Press, 1993.

Page, John M. "The East Asian Miracle: An Introduction." *World Development* 22, no. 4 (1994): 615–25.

Palmer-Jones, R., and K. Sen. "On India's Poverty Puzzles and Statistics of Poverty." *Economic and Political Weekly* 36 (2001): 211–7.

Panagariya, Arvind. *India: The Emerging Giant.* New York, NY: Oxford University Press, 2008.

Panagariya, Arvind. "Avoiding Lopsided Spatial Transformation." In *Reshaping Tomorrow: Is South Asia Ready for the Big Leap?*, edited by Ejaz Ghani, 143–67. New Delhi, India: Oxford University Press, 2011.

Panda, Sitakanta. "Political Connections and Elite Capture in a Poverty Alleviation Programme in India." *Journal of Development Studies* 51, no. 1 (2015): 50–65.

Pande, Rohini. "Can Informed Voters Enforce Better Governance? Experiments in Low-Income Democracies." *Annual Review of Economics* 3, no. 1 (2011): 215–37.

Pandey, Priyanka, Sangeeta Goyal, and Venkatesh Sundararaman. "Community Participation in Public Schools: The Impact of Information Campaigns in Three Indian States." World Bank Policy Research Working Paper 4776, World Bank, Washington, DC, 2008a.

Pandey, Priyanka, Sangeeta Goyal, and Venkatesh Sundararaman. "Public Participation, Teacher Accountability, and School Outcomes: Findings from Baseline Surveys in Three Indian States." World Bank Policy Research Working Paper 4777, World Bank, Washington, DC, 2008b.

Pandita, Rahul. *Hello, Bastar: The Untold Story of India's Maoist Movement.* New Delhi, India: Tranquebar Press, 2011.

Papola, T. S. "Employment Trends in India." New Delhi, India: Institute for Studies in International Development, 2005. Accessed April 25, 2016. http://isidev.nic.in/pdf/EmployTrenz.PDF.

Parikh, P. P., and S. P. Sukhatme. "Women Engineers in India." *Economic and Political Weekly* 39, no. 2 (2004): 193–201.

Paris, Thelma, Abha Singh, Joyce Luis, and Mahabub Hossain. "Labour Out-migration, Livelihood of Rice Farming Households and Women Left Behind: A Case Study in Eastern Uttar Pradesh." *Economic and Political Weekly* 40, no. 25 (2005): 2522–9.

Patel, Reena, and Mary Jane Parmentier. "The Persistence of Gender Roles in the Technology Sector: A Study of Female Engineers in India." *Information Technologies and International Development* 2, no. 3 (2005): 29–46.

Patnaik, Utsa. "Trends in Urban Poverty under Economic Reform: 1993–94 to 2004–05." *Economic and Political Weekly* 45, no. 94 (2007): 42–53.

Peters, Thomas J., and Robert H. Waterman, Jr. *In Search of Excellence: Lessons from America's Best-run Companies.* New York, NY: Harper and Row, 1982.

Pettigrew, Thomas F., and Linda R. Tropp. "A Meta-analytical Test of Inter-group Contact Theory." *Journal of Personality and Social Psychology* 90, no. 5 (2006): 751–83.

Picherit, David. "Neither a Dog, Nor a Beggar: Seasonal Labor Migration, Development and Poverty in Andhra Pradesh." In *Persistence of Poverty in India*, edited by Nandini Gooptu and Jonathan Parry, 261–90. New Delhi, India: Social Science Press, 2014.

Pieters, Janneke. "Growth and Inequality in India: Analysis of an Extended Social Accounting Matrix." *World Development* 38, no. 3 (2010): 270–81.

Pietrobelli, Carlo, and Roberta Rabellotti. "Global Value Chains Meet Inno-vation Systems: Are There Learning Opportunities for Developing Coun-tries?" *World Development* 39, no. 7 (2011): 1261–9.

PRB. *The Urban-Rural Divide in Health and Development.* Population Ref-erence Bureau, 2015. Accessed September 15, 2015. www.prb.org/pdf15/urban-rural-datasheet.pdf.

Porter, Michael E. "Location, Competition, and Economic Development: Local Clusters in a Global Economy." *Economic Development Quarterly* 14, no. 1 (2000): 15–34.

Potter, David. *India's Political Administrators: From ICS to IAS.* New Delhi, India: Oxford University Press, 1996 [1986].

Prahalad, C. K. *The Fortune at the Bottom of the Pyramid: Eradicating Poverty through Profits.* Singapore: Pearson Education, 2005.

Pritchett, Lant, and Amanda Beatty. "The Negative Consequences of Over-ambitious Curricula in Developing Countries." Working Paper, Harvard Kennedy School of Government, 2012. Accessed May 2, 2015. www.hks.harvard.edu/fs/lpritch/Education%20-%20docs/Pritchett%20Beatty%20Overambitious%201%20Feb%202012.pdf.

Pritchett, Lant, and Rinku Murgai. "Teacher Compensation: Can Decentralization to Local Bodies Take India from Perfect Storm through Troubled Waters to Clear Sailing?" Preliminary draft, 2006.

Pritchett, Lant, and Varad Pande. "Making Primary Education Work for India's Rural Poor: A Proposal for Effective Decentralization." Social Development Paper 95, South Asia Series. World Bank, Washington, DC, 2006.

Pritchett, Lant, and Michael Woolcock. "Solutions When the Solution Is the Problem: Arraying the Disarray in Development." *World Development* 32, no. 5 (2004): 191–212.

Priyam, Manisha. "Political Ethnography as a Method for Understanding Urban Politics and Elections in India." *Studies in Indian Politics* 4, no. 1 (2016): 119–27.

Przeworski, Adam. "Institutions Matter?" *Governance and Opposition* 39, no. 4 (2004): 527–40.

Putnam, Robert. *Our Kids: The American Dream in Crisis*. New York, NY: Simon and Schuster, 2015.

Rajagopal, Arvind. "Thinking about the New Indian Middle Class: Gender Advertising, and Politics in an Age of Globalisation." In *Signposts: Gender Issues in Post-Independence India*, edited by Rajeswari Sundar Rajan, 57–100. New Delhi, India: Kali for Women, 1999.

Rajagopalan, C., and Jaspal Singh. "The Indian Institutes of Technology: Do They Contribute to Social Mobility?" *Economic and Political Weekly* 3, no. 14 (1968): 565–70.

Rajasekhar, Durgam. (2008). "Social Security for Unorganized Workers in India: Status and Issues." *India Economy Review* V: 125–31.

Ramachandran, H., and S. V. Subramanian. "Slum Household Characteristics in Bangalore: A Comparative Analysis (1973 and 1992)." In *Living in India's Slums: A Case Study of Bangalore*, edited by H. Schenk, 65–88. New Delhi, India: Manohar, 2001.

Ramachandran, V. K., and Vikas Rawal. "The Impact of Liberalization and Globalization on India's Agrarian Economy." *Global Labour Journal* 1, no. 1 (2009): 56–91.

Rangarajan, Chakravarthi, and S. Mahendra Dev. "Counting the Poor: Measurement and Other Issues." *Economic and Political Weekly* 50, no. 2 (2015): 70–4.

Rangarajan, Chakravarthi, Suryadevara M. Dev, K. Sundaram, et al. *Report of the Expert Group to Review the Methodology for Measurement of Poverty*. New Delhi, India: Planning Commission, Government of India, 2014.

Ranis, Gustav, Frances Stewart, and Alejandro Ramirez. "Economic Growth and Human Development." *World Development* 28, no. 2 (2000): 197–219.

Rao, Gautam. "Familiarity Does *Not* Breed Contempt: Diversity, Discrimination and Generosity in Delhi Schools." Working paper, 2013. Accessed April 16, 2016. https://sites.google.com/site/graoeconomics/.

Rao, M. Govinda, and Mita Choudhury. "Health Care Financing Reforms in India." Working paper 2012-100, National Institute of Public Finance and Policy, 2012. Accessed April 2, 2016. www.nipfp.org.in/media/medialibrary/2013/04/wp_2012_100.pdf.

Rao, Vijayendra, and Paromita Sanyal. "Dignity through Discourse: Poverty and the Culture of Deliberation in Indian Village Democracies." *Annals of the American Academy of Political and Social Science* 629, no. 1 (2010): 146–72.

Ravallion, Martin. "Poverty Lines across the World." World Bank Policy Research Working Paper 5284, World Bank, Washington, DC, 2010.

Ravallion, Martin. "A Comparative Perspective on Poverty Reduction in Brazil, China, and India." *World Bank Research Observer* 26, no. 1 (2011): 71–104.

Ravallion, Martin. "MNREGA: Vision and Reality." IdeasforIndia.com, 2016. Accessed April 9, 2016. www.ideasforindia.in/article.aspx?article_id=1598.

Rawal, Vikas. "Ownership Holdings of Land in Rural India: Putting the Record Straight." *Economic and Political Weekly* 43, no. 10 (2008): 43–47.

Ray, Debraj. "Aspirations, Poverty, and Economic Change." In *Understanding Poverty*, edited by Abhijit Banerjee, Roland Benabou, and Dilip Mookherjee, 409–21. Oxford, UK: Oxford University Press, 2006.

Reddy, A. Bheemeshwar. "Changes in Intergenerational Occupational Mobility in India: Evidence from National Sample Surveys, 1983–2012." *World Development* 76 (2015): 329–43.

Reddy, A. Bheemeshwar, and Madhura Swaminathan. "Intergenerational Occupational Mobility in Rural India: Evidence from Ten Villages." *Review of Agrarian Studies* 4, no. 1 (2014): 95–134.

Reddy, D. Narasimha, and Srijit Mishra. "Agriculture in the Reforms Regime." In *Agrarian Crisis in India*, edited by D. Narasimha Reddy and Srijit Mishra, 3–43. New Delhi, India: Oxford University Press, 2009.

Reddy, G. Ram, and G. Haragopal. "The Pyraveerkar: The 'Fixer' in Rural India." *Asian Survey* 25, no. 11 (1985): 1147–62.

Reddy, Sanjay G. "The New Global Poverty Estimates – Digging Deeper into a Hole." International Poverty Centre, United Nations Development Programme, 2008. Accessed October 23, 2016. www.ipc-undp.org/pub/IPCOnePager65.pdf.

Reddy, Sanjay G., and Thomas W. Pogge. "How Not to Count the Poor." 2002. Accessed April 4, 2016. http://thomaspogge.com/how-not-to-count-the-poor/.

Reed, Megan. "Ensuring Education for the Children of India's Migrants." *Transitions: An India in Transition Blog*. June 30, 2014. Accessed October 21, 2015. https://indiaintransition.com/2014/06/30/ensuring-education-for-the-children-of-indias-migrants/.

Reid, Thomas R. *The Healing of America: A Global Quest for Better, Cheaper, and Fairer Health Care*. New York, NY: Penguin Press, 2009.

Reinikka, Ritva, and Jakob Svensson. "The Power of Information: Evidence from a Newspaper Campaign to Reduce Capture." Working paper, IIES, Stockholm University, Sweden, 2004.

Roberts, Gregory D. *Shantaram: A Novel*. New York, NY: St. Martin's Griffin, 2005.

Rodgers, Gerry, and Janine Rodgers. "Inclusive Development? Migration, Governance and Social Change in Rural Bihar." *Economic and Political Weekly* 46, no. 23 (2011): 43–50.

Rodrik, Dani. "Growth versus Poverty Reduction: A Hollow Debate." *Finance and Development* 37, no. 4 (2000): 8–9.

Rodrik, Dani. *One Economics, Many Recipes: Globalization, Institutions, and Economic Growth*. Princeton, NJ: Princeton University Press, 2007.

Rodrik, Dani, and Francisco Rodriguez. "Trade Policy and Economic Growth: A Skeptic's Guide to the Cross-National Evidence." In *Macroeconomics Annual 2000*, edited by Ben Bernanke and Kenneth S. Rogoff. Cambridge, MA: MIT Press for NBER, 2001.

Roemer, John E. "Equality of Opportunity." In *Meritocracy and Economic Inequality*, edited by Kenneth Arrow, Samuel Bowles, and Steven Durlauf, 17–32. Princeton, NJ: Princeton University Press, 2000.

Rogaly, Ben, Daniel Coppard, Abdur Safique, et al. "Seasonal Migration and Welfare/Illfare in Eastern India: A Social Analysis." In *Labour Mobility and Rural Society*, edited by Arjan De Haan and Ben Rogaly, 89–114. New York, NY: Frank Cass, 2002.

Roy, Ananya. "Why India Cannot Plan Its Cities: Informality, Insurgence, and the Idiom of Urbanization." *Planning Theory* 8, no. 1 (2009): 76–87

Roy, Manoj, David Hulme, and Ferdous Jahan. "Contrasting Adaptation Responses by Squatters and Low-Income Tenants in Khulna, Bangladesh." *Environment and Urbanization* 25, no. 1 (2013): 157–76.

Roychowdhury, Supriya. "Labour and Economic Reforms: Disjointed Critiques." In *Politics of Economic Reforms in India*, edited by Jos Mooij, 264–90. New Delhi, India: Sage, 2005.

Rudolph, Lloyd I., and Susanne H. Rudolph. *In Pursuit of Lakshmi: The Political Economy of the Indian State*. Chicago, IL: University of Chicago Press, 1987.

Rueda, David, Erik Wibbels, and Melina Altamarino. "The Origins of Dualism." n.d. Accessed April 12, 2016. http://users.ox.ac.uk/%7Epolf0050/Ch3_RuedaWibbelsAltamirano.pdf.

Sachs, Jeffrey, D. *The End of Poverty: Economic Possibilities for Our Times.* New York, NY: Penguin Press, 2005.

Sah, D. C., and Amita Shah. "Migration in Remote Tribal Areas: Evidence from Southwestern Madhya Pradesh." *Indian Journal of Agricultural Economics* 60, no. 2 (2005): 184–204.

Sainath, Palagummi. (2009). "The Largest Waves of Suicides in History." *The Hindu*, February 16, 2009.

Sainath, Palagummi. (2010). "Farm Suicides: A 12-year Saga." *The Hindu*, January 25, 2010.

Saith, Aswani. "Poverty Lines versus the Poor: Method versus Meaning." *Economic and Political Weekly* 40, no. 43 (2005): 4601–10.

Sanyal, Kalyan, and Rajesh Bhattacharya. "Beyond the Factory: Globalisation, Informalisation of Production, and the New Locations of Labour." *Economic and Political Weekly* 44, no. 22 (2009): 35–44.

Sarin, Ankur, and Swati Gupta. "Quotas under the Right to Education: Not Leading towards an Egalitarian Education System." *Economic and Political Weekly* 49, no. 38 (2014): 65–72.

Sarkar, Sandip, and Balwant Singh Mehta. "Income Inequality in India: Pre- and Post-reform Periods." *Economic and Political Weekly* 45, no. 37 (2010): 45–55.

Sassen, Saskia. *The Global City.* Princeton, NJ: Princeton University Press, 2001.

Saxena, Naresh C. *Report of the Expert Group to Advise the Ministry of Rural Development on the Methodology for Conducting the Below Poverty Line (BPL) Census for the 11th Five-Year Plan.* New Delhi, India: Ministry of Rural Development, Government of India, 2009.

Schelzig, Karin. "Escaping Poverty: Behind the Numbers." *Public Administration and Development* 21, no. 3 (2001): 259–69.

Schenk, H. "Living in Bangalore's Slums." In *Living in India's Slums: A Case Study of Bangalore*, edited by H. Schenk, 17–37. New Delhi, India: Manohar, 2001.

Schneider, Mark, and Neelanjan Sircar. "Whose Side Are You On? Identifying Distributive Preferences of Local Politicians in India." Paper presented at the Annual Meeting of the Midwest Political Science Association, 2014.

Schumpeter, Joseph. *Capitalism, Socialism, and Democracy.* New York, NY: Harper Colophon Books, 1950.

Scott, Christopher. "Mixed Fortunes: A Study of Poverty Mobility among Small Farm Households in Chile, 1968–86." *Journal of Development Studies* 36, no. 6 (2000): 155–80.

Scott, J. C. *Domination and the Arts of Resistance: Hidden Transcripts.* New Haven, CT: Yale University Press, 1990.

Scott, James C. *Weapons of the Weak: Everyday Forms of Peasant Resistance.* New Haven, CT: Yale University Press, 1985.

Scott, James C. *Seeing Like a State: How Certain Schemes to Improve the Human Condition Have Failed*. New Haven, CT: Yale University Press, 1999.

Scott, R. W. "The Adolescence of Institutional Theory." *Administrative Science Quarterly* 32, no. 4 (1987): 493–511.

Sen, Abhijit, and M. S. Bhatia. *The State of the Indian Farmer: A Millennium Study*, Vol. 14, *Cost of Cultivation and Farm Income*. New Delhi, India: Academic Foundation and Ministry of Agriculture, 2004.

Sen, Abhijit, and Himanshu. "Poverty and Inequality in India – I and II," *Economic and Political Weekly* 39, no. 38 (2004): 4247–63; and vol. 39, no. 39 (2004): 4361–75.

Sen, Amartya. *Development as Freedom*. New York, NY: Random House, 1999.

Sen, Amartya. "Globalization, Inequality and Global Protest." *Development* 45, no. 2 (2002): 11–16.

Sen, Binayak. "Drivers of Escape and Descent: Changing Household Fortunes in Rural Bangladesh." *World Development* 31, no. 3 (2003): 513–34.

Sen, Gita, Aditi Iyer, and Asha George. "Structural Reforms and Health Equity: A Comparison of NSS Surveys, 1986–87 and 1995–96." *Economic and Political Weekly* 37, no. 14 (2002): 1342–52.

Sethi, Aman. *A Free Man: A True Story of Life and Death in Delhi*. New York, NY: W. W. Norton, 2013.

Shah, Alpa. "The Labour of Love: Seasonal Migration from Jharkhand to the Brick Kilns of Other States in India." *Contributions to Indian Sociology* 40, no. 1 (2006): 91–118.

Shah, Amita, and D. C. Sah. "Chronic Poverty in a Remote Rural District in Southwest Madhya Pradesh: A Multidimensional Analysis of its Extent and Causes." CPRC-IIPA Working Paper 5, Indian Institute of Public Administration, New Delhi, 2003.

Shah, Svati P. *Street Corner Secrets: Sex, Work, and Migration in the City of Mumbai*. Durham, NC: Duke University Press, 2014.

Sharma, Mihir. *Restart: The Last Chance for the Indian Economy*. New Delhi, India: Vintage, 2015.

Sharma, Sonal, and Eesha Kunduri. "Of Law, Language, and Labour: Situating the Need for Legislation in Domestic Work." *Economic and Political Weekly* 50, no. 28 (2015), web exclusive. Accessed January 29, 2016. http://www.epw.in/journal/2015/28/web-exclusives/law-language-and-labour.html.

Sheth, D. L. "Secularization of Caste and the Making of a New Middle Class." *Economic and Political Weekly* 34, no. 34 (1999): 2502–10.

Shourie, Arun. *Falling Over Backwards*. New Delhi, India: Rupa, 2006.

Shrivastava, Aseem, and Ashish Kothari. *Churning the Earth: The Making of Global India*. New Delhi, India: Penguin, 2012.

Shukla, Rajesh. *How India Earns, Spends, and Saves: Unmasking the Real India*. New Delhi, India: Sage, 2010.

Shukla, Srilal. *Raag Darbari: A Novel*. New Delhi, India: Penguin Books, 1968 [1992].

Singh, Abhishek, et al. "Infant and Child Mortality in India in the Last Two Decades: A Geospatial Analysis." *PLoS One*, 6, no. 11 (2011): e26856.

Singh, Bhrigupati. *Poverty and the Quest for Life: Spiritual and Material Striving in Rural India*. Chicago, IL: University of Chicago Press, 2015.

Singh, Charan. *Economic Nightmare of India: Its Cause and Cure*. New Delhi, India: National Press, 1981.

Singh, D. P. "Poverty and Migration: Does Moving Help?" In *India: Urban Poverty Report*, 50–76. New Delhi, India: Oxford University Press, 2009.

Singh, Nirvikar, Laveesh Bhandari, Aoyu Chen, and Aarti Khare. "Regional Inequality in India: A Fresh Look." *Economic and Political Weekly* 38 (2003): 1069–73.

Singh, Prerna. *How Solidarity Works for Welfare: Subnationalism and Social Development in India*. New York, NY: Cambridge University Press, 2015.

Singh, R. P., and Hans Binswanger. "Income Growth in Poor Dryland Areas of India's Semi-arid Tropics." *Indian Journal of Agricultural Economics* 48, no. 1 (1993): 51–64.

Singh, Sukhpal. "Implications of FDI in Food Supermarkets." *Economic and Political Weekly* 45, no. 34 (2010): 17–20.

Singh, Sukhpal. "New Markets for Smallholders in India: Exclusion, Policy and Mechanisms." *Economic and Political Weekly* 47, no. 52 (2012): 95–105.

Sinha, Amarjeet. *An India for Everyone: A Path to Inclusive Development*. New Delhi, India: Harper Collins, 2013.

Sinha, Aseema. *The Regional Roots of Developmental Politics in India: A Divided Leviathan*. Bloomington: Indiana University Press, 2005.

Sinha, Aseema. "Business and Politics." In *Oxford Companion to Politics in India*, edited by Niraja Gopal Jayal and Pratap Bhanu Mehta, 459–76. New Delhi, India: Oxford University Press, 2010.

Sinha, Saurabh, and Michael Lipton. (1999). "Damaging Fluctuations, Risk and Poverty: An Overview." In *Background paper for the World Development Report 2000/2001*. Poverty Research Unit, University of Sussex, 1999. Accessed May 4, 2014. www1.worldbank.org/prem/poverty/wdrpoverty/background/sinhaliptn.pdf.

Srinivasan, T. N. "The Unsatisfactory State of Global Poverty Estimation." *inFocus* (September 2004). Accessed September 27, 2016. www.ipc-undp.org/pub/IPCPovertyInFocus4.pdf.

Sriram, M. S. "Identity for Inclusion: Moving Beyond Aadhaar." *Economic and Political Weekly* 49, no. 28 (2014): 148–54.

Sriram, M. S. *Inclusive Finance India Report 2016*. New Delhi, India: Sage, 2016.

Srivastava, Ravi. "Labour Migration, Inequality, and Development Dynamics in India." *Indian Journal of Labour Economics* 54, no. 3 (2011): 373–85.

Srivastava, Ravi, and Richa Singh. "Rural Wages during the 1990s: A Re-estimation." *Economic and Political Weekly* 41, no. 38 (2006): 4053–62.

Srivastava, Ravi, and S. K. Sasikumar. "An Overview of Migration in India, Its Impacts and Key Issues." Presented at the Regional Conference on Migration, Development and Pro-Poor Policy Choices in Asia, 2003.

Standing, Guy. "From Cash Transfers to Basic Income: An Unfolding Indian Agenda." *Indian Journal of Labour Economics* 57, no. 1 (2014): 111–37.

Stiglitz, Joseph E. *Globalization and Its Discontents*. New York, NY: Norton, 2002.

Stiglitz, Joseph E. *The Price of Inequality: How Today's Divided Society Endangers Our Future*. New York, NY: Norton, 2013.

Subbaraman, Ramnath, Jennifer O'Brien, Tejal Shitole, et al. "Off the Map: The Health and Social Implications of Being a Non-notified Slum in India." *Environment and Development* 24, no. 2 (2012): 643–63.

Subramanian, Arvind. *India's Turn: Understanding the Economic Transformation*. New Delhi, India: Oxford University Press, 2008.

Subramanian, S. V., Shailen Nandy, Michelle Irving, et al. "The Mortality Divide in India: The Differential Contributions of Gender, Caste, and Standard of Living across the Life Course." *American Journal of Public Health* 96, no. 5 (2006): 818–25.

Subramanian, Sreenivasan. (2010a). "Identifying the Income-Poor: Some Controversies in India and Elsewhere." *Discussion paper 46*, Courant Research Centre, 2010.

Subramanian, Sreenivasan. "Poverty, Equity and Growth in Developing and Transitional Countries: Statistical Methods and Empirical Analysis." *Discussion paper 46*, University of Goettingen, 2010b. Accessed April 29, 2015. www.uni-goettingen.de/crc-peg

Subramanian, T. S. R. *Journeys through Netaland and Babudom*. New Delhi, India: Rupa, 2004.

Sundar, Nandini. "Bastar, Maoism and Salwa Judum." *Economic and Political Weekly* 41, no. 29 (2006): 3187–92.

Sundar, Ramamani, and Abhilasha Sharma. "Morbidity and Utilisation of Healthcare Services: A Survey of Urban Poor in Delhi and Chennai." *Economic and Political Weekly* 37, no. 47 (2002): 4729–40.

Sundaram, Krishnamurthy, and Suresh Tendulkar. "Poverty in India in the 1990s: Revised Results for All-India and 15 Major States for 1993–94." *Economic and Political Weekly* 38 (2003): 4865–72.

Sundari, S. "Migration as a Livelihood Strategy: A Gender Perspective." *Economic and Political Weekly* 40, no. 22–23 (2005): 2295–303.

Swidler, Ann. "Culture in Action: Symbols and Strategies." *American Sociological Review* 51, no. 2 (1986): 273–86.

Tendler, Judith. *Good Government in the Tropics*. Baltimore, MD: Johns Hopkins University Press, 1997.

Thachil, Tariq. "Do Rural Migrants Divide Ethnically in the City? Ethnographic and Experimental Evidence from Urban India." APSA 2014 Annual Meeting Paper, 2014a. Accessed July 14, 2016. http://www .academia.edu/15018531/Do_Internal_Migrants_Divide_or_Unite_ Across_Ethnic_Lines_Ethnographic_and_Experimental_Evidence_from_ Urban_India.

Thachil, Tariq. *Elite Parties, Poor Voters: How Social Services Win Votes in India*. New York, NY: Cambridge University Press, 2014b.

Thorat, Sukhdeo, and Paul Attewell. "The Legacy of Social Exclusion – a Correspondence Study of Job Discrimination in India." *Economic and Political Weekly* 47, no. 42 (2007): 4141–5.

Thorat, Sukhdeo, and Amaresh Dubey. "Has Growth Been Socially Inclusive during 1993/94–2009/10?" *Economic and Political Weekly* 48, no. 10 (2012): 43–53.

Tilak, Jandhyala B. G. "Post-elementary Education, Poverty and Development in India." *International Journal of Educational Development* 27, no. 4 (2007): 435–45.

Topalova, Petia (2008): "India: Is the Rising Tide Lifting All Boats?" Working paper 08/54, International Monetary Fund, 2008. Accessed April 23, 2013. www.imf.org/external/pubs/ft/wp/2008/wp0854.pdf.

Toyama, Kentaro. *Geek Heresy: Rescuing Social Change from the Cult of Technology*. New York, NY: Public Affairs, 2015.

Tully, Mark. *India's Unending Journey: Finding Balance in a Time of Change*. London, UK: Rider, 2007.

Tumbe, Chinmay. "Migration and Remittances in India: Historical, Regional, Social and Economic Dimensions." Unpublished doctoral dissertation, Indian Institute of Management Bangalore, 2012.

UNDP. *Democracy in Latin America: Towards a Citizens' Democracy*. New York, NY: United Nations Development Programme, 2004.

Unni, Jeemol, and Uma Rani. "Informal Workers in Ahmedabad City." In *Indian Cities in Transition*, edited by Annapurna Shaw, 217–37. Chennai, India: Orient Longman, 2007.

Unni, Jeemol, and G. Raveendran. "Growth of Employment (1993–94 to 2004–05): Illusion of Inclusiveness?" *Economic and Political Weekly* 42, no. 3 (2007): 196–9.

Upadhya, Carol. "Employment, Exclusion and 'Merit' in the Indian IT Industry." *Economic and Political Weekly* 42, no. 20 (2007): 1863–68.

Uphoff, Norman, Milton Esman, and Anirudh Krishna. *Reasons for Success: Learning from Instructive Experiences in Rural Development*. West Hartford, CT: Kumarian Press, 1998.

Vaidyanathan, A. "Poverty and Development Policy." *Economic and Political Weekly* 36, no. 21 (2001).

Vaidyanathan, A. "Some Notes on the Indian Economy in Crisis: Assessments and Prospects." *Economic and Political Weekly* 49, no. 24 (2014): 108–17.

Vakulabharanam, Vamsi. "Does Class Matter? Class Structure and Worsening Inequality in India." *Economic and Political Weekly* 45, no. 29 (2010): 67–76.

Vakulabharanam, Vamsi, and Sripad Motiram. "Political Economy of Agrarian Distress in India since the 1990s." In *Understanding India's New Political Economy: A Great Transformation?* edited by Sanjay Ruparelia, 101–26. New York, NY: Routledge, 2011.

Vakulabharanam, Vamsi, and Sripad Motiram. "Understanding Poverty and Inequality in Urban India since Reforms: Bringing Quantitative and Qualitative Approaches Together." *Economic and Political Weekly* 47, no. 47–48 (2012): 44–52.

Varshney, Ashutosh. *Democracy, Development and the Countryside: Urban-Rural Struggles in India*. Cambridge, UK: Cambridge University Press, 1995.

Varshney, Ashutosh. *Ethnic Conflict and Civic Life: Hindus and Muslims in India*. New Haven, CT: Yale University Press, 2002.

Vasudeva Dutta, Puja. "Returns to Education: New Evidence for India, 1983–1999." *Education Economics* 14, no. 4 (2006): 431–51.

Verba, Sidney, Kay Lehman Schlozman, and Henry Brady. *Voice and Equality: Civic Voluntarism in American Politics*. Cambridge MA: Harvard University Press, 1995.

Verma, Arvind. *The Indian Police: A Critical Evaluation*. New Delhi, India: Regency, 2005.

Verma, Pavan K. *The Great Indian Middle Class*. New Delhi, India: Penguin Books, 1998.

Vijay, G. "Migration, Vulnerability and Insecurity in New Industrial Labour Markets." *Economic and Political Weekly* 40, no. 22–23 (2005): 2304–12.

Virmani, Arvind. *Propelling India from Socialist Stagnation to Global Power*. New Delhi, India: Academic Foundations, 2006.

Visaria, Pravin. "Poverty in India during 1994–98." Working paper, Institute of Economic Growth, Delhi, 1999.

Wade, Robert. *Village Republics: Economic Conditions for Collective Action in South India.* San Francisco, CA: Institute for Contemporary Studies, 1994.

Wade, Robert. "Is Globalization Reducing Poverty and Inequality?" *World Development* 32, no. 4 (2004): 567–89.

Wadhawan, Neha. "Living in Domesti-City: Women and Migration for Domestic Work from Jharkhand." *Economic and Political Weekly* 48, no. 43 (2013): 47–54.

Wadhwa, Wilima. "Government vs. Private Schools: Have Things Changed?" ASER Centre, 2014. Accessed October 23, 2016. img.asercentre.org/docs/Publications/ASER%20Reports/ASER%202014/Articles/wilimawadhwa.pdf.

Wadley, Susan. *Struggling with Destiny in Karimpur, 1925–1984.* Berkeley: University of California Press, 1994.

Walker, Thomas S., and James G. Ryan. *Village and Household Economies in India's Semi-arid Tropics.* Baltimore, MD: Johns Hopkins University Press, 1990.

Wang, Xiaobing, Jennifer Piesse, and Nick Weaver. "Mind the Gaps: A Political Economy of the Multiple Dimensions of China's Rural–Urban Divide." Working paper 152. Brooks World Policy Institute, Manchester, UK, 2011.

Weiner, Myron. *Political Change in South Asia.* Calcutta, India: K. L. Mukhopadhyay, 1963.

Weiner, Myron. *The Indian Paradox: Essays in Indian Politics.* New Delhi, India: Sage, 1989.

Weiner, Myron. *The Child and the State in India: Child Labor and Education Policy in Comparative Perspective.* Princeton, NJ: Princeton University Press, 1990.

Weinstein, Liza. *The Durable Slum: Dharavi and the Right to Stay Put in Globalizing Mumbai.* New Delhi, India: Orient Blackswan, 2014.

Weisskopf, Thomas E. "Why Worry about Inequality in the Booming Indian Economy?" *Economic and Political Weekly* 46, no. 47 (2011): 41–51.

Whang, In-Joung. *Management of Rural Change in Korea.* Seoul: Seoul National University Press, 1981.

Whitehead, Margaret, Goran Dahlgren, and Timothy Evans. "Equity and Health Sector Reforms: Can Low-Income Countries Escape the Medical Poverty Trap?" *Lancet* (September 8, 2001): 833–6.

Whittaker, D. Hugh, Tianbiao Zhu, Timothy Sturgeon, Mon Han Tsai, and Toshie Okita. "Compressed Development." *Studies in Comparative International Development* 45, no. 4 (2010): 439–67.

Wilkinson, Richard, and Kate Pickett. *The Spirit Level: Why Greater Equality Makes Societies Stronger.* New York, NY: Bloomsbury Press, 2009.

Wilkinson, Steven. *Votes and Violence: Electoral Competition and Ethnic Riots in India*. New York, NY: Cambridge University Press, 2004.

Witsoe, Jeffrey. *Democracy against Development: Lower-Caste Politics and Political Modernity in Postcolonial India*. Chicago, IL: University of Chicago Press, 2013.

World Bank. "Engendering Development." *World Bank Policy Research Report*, Washington, DC: World Bank, 2001.

World Bank. "Inclusive Growth and Service Delivery: Building on India's Success." *Development Policy Review*. Washington, DC: World Bank, 2006.

World Bank. *World Development Report 2009: Reshaping Economic Geography: Overview*. Washington, DC: World Bank, 2009.

World Bank. *Perspectives on Poverty in India: Stylized Facts from Survey Data*. Washington, DC: World Bank, 2011a.

World Bank. *Social Protection for a Changing India: Main Report*. Washington, DC: World Bank, 2011b.

World Bank. *Global Monitoring Report 2013*. Washington, DC: World Bank, 2013.

World Bank. *Monitoring Global Poverty: Report of the Commission on Global Poverty*. Washington, DC: World Bank, 2017. Accessed October 25, 2016. openknowledge.worldbank.org/bitstream/handle/10986/25141/9781464809613.pdf.

Wu, Xiaogang, and Donald J. Treiman. "Inequality and Equality under Chinese Socialism: The Hukou System and Intergenerational Occupational Mobility." *American Journal of Sociology* 113, no. 2 (2007): 415–45.

Xie, Yu, and Xiang Zhou. "Income Inequality in Today's China." *Proceedings of the National Academy of Sciences of the United States of America*, 111, no. 19 (2014): 6928–33.

Xu, Ke, David B. Evans, Kei Kawabata, et al. "Household Catastrophic Health Expenditure: A Multi-country Analysis." *Lancet* 362, no. 9378 (2003): 111–7.

Yadav, Yogendra. "Reconfiguration in Indian Politics: State Assembly Elections, 1993–95." *Economic and Political Weekly* (January 13, 1996): 95–104.

Yadav, Yogendra. "Electoral Politics in the Time of Change: India's Third Electoral System, 1989–99." *Economic and Political Weekly* (August 21, 1999): 2391–9.

Yadav, Yogendra. "Understanding the Second Democratic Upsurge: Trends of Bahujan Participation in Electoral Politics in the 1990s." In *Transforming India: Social and Political Dynamics of Democracy*, edited by F. Frankel, Z. Hasan, R. Bhargava, and B. Arora, pp. 120–45. New Delhi, India: Oxford University Press, 2000.

Young, Stephen, and Craig Jeffrey. "Making Ends Meet: Youth Enterprise at the Rural–Urban Intersections." *Economic and Political Weekly* 47, no. 30 (2012): 45–51.

Zacharias, Ajit, and Vamsi Vakulabharanam. "Caste Stratification and Wealth Inequality in India." *World Development* 39, no. 10 (2011): 1820–33.

Zakaria, Fareed. *The Future of Freedom: Illiberal Democracy at Home and Abroad.* New York, NY: W. W. Norton, 2003.

Zhang, Xiaobo, and Kevin H. Zhang. "How Does Globalization Affect Regional Inequality within a Developing Country? Evidence from China." *Journal of Development Studies* 39, no. 4 (2003): 47–67.

Zhao, Zhongwei. "Income Inequality, Unequal Health Care Access, and Mortality in China." *Population and Development Review* 32, no. 3 (2006): 461–83.

Zimmerman, Laura. "Why Guarantee Employment? Evidence from a Large Indian Public-Works Program." 2013. Accessed April 9, 2016. www.terry.uga.edu/media/events/documents/zimmermann.pdf.

INDEX

Abdul Kalam, 44
agglomeration effects, 49
agglomerations, 28
agricultural labor, wage of, 40
agriculture, 27, 37, 39–40, 81, 88–89,
    108, 156, 166, 172, 211
  decline of, 37
  de-peopling of, 47
  highest-paying alternative to, 41
  in rural households, 40
  investing in, 88
  irrigation failures, 85
  productivity/yields, 37–38, 40
  public investments in, 39–40
  state support to, 38–39
aspirations, 22, 97, 102, 142, 143
attitudes, 16, 20, 47, 65–66, 96, 114, 120,
    130–33, 134, 135–36

beliefs, 20, 22, 51, 65, 66, 96, 128–32,
    142, 146
below poverty line (BPL), 3, 91
Bengaluru, 10, 56, 58, 59–60, 69–70, 88,
    102, 139–40, 179, 190
Bentinck, William, 130
beyond–5-km villages, 26, 33–36, 40,
    42–43, 45, 48, 55, 64, 90, 95, 199,
    203
BJP, 15, 204
blue-polygon people, 55–57, 65, 181,
    183

blue-polygon slums
  of Bengaluru, 209
  Svati Shah study on Mumbai,
    209

capacities, 7, 23, 47, 64, 91, 103, 120,
    125, 147, 153, 176
  diverse, 193
  for self-improvement, 29
caste compositions, 7, 20, 66, 157
caste conflict, 139, 147
casual labor, 40, 57. *See* labor; mazdoors,
    see also under migration/migrants
central government, 166–67
centralization, 157, 166. *See also*
    decentralization
cities, 16–17, 31–34, 70–71
  and villages, 17, 33, 44, 48
  globalization and, 51
  investing in, 55, 70
  largeset, 33
  largest, 51
  resources to big cities, 36
Citizen Report Cards, 149
civil services, 108, 109, 147, 157, 174.
    See also governance; public,
    street-level bureaucrats
civil society, 4, 5, 150, 166, 177
Congress Party, 16
Contract Labor (Abolition and
    Regulation) Act, 1970, 213

corporate social responsibility (CSR), 24, 246

corruption, 10, 19, 35, 90, 150, 157, 159, 176, 245

Dalits, biases against, 132. *See also* caste
death rates, 52. *See also* healthcare
debts with high-interest, 85
decentralization, 145, 154, 168, 174, 231. *See also* centralization
defeatism, culture of, 160
democracy, 4–5, 25, 44, 144–45, 152, 153–54, 166, 170, 171, 172, 193
  and poverty, 4
  inequality in, 153
  information and, 116
  representative, 171
democratic upsurge, 132
demonetization policy, 189
desire system, 161
developing countries, 10, 16, 25–26, 49, 71, 77, 79, 81, 122
  as largely agrarian, 9, 55, 71, 94, 190, 196
  elites in, 26
development, 4, 5–7, 9–10, 16, 20, 22–23, 42–43, 65, 175, 190
  microclimates of, 179–82
  practice, 7, 23
  problems of, 23, 175, 181
  programs of, 7, 9
  tasks of, 22–23, 136
dollar-economy and rupee-economy, 9–13, 48, 62, 153–54, 162, 173
droughts, 57, 85
dwelling units, shortage of, 215

economic
  development, 38, 47–48, 65, 97, 167, 191
  growth, 2, 4–5, 10, 48–50, 51, 53, 70, 77, 78, 80, 89, 92–93, 178–79
education, 1–3, 20, 60–61, 63–64, 131–32, 150, 156, 166, 176
  cost of, 68
  gender gap in, 34
  investments in, 54
  privatization of, 121
  quaity of, 123

quality of, 20, 78, 103, 108, 114, 117, 118, 145, 192–93
  technology and, 45
educational. *See also* school education
  institutions, 43, 108–10, 114, 131
  investments, 64
educational systems, 64, 121–23
elections, 5, 35, 154
electoral democracy, 154, 171, 173
elites, 25–26, 66, 130, 131, 132, 134, 171
employment, 4, 40, 47, 52, 54, 60, 61–63, 88–89, 91, 124, 180
  alternative, 40
  and state unemployment benefits, 66
  flexible arrangements, 66
  growth of good-quality, 63
  structure of, 62. *See also* labor
English-medium schools, 41
epidemic outbreaks, 13, 207
equality, 192
  educational, 121
  global, 190
  opportunity of, 25, 51, 60, 67
  politics of growing, 50
  toleration of, 129
expectations, 43, 114, 181

farm families, 28, 40. *See also* agriculture
farmers
  contractors, 39
  of medium level, 27, 41
funeral feasts, 85

Gandhi, Mahatma, 44, 204
GDP, 53, 61
global inequality, 190
globalization, 3, 10, 11, 13, 16–17, 18, 25–26, 36, 37, 39, 42, 43, 49–50, 51, 61, 190–91
  making English as universal language, 133
  of economy, 17
globalized growth, 11, 12, 16, 49, 60–61, 86, 153, 166, 172
GNP, 63, 86, 94
governance, 9, 35, 36, 37, 43, 46–47, 69–70, 94–95, 120, 151–53, 166–67, 170–71, 174–75

governance (*cont.*)
  administrative stretch, 151, 153, 166–70, 173
  and public, 152
  and public administration, 166, 167
  chain of, 46, 152, 161, 162, 177
  local, 184
  processes of, 183
gram sabhas, 168–69. *See also* panchayats
grass roots, 23–24, 46, 124, 153–54, 170–72, 174–75, 177
  empowering, 24
  institutions of, 170

handouts/free things/or subsidized things, 28–29, 91, 92
healthcare, 15, 25, 34, 45, 46, 78, 85–87, 90, 94–95, 145, 150, 185–86
  and poverty, 85
  expenditures on, 78
higher education, 34, 43, 99, 103, 109, 114, 128, 135, 139, 141
high-variance society, 190–93

illiteracy, 2. *See also* education
Indian Administrative Service (IAS), 9, 108, 110, 111, 125
Indian Police Service (IPS), 155, 244
Indian society, 13, 31. *See also* caste differences
  layering of, 13
Indira Awaas Yojana, 91
inequalities, 4, 13, 15, 26, 33, 129
informal sector, 43, 60, 61, 89, 102
informal work arrangements, formalization of, 66
information
  for participation, 185
  gaps, 136, 141
  job-related, 157
information age, 148
information-poor society, 16, 20
infrastructures, 42, 70
initiatives, 95, 96, 122, 144, 147–49, 157, 167, 170, 174, 182, 186
  top-down, 187
innovation, 184–85. *See also under* institutional
  local, 24, 90, 175, 185

national, 192
process of bottom-up, 24, 177, 187
social, 25
institutional
  designs, 46, 47, 169
  innovation, 154, 184–85, 187, 192
institutions, 5, 43, 44–47, 72, 107, 108–10, 114, 167–70, 171, 184–88, 191–92
  as innovating, 184–88
  disconnectedness, 69. *See also under* grass roots
  local, 177, 184
intergenerational. *See also* social mobility
intergenerational mobility, 28, 57, 59, 101
intermediate classes, 241
International Monetary Fund (IMF), 10
investigations, 58, 76, 77, 85, 89, 91, 100, 103, 147, 165
investments, 38, 48, 51, 54–55, 63–64, 70, 148, 161, 172, 190
  in cities, 72. *See also* cities
  in financial markets, 10

Jaipur, 58, 60, 69, 208, 210, 211
jobs, 18
  creators, 5, 44, 54, 64, 73, 103
  formal, 12, 89
  higher-paying, 54, 61, 64, 99, 102, 103
  low-paying, 60, 61–62, 89, 114

labor, 19, 20, 28, 30, 40–41, 42–43, 53, 61–63, 65–66, 133
  agricultural, 40–41, 42. *See also* farmers
  casual, 57
  informalization of, 213
  intensive manufacturing, 30
  labor chowks (nakas), 31
  non-agricultural, 40–41
  skilled, 49, 63
land reforms, 201
landholdings, 27–28, 36, 37–38, 52, 89
libraries, 49, 114, 126, 128, 148
lifestyles, 13, 16, 26, 27, 30–32, 50, 59, 66, 89, 133, 147
literacy, 7
  public investments in, 44

loans, 68, 81–82, 126, 189
local organizations, 184
local politics, 162–63

Macaulay, Thomas, 130
Make in India, 63
manufacturing sector, 62–63
marginalized, 127, 187. *See also* poor
mazdoor, 31
mazdoors, 2, 12, 25, 28, 41, 44, 47, 54, 99, 132, 181–82. *See also* labor
mediators, 162, 163, 164–65, 174
medical insurance, 95
medicines, commercialization of, 86
Members of Parliament, dynastic of, 172
metropolitan bias, 205. *See also* urban bias
microfinance, 82
Mid-day Meal program, 91
middle class, 10, 30, 66, 115, 131, 191
English language and, 131, 133
of urban, 52, 54, 194
migration/migrants, 28, 43. *See also* rural-urban migration
circular/seasonal, 28, 206, 207, 209
internal, 18, 55, 71
laborers, 34
short-term single, 55
minimum living standards, 192
MLAs, 159–60, 164
MNREGA, 90–92, 221, 242
mobility, 76, 182
social, 22, 60, 89, 101, 111, 116, 124, 142, 143, 145
upward, 18, 19, 59, 71, 75, 97, 124, 125, 133, 155, 178, 181, 192, 211
modernization, 27, 51, 53, 69
motivation, 113, 123
movement of people, 52, 156. *See also* migration/migrants
municipalities, 168. *See also* panchayats

National Rural Health Mission, 220, 242
National Rural Livelihoods Mission, 220, 242
Naxalite or Maoist movement, 42
Nehru, Jawaharlal, 103, 157
newspapers, 134, 148, 153

NGO, 148
NGOs, 7, 19, 24, 57, 68, 72, 87, 95, 97, 123, 126, 186

Olympic medals/games, 45, 104–06, 111, 125, 143
ordinary citizens, 35, 149, 152, 161–62, 166, 168, 171, 173
outliers, 107, 111–12, 113–14

Panchayati Raaj Institutions (PRIs), 243
panchayats, 46–47, 161, 163, 168, 169, 184
elections of, 134
parent-teacher associations, 145, 168, 170. *See also* school education; English-medium schools
Patna, 56, 58, 69, 208
policy makers, 4, 13, 76, 92, 191
poor, 13–15, 19–20, 43, 74–77, 79–90, 91–97, 103–04, 134, 181–82. *See also* (marginalized)
households, 40, 89, 92, 143
population, 10–11, 14–16, 17, 19, 27–28, 43, 76–77, 79–80, 104–07, 109, 131, 132
growth, 28, 52, 128
of India, 14, 16, 17, 92
of rural, 17, 33, 48, 136, 191
poverty, 4, 5–8, 12, 18–19, 47, 57, 75–76. *See also* drought
and antipoverty programs, 91
and family size, 86
as growing, 75
as part of existence, 146
culture of, 219
definition of, 77. *See also* poverty line
dynamics of, 8, 83, 219
escaped, 8, 83–84, 86, 87–89, 90
falling into, 18–19, 79, 82–86
in developing countries, 77
prevention of future, 84
rates among SCs and STs, 218
reduction, 5, 19, 51, 70, 76–77, 78–80, 83, 87, 90, 125, 157, 222
tracking, 96
poverty line, 76–77, 78–80, 84, 86, 87, 89, 93, 128, 129, 217. *See also* below poverty line (BPL)

preparation-side factors, 54, 60, 65, 103
primary schools, 6, 46, 64, 113, 117, 131.
    See also public school systems;
    school education
privatization, 121, 166
productivity, 17, 36, 37, 38, 40
Provision of Urban Amenities to Rural
    Areas (PURA), 204
public
    administration, 9, 72, 151, 156, 166,
        167, 173–74
    officials, 3–4, 35, 36, 45, 69, 153, 159,
        161, 168, 176
    street-level bureaucrats, 158, 161,
        174
public investments, 18, 39, 44, 48, 121,
    203
    in agriculture, 39
public school systems, 2, 36, 64, 66, 119,
    122, 128. *See also* education;
    education system
public–private partnerships, 246
purchasing power parity (PPP), 49, 79,
    93
    exchange rate, 217

recruitments, 148, 151, 174
    as constable, 155
    discrimination at, 114
    English speakers and, 133
    forest department, 239
    in IAS, 110, 111
    of public employees, 154–58
    single-entry system of, 156
resource allocation, 37, 44, 182
rich countries, 9, 15, 26, 52, 54, 65, 192.
    See also developing countries
Right to Education Act, 120, 228
Right to Information Act, 170,
    238
rights, and poorer people, 92
rights-based initiatives, 223
roads, 2, 5, 34, 48, 59, 70–71, 72, 150,
    178
role models, 20, 22, 45, 103, 112, 114,
    115, 125–26, 142, 148, 182
rootlessness, 66
    and urbanization, 53
runaway children, 137

rural areas, 2, 16–18, 27–29, 36, 38–39,
    42, 48–50, 108, 134, 190–91
    households, 33, 40, 41
    investing in, 55
    population in, 27
rural employment guarantee program, 19
rural employment gurantee program. *See
    also* MNREGA
rural-urban migration, 17. *See also*
    migration/migrants

Samuel Undong program, 205
sanitation, 58, 150, 191
Sarva Shiksha Abhiyan, 228
Scheduled Caste. *See also under* poverty
scheduled castes (SCs), 20, 46, 56, 82,
    107, 109–10, 114, 128, 141
    Dalits, 128, 132
scheduled tribes (STs), 20, 46, 56, 82,
    107, 109–10, 114, 128
school education, 2, 23, 57, 114, 117,
    119, 120
    and governance, 120, 122
    backlash against, 124
    English-medium schools, 111
    exchanges among rural and elite urban
        schools, 147
    privatization of, 121
    school vouchers, 121
    technology and, 123
schoolteachers. *See* teachers
Singh, Manmohan, 43
skill development, 54, 125, 166
skills premium, 60–61
    and link to college premium, 12
slum dwellers
    Benjamin on, 214
    police brutality on, 213
Slumdog Millionaire, 20
slums, 18, 54–60, 67–69, 71, 109, 110,
    148, 165, 179
    and land ownership, 213
    Bengaluru's blue-polygon, 55–57
    children, 138, 146
    dwellers, 58, 132, 152
    in Jaipur, 60
    in Mumbai, 56, 211
    swellers, 69
Smart Cities, 71. *See also* cities

social
  change, 173
  justice, 97, 107. *See also* mobility, social
  security, 202
  welfare, 125, 129, 134
soft factors, 20, 67, 127, 128, 130, 142,
  143
specialized education, 11–12. *See also*
  higher education
splintered urbanism, 214
state governments, 46, 70, 95, 123, 124,
  134, 136, 167
  transfer of officials and, 160
stereotypes, 138–39, 146
strategies, 16, 179, 190
  macro, 179
  micro, 179
subsidiarity, 166, 167, 168
supply-side factors, 54, 60, 63,
  65
  weaknesses of, 18, 103

talent development, 125, 192
talent pool, 35, 45, 109
Targeted Public Distribution System
  (TPDS), 91
teachers, 6, 22–24, 35–36, 69, 113–16,
  118–20, 121–23, 125, 128, 140–41,
  143, 147, 153, 158, 162, 167, 174,
  176, 224
  and authority, 174
  as voucher-based, 122
  deputation of, 118
  mass recruitment of, 220
  motivation of, 115, 119–20, 140,
  167
  performance of, 23
  training, 113, 119

technology, 13, 42, 63, 71, 153, 157, 166,
  175, 192
  and employment, 192
  robots, 175
tiered state, 16, 67–70, 151, 154–57, 167,
  172, 173, 177
towns, 17, 25, 32–35, 36, 41, 42, 51, 55,
  66, 70, 99
  and 'city', 199
Trump, Donald, 26

urban
  and rural, 44, 100, 139, 191
  bias, 191
  centers, 33, 49
  development agencies, 70
  poor, 66
  population, 52, 191
urbanization, 18, 36, 42, 43, 51, 53,
  54–55, 72, 181

values, 20, 65, 67, 96, 120, 128–31,
  132–33, 137, 146. *See also* attitudes;
  beliefs
  as practical, 129
  biased, 96, 138
  shared conceptions, 65
villages, 16–17, 18, 120, 125, 180–82
  closer to towns, 17
  investing in, 18

wedding ceremonies, expensive, 75, 85
workers. *See also* labor
  of manufacturing sector, 212
  wages of, 201
workforce, 61, 64, 159. *See also* labor;
  workers
world wealth distribution, 14

CPSIA information can be obtained
at www.ICGtesting.com
Printed in the USA
LVHW012309130820
663131LV00002B/345

9 781108 402507